QuarkXPress for Windows Desig[...]

MW00837167

Overview

QuarkXPress has a wealth of shortcuts for design-oriented publishing tasks. Those listed here are the ones you'll likely use day to day, although they are by no means all the options available. For more shortcuts and detailed explanations of QuarkXPress's tools, consult the *QuarkXPress for Windows Designer Handbook* or the *Using QuarkXPress* manual.

Special Characters

Open double quote (")	Alt+Shift+[
Close double quote (")	Alt+Shift+]
Open single quote (')	Alt+[
Close single quote (')	Alt+]
Registered trademark (®)	Alt+Shift+R
Trademark (™)	Alt+Shift+2
Copyright (©)	Alt+Shift+C
Paragraph (¶)	Alt+Shift+7
Section (§)	Alt+Shift+6
Dagger (†)	Alt+Shift+T
Bullet (•)	Alt+Shift+8

Enter Symbol (one character at a time)
Symbol typeface	Ctrl+Shift+Q
Zapf Dingbats typeface	Ctrl+Shift+Z

Special Spaces
Nonbreaking standard space	Ctrl+spacebar
En space	Ctrl+Shift+6
Nonbreaking en space	Ctrl+Alt+Shift+6
Punctuation (thin) space	Shift+spacebar
Nonbreaking punctuation space	Ctrl+Shift+spacebar
Flexible space	Ctrl+Shift+5
Nonbreaking flexible space	Ctrl+Alt+Shift+5

Note: A flexible space's width is user-defined; a good setting is 200%, which is an em space.

Special Hyphens and Dashes
Discretionary hyphen	Ctrl+hyphen
Nonbreaking standard hyphen	Ctrl+Shift+hyphen
En dash (–) (nonbreaking)	Ctrl+=
Em dash (—)	Ctrl+Shift+=
Nonbreaking em dash (—)	Ctrl+Alt+Shift+=

Page Numbering and References
Current text box/page	Ctrl+3
Previous text box in chain	Ctrl+2
Next text box in chain	Ctrl+4

Typographic Controls

Reduce kerning or tracking	
in ¹⁄₂₀-em units (−10)	Ctrl+Shift+{
in ¹⁄₂₀₀-em units (−1)	Ctrl+Alt+Shift+{
Increase kerning or tracking	
in ¹⁄₂₀-em units (+10)	Ctrl+Shift+}
in ¹⁄₂₀₀-em units (+1)	Ctrl+Alt+Shift+}
Reduce point size 1 point	Ctrl+Alt+Shift+<
to next default size	Ctrl+Shift+<
Increase point size 1 point	Ctrl+Alt+Shift+>
to next default size	Ctrl+Shift+>
Increase leading 1 point	Ctrl+Shift+"
by 0.1 points	Ctrl+Alt+Shift+"
Decrease leading 1 point	Ctrl+Shift+:
by 0.1 points	Ctrl+Alt+Shift+:
Shift baseline up 1 point	Ctrl+Alt+Shift+)
Shift baseline down 1 point	Ctrl+Alt+Shift+(

Positional Typographic Controls
Insert indent	Ctrl+\
Insert right-indent tab	Shift+Tab
Insert new line	Shift+Enter
Insert discretionary new line	Ctrl+Enter
Insert new column	keypad Enter
Insert new box	Shift+keypad Enter

Text Formatting

Plain (normal)	Ctrl+Shift+P
Bold	Ctrl+Shift+B
Italic	Ctrl+Shift+I
Underline all	Ctrl+Shift+U
Underline words only	Ctrl+Shift+W
Strikethrough	Ctrl+Shift+/
All caps	Ctrl+Shift+K
Small caps	Ctrl+Shift+H
Superscript	Ctrl+Shift+)
Subscript	Ctrl+Shift+(
Character formatting	Ctrl+Shift+D

Paragraph Formatting

Alignment
Left	Ctrl+Shift+L
Justified	Ctrl+Shift+J
Right	Ctrl+Shift+R
Centered	Ctrl+Shift+C
Leading	Ctrl+Shift+E
Paragraph formatting	Ctrl+Shift+F
Rules	Ctrl+Shift+N
Tabs	Ctrl+Shift+T

QuarkXPress for Windows Designer Handbook

IDG BOOKS QUICK REFERENCE CARD

Basic Editing

Undo	Ctrl+Z
Select All	Ctrl+A
Copy	Ctrl+C
Cut	Ctrl+X
Paste	Ctrl+V
Find/Change	Ctrl+F
Check spelling in story	Ctrl+Alt+W

Moving the Text Pointer

Previous word	Ctrl+←
Next word	Ctrl+→
Previous paragraph	Ctrl+↑
Next paragraph	Ctrl+↓
Start of line	Home
End of line	End
Start of story	Ctrl+Home
End of story	Ctrl+End

Highlighting text

Add Shift to the above shortcuts. In addition, there are the following shortcuts:

Previous character	Shift+←
Next character	Shift+→
Previous line	Shift+↑
Next line	Shift+↓

Scrolling and Views

Go to specific page	Ctrl+J
First page	Ctrl+PgUp
Previous page	Shift+PgUp
Next page	Shift+PgDn
Last page	Ctrl+PgDn
Fit page in window	Ctrl+0
Actual size	Ctrl+1
200%	Ctrl+right mouse
Show/hide rulers	Ctrl+R
Show/hide invisibles	Ctrl+I
Show Measurements palette	Ctrl+Alt+M

Major Dialog Boxes

New	Ctrl+N
Open	Ctrl+O
Save	Ctrl+S
Save As	Ctrl+Alt+S
Print	Ctrl+P
Printer Setup	Ctrl+Alt+P
General Preferences	Ctrl+Y
Typographic Preferences	Ctrl+Alt+Y
Exit	Ctrl+Q

Box Controls (Item tool active)

Modify	Ctrl+M
Frame	Ctrl+B
Runaround	Ctrl+T
Duplicate	Ctrl+D
Step and Repeat	Ctrl+Alt+D
Delete	Ctrl+K
Group	Ctrl+G
Ungroup	Ctrl+U
Lock	Ctrl+L
Keep box height, width equal	Shift+drag handle
Maintain box aspect ratio	Alt+Shift+drag

Graphics (Content tool active)

Positioning and Sizing

Center graphic in box	Ctrl+Shift+M
Fit graphic to box size	Ctrl+Shift+F
Maintain aspect ratio	Ctrl+Alt+Shift+F
Scale box and graphic	Ctrl+drag handle
Keep box height, width equal	Ctrl+Shift+drag
Maintain aspect ratio	Ctrl+Alt+Shift+drag
Scale graphic larger by 5%	Ctrl+Alt+Shift+>
Scale graphic smaller by 5%	Ctrl+Alt+Shift+<
Moving Graphics in Box	
Left by 1 point	←
by 0.1 points	Alt+←
Right by 1 point	→
by 0.1 points	Alt+→
Up by 1 point	↑
by 0.1 points	Alt+↑
Down by 1 point	↓
by 0.1 points	Alt+↓

TIFF Gray-Scale Image Control

Normal	Ctrl+Shift+N
Negative	Ctrl+Shift+hyphen
High contrast	Ctrl+Shift+H
Posterized	Ctrl+Shift+P
Custom contrast	Ctrl+Shift+C
Custom screen	Ctrl+Shift+S

Runaround Polygon Picture Boxes

Create a handle	Ctrl+click on line
Delete a handle	Ctrl+click on handle
Constrain line/handle to nearest of 0°, 45°, or 90°	Shift+drag handle
Suspend text reflow	hold spacebar
Delete runaround polygon	Ctrl+Shift+click

QuarkXPress
for Windows
Designer HANDBOOK

Colin -
Thanks for
all your help!
Best wishes -
Barbara Assadi

QuarkXPress
for WINDOWS
Designer HANDBOOK

By Barbara Assadi and Galen Gruman

Foreword by Fred Ebhrami
President, Quark Inc.

IDG BOOKS

IDG Books Worldwide, Inc.
An International Data Group Company
San Mateo, California 94402

QuarkXPress for Windows *Designer* Handbook

Published by
IDG Books Worldwide, Inc.
An International Data Group Company
155 Bovet Road, Suite 610
San Mateo, CA 94402
415-312-0650

Library of Congress Catalog Card No.: **92-74311**

ISBN **1-878058-45-2**

Printed in the United States of America

10 9 8 7 6 5 4 3 2 1

Distributed in the United States by IDG Books Worldwide, Inc.

Distributed in Canada by Macmillan of Canada, a Division of Canada Publishing Corporation; by Woodslane Pty. Ltd. in Australia; and by Computer Bookshops in the U.K.

For information on translations and availability in other countries, contact Marc Jeffrey Mikulich, Foreign Rights Manager, at IDG Books Worldwide. Fax: 415-358-1260.

For sales inquiries and special prices for bulk quantities, write to the address above or call IDG Books Worldwide at 415-312-0650.

Dedication

To my husband, Khossrow, for taking care of everything all those nights and weekends when I sat glued to my computer.

— Barbara Assadi

To Angela Burgess, a good friend and strong colleague for many years, who more than anyone I know epitomizes an enabler.

— Galen Gruman

To the reviews editors at *InfoWorld* — particularly Serge Timacheff and Kyla Carlson — who for several years have encouraged us to deeply explore desktop publishing, and who have challenged us to keep at least a step ahead of this complex, exciting, and ever-changing technology. And to each other, for making the whole greater than the sum of its parts.

— B.A. and G.G.

Illustrations used in the screen shots were created by Colin M. Foden.

Acknowledgments

Many people helped us develop this book. We thank them all for their role in making the project a reality. At IDG Books Worldwide: Janna Custer, the project editor; Julie King, the copy editor; and Michael "Mac" McCarthy (our former reviews editor at *InfoWorld* and now editor-in-chief at *SunWorld*), the technical reviewer. For the real-world examples used in Appendix A, "Applications Tips": Angela Burgess, managing editor of *IEEE Software*; John Frick Jr., art director, and Robert Francisco, graphic designer, Pacific Mutual Life Insurance Company; Jeff Gregory, documentation specialist, Quark Inc.; and Michael Haggerty, associate editor of *IEEE Computer Graphics and Applications*. For the animal and environment illustrations used throughout the screen shots in our example documents: Colin M. Foden. Special thanks to Edgar R. Lehman and Stephen T. O'Hare, Pacific Mutual Life Insurance Company, for their encouragement and support.

(The publisher would like to give special thanks to Patrick J. McGovern, without whom this book would not have been possible.)

About the Authors

Barbara Assadi and Galen Gruman have used, taught, and reviewed desktop-publishing technology for many years, on both Macintosh and PC platforms. Fluent in all the major desktop-publishing programs, they regularly review publishing technology for the computer trade weekly *InfoWorld,* serving as members of the publication's review board.

One of their *InfoWorld* articles, published in 1990, still stands as a landmark and has since been much imitated. That article was the first to compare a number of desktop publishing programs, not by evaluating individual features (hyphen-ation-exception dictionaries, graphics scaling, and so on), but by actually applying the programs to the process of publishing a complex document. This article and caused more than one product developer to reconsider approaches to user needs for desktop publishing software.

Assadi began following developments in desktop publishing in the early 1980s, first as a user of publishing systems and later as a consultant to businesses interested in setting up electronic publishing systems. She uses desktop publishing systems in her current position as communications manager at Pacific Mutual Life Insurance Company. In addition to reviewing desktop publishing and word processing products for *InfoWorld,* she lectures and consults on topics related to desktop publishing. She lives in California with her husband, Khossrow, and three children.

Gruman was an early advocate of PC-based desktop publishing. He helped bring it to a magazine group back when desktop publishing was a suspect technology and a PC was considered incapable of doing anything but word processing. Gruman is president of the Computer Press Association (the international association for computer journalists) and a free-lance writer. When he's not working, he usually can be found on his bicycle.

Credits

President and Publisher
John J. Kilcullen

Publishing Director
David Solomon

Project Editor
Janna Custer

Acquisitions Editor
Terrie Lynn Solomon

Managing Editor
Mary Bednarek

Editors
Julie King
Diane Steele

Technical Reviewer
Michael E. McCarthy

Production Director
Lana J. Olson

Editorial Assistant
Megg Bonar

Text Preparation
Mary Ann Cordova
Dana Bryant Sadoff

Proofreading
Michael D. Welch

Indexer
Joan Dickey

Book Design and Production
Francette M. Ytsma
Peppy White
(*University Graphics, Palo Alto, California*)

university **g** raphics

About IDG Books Worldwide

Welcome to the world of IDG Books Worldwide.

IDG Books Worldwide, Inc., is a division of International Data Group (IDG), the world's largest publisher of computer-related information and the leading global provider of information services on information technology. IDG publishes over 185 computer publications in 60 countries. Thirty million people read one or more IDG publications each month.

If you use personal computers, IDG Books is committed to publishing quality books that meet your needs. We rely on our extensive network of publications, including such leading periodicals as *InfoWorld, PC World, Computerworld, Macworld, Publish, Network World,* and *SunWorld,* to help us make informed and timely decisions in creating useful computer books that meet your needs.

With every IDG book, we strive to bring extra value and skill-building instruction to the reader. Our books are written by experts, with the backing of IDG periodicals, and with careful thought devoted to issues such as audience, interior design, use of icons, and illustrations. Our editorial staff is a careful mix of high-tech journalists and experienced book people. Our close contact with the makers of computer products helps ensure accuracy and thorough coverage. Our heavy use of personal computers at every step in production means we can deliver books in the most timely manner.

We are delivering books of high quality at competitive prices on topics customers want. At IDG, we believe in quality, and we have been delivering quality for over 25 years. You'll find no better book on a subject than an IDG book.

John Kilcullen
President and Publisher
IDG Books Worldwide, Inc.

IDG Books Worldwide, Inc. is a division of International Data Group. The officers are Patrick J. McGovern, Founder and Board Chairman; Walter Boyd, President; Robert A. Farmer, Vice Chairman, International Data Group's publications include: **ARGENTINA's** Computerworld Argentina, InfoWorld Argentina; **ASIA's** Computerworld Hong Kong, PC World Hong Kong, Computerworld Southeast Asia, PC World Singapore, Computerworld Malaysia, PC World Malaysia; **AUSTRALIA's** Computerworld Australia, Australian PC World, Australian Macworld; **AUSTRIA's** Computerwelt Oesterreich, PC Test; **BRAZIL's** DataNews, Mundo IBM, Mundo Unix, PC World, Publish; **BULGARIA's** Computerworld Bulgaria, Ediworld, PC World Express; **CANADA's** ComputerData, Direct Access, Graduate Computerworld, InfoCanada, Network World Canada; **CHILE's** Computerworld, Informatica; **COLUMBIA's** Computerworld Columbia; **CZECHOSLOVAKIA's** Computerworld Czechoslovakia, PC World Czechoslovakia; **DENMARK's** CAD/CAM WORLD, Communications World, Computerworld Danmark, Computerworld Focus, Computerworld Uddannelse, LAN World, Lotus World, Macintosh Produktkatalog, Macworld Danmark, PC World Danmark, PC World Produktguide, Windows World; **EQUADOR's** PC World; **EGYPT's** PC World Middle East; **FINLAND's** Mikro PC, Tietoviikko, Tietoverkko; **FRANCE's** Distributique, GOLDEN MAC, InfoPC, Languages & Systems, Le Guide du Monde Informatique, Le Monde Informatique, Telecoms & Reseaux; **GERMANY's** Computerwoche, Computerwoche Focus, Computerwoche Extra, Computerwoche Karriere, edv aspekte, Information Management, Macwelt, Netzwelt, PC Welt, PC Woche, Publish, Unit; **HUNGARY's** Computerworld SZT, PC World; **INDIA's** Computers & Communications; **ISRAEL's** Computerworld Israel, PC World Israel; **ITALY's** Computerworld Italia, Lotus Magazine, Macworld Italia, Networking Italia, PC World Italia; **JAPAN's** Computerworld Japan, Macworld Japan, SunWorld Japan; **KOREA's** Computerworld Korea, Macworld Korea, PC World Korea; **MEXICO's** Compu Edicion, Compu Manufactura, Computacion/Punto de Venta, Computerworld Mexico, MacWorld, Mundo Unix, PC World, Windows; **THE NETHERLANDS'** Computer! Totaal, LAN Magazine, Lotus World, MacWorld Magazine; **NEW ZEALAND's** Computerworld New Zealand, New Zealand PC World; **NIGERIA's** PC World Africa; **NORWAY's** Computerworld Norge, C/world, Lotusworld Norge, Macworld Norge, Networld, PC World Ekspress, PC World Norge, PC World's Product Guide, Publish World, Student Guiden, Unix World, Windowsworld, IDG Direct Response; **PERU's** PC World; **PEOPLES REPUBLIC OF CHINA's** China Computerworld, PC World China, Electronics International; **IDG HIGH TECH** Newproductworld, Consumer Electronics New Product World; **PHILLIPPINES'** Computerworld, PC World; **POLAND's** Computerworld Poland, PC World/Komputer; **ROMANIA's** InfoClub Magazine; **RUSSIA's** Computerworld-Moscow, Networks, PC World; **SOUTH AFRICA's** Computing S.A.; **SPAIN's** Amiga World, Autoedicion, Communicaciones World, Computerworld Espana, Macworld Espana, Network World, PC World Espana, Publish, Sunworld; **SWEDEN's** Attack, CAD/CAM World, ComputerSweden, Corporate Computing, Lokala Natverk/LAN, Lotus World, MAC&PC, Macworld, Mikrodatorn, PC World, Publishing & Design (CAP), Datalngenjoren, Maxi Data, Windows World; **SWITZERLAND's** Computerworld Schweiz, Corporate Computing, Macworld Schweiz, PC & Workstation; **TAIWAN's** Computerworld Taiwan, Global Computer Express, PC World Taiwan; **THAILAND's** Thai Computerworld; **TURKEY's** Computerworld Monitor, Macworld Turkiye, PC World Turkiye; **UNITED KINGDOM's** Lotus Magazine, Macworld, Sunworld; **UNITED STATES'** AmigaWorld, Cable in the Classroom, CIO, Computerworld, DOS Resource Guide, Electronic News, Federal Computer Week, GamePro, inCider/A+, IDG Books, InfoWorld, InfoWorld Direct, Macworld, Multimedia World, Network World, NeXTWORLD, PC Games, PC World, PC Letter, Publish, RUN, SunWorld, SWATPro; **VENEZUELA's** Computerworld Venezuela, MicroComputer-world Venezuela; **YUGOSLAVIA's** Moj Mikro.

 The text in this book is printed on recycled paper.

x

Contents at a Glance

Table of Contents

Foreword

By Fred Ebrahimi, President, Quark, Inc.

In 1988, I became aware of Barbara Assadi and Galen Gruman when I read their product reviews in *InfoWorld*. Early on, I recognized that these two people have an understanding of the desktop-publishing field that goes much deeper than just knowing how to evaluate a program feature by feature. Bringing their own solid publishing backgrounds into play, they were the first to approach product reviews from a basis of understanding the intricacies of the publishing process.

I had the privilege of meeting Barbara and Galen at computer publishing trade shows, and I took advantage of the time to talk with them about the direction of desktop publishing and to get their feedback on some of our own product ideas. To put it simply, when it comes to publishing on the computer, these two know their stuff. You will recognize that as you use this book, which guides you through the process of creating a variety of documents on QuarkXPress for Windows. Regardless of whether you are a beginner or an expert, you will find value in these pages, as two industry experts share their insights on the best ways to use this program.

— Fred Ebrahimi, President, Quark, Inc.

Introduction

■ ■

Welcome to *The QuarkXPress for Windows Designer Handbook* — your personal guide to a powerful, full-featured publishing program. The program offers precise control over all aspects of page design within today's leading operating environment, Microsoft Windows. Our goal is to guide you each step of the way through the publishing process, showing you as we go how to make QuarkXPress for Windows work for you. You'll also learn tips and tricks about publishing design itself that you can use in any document, whether created in QuarkXPress or not.

QuarkXPress does more than offer a wide range of desktop publishing capabilities to sophisticated designers who develop magazines, books, ads, and product brochures. It also gives the power of the press to individuals and groups who use the program's impressive set of publishing tools to communicate their thoughts, dreams, and philosophies.

The market for QuarkXPress knows no limits in terms of publishing applications. It also knows no national boundaries. The program is sold throughout the world, and its founders take pride in enabling people to communicate. Quark Inc. regards this responsibility seriously and keeps a wide range of users in mind when developing software to serve them.

Simply put, the philosophy of the people who give us QuarkXPress is to provide the best possible publishing tools to those who strive to educate, inform, and document the world in which we live.

What This Book Offers

Since QuarkXPress comes with good documentation chock full of examples, why do you need this book? In a phrase, "to see the bigger picture." Publishing design involves much more than understanding a particular program's tools — it involves knowing when, how, and, most important, *why* to use them. In this book, we help you realize the potential of QuarkXPress by applying its tools to real-world publishing design needs.

Desktop publishing users in general, and QuarkXPress users in particular, are an interesting bunch of people. Some have years of high-end, creative, design-intensive experience, Others are just getting started in publishing, perhaps by producing simple newsletters or flyers to advertise a community event.

Desktop publishing users fall into several classes:

- Experienced designers new to desktop technologies.
- Novice designers new to desktop technologies.
- Designers new to QuarkXPress but who are familiar with other desktop technologies.
- Designers familiar with Macintosh publishing tools who are new to Windows.

No matter which class applies to you, you'll find that this book addresses your needs. The key word here is "designers." That doesn't mean you have a degree in design or have 10 years' experience producing national ad campaigns — it means that you are responsible for developing and implementing the look of documents, whether a four-page company newsletter or a four-color billboard ad. The basic techniques and issues are the same for both ends of the spectrum. And we, of course, cover in detail the specialized needs — such as table creation, image control, and color output — of high-end designers. (For those just learning about such advanced techniques, be sure to read the sidebars that explain the underlying issues.)

Regardless of your level of experience with desktop publishing, this book will help you use QuarkXPress. It is written with plenty of detail for experienced designers, while including enough step-by-step introductory material for the newest user. What distinguishes this book from the rest is that it does not attempt to substitute for the documentation that accompanies QuarkXPress. Instead, it guides you through the *process* of publishing a document, regardless of whether that document is your first or your 1,000th. If you're new to Microsoft Windows, you'll appreciate how this book also includes information on getting started with the Windows operating environment.

How This Book Is Organized

We've arranged the book into broad sections covering the basic aspects of publishing design, as well as aspects related to implementing your designs (such as printing issues). These sections reflect the typical groupings of tasks and issues in an everyday publishing environment.

Part I: QuarkXPress Fundamentals

Users new to desktop publishing, QuarkXPress, or Windows will find information in this part for understanding the basic elements and tools in the program.

Chapter 1, The Philosophy Behind QuarkXPress, explains how the program arranges its tools and features, as well as the basic process used for creating documents in QuarkXPress.

Chapter 2, Basic Elements, details the QuarkXPress environment — the icons used in the program, the menu structure, and the tools used to implement your design elements.

Chapter 3, The Windows Environment, explains Windows for users new to this platform. QuarkXPress users familiar with the Macintosh will find it particularly helpful because the differences between the two environments are highlighted.

Part II: Document Preparation

Before you can lay out a specific document, you must prepare the text, graphics, and basic layout structure. The chapters in this part shows you how to lay the groundwork for your documents.

Chapter 4, Customizing QuarkXPress, shows you how to customize the QuarkXPress interface and set global settings that will affect your entire document or, in some cases, all future documents.

Chapter 5, Understanding Master Pages, explains the powerful master page tool that lets you define a layout structure once and have QuarkXPress implement it on any number of pages, which saves a lot of labor.

Chapter 6, Creating Style Sheets, explains another powerful tool, the style sheet, which lets you define typographic settings that you can apply to any number of paragraphs.

Chapter 7, Preparing Files for Import, details the steps you need to take — as well as the ones you should avoid — in the programs that create your text and graphics.

Part III: Page Layout

The heart of publishing is layout — how your document's elements are arranged. This part explains both QuarkXPress's layout tools and general layout techniques.

Chapter 8, Getting Started with Layout, explains the basic layout tools in QuarkXPress and how to use them.

Chapter 9, Working with Text, details how to use the layout tools for text elements, including multicolumn layout and rotated text.

Chapter 10, Working with Picture Boxes, details how to use the layout tools for graphics elements, including wraparound, rotation, and borders.

Chapter 11, Additional Layout Features, explains how to use advanced tools, such as section numbering, as well as how to combine text and graphics layout techniques.

Part IV: Typography and Text

As fundamental as layout is *typography* — the appearance of text. This part explains both the typographic tools in QuarkXPress and general typographic techniques.

Chapter 12, Understanding Character Spacing, explains how to control the appearance of text through character-spacing settings, such as point size, tracking, and special spaces.

Chapter 13, Understanding Paragraph Spacing, is about how to control the appearance of text through paragraph-spacing settings, such as leading, hyphenation, and indents.

Chapter 14, Working with Typefaces, teaches you about the many varieties of typefaces and how to use them. We concentrate on explaining the appropriate uses of type styles like boldface, small caps, and italics that are used in most documents.

Chapter 15, Using Special Effects and Elements, focuses on design-intensive typography, such as creating bulleted lists, rotated text, drop caps, and colored text.

Chapter 16, Using Tabs, explains how to set and use tab stops, particularly to create tables.

Chapter 17, Editing Text, explains how to combine typographic features to make text fit the available space, as well as how to use text-editing features like spell checking and find and replace.

Part V: Graphics

The third fundamental component of publishing is graphics. This part explains how to manipulate imported graphics and create your own in QuarkXPress.

Chapter 18, Using the Modify Command, explains how to manipulate imported graphics — resize, crop, rotate, slant, and distort.

Chapter 19, Creating Graphics in QuarkXPress, teaches you how to use the several picture box shapes and ruling lines in combination to create simple graphics.

Chapter 20, Working with Bitmap Images, covers the tools that let you manipulate bitmap images, particularly gray-scale ones, to change their appearance or prepare them for output on high-resolution printers.

Chapter 21, Working with Color, explains how to create colors in QuarkXPress, how to apply colors to text and graphics, and what to watch out for when outputting color separations.

Part VI: Document Management

Publishing is based on integrating multiple elements, and desktop publishing is no exception. This part covers QuarkXPress's tools to organize your document's elements and explains production-management techniques that can streamline your operation.

Chapter 22, Using Libraries, covers the QuarkXPress feature that lets you put common text and graphics elements into files that any document can access.

Chapter 23, Linking to Source Files, explains how to ensure that your layout reflects the latest versions of your text and graphics, as well as how to work with the new "live link" features offered by Windows.

Chapter 24, Using QuarkXPress in a Workgroup Environment, guides you past the production-management pitfalls that snare many desktop publishers not experienced in managing a collection of single-user computers in a multiple-user production environment.

Part VII: Printing

Ultimately, you will print your document. This part explains how to set your printer up, how to control your printer from QuarkXPress, and how to work with service bureaus.

Chapter 25, Setting Up Printers, explains how to set up your printer both in Windows and in QuarkXPress.

Chapter 26, Printing Techniques, explains the options available for both PCL 5 and PostScript printers, showing you what effects are available and how to implement them. It also guides you through the process of working with your service bureau to ensure that they print what you expect.

Part VIII: Appendixes

Appendix A, Application Tips, presents real-world examples that incorporate the many techniques offered by QuarkXPress. We show what techniques designers of nine real publications used and how they used them.

Appendix B, Installing and Reconfiguring QuarkXPress, covers installation and configuration. If you upgrade your system, you may find you need to reinstall QuarkXPress. Or, as you gain experience using QuarkXPress, you may want to reconfigure its installation to add or remove features and filters. This appendix shows you how to do both.

Appendix C, Extending QuarkXPress's Capabilities, covers the third-party utilities that have been developed to enhance QuarkXPress. XTensions add functions to QuarkXPress for specific user neeeds, such as special color blends and table editing.

How to Read This Book

If you are a novice publisher or designer, we suggest you read the book in order. The process of page design is presented in increasing levels of sophistication — you first learn how (and why) to create a template, then how to work with common elements such as text, and finally how to use special effects and deal with high-end publishing issues such as output controls and image manipulation.

If you are experienced, read the book in any order you want — pick those chapters or sections that cover the design issues you want to know more about, either as basic design issues or as QuarkXPress implementation issues.

Whether you read the book sequentially or nonsequentially, you'll find the many cross-references helpful. Publishing design is successful ultimately because the result is more than the sum of its parts — and the tools used to create and implement your designs cannot be used in isolation. Because this is true, it is impossible to have one "right" order or grouping of content; the cross-references let you know where to get additional information when what you're seeking to understand or learn doesn't fit into the way we've organized this book.

Conventions Used in This Book

Before we begin showing you the ins and outs of using QuarkXPress for Windows, we need to spend a few minutes reviewing the terms and conventions used in this book.

QuarkXPress for Windows commands

The QuarkXPress for Windows commands that you select using the program menus appear in this book in normal typeface, but are distinguishable because a single letter in the command is underlined, as in Edit. You can access the command by pressing the Alt key as you press the underlined key: To access the Edit menu, you press the Alt key as you press the E key.

When you choose some menu commands, a related pull-down menu or a drop-down list box appears. If we describe a situation in which you need to select one menu and then choose a command from a secondary menu or list box, we use an arrow symbol. For example, *Choose View ⇨ Thumbnails to display the pages in thumbnail (reduced) view* means that you should choose the Thumbnails command from the View menu.

Mouse conventions

Because you use a mouse to perform many functions in QuarkXPress, you need to be familiar with the following terms and instructions:

- **Pointer:** This is the small graphic icon that moves on the screen as you move your mouse. The pointer takes on different shapes depending on the tool you select, the current location of the mouse, and the function you are performing.

- **Click:** Quickly press and release the left mouse button once. Sometimes, you are instructed to *click the box* or *click the button.* To do this, use the mouse to move the pointer into position over the box or button before you click.

- **Double-click:** Quickly press and release the left mouse button twice.

- **Drag:** Dragging is used for moving and sizing items in a QuarkXPress document. To drag an item, position the mouse pointer on it. Press and hold down the left mouse button and then slide the mouse across a flat surface to "drag" the item.

Icons

You will notice special graphic symbols, or *icons,* used throughout this book. We use these icons to call your attention to points that are particularly important or worth noting. The following icons are used in this book:

The Note icon sits next to an explanation about why QuarkXPress behaves in a certain way.

The Tip icon indicates that the accompanying paragraph includes a tip or an idea about how to use a QuarkXPress feature.

The Caution icon alerts you to a warning about potential unwanted effects of using a QuarkXPress feature.

The Mac icon calls attention to an accompanying description of a feature that works differently on the Mac version of QuarkXPress.

The Design Tip icon accompanies paragraphs that include information on how to use a publishing technique (this is general publishing advice and is not necessarily specific to QuarkXPress).

 The Cross-Reference icon means the paragraph includes a reference to information contained in another part of the book.

Closing Remarks

Publishing is an exciting field, and desktop publishing has brought that excitement to the masses, revolutionizing communications and giving deeper meaning to "freedom of the press." We've been excited about desktop publishing from the early days, and we hope that you share that enthusiasm (or that we infect you with it!).

Desktop publishing is an ever-changing field. QuarkXPress has evolved significantly since its first version on the Macintosh, and its chief competitors (worthwhile programs in their own right for a variety of users) Aldus PageMaker and Ventura Publisher also continue to evolve, as do the computers we all run them on. Despite this evolution, the principles of publishing remain the same, so we hope that you'll find this book's advice valuable over the years, even when you're using QuarkXPress 6.0.

PART I

QuarkXPress Fundamentals

If you are new to desktop publishing in general or are just beginning to work with Windows, you will find this section to be particularly useful. By the time you finish reading it, you'll have the basics you need to go on and learn more about the program's powerful publishing tools.

In this section, we discuss the basics of QuarkXPress, including its set of text and picture tools and its user interface. We also introduce fundamental facts about working in a Windows operating environment.

If you are familiar with the Macintosh version of QuarkXPress and know how to use Windows, you can skip this section and move on to the next. If not, rest easy. You are about to begin learning how to use the most powerful and comprehensive publishing program yet developed to run under Windows.

QuarkXPress has plenty of features but, if you take it a step at a time, it is not difficult to learn. Some words of advice: Use it whenever you can so you get plenty of practice. The more you use QuarkXPress, the better you'll be and the more features you will know how to use as you create a wide range of professional documents.

CHAPTER 1

What Is QuarkXPress?

The QuarkXPress Method

QuarkXPress takes a structured approach to publishing. It is *box-based,* meaning that you build pages by assembling a variety of boxes in a logical manner. First, you set up the basic framework of the document — the page size and orientation, margins, number of columns, and so on. Then you fill that framework with text, pictures, and lines.

Before you can put text on a QuarkXPress page, you need a text box. You can tell QuarkXPress to create text boxes automatically for you, or you can draw them with the Text Box tool (the full set of QuarkXPress tools is described in Chapter 2). If you want to add pictures to a page, you need a picture box. You draw picture boxes using one of four Picture Box tools, each of which creates a different shape of box. You can put frames around picture boxes and text boxes; you also can resize, rotate, and apply color to both types of boxes.

If you simply want to put a line on a page, however, you don't need a text or picture box. You can draw lines anywhere on a page by using one of two Line tools, and you can specify the style and thickness of the lines you draw.

This, in very simple terms, is the publishing philosophy of QuarkXPress. In the right hands, it can generate truly impressive results.

Terms You Should Know

The accessibility of desktop publishing tools brought an arcane dialect to the masses. Not too long ago, only a few publishing professionals knew — or cared — what the words *pica, kerning, crop,* or *Pantone* meant. Now, almost everyone who wants to produce a nice-looking report or a simple newsletter encounters these terms in the menus and manuals of their layout programs. Unfortunately, the terms sometimes are used incorrectly or are replaced with general terms to make nonprofessional users feel less threatened, but that confuse a professional printer or someone who works in a service bureau. Here are definitions of some of the basics terms you need to know, grouped by publishing task.

Typography terms

Typography terms include words that describe the appearance of text in a document. These terms refer to such aspects of typography as the amount of space between lines, characters, and paragraphs and the size and style of the typeface used.

Characters

A *font* is a set of characters at a certain size, weight, and style (for example, 10-point Palatino Bold). This term now is used often as a synonym for *typeface*, which is a set of characters at a certain style in *all* sizes, weights, and stylings (for example, Palatino). A *face* is a combination of a weight and styling at all sizes (for example, Palatino Bold Italic). A *font family* is a group of related typefaces (for example, the Franklin family includes Franklin Gothic, Franklin Heavy, and Franklin Compressed).

Weight describes typeface thickness. Typical weights, from thinnest to thickest, are *ultralight, light, book, medium, demibold, bold, heavy, ultrabold,* and *ultra heavy.*

Type can have one of three basic *stylings*: *Roman* type is upright type; *oblique* type is slanted type; and *italic* type is both slanted and curved (to appear more like calligraphy than roman type). Type also may be *expanded* (widened), *condensed* (narrowed), or *compressed* (severely narrowed).

The *x-height* refers to the height of the average lowercase letter (this is based on the letter *x*). The greater the height, the bigger the letter looks when compared to letters in other typefaces that are the same point size but have a smaller x-height. *Cap height* is similar; it refers to the size of the average uppercase letter (based on the letter *C*).

In a letter such as *q*, the part of the letter that goes below the baseline is called a *descender*. The part of a letter that extends above the x height (as in the letter *b*) is called an *ascender*.

A *serif* is a horizontal stroke used to give letters visual character. The strokes on the upper-left and bottom of the letter *p* in a typeface such as Times are serifs. *Sans serif* means that a typeface does not use these embellishments — Helvetica is an example of a sans serif typeface.

Measurement units

A *pica* is a measurement unit used to specify the width and depth of columns and pages. A pica is just a little less than ⅙ of an inch (most people round up to an even ⅙-inch). A *point* is a measurement used to specify type size and the space between lines. There are 12 points in a pica, so there are about 72.27 points to the inch — most people round down to 72 per inch. A *cicero* is a unit of measure used in many parts of Europe. One inch equals about 5.62 ciceros.

The terms *em*, *en*, and *punctuation space* (also called a *thin space*) are units of measurement that reflect, respectively, the horizontal space taken up by a capital *M*, capital *N*, and lowercase *t*. Typically, an em space is the same width as the current point size; an en space is ½ of the current point size; and a punctuation (thin) space is ¼ of the current point size. In other words, for 12-point type, an em is 12 points wide, an en space is 6 points, and a punctuation or thin space is 3 points. A *figure space* refers to the width of a numeral, which usually is the same as an en. (In most typefaces, all numerals are the same width so that tables align naturally.)

Spacing

Leading, also called *line spacing*, refers to the space from the base of one line (the *baseline*) to another. (Leading is named after the pieces of lead once used to space out lines.)

Tracking determines the overall space between letters within a word. If you increase tracking, space increases globally (throughout your entire document). *Word spacing* defines the preferred, minimum, and maximum spacing between words. *Letter spacing* (sometimes called *character spacing*) defines the preferred, minimum, and maximum spacing between letters. QuarkXPress uses your preferred spacing specifications unless you justify the text; if you justify text, the program spaces letters and words within the limits you set for maximum and minimum spacing.

Kerning refers to an adjustment of the space between two letters. You kern letters to accommodate their specific shapes. For example, you probably would use tighter kerning in the letter pair *to* than in *oo*, because *to* looks better if the *o* fits partly under the *t*. *Pair kerning* is a table, called the *kerning table* in QuarkXPress, that indicates the letter pairs you want the publishing program to kern automatically.

Justification adds space between words (and sometimes between letters) so that each line of text aligns at both the left and right margin of a column or page. *Ragged right* and *flush left* both refer to text that aligns against a column's left margin but not its right margin; *ragged left* and *flush right* text aligns against the right margin but not the left margin. *Centered* text is aligned so that there is equal space on both margins. *Justification* also is used to refer to the type of spacing used: justified, ragged right, centered, or ragged left.

Vertical justification adds space between paragraphs (and sometimes between lines) so that the tops and bottoms of each column on a page align. (This often is confused with *column balancing*, which ensures that each column has the same number of lines.) *Carding* is a vertical-justification method that adds space between paragraphs in one-line increments. *Feathering* uses fractional-line spaces between paragraphs.

Paragraphs

You typically indicate a new paragraph with an *indent*, which inserts a space (typically an em space in newspapers and magazines) in front of the paragraph's first letter. An *outdent* (also called an *exdent*) shifts the first character past the left margin and places the other lines at the left margin; this paragraph alignment typically is used in lists. A *block indent* moves an entire paragraph in from the left margin, a style often used for long quotes. A *hanging indent* is like an outdent, except that the first line begins at the left margin and all subsequent lines are indented.

A *bullet* is a character (often a filled circle) used to indicate that a paragraph is one element in a list of elements. Bullets can be indented, outdented, or kept at the left margin. A *drop cap* is a large capital letter that extends down several lines into the surrounding text (the rest of the text wraps around it). Drop caps are used at the beginning of a section or story. A *raised cap* is the same as a drop cap except that it does not extend down into the text; instead, it rests on the baseline of the first line and extends several lines above the baseline.

Style sheets contain named sets of such attributes as spacing, typeface, indent, leading, and justification. A set of attributes is known as a *style* or *style tag*. Essentially, styles are formatting macros. You *tag* each paragraph with the name of the style you want to apply. Any formatting changes made to one paragraph are automatically reflected in all other paragraphs tagged with the same style.

Hyphenation

A *hyphen* is used to indicate the division of a word at the end of a line and to join words that combine to modify another word. *Hyphenation* is determining where to place the hyphen in split words. *Consecutive hyphenation* determines how many lines in a row can end with a hyphen (more than three hyphens in a row is considered bad typographic practice). The *hyphenation zone* determines how far from the right margin a hyphen can be inserted to split a word.

An *exception dictionary* lists words with nonstandard hyphenations. You can add words that the publishing program's default dictionary does not know and override the default hyphenations for words such as *project* that are hyphenated differently as a noun (*proj-ect*) than as a verb (*pro-ject*). Placing a *Discretionary hyphen* (also called a *soft hyphen*) in a word tells the program to hyphenate the word at that place if the word must be split. A discretionary hyphen affects only the word in which it is placed.

Layout terms

Document layout — the placement of text, pictures, and other items on a page — involves many elements. A brief primer on layout terms follows; you'll find more detailed explanations later in this book, particularly in Chapter 8, "Getting Started with Layout."

Design elements

A *column* is a block of text. When you place two or more columns side by side, the space between columns is called the *gutter*. (In newspapers and magazines, gutter space usually is one or two picas.)

The *margin* is the space between the edge of a page and the nearest standard block of text. Some designers allow text or graphics to intrude into the margin for visual effect.

A *bleed* is a graphic element or block of color that extends to the trimmed edge of the page.

A *wrap* refers to a textual cutout that occurs when a column is intruded by graphics or other text. The column margins are altered so that the column text goes around — wraps around — the intruding graphic or text instead of being overprinted by the intruding element. A wrap can be rectangular, polygonal, or curved, depending on what the text wraps around and the capabilities of the layout program; QuarkXPress supports all three shapes.

A *folio* is the page number and identifying material (such as the publication name or month) that appears at the bottom or top of every page.

White space is the part of the page left empty to create contrast to the text and graphics. White space provides visual relief and emphasizes the text and graphics.

Most desktop publishing programs use *frames* to hold layout elements (text and graphics) on a page; QuarkXPress refers to these frames as *boxes*. Using a mouse, you can delete, copy, resize, or otherwise manipulate boxes in your layout. The boxes that hold layout elements can have ruling lines around them; Quark calls these lines *frames*. You can create a *template* by filling a document with empty boxes and defining style tags in advance; you then can use the template repeatedly to create documents that use the same boxes and styles.

Image manipulation

Cropping an image means to select a part of it for use on the page. *Sizing* an image means to determine how much to reduce or enlarge the image (or part of the image). Sizing also is called *scaling*. With layout programs, you often can *distort* an image to size it differently horizontally than vertically, which creates special effects such as compressing or stretching an image.

Reversing (also called *inverting* in some programs) exchanges the black and white portions of an image, which is like creating a photographic negative.

Layout tools

Galleys are single columns of type that are not laid out in any sort of page format. Publishers typically use galleys to check for proper hyphenation and proof for errors; galleys also are sent to authors for proofreading, so corrections can be made before the text is laid out.

A *grid* is the basic layout design of a publication. It includes standard positions of folios, text, graphics, bylines, and headlines. A layout artist modifies the grid when necessary. Grids also are called *templates*. A *dummy* is a rough sketch of the layout of a particular story. *Guidelines* show the usual placement of columns and margins in the grid. In some programs, guidelines are nonprinting lines you can use to ensure that elements align.

An *overlay* is a piece of transparent paper or film laid over a layout board. On the overlay, the artist can indicate screens in a different color or overprinted material such as text or graphics. Some programs have electronic equivalents of overlays.

Production terms

Registration marks tell a printer where to position each negative relative to other negatives (the registration marks must line up when the negatives are superimposed). *Crop marks* tell a printer where to cut the negatives; anything outside the crop marks is not printed. Crop marks are used both to define page size and to indicate which part of an image is to be used.

A *screen* is an area printed at a particular percentage of a color (including black). For example, the border of a page may have a 20-percent black screen.

Spot color is a single color applied at one or more places on a page, such as for a screen or as part of an illustration. You can use more than one spot color per page. Spot colors can be process or Pantone colors.

A *process color* refers to any of the four primary colors in publishing: cyan, magenta, yellow, and black (known as a group as *CMYK*). A *Pantone Matching System color* (called *Pantone* or *PMS* for short) is an industry standard for specifying a color. The printer uses a premixed ink based on the Pantone number you specify; you look up these numbers in a table of colors. *Four-color printing* is the use of the four process colors in combination to produce most other colors. A *color separation* is a set of four photographic negatives — one filtered for each process color — shot from a color photograph or image. When overprinted, the four negatives reproduce that image. A *build* attempts to simulate a Pantone color by overprinting the appropriate percentages of the four process colors.

Trapping refers to the technique of extending one color so that it slightly overlaps an adjoining color. Trapping is done to prevent gaps between two abutting colors; such gaps sometimes are created by the misalignment of color plates on a printing press.

Global Control vs. Local Control

The power of desktop publishing in general, and QuarkXPress in particular, is that it enables you to automate time-consuming layout and typesetting tasks while at the same time letting you customize each step of the process according to your needs. You can use *global* controls to establish general settings for layout elements and then use *local* controls to modify those elements to meet specific publishing requirements. The key to using global and local tools effectively is to know when each is appropriate.

Global tools include:

- Style sheets (covered in Chapter 6)
- Hyphenation and justification (H&J) sets (Chapter 13)
- Master pages (Chapter 5)
- Libraries (Chapter 22)
- Sections (Chapter 11)
- General preferences and application preferences (Chapter 4)

Styles and master pages are the two main global settings you can expect to override locally throughout a document. This is no surprise, because the layout and typographic functions that styles and master pages automate are the fundamental components of any document.

Local tools include:

- Character and paragraph tools (Chapters 12 and 13)
- Text Box and Picture Box tools (Chapters 9 and 10)
- Graphics tools (Part V)

In many cases, it's obvious which tool to use. If you maintain certain layout standards throughout a document, for example, using master pages is the obvious approach. Using styles is the best solution if you want to apply standard character and paragraph formatting throughout a document. When you work with special-case documents, such as a single-page display ad, it doesn't make much sense to spend time designing master pages and styles — it's easier just to format elements on-the-fly.

In other cases, it's harder to decide which tool is appropriate. For example, you can control page numbering on a global basis through the Section dialog box (accessed via Page ⇨ Section). But you also can change page numbering within a document by moving to the page on which you want to change a page number, invoking the Section dialog box, and selecting new settings.

Another situation in which you can choose between local or global controls is specifying measurement values. Regardless of the default measurement unit, you can use any unit when entering measurements in a QuarkXPress dialog box. If, for example, the default measurement is picas but you're accustomed to working with inches, go ahead and enter measurements in inches. QuarkXPress accepts any of the following measurement units:

- " (for inches)
- p (for picas)
- pt (for points)

- cm (for centimeters)
- mm (for millimeters)
- c (for ciceros)

 You can enter fractional picas in two ways: in decimal format, as in *6.5p*; and in picas and points, as in *6p6*. Either of these settings results in a measurement of 6 ½ picas. Note that if you use points, you must place them after the *p*.

Summary

▶ QuarkXPress is box-based, meaning that you build pages by assembling a variety of boxes and then filling the boxes with text or pictures.

▶ You'll find it easier to use QuarkXPress if you familiarize yourself with basic publishing terminology.

▶ Use global controls to establish general settings for layout elements.

▶ Use local controls to modify elements to meet specific publishing requirements.

Basic Elements

CHAPTER 2

In This Chapter

▶ Choosing hardware and software to use with QuarkXPress

▶ Using QuarkXPress menus and palettes

▶ Selecting items to make them active

Hardware and Software Recommendations

We recommend that you have at least the following hardware and software to use QuarkXPress:

- A computer with an 80386 (or better) processor, running at 20 MHz (or faster); 6 to 8 megabytes of RAM; and a 120MB (or more) hard disk

- A color or gray-scale monitor with an 8-bit video card (if you use lots of high-end color, a color monitor and a 16- or 24-bit video card)

- A mouse

- Windows 3.1 (or better) and DOS 5.0 (or better)

- A separate word processing program, a separate graphics program and, if you will be using a scanner, a separate image-editing program

- As many type fonts as you can manage — the more the better

QuarkXPress for Windows runs on computers equipped with earlier versions of DOS, but the versions recommended here give you best performance. The program may run on Windows 3.0, but it was not designed to do so. If you have Windows 3.0, we strongly suggest that you upgrade to a more current version.

The Document Window

The QuarkXPress *user interface* — the way in which you communicate and work with QuarkXPress for Windows — has a number of similarities to the interfaces used by other programs designed to run under Microsoft Windows. If you use other Windows programs, you may be familiar with such QuarkXPress interface components as the menu bar at the top of the document window and the Tool palette. The rest of this chapter explains the basics of using QuarkXPress interface components.

When you open a document in QuarkXPress, the program displays a document window containing the elements shown in Figure 2-1.

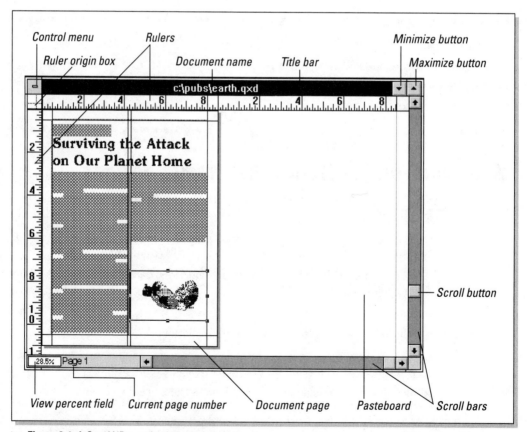

▶ **Figure 2-1:** A QuarkXPress document window.

- The *ruler origin box* lets you reset and reposition the ruler origin, which is the point at which the side and top rulers are 0 (zero).

- The *Control menu* lets you restore, move, size, minimize, maximize, and close an open document window.

- The name of the open document appears on the *title bar*, located beneath the menu bar. You can move the document window around in the screen display area by clicking and dragging the title bar.

- The *vertical* and *horizontal rulers* on the left and top of the window reflect the measurement system currently in use.

- The *pasteboard* is a work area around the document page. You can temporarily store text boxes, picture boxes, or lines on the pasteboard. Items on the pasteboard do not print.

- QuarkXPress displays a shadow effect around the document page. The shadow indicates where the pasteboard begins.

- If you click the *maximize* or *minimize buttons,* the document window enlarges to its maximum size or reduces to a small icon.

- The *View Percent field* shows the magnification level of the currently displayed page. To change the magnification level, enter a value between 10 and 400 percent in the field and then press Enter.

- Use the *scroll bars, buttons,* and *arrows* to maneuver the document page within the document window.

QuarkXPress Menus

The menu bar appears across the top of the document window. To display, or "pull down," a menu, click the menu title or press the Alt key together with the underlined letter in the menu name. To open the File menu, for example, press Alt+F.

After a menu appears, you can select any of the active menu commands. QuarkXPress displays inactive menu commands with dimmed ("grayed-out") letters; these commands are not currently available to you.

If an arrowhead appears to the right of a menu command, QuarkXPress displays a second, associated menu when you choose that command. Sometimes this secondary menu appears automatically when you highlight the first menu command; other times, you must press the right-arrow key or press Enter to open the secondary menu. Figure 2-2 shows the Style menu and the secondary menu that appears when you select the Type Style menu command.

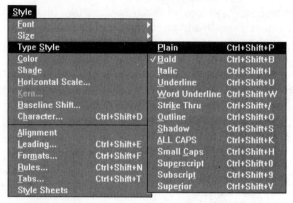

▶ **Figure 2-2:** Selecting menu items in QuarkXPress.

Dialog Boxes

Dialog boxes appear if you choose a menu command whose name is followed by an ellipsis (. . .). Figure 2-3 shows an example of a dialog box.

Through dialog boxes, you can set specifications that relate to the menu command or enter values that affect how QuarkXPress applies the command to your document. Some dialog boxes also contain *drop-down lists;* in Figure 2-3, the small box containing tab options (the box with the down-pointing arrow in the upper-right corner) is a drop-down list. If a down-pointing arrow appears next to an item in the dialog box, a drop-down list is available.

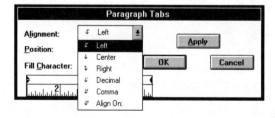

▶ **Figure 2-3:** A dialog box and drop-down list.

Keyboard Shortcuts

You can select many QuarkXPress functions in a variety of ways. Some functions are available through pull-down menus, some through palettes, some through keyboard shortcuts — and some are available through all three options. When you first begin using the program, you probably will be like most new users and access functions by using menus. But as you gain familiarity with QuarkXPress, you can save time by using keyboard shortcuts instead of menus to access functions.

Suppose you want to move from page one of a document to page three, for example. You can change pages by choosing Go To from the Page menu, or you can use the keyboard shortcut: Press and hold the Ctrl key while you press the J key. In this book, we write this key combination as follows: *Ctrl+J.* We use the same format for all keyboard shortcuts.

Palettes

To make it easy for you to perform common desktop publishing functions, QuarkXPress offers a set of *palettes.* You can display palettes while a document is open, which enables you to access palette functions without using the pull-down menus. You'll discover that using the palettes really speeds up the process of creating documents in QuarkXPress. In fact, you'll probably find yourself using a couple of the palettes — the Tool palette and the Measurements palette — all the time.

The Tool palette

When you open QuarkXPress, the Tool palette, shown in Figure 2-4, appears on the left side of the screen. (If the palette is not visible, select Show Tools from the View menu.) This palette displays tools you use to create, change, link, view, and rotate text boxes, picture boxes, and lines.

To activate a tool on the palette, use the mouse to position the cursor above the tool icon and then click the mouse button. Depending on the tool you select, the cursor takes on a different look to reflect the function the tool performs. When you click the Linking tool, for example, the cursor changes to look like links in a chain.

▶ **Figure 2-4:** The Tool palette.

In the chapters that follow, we explain in greater detail many of the functions you can perform with the Tool palette. But here are brief descriptions of each tool.

Item tool

 When you want to change the shape, location, or presence of a text box, picture box, or line, use the Item tool. The Item tool enables you to select, move, group, ungroup, cut, copy, and paste text boxes, picture boxes, lines, and groups. When you click the Item tool on a box, the box becomes active, meaning that you can change or move it. Sizing handles appear on the sides of the active box; you can click and drag these handles to make the box a different size.

Content tool

 If you want to make changes to the contents of a text box or picture box, use the Content tool. Functions you can perform with the Content tool include *importing* (putting text into a text box or putting a picture into a picture box), cutting, copying, pasting, and editing text.

To edit text in a text box, first select the Content tool. Then select the areas of text you want to edit by clicking and dragging the Content tool to highlight the text or by using different numbers of mouse button clicks, as follows:

- **To position the cursor:** Use the mouse to move the pointer (it looks like a large capital I) to the desired location and click the mouse button once.

- **To select a single word:** Use the mouse to move the pointer within the word and click the mouse button twice.

- **To select a line of text:** Use the mouse to move the pointer within the line and click the mouse button three times.

- **To select an entire paragraph:** Use the mouse to move the pointer within the paragraph and click the mouse button four times.

- **To select the entire document:** Use the mouse to move the cursor anywhere within the document and click the mouse button five times.

 In a picture box, the Content tool cursor changes to a hand shape. You can use this tool in a picture box to move around within the box. You can also use it when manipulating the picture's contents, such as applying shades, colors, or printing effects. See Chapter 20, "Working with Bitmap Images," and Chapter 21, "Working with Color."

Rotation tool

 The Rotation tool lets you click a text box, picture box, or line and rotate it by dragging it to the angle you want. As you will learn later in this book, you can rotate items on a page in other ways, which include using the Measurements palette and the Modify command in the Item menu. See Chapter 9, "Working with Text," Chapter 10, "Working with Picture Boxes," and Chapter 11, "Additional Layout Features."

Zoom tool

 Depending on what you are doing, you may want to change the magnification of the page on-screen. The Zoom tool lets you reduce or enlarge the view you see in the document window. When you select the Zoom tool, the cursor looks like a small magnifying glass; when you hold the cursor over the document window and click the mouse button, QuarkXPress changes the magnification of that section of the screen up or down in increments of 25 percent.

Text Box tool

 In QuarkXPress, you can import text from a word processor file or enter text directly onto a document page. But whichever method you choose, you need to create a text box to hold the text. You can instruct QuarkXPress to create text boxes on each page of the document automatically. Sometimes, though, you need to create a text box manually — which you do using the Text Box tool.

To create a text box, select the Text Box tool and place the cursor at the approximate location where you want the box to appear. Click the mouse button and hold it down as you drag the box to size.

 See Chapter 9, "Working with Text," for more information about creating text boxes.

Picture Box tools

Picture boxes hold graphics that you import from graphics programs. QuarkXPress offers four Picture Box tools. Using these tools, you can draw four different box shapes:

 ■ **Rectangle Picture Box tool:** Use this to create rectangular or square picture boxes.

 ■ **Rounded Rectangle Picture Box tool:** Use this tool to create picture boxes that are rectangular but have rounded corners. You can change the curve of the corners by using the Modify command in the Item menu.

 ■ **Oval Picture Box tool:** This tool enables you to create oval or circular picture boxes.

 ■ **Polygon Picture Box tool:** Using this tool, you can create any shape of picture box you want. The only restriction is that the box must have at least three sides.

You create the first three styles of picture boxes (rectangle, rounded rectangle, and oval) in the same manner as text boxes: Place the cursor at the approximate spot you want the box to appear on the page, click the mouse button, and hold it down as you drag the box to size.

To create a polygon picture box, draw the first line in the box and click the mouse button once to end the line. Continue drawing the lines of the box, clicking the mouse button once to end each line. Close the box by connecting the final line to the originating point of the polygon.

Line tools

The two Line tools enable you to draw lines, or rules. After you draw a line, you can change its thickness (*weight*) or line style (dotted line, double line, and so on). The Orthogonal Line tool (top) draws horizontal and vertical lines. The Diagonal Line tool (bottom) draws lines at any angle.

QuarkXPress calls the Diagonal Line tool simply the Line tool. We use *Diagonal Line tool* so it is not confused with the Orthogonal Line tool.

To use either of these tools, click the tool to select it and position the cursor at the point where you want the line to begin. Click the mouse button and hold it as you draw the line. When the line is approximately the length you want, release the mouse button. After you draw a line, use the Measurements palette to select the line weight and line style.

For more specifics on drawing lines, see Chapter 11, "Additional Layout Features."

Linking and Unlinking tools

The bottom two tools in the Tool palette are the Linking tool (top) and the Unlinking tool (bottom). The Linking tool enables you to link text boxes together so that overflow text flows from one text box into another. You use the Unlinking tool to break the link between text boxes.

Linking is particularly useful when you want to jump text — for example, when a story starts on page one and jumps to (continues on) page four. Chapter 9 covers linking in more detail.

The Measurements palette

The Measurements palette is one of the best inventions we have ever come across. This palette displays information about the position and attributes of any selected page element, and it enables you to enter values to change those specifications. You invoke the measurements palette by choosing View ⇨ Show Measurements.

The information displayed on the Measurements palette depends on the element currently selected. When you select a text box, the Measurements palette displays the text box position coordinates (X: and Y:), size (W: and H:), amount of rotation, and number of columns (Cols:), as shown in Figure 2-5. Using the

X: 0.5"	W: 7.5"	△ 0°		auto		Souvenir-Demi	▼ 24 pt ▼
Y: 0.5"	H: 2.417"	Cols:1				P B I O S Q U W K K	

▶ **Figure 2-5:** The Measurements palette when a text box is selected.

up- and down-pointing arrows on the palette, you can modify the leading of the text box; use the right- and left-pointing arrows to adjust kerning or tracking for selected text.

You can specify text alignment — left, center, right, or justified — by using the alignment icons. In the type section of the palette, you can control the font, size, and type style of selected text. Chapter 12, "Understanding Character Spacing," Chapter 13, "Understanding Paragraph Spacing," and Chapter 14, "Working with Typefaces," cover these features in detail.

If you select a picture box, the Measurements palette displays the picture box position coordinates (X: and Y:), size (W: and H:), amount of box rotation, corner radius, reduction or enlargement percentage (X%: and Y%:), repositioning coordinates (X+: and Y+:), amount of picture rotation within the box, and amount of slant. Figure 2-6 shows the Measurements palette for a picture box.

X: 4.333"	W: 3.667"	△ 0°	X%: 60%	X+: 0.128"	△ 0°
Y: 7.525"	H: 2.277"	⊾ 0"	Y%: 60%	Y+: 0.333"	⟋ 0°

▶ **Figure 2-6:** The Measurements palette when a picture box is selected.

When you select a line, the Measurements palette displays the location coordinates (X: and Y:), line width, line style, and endcap (line ending) style. The line style list box lets you select the style for the line. Figure 2-7 shows the Measurements palette for a line.

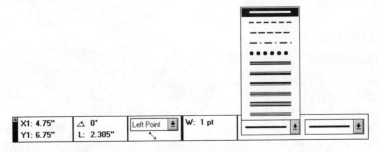

▶ **Figure 2-7:** The Measurements palette for a line.

The Document Layout palette

You can use the Document Layout palette, shown in Figure 2-8, to create, name, delete, move, and apply master pages. You also can add, delete, and move document pages. To display the Document Layout palette, choose Show Document Layout from the View menu. Chapter 5, "Understanding Master Pages," and Chapter 11, "Additional Layout Features," cover this feature in detail.

The Colors palette

▶ **Figure 2-9:** The Colors palette.

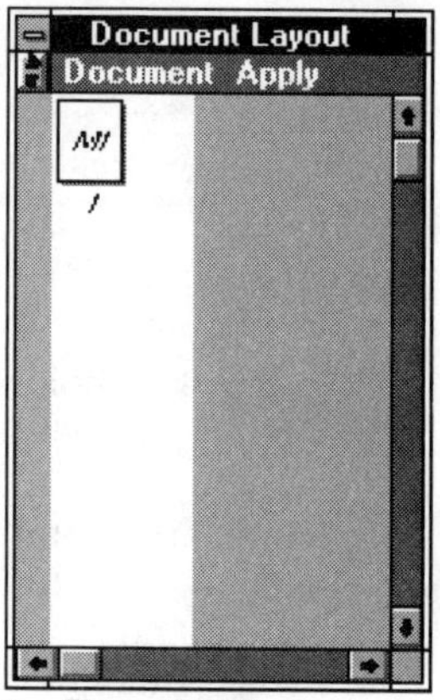

▶ **Figure 2-8:** The Document Layout palette.

Figure 2-9 shows the Colors palette. Using this palette, you can designate the color and shade (percentage of color) you want to apply to text, pictures, and backgrounds of text and picture boxes. You also can produce color blends, using one or two colors, to apply to box backgrounds. To display the Colors palette, choose Show Colors from the View menu. Chapter 21, "Working with Color," covers color in more detail.

The Style Sheets palette

The Style Sheets palette displays the names of the style tags attached to selected paragraphs and also enables you to apply style sheets to paragraphs. To display the Style Sheets palette, shown in Figure 2-10, choose Show Style Sheets from the View menu.

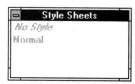

▶ **Figure 2-10:** The Style Sheets palette.

The Trap Information palette

In the Trap Information palette, shown in Figure 2-11, you can set or change trapping specifications for selected items. (*Trapping* controls how one color in a document prints next to another color.) Don't use this palette unless you know what you are doing — it is considered an expert feature. You use this palette to set custom trapping for selected items; you can specify a setting from –36 to 36 points. To display the Trap Information palette, choose Show Trap Information from the View menu. Chapter 26, "Printing Techniques," covers trapping in detail.

Trap Information

| Background: | Default | ± | Overprint | ? |

▶ **Figure 2-11:** The Trap Information palette.

Library palettes

You can store a layout element (text or picture box, line, or group) in a library palette by dragging the element from the document or the pasteboard into an open Library palette. You then can use items stored in the library in other documents. To open a library palette, like that shown in Figure 2-12, choose Library from the Utilities menu. Chapter 22, "Using Libraries," covers this topic in detail.

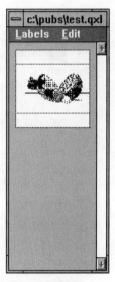

c:\pubs\test.qxl

Labels   Edit

▶ **Figure 2-12:** A library palette.

Variations of the Mouse Pointer

Like all Windows programs, QuarkXPress reminds you what tool is active by changing the mouse pointer (also called the *cursor*) to reflect the current tool. Some tools you'll see all the time, others only occasionally because they are used for specialized features. Following are the various renditions of the mouse pointer you can expect to see in QuarkXPress.

Common mouse pointers

You'll frequently come across the following mouse pointers:

- **Standard pointer:** This pointer appears as you move through dialog boxes, menus, and windows. It also appears as you move over nonselected elements.

- **Creation pointer:** This pointer appears if you have selected a box or line tool. To create a rectangular or oval box, click and hold down the mouse button at one corner of the box and drag the mouse to the opposite corner, then release the button. (Hold the Shift key to keep the box a perfect square or circle.) For a polygon box, click each point in the polygon and return to the first point when done (the creation pointer changes to an oval (▢) to indicate you are over the first point). For a line, click and hold down the mouse button at one end and drag it to the line's end, and then release the button. Parts III and V cover text box, picture box, and line creation.

- **Sizing pointer:** This pointer appears if you select one of the handles on a text or picture box (with either the Item or Content tool selected) or on a line. You can resize the item by holding down the mouse button and dragging the handle. Parts III and V cover text box, picture box, and line manipulation.

- **Item pointer:** This pointer appears if the Item tool is selected and you have selected a box or line. You can move the selected item by holding down the mouse button and dragging the item. Parts III and V cover text box, picture box, and line manipulation.

- **Lock pointer:** This pointer appears if the Item tool is selected and you have selected a locked text box, picture box, or line. This indicates that the box will not move if you try to drag it (you can move it, however, by changing the coordinates in the Measurements palettes or via Item ⇨ Modify). Part III covers text box, picture box, and line manipulation.

- **I-beam (text) pointer:** This pointer appears if the Content tool is selected and you select a text box. If the cursor is blinking, any text you type inserts where the cursor appears. If the cursor is not blinking, you must click at the location in the text box where you want to edit text. Part IV covers text manipulation.

- **Grabber pointer:** This pointer appears if the Content tool is selected and you have selected a picture box containing a graphic. You can move the graphic within the box by holding down the mouse button and dragging the item. Parts III and VI cover text box, picture box, and line manipulation.

- **Zoom-in pointer:** This pointer appears if you select the Zoom tool and click the left mouse button (this zooms in by the predefined amount, which by default is 25 percent). You can also select an area to zoom into by clicking the mouse at one corner of the area of interest, holding the mouse button down, dragging the mouse to the opposite corner, and then releasing the button. Chapter 4 covers zoom preference settings; Chapter 8 covers the different views to use while working on layouts.

- **Zoom-out pointer:** This pointer appears if you select the Zoom tool and hold the Ctrl key down while clicking the left mouse button (this zooms out by the predefined amount, which by default is 25 percent). Chapter 4 covers zoom preference settings; Chapter 8 covers using different views while working on layouts.

- **Rotation pointer:** This pointer and the rotation guide target appear when you select the Rotate tool. Hold the mouse button down and move the pointer around the target until you have achieved the desired rotation. The line connecting the target to the pointer can be made larger or smaller by moving the pointer further away or closer to the target; the further away the pointer from the target, the finer rotation increments you can control. Chapter 10 covers rotation for picture boxes; Chapter 15 covers rotation for text boxes.

- **Link pointer:** This pointer appears if you select the Link tool. Click the pointer on the first text box and then on the second text box in the chain of boxes you want text to flow through. If there are more boxes, select them in the flow order as well. You can switch pages while this tool is active to flow text across pages. Chapter 9 covers linking.

- **Unlink pointer:** This pointer appears if you select the Unlink tool. Click the pointer on the first text box and then on the second text box in the chain of boxes you want to sever the text flow between. If there are more boxes to unlink, repeat this process. You can switch pages while this tool is active to unlink text flow across pages. Chapter 9 covers linking.

Specialized pointers

The following pointers are those you'll run across less often:

- **Library pointer:** This pointer appears in the current library window if you have selected a library element and are moving it, either within the window or to another open library window. Libraries are covered in Chapter 22.

The following three pointers appear only in the Document Layout palette, accessed via <u>V</u>iew ➪ <u>D</u>ocument layout. For details on master pages, see Chapter 5.

- **Insert Master Page pointer:** This pointer appears in the Document Layout palette when Masters appears in its menu (after you select the Insert option from the Masters menu). Move the pointer to the location in the list of master pages where you want the new master page to be inserted.

- **Facing Master Pages pointer:** When Masters appears in the Document Layout palette menu, this pointer appears as you move the Insert Master Page pointer over an existing master page (if you selected Blank Facing Master from the Masters ➪ Insert menu).

- **Single Master Page pointer:** When Masters appears in the Document Layout palette menu, this pointer appears as you move the Insert Master Page pointer over an existing master page (if you selected Blank Single Master from the Masters ➪ Insert menu).

Active and Selected Items

Throughout this book, you'll see instructions such as *select the text box* or *apply the change to the active line*. *Selecting* an item is the same as *activating* it — which you must do before modifying an item in QuarkXPress. If you want to make a change to an entire item, select or activate the item by clicking on it with the Item tool. If you want to make a change to the item's contents, click the Content tool on the item.

When an item is selected or active, you see small black boxes, or sizing handles, on its sides and corners, as illustrated in Figure 2-13.

▶ **Figure 2-13:**
QuarkXPress displays sizing handles on the sides and corners of an active item.

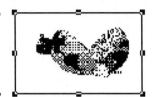

Summary

▶ When you choose a menu command that has an arrowhead to its right, QuarkXPress displays a secondary, associated menu.

▶ A dialog box appears when you choose a menu command that has an ellipsis to its right.

▶ Use keyboard shortcuts and palettes to save time when using QuarkXPress.

The Windows Environment

∎∎∎

In This Chapter

▶ Understanding and customizing the Windows interface

▶ Creating and modifying program groups

▶ Loading programs automatically and loading the right program for each file type

▶ Moving between programs

▶ Manipulating files

▶ Installing PostScript and TrueType fonts

▶ Determining which fonts download to printers

∎∎∎

Understanding the Benefits of Windows

Windows 3.0 provided PC users the graphical environment needed to do the kind of publishing traditionally done on a Macintosh. And the speed and ease of use that Windows 3.1 offers rival that of the Macintosh, even if some aspects of Windows are worse, some better, and some simply different. (Although Ventura Publisher and Aldus PageMaker existed in PC versions before Windows 3.0, PC-based publishers did not have many other necessary tools, especially for high-end graphics. They also lacked the ability to run multiple programs simultaneously, to move elements between different programs, and to work with a consistent set of tools, fonts, and device drivers.)

If you are using Windows 3.0, upgrade to Windows 3.1, which is both significantly faster and offers built-in type scaling for TrueType fonts (you'll still want Adobe Type Manager for your PostScript fonts). Version 3.1 also offers features

that make it easier to use, such as drag-and-drop printing, the ability to load selected programs automatically when you load Windows, and an improved File Manager. QuarkXPress was designed for Windows 3.1, not 3.0, and it may not work properly if you run it in Windows 3.0.

If you are an experienced Windows user, you can skip this chapter. But if you are a Mac user who is now also using Windows or a DOS user who moved to Windows because of QuarkXPress, read on. For a comprehensive look at Windows, we recommend *Windows 3.1 Secrets*, by Brian Livingston, and for a thorough introduction to DOS, *DOS for Dummies*, by Dan Gookin (both published by IDG Books Worldwide).

Using the Windows Interface

To open the Windows program, type **WIN** and press Enter at the DOS prompt, which usually looks something like C:>. When you start Windows, what first appears is a program called *Program Manager*. Figure 3-1 shows Program Manager and labels its main elements. The Program Manager screen elements are:

- **Title bar:** The title bar tells you what group or program is displayed in a particular window. Active title bars have a different color than inactive title bars. (You can set these colors; the process is explained later.) In this figure, Program Manager and Publishing are active windows. (Program Manager is always active when it is the currently running application.)

- **Menu bar:** The menu bar lists menu items. The underlined characters indicate keyboard access: Holding the Alt key and typing the underlined letter is the same as clicking the menu option with the mouse. Items that are not available are grayed out (which usually means they are not applicable for the current operation or item). When you pull down a menu, some menu items have a keyboard shortcut listed to their right; you can use the shortcut keys to access those menu options directly, bypassing the need to select a series of menu options. An ellipsis (. . .) after a menu option means that when you select the option, a dialog box appears offering more options. A right-pointing arrowhead to the right of a menu option means that when you select that option, a submenu appears next to the first menu.

In Windows, you can single-click a menu item to make its pull-down menu appear. You do not have to hold down the mouse button to keep the pull-down menu displayed, as you do when using the Macintosh. But if you do keep the mouse button pressed, that's fine too.

- **Program group window:** In Figure 3-1, all of the open windows are program windows, which contain icons for programs in a particular group. In this figure, the program currently selected, QuarkXPress 3.1, is highlighted.

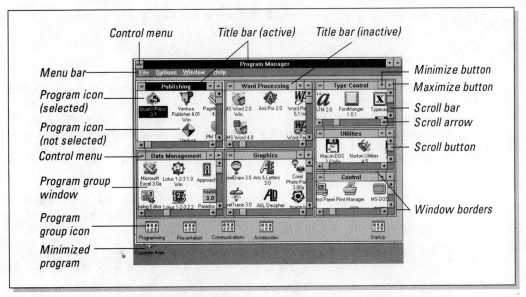

▶ **Figure 3-1:** Program Manager screen elements.

■ **Program icon:** Program icons visually differentiate programs. Some programs even let you change their icons (covered later in this chapter). Icon libraries are available on many bulletin boards, so you can customize icons or use icons for DOS applications that otherwise have no program-specific visual representation. Double-clicking an icon opens its corresponding program.

■ **Program group icon:** At the bottom of the screen are several closed, or *minimized,* program groups, each represented by a miniature program group icon. Double-clicking such icons opens corresponding program groups. (See further for definitions of *minimized* and *maximized,* two terms that apply to both program windows and program groups.)

■ **Window borders:** Use window borders to resize a window. By selecting a window directly on a border corner, you can simultaneously change the window's height and width. Selecting only a side border lets you change just the width or the height of the window.

■ **Scroll bar:** The scroll bar lets you move around within a window, and appears only when a window is too small to reveal all of its contents. You can click the scroll buttons (the arrows) or drag the scroll slider to access elements of a window that may be out of view. You can also click on the scroll bar itself: Clicking above the scroll slider scrolls a window up one page; clicking below the scroll slider scrolls a window down one page.

Drag means to select an item with the mouse and keep the mouse button pressed while moving the selected item.

- **Minimize button:** This button closes a window and reduces (*minimizes*) it to an icon. If you minimize a program window, such as an open document in QuarkXPress, the program icon appears at the bottom of the screen with the name of the file beneath it (the program is still running). If you minimize a program group, the program-group icon appears. Minimized programs appear outside the Program Manager window; minimized program groups, on the other hand, always appear within Program Manager, since these kinds of windows are a part of the Program Manager program.

- **Maximize button:** Selecting this button *maximizes* a window, causing it to occupy the full screen. When you work in programs such as QuarkXPress for Windows or your word processor, you'll have more space to work in if you maximize your windows.

- **Restore button (⬍):** This makes a full-screen window take its normal size (the default size or the size you specified via the resize borders).

- **Control menu:** Selecting the button in the upper-left corner of any window opens the Control menu, from which you restore, move, size, minimize, and maximize windows, switch to another window, or close the current window. Double-clicking the Control button closes the current window or exits the application. The Control menu also lets you switch to other programs, which is one of its most useful features; this feature is covered later in this chapter.

- **Drop-down button (⬍):** This button, found in dialog boxes, drops down a list of options available for a current field. This is most commonly used for options whose number depends on your system setup (for example, a typeface list). Often, entering the first letter or so of the option you want causes the drop-down list to jump to the first option that begins with those letters.

In Windows 3.1, the default command Options ➪ Save Settings on Exit automatically saves all changes to window sizes and locations, to elements within program groups, and to the open or closed status of a program group.

Working with Program Groups

The Program Manager lets you organize applications into *program groups*. This enables you to arrange and access applications by type. A program group is not the same as a Macintosh folder or DOS directory. Folders and directories are physical spaces on the computer's hard disk. A group is *logical* space: The elements in it can be from any directory; only the icons are grouped together, usually by similar types (such as word processing), in a common window. You can put the same program in more than one group, even if it is installed on the hard disk just once. Groups let you organize your programs in whatever arrangement makes sense to you.

When you install Windows, it creates the following groups: Main, Accessories, Games, StartUp, and Applications. Some programs create their own groups when you install them. For example, Aldus programs, including PageMaker and Persuasion, automatically install themselves into a group called Aldus. Others give you the choice of whether to create a group (QuarkXPress is an example), and still others let you specify any existing group in which to install them.

It doesn't matter into what groups and in what form you initially install your programs: you can completely customize and change an icon's location later. You can get rid of groups you don't want, add ones you do, and rename existing groups so their names better match your preferences. Figure 3-1 shows how we organized our applications into task-oriented groups. Program groups we frequently use stay open, while those we use less often are minimized along the bottom of the screen. This makes it easy to access our most-used programs without making it hard to get to other programs. The following steps show you how to add new program groups, enabling you to then organize your program icons as you see fit.

▶ Steps: Adding new program groups

Step 1. Select File ➪ New from Program Manager. The New Program Object dialog box, shown in Figure 3-2, appears.

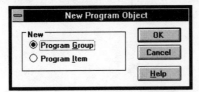

▶ **Figure 3-2:** The New Program Object dialog box.

Step 2. Select the Program Group option and choose OK. This action opens another dialog box, Program Group Properties, shown in Figure 3-3.

Program Group Properties

Description: Photo Editors

Group File: photo.grp

OK

Cancel

Help

▶ **Figure 3-3:** The Program Group Properties dialog box.

Step 3.   In the Description field, enter the name you want to assign to the new group. (This name will appear on the group's title bar.)

 You also can enter a name in the Group File field. Windows uses this name for the internal file it creates to store information about the group, such as what icons are in it. If you do not enter a name, Windows automatically creates a name based on the first eight characters (not including any spaces) of the description. If you enter a name, make sure it has eight characters or fewer, not counting the GRP extension. (You do not need to enter the GRP extension — Windows adds it automatically.)

Step 4.   A new, empty window appears. You can add programs to this window and resize or move it wherever you want.

Once you've created a group, you can add and move program items to it. You can also size the group window and place it anywhere you want in the Program Manager window.

Placing program items into groups

There are three ways to put application icons — called *program items* in Windows — into a program group. You can drag and drop a program item from an existing group into a new group. You can drag and drop a program's EXE file from File Manager to a group window in Program Manager. You also can add an item, either for the first time or as a copy of an item installed in another group, through a command sequence in Program Manager.

▶ Steps: Moving program items from one group to another

Step 1. Open the group window that contains the item you want to move (double-click the minimized icon or select the group name from the Window menu).

 If you cannot find a group on your screen, use the Window menu to select the desired group, as shown in Figure 3-4. This menu is limited to nine window names; if you have more than that, the last option is More Windows. If you select More Windows, the Select Window dialog box appears and offers a scroll list of all program groups. This dialog box is also shown in Figure 3-4, but in practice, the dialog box and Window menu do not actually appear together on-screen.

▶ **Figure 3-4:** The Window menu and the Select Window dialog box.

Step 2. Make sure the program group you intend to move the icon to is either open or that its minimized program group icon is visible on-screen.

Step 3. Find the icon or program item you want to move. Select and drag the item to the other window or minimized program group icon.

Step 4. Release the mouse button after you position the item in the window or on the minimized program group icon.

Most Windows programs' EXE files are embedded with information about their Program Manager-associated icons. You can, therefore, simply drag the File Manager icon of a program's EXE file directly to a program group in Program Manager. To do this, however, you must have both File Manager and Program Manager open and visible on your screen. The disadvantage to this method is that you may have to resize several windows in order to achieve your goal. The advantage is that you don't have to remember the somewhat more complicated steps that follow these, for adding a program item to a group.

▶ Steps: Moving a program's EXE file from File Manager to Program Manager

Step 1. From Program Manager, double-click the File Manager icon to run the File Manager program. Use the window-sizing method described earlier under "Using the Windows Interface," in the section "Window borders," to resize File Manager so that it takes up one-half of your screen.

Step 2. Make sure the program group in Program Manager you intend to move the icon to is either open or that its minimized program group icon is visible on-screen.

Step 3. Open the directory in File Manager that contains the EXE file of the program you want to have represented in Program Manager and locate the EXE file.

Step 4. Select and drag the EXE file to the window or minimized program group icon in Program Manager and release the mouse button.

You'll need to add program items to a group, not just move existing program items, when you have a program (such as a DOS program) previously installed on your system that Windows doesn't know about and hasn't created an icon for.

▶ Steps: Adding a program item to a group

Step 1. Select File ⇨ New to open the New Program Object dialog box.

Step 2. Select Program Item and choose OK, as shown in Figure 3-5. The Program Item Properties dialog box appears, as shown in Figure 3-6.

▶ **Figure 3-5:** Select Program Item to add a new application to a group.

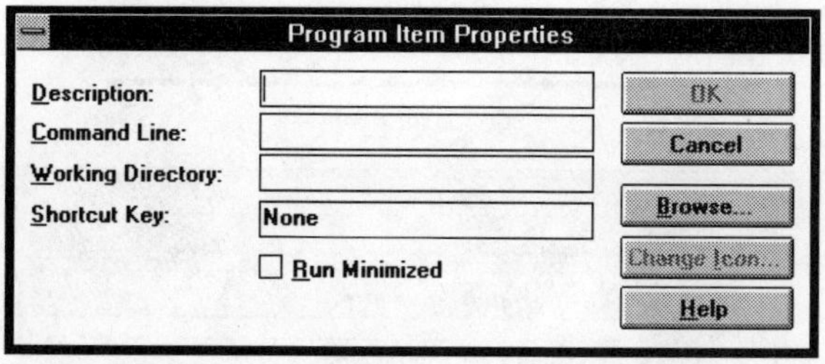

▶ **Figure 3-6:** The Program Item Properties dialog box.

Step 3. If you know all the information needed, enter it in the appropriate fields in the Program Item Properties dialog box: In the Description field, enter the name you want to appear under the icon. In the Command Line field, enter the name of the program file, including the drive and directory location. In the Working Directory field, indicate where related items might be located (this is usually the same as the directory for the program). If you want, enter a key combination that you can use as a shortcut key in the Shortcut Key field. The key combination you select must be in the form Ctrl+Alt+*character*.

If you don't know the Command Line and Working Directory information, that's OK. Use the Browse button to find the program you want to add (Figure 3-7 shows the resulting dialog box. Scroll through your drives and directories using the options at the right side of the Browse dialog box. Single-click the drive shown to get a list of other drives. Double-click the folder that contains the program. Any folders (actually, these are DOS directories) currently open are displayed with an open-folder icon. The folders are arranged so that subdirectories appear below the current directory, while parent directories appear above. When the program filename appears in the File Name field, double-click it and choose OK. You can then edit the Description and Shortcut Key fields as desired.

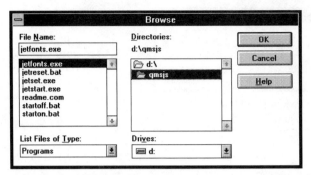

▶ **Figure 3-7:** The Browse dialog box.

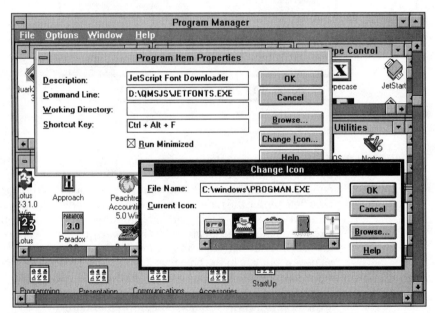

▶ **Figure 3-8:** The completed Program Item Properties dialog box and the Change Icon
dialog box.

Step 4. Figure 3-8 shows the completed dialog box with information for our
font loader, which resides on drive D: in the \QMSJS directory.

Step 5. Some programs, including QuarkXPress, offer you a choice of icons.
Others, like our DOS program, have no icon, so you must use an icon
library to select an icon for it. Use the Change Icon dialog box to select
an alternative or new icon. Choosing OK makes that icon the one that
Windows displays. Here, we used one of the icons supplied in the
Windows Program Manager.

Copying a program item to another group

You can also place a copy of a program item in as many program groups as you want. That way, the application can be launched from both windows. First, open the program group window containing the item you want to copy. Then, hold down the Ctrl key while selecting and dragging the icon to another group (either into an open window or onto the group icon).

 If the program is already installed in one program group, it will be unaffected by changes made in a different group. Thus, you can have different keyboard shortcuts or different icons for the same program in different program groups.

Using the StartUp group

Windows 3.1 has a new, special group called StartUp. Any program in that group loads immediately after you load Windows. If you use one or more programs all the time, you can place copies of their icons in the StartUp group window (press and hold the Ctrl key before you select the icon and move it; otherwise, it is moved out of the original group, not just copied). For example, if you use QuarkXPress every day, put it in the StartUp group; Quark automatically loads when you start Windows, and you don't have to locate the icon first. You also may want to have programs such as Print Manager (described in Part VII), Character Map (described in Chapter 14's "Using Character Map" section), a screen-capture program, or a word processor in your StartUp group.

You may want some programs you put in the StartUp program group, such as Print Manager and Character Map, to be available as minimized programs so they're immediately accessible. For such programs, check the Run Minimized box in the Program Item Properties dialog box when you add the program to the StartUp group. (The next section explains how to open the Program Item Properties dialog box if you forget to check this option when adding an item to the StartUp group.)

You can also place a file associated with a program in the StartUp group (the process is described later in this chapter); doing so causes that file's application to be launched and the file automatically opened.

Modifying groups

If you want to change program item *properties* — such as the icon or program description — select (single-click) the group that contains the program. Then select File ⇨ Properties to open the Program Item Properties dialog box and enter your changes. Choose OK to activate them.

To delete a program item, highlight it and select File ⇨ Delete. To delete a program group, minimize it, highlight it, and select File ⇨ Delete. Or, just single-click it and press the Delete key.

Deleting a program item (or file) does not remove the program (or file) from your disk. You must use DOS commands or the Windows File Manager to delete those files and directories.

Switching Between Programs

One of Windows' most powerful capabilities is *task switching,* which lets you jump from one program to another without quitting the first program. This capability also means you can move elements — text, charts, graphics, data — directly from one program to another through the Windows *Clipboard,* which is a scratch pad that holds the last element copied or cut. There are several ways to switch between programs:

■ If you assigned a keyboard shortcut for a program and that program is running (whether in an open window or minimized), enter the shortcut (the keyboard command).

■ If any portion of a program's window is visible, just click anywhere on that window to switch to the program.

■ If the program is minimized and you can see the minimized icon at the bottom of your screen, double-click the minimized icon to restore that program's window.

■ If the program is running, but you can't see its window or minimized icon, use the Windows Task List, shown in Figure 3-9. Access the Task List via the keyboard shortcut Ctrl+Esc or via the Control menu's Switch To option. Double-click the program you want to switch to (or single-click it and choose Switch To). You can close a program by selecting the End Task button.

■ If the program is not running, switch to the Program Manager (in the same way you switch to any program). Move to the group that contains the program you want and double-click that program. You also can select File ⇨ Run to start a program that has not been added to a group (such as a DOS program).

Mac users will recognize the Task List as similar to System 6's MultiFinder and System 7's multitasking.

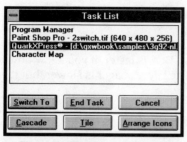

▶ **Figure 3-9:** The Windows Task List.

 When running on a 386- or 486-based PC, Windows 3.1 can handle DOS programs almost as if they were Windows programs. It can minimize them, associate icons with them, resize their windows, and even cut-and-paste or copy information from them into Windows programs, as Figure 3-10 shows. (These capabilities don't exist from Windows back to DOS.) To use these capabilities, make sure Windows is running under 386 Enhanced mode. Establish this setting in the Control Panel, which is found in the Main group unless you move it.

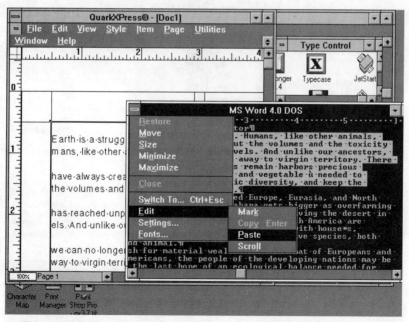

▶ **Figure 3-10:** Copying and pasting information from a Word for DOS file into QuarkXPress.

Working with Files

To work with files, use the File Manager or the DOS prompt (both are in the Main group, unless you move them). DOS is faster, if you know how to use its dozen or so common commands. The File Manager is slower, but it is more visual.

Using the Windows File Manager

Figure 3-11 shows the Windows File Manager. At the left is a directory tree for drive C: (select the drive you want to view from the drive icons at the top of the File Manager screen). In Figure 3-11, the \WINDOWS directory is selected, so its subdirectories are displayed. All the files in the \WINDOWS directory are shown at the right in Figure 3-11. The files are sorted by type, with data files listed first, then programs, then Windows resources (programs and settings used internally by Windows programs), and finally, subdirectories. You can change the sort options and list the files in a different order by making a selection in the View menu, which you can see in the middle of Figure 3-11.

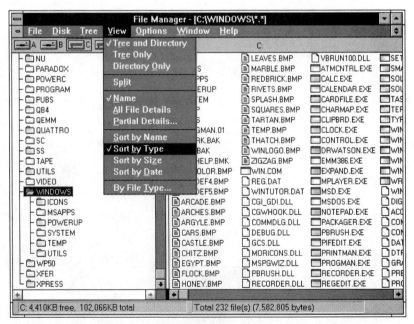

▶ **Figure 3-11:** The Windows File Manager.

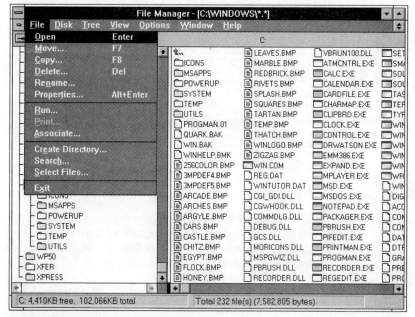

▶ **Figure 3-12:** The File menu.

Choose from the options in the File menu, shown in Figure 3-12, to delete, rename, move, or copy a file. The File menu contains the equivalent functions to DOS file-management commands. The File menu also offers options that let you search for files and select files that share common names or extensions.

In DOS and Windows, you use wildcards to select multiple files that have at least part of their names in common. There are two wildcards: the asterisk (*) and the question mark (?). The asterisk wild card stands for "any number of characters," so the expression Q*.QDT instructs the program to look for any file whose name begins with a Q and has the extension QDT, no matter how many letters follow the first Q. The expression Q*.* instructs the program to search for any file whose name begins with a Q, regardless of the extension. The expression Q?.QDT, by contrast, specifies any two-letter file that begins with a Q and has the extension QDT. Using wildcards makes it easy to copy, delete, rename, or select many files at once without having to select each one individually, as you do with a Mac.

Associate		
File with Extension: QXD		OK
Associate With:		Cancel
XPress.exe		
(None)		Browse...
Calendar File (calendar.exe)		
Card File (cardfile.exe)		Help
Media Player (MPlayer.exe)		
Paintbrush Picture (pbrush.exe)		

▶ **Figure 3-13:** The Associate dialog box.

Associating files with programs

Through the File ➪ Associate menu option in the File Manager, you can tell Windows what program to run when you double-click a file in File Manager (or in a Program Manager program group) that has a particular filename extension. Figure 3-13 shows the Associate dialog box.

The Associate feature in Windows is similar to the Mac feature that lets you double-click a file to open it and the associated program. On a Mac, the System determines the association from the file's resource fork, which is read when you double-click the file icon. This association is automatically created when you save a file. In Windows, you make this connection through the Associate dialog box. But after you associate an extension with a program, Windows knows to associate all files that have that extension with the desired program. To associate a file extension with a program, use the following steps.

▶ **Steps: Associating a file extension with a program**

Step 1. Select File ➪ Associate to open the Associate dialog box. Enter the file extension in the Files with Extension field. Do not enter the period. (If you single-click a file before entering this dialog box, its extension appears in the field. If you select a resource or program, no extension appears, since Windows knows that files with those extensions are not meant to be used by programs.)

Step 2. Scroll through the list of programs in the Associate With list box or, if the program you want is not listed, use the Browse button to find it.

In some cases, Windows automatically knows what program to associate with an extension, because the program does the association upon installation. QuarkXPress is such a program. Sometimes, different programs use the same extension for their files. You must select one program to use with the Associate feature, because you cannot associate the same extension with two different programs.

```
[Extensions]
doc=D:\WINWORD\WINWORD.EXE ^.DOC
dot=D:\WINWORD\winword.exe ^.dot
smm=d:\amipro\amipro.exe ^.smm
sam=D:\AMIPRO\amipro.exe ^.sam
cal=calendar.exe ^.cal
crd=cardfile.exe ^.crd
trm=terminal.exe ^.trm
txt=notepad.exe ^.txt
ini=notepad.exe ^.ini
pcx=D:\CORELDRW\PHOTOPNT\corelpnt.exe ^.pcx
bmp=pbrush.exe ^.bmp
wri=write.exe ^.wri
rec=recorder.exe ^.rec
rtf=D:\WINWORD\winword.exe ^.rtf
cdr=D:\CORELDRW\DRAW\coreldrw.exe ^.cdr
QXD=XPress.exe ^.qxd
qxt=XPress.exe ^.qxt
ctl=aldsetup.exe ^.ctl
tbl=TE.exe ^.tbl
```

▶ **Figure 3-14:** File extension associations are stored in the WIN.INI file.

A fast way to associate file extensions with a program is to edit the WIN.INI file directly. (The WIN.INI file contains many of the Windows settings.) This is especially appropriate if you work on several different PCs and you want to ensure that they all are set up the same way. Figure 3-14 shows the part of WIN.INI that contains associations (the QuarkXPress settings for documents and templates are highlighted). Before you edit WIN.INI (which resides in the \WINDOWS directory), be sure to make a backup copy of the file, in case you damage it during the edit. The associations are listed under the [Extensions] label. Note that the caret character (^) is used instead of the standard DOS asterisk (*) wildcard. Make sure you save WIN.INI as an ASCII (text-only) file when you finish editing. You must restart Windows for any changes to take effect.

Placing files in program groups

While the Program Manager is designed primarily to display applications in logical groups (by function or task) instead of physical groups (by disk and directory locations), you can also place files in program groups. Mac users have been accustomed to this from the start, but the capability is new to Windows.

Just as program items are visual representations of the actual applications, file items placed in a program group are visual representations of the actual files. If you delete a file item from a program group, you have simply removed the file from the group, not deleted the file from the disk. And moving a file item from one group to another does not move it from directory to another. To physically move, delete, rename, or otherwise manipulate files, you must use the File Manager or DOS. (This is different from the Mac where the equivalents of the Program Manager and File Manager are merged into one system.) To move a file into a program group, take the following steps.

▶ Steps: Moving a file into a program group

Step 1. Run the File Manager and move to the disk and directory that contains the file(s) you want to place in a program group.

Step 2. Make sure the File Manager and Program Manager windows are arranged so you can see the filename you want to place in a program group as well as the group itself (either its open window or minimized icon).

Step 3. Click and drag the filename into the group.

The file will appear in the group with the same icon as the application that file is associated with. Thus, a QXD file (a QuarkXPress document) will appear with the QuarkXPress icon.

If the file you have placed into a program group is not associated with a particular application, the file will have an "empty window" icon that represents unassociated file types, and Windows will display an alert box that tells you no application is associated with the file type. You have the option of canceling the placement of the file. (File association is covered in the previous section.)

If the file you place from the File Manager into a program group is associated with an application, Windows will put the application's icon with the filename below it in the program group. If the application is a Windows application, its icon will be loaded with it. Otherwise, you must modify the item properties as described earlier in this chapter.

Working with Fonts

QuarkXPress can do wonders with type in either the TrueType or PostScript Type 1 formats, as Chapter 15 describes. But for QuarkXPress to see typefaces, you must install them properly in Windows. Even though Adobe Type Manager 2.0 simplified font installation and Windows 3.1 brought TrueType to Windows, there are still a few tricks and cautions you should know about.

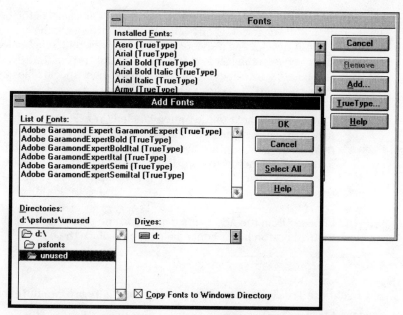

▶ **Figure 3-15:** The Windows Fonts dialog box and its Add Fonts dialog box.

Using TrueType fonts

To install TrueType fonts, either use the installer that came with your typefaces or select the Fonts icon in the Windows Control Panel. The Windows Fonts dialog box (which appears when you select the icon) and its Add Fonts dialog box are shown in Figure 3-15.

▶ **Steps: Installing TrueType fonts through the Fonts dialog box**

Step 1. Open the Control Panel (which is in the Main group unless you move it) and double-click the Fonts icon.

Step 2. Windows displays any installed TrueType fonts in the Fonts dialog box. Choose Add to add more TrueType fonts.

Step 3. Use the Directories and Drives fields to search for directories that contain TrueType font files. (Only TrueType fonts are displayed.)

Step 4. Select the files you want to install. A single click selects the current font only while deselecting any others. Ctrl+click selects the current font without deselecting previously selected fonts. Shift+click selects all fonts between the last font selected and the current font. To select all files listed, choose Select All. You can deselect specific files by using Shift+click and Ctrl+click as just described.

Step 5. Check the box next to the option labeled Copy Fonts to Windows Directory. This copies fonts into the \WINDOWS\SYSTEM directory. If you do not check this option, Windows can still install your TrueType fonts. But it is better to copy the files, so all installed files are in one place. If you installed your fonts from a floppy disk, you must check this box.

Step 6. Choose OK in the Add Fonts dialog box and then double-click the Control button in the Fonts dialog box to close the box.

If you choose TrueType in the Fonts dialog box, there are two further options:

- **Enable TrueType Fonts:** You must check this option for TrueType fonts to be available in your programs.

- **Show Only TrueType Fonts in Applications:** If you check this option, only TrueType fonts are available, even if you install Adobe Type Manager or other type scalers. There is little reason to use this option unless you use only TrueType fonts and you don't want the low-quality Windows bitmap fonts (such as Helv and Tms Rmn) to be available.

Using PostScript fonts

If you use PostScript typefaces, make sure you also use Adobe Type Manager 2.0 or later. You likely have ATM, since many vendors bundle it with their software. If you don't have it, it's a worthwhile investment. This type scaler makes sure your text displays cleanly and crisply at all sizes. Without a type scaler, text can look jagged or blocky on-screen, though fonts will print smoothly. The type scaler also lets you print PostScript Type 1 fonts on non-PostScript printers — it automatically converts the PostScript format to the printer's format when printing.

PostScript fonts come in two versions: Type 1 and Type 3. Type 1 fonts are the most common; they consist of an outline that a type scaler can use to create crisp text at any size. Type 3 is a bitmap version, which means that the type does not scale well.

Installing PostScript fonts

To install PostScript typefaces, double-click the Adobe Type Manager icon to invoke the ATM Control Panel. Any fonts already installed appear in the Installed ATM Fonts list. The following steps provide the details.

▶ Steps: Using Adobe Type Manager to install PostScript fonts

Step 1. To add fonts, open the ATM Control Panel and select the Add button, which opens the Add ATM Fonts dialog box, as shown in Figure 3-16.

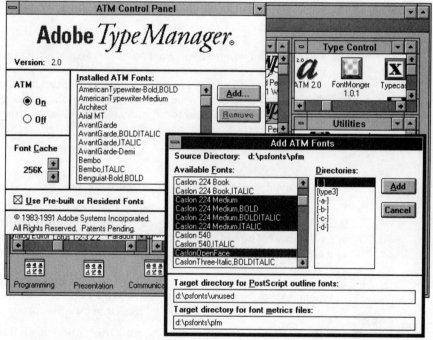

▶ **Figure 3-16:** The Adobe Type Manager ATM Control Panel and Add ATM Fonts dialog box.

Step 2. Use the Directories list box to locate the directory that contains your printer font metric files (these have the extension PFM). When you locate the directory (usually called \PSFONTS\PFM), a list of all available fonts appears.

Step 3. Select the fonts you want to install. (All fonts available — even those previously installed — appear.) Select fonts by clicking them. A regular click selects the current font only, deselecting any others. Ctrl+click selects the current font without deselecting previously selected fonts. Shift+click selects all fonts between the last font selected and the current font.

Step 4. Edit the locations in the fields labeled Target Directory for PostScript Outline Fonts and Target Directory for Font Metrics Files. Typically, the outline fonts directory is \PSFONTS, while the metrics directory is \PSFONTS\PFM. (The drive depends on what drive you installed ATM on.)

Step 5. Choose Add and then choose Exit.

Step 6. You are asked whether you want to restart Windows. If you do restart Windows, all your changes are implemented. If you don't, you won't see the changes until you exit Windows and later restart it. Unless you have a reason not to, restart Windows. (Don't worry about losing unsaved data — you are prompted to save any unsaved files before Windows actually restarts.)

Other options available in the Add ATM Fonts dialog box are:

■ **Font Cache:** This feature reserves system memory exclusively for ATM. It uses that memory to hold typefaces you frequently use, which speeds screen redraw. The best setting depends on how much memory you have and how many programs you typically have open. A number between 128KB and 512KB works well for most setups. The more memory installed in your computer, the higher number you can use. But unless you use a lot of typefaces regularly, there's no reason to allocate more than 512KB to ATM, since that memory is no longer available for other programs.

■ **Use Pre-Built or Resident Fonts:** Checking this option box tells ATM to use the size-specific bitmap fonts provided with Windows whenever you select a typeface at one of those supplied sizes. This means less work for ATM and quicker screen redraw. (Printing still uses ATM.) There is rarely reason to uncheck this box.

Although you might consider using different directories to keep track of typefaces used for different projects, we don't recommend this. It can result in typefaces being scattered across your hard disk and thus hard to find. After all, you can't tell ATM to use fonts from only certain directories, so the benefit of having font files in different directories is questionable.

Should you use TrueType or PostScript fonts?

The most basic question about fonts usually is whether you should use TrueType or PostScript fonts. The answer depends on the work you do. If you produce newsletters, magazines, ads, or brochures that you output on a typesetter or image setter, use PostScript, because that is the standard format on these devices. If you output to a laser printer, TrueType is probably the better bet, because it prints faster in most cases, especially if you print to a non-PostScript printer. However, you do not have to use one font format exclusively:

■ If you see a TrueType typeface that you want to use in your typeset document, use it — Windows converts TrueType fonts into PostScript format when printing to a PostScript device (or to a file designated for use by a PostScript device). The drawback is that this conversion process may make your files larger, because Windows must download the converted TrueType font file into your document. This isn't required when you use PostScript fonts, because you can set up Windows so that it assumes the typesetter has your stan-

dard PostScript fonts in its memory. Windows then just tells the printing device what typefaces to use, not how to create them. (These settings are described in Part VII, which explains printing in detail.)

■ Conversely, if you have PostScript typefaces, there's no reason to give them up if you switch to TrueType. On a PostScript printer, you can use both formats. On other printers, all you need is a program such as Adobe Type Manager or Bitstream FaceLift to translate PostScript font files into a format the printer can use (which is exactly what Windows' built-in TrueType type scaler does).

Don't base decisions about whether to use TrueType or PostScript fonts on assumptions about quality. Both technologies provide excellent results, so any quality differences are due to the font manufacturer's standards. If you purchase typefaces from recognized companies, you don't need to worry. (Many smaller companies produce high-quality fonts as well.)

Downloading PostScript fonts

If you use TrueType, Adobe Type Manager, or another type scaler, fonts are downloaded to the printer each time you use them. But there are times when you do not want fonts downloaded to the printer, especially if you use a PostScript printer. For example, PostScript printers come with several preloaded fonts (typically Courier, Helvetica, Helvetica Narrow, Times, New Century Schoolbook, Bookman, Palatino, Avant Garde, Zapf Chancery, Zapf Dingbats, and Symbol), and it doesn't make sense to download those fonts to the printer if they are already there. Also, many printers can store fonts in memory or on disk, and it is faster to download fonts to the printer once and leave them there, available for use in future documents.

Controlling font downloading for PostScript printers can be critical if you work with a service bureau. You may use a laser printer for proofing and then print the document to file for output at a service bureau. In this situation, you probably expect your service bureau to have downloaded all fonts to its typesetter, so you don't want those fonts downloaded by Windows when it prints to file. (If you give your service bureau a QuarkXPress document, and the bureau opens the document in its copy of QuarkXPress and prints directly from there, this is not an issue.) But you may use some typefaces for which your service bureau doesn't have font files, such as special decorative typefaces or typefaces you create yourself. In this case, you *do* want fonts to download.

By editing the WIN.INI settings file in the \WINDOWS directory, you can determine precisely which fonts download to which printer. For each installed PostScript printer configuration, Windows has a printer entry that lists such details as the basic parameters of printer trays as well as the name of each PostScript font and the download information for each font. Figures 3-15 and 3-16 show customized download information.

Figure 3-17 shows the settings for a laser printer. (Although 151 fonts are installed, only the first 11 are shown here.) Each line includes a font number (`softfontx=`), which Windows uses internally, followed by the location and name of the printer metric file (PFM), which is used to space characters correctly on-screen. For all but four of the fonts (10–13), the PFM file is followed by a comma and the name of the printer outline file (PFB), which is what Windows downloads to the printer for that font. The four fonts that have no PFB information are the four faces of the Bookman typeface. This typeface is preinstalled in most PostScript laser printers, so we removed the download information to speed up the printing of documents that use these fonts.

Notice that in Figure 3-17, fonts 3, 4, 5, and 8 aren't listed. This is because they had been deleted earlier. This can be confusing if you are editing the WIN.INI file. The number of fonts indicated (here, 151) is the total number of fonts currently installed, not the highest-numbered ID (softfontx) used.

```
[PostScript,LPT2]
device=12
feed1=1
feed15=1
softfonts=151
softfont1=m:\psfonts\pfm\atb_____.pfm,m:\psfonts\unused\atb_____.pfb
softfont2=m:\psfonts\pfm\atm_____.pfm,m:\psfonts\unused\atm_____.pfb
softfont6=m:\psfonts\pfm\beb_____.pfm,m:\psfonts\unused\beb_____.pfb
softfont7=m:\psfonts\pfm\be_____.pfm,m:\psfonts\unused\be_____.pfb
softfont9=m:\psfonts\pfm\bdps____.pfm,m:\psfonts\unused\bdps____.pfb
softfont10=m:\psfonts\pfm\bkd_____.pfm
softfont11=m:\psfonts\pfm\bkdi____.pfm
softfont12=m:\psfonts\pfm\bkl_____.pfm
softfont13=m:\psfonts\pfm\bkli____.pfm
softfont14=m:\msfonts\pfm\ca_____.pfm,m:\psfonts\unused\ca_____.pfb
softfont15=m:\psfonts\pfm\carta___.pfm,m:\psfonts\unused\carta___.pfb
```

▶ **Figure 3-17:** WIN.INI download settings for a laser printer.

```
[PostScript,FILE]
device=12
feed1=1
softfonts=151
softfont1=m:\psfonts\pfm\atb_____.pfm
softfont2=m:\psfonts\pfm\atm_____.pfm
softfont6=m:\psfonts\pfm\beb_____.pfm
softfont7=m:\psfonts\pfm\be_____.pfm
softfont9=m:\psfonts\pfm\bdps____.pfm
softfont10=m:\psfonts\pfm\bkd_____.pfm
softfont11=m:\psfonts\pfm\bkdi____.pfm
softfont12=m:\psfonts\pfm\bkl_____.pfm
softfont13=m:\psfonts\pfm\bkli____.pfm
softfont14=m:\psfonts\pfm\ca_____.pfm
```

▶ **Figure 3-18:** WIN.INI download settings for a typesetter.

Figure 3-18 shows the same download settings for a typesetter. However, none of the fonts lists a PFB file for downloading, because we have our service bureau download the fonts into the typesetter's memory. This speeds printing and keeps our files smaller.

When you use Adobe Type Manager to install fonts, it assumes that you want all fonts downloaded, and it includes the PFB part of the softfont*x* line for all PostScript printers installed. You must edit WIN.INI in a word processor to change these settings for fonts you do not want downloaded. Part VII covers printer setup in more detail.

Before you edit WIN.INI, be sure to make a backup copy of it, in case something goes wrong, and save the file as an ASCII (text-only) file. You must restart Windows for the changes to take effect.

Translating TrueType to PostScript

Other important printer settings are controlled through the Windows Advanced Options dialog box, which you open via the Printers option in Control Panel. This is where you tell Windows how to handle TrueType fonts when you use a PostScript printer. To establish these settings, you must invoke the Substitution dialog box through the following series of dialog boxes, as shown in Figure 3-19: Control Panel ⇨ Printers ⇨ Setup ⇨ Options ⇨ Advanced. If you don't have a PostScript printer installed, the Advanced button won't appear in the Options dialog box. (The Windows Control Panel is found in the Main program group, unless you move it elsewhere.)

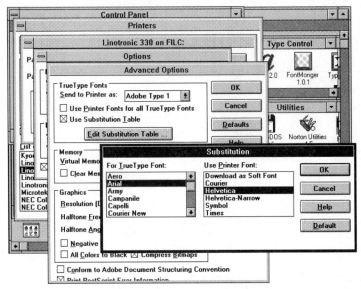

▶ **Figure 3-19:** The Advanced Options dialog box and its Substitution dialog box.

First, you have the option to specify how Windows sends TrueType fonts to a PostScript printer. The Send to Printer as: drop-down list box (in the Advanced Options dialog box) gives you two options:

- **Adobe Type 1:** This translates TrueType fonts into PostScript outlines. Most people should use this setting.

- **Bitmap (Type 3):** This setting translates TrueType fonts into PostScript bitmaps. Avoid this setting, because it results in larger files (bitmaps take more space than outlines) and may take longer to print. Some printers prefer Type 3 fonts because of their machine setup, but unless you are asked to provide fonts in Type 3 format, don't.

Three options in the Advanced Options dialog box enable you to control how Windows handles TrueType fonts that have PostScript equivalents:

- **Use Printer Fonts for All TrueType Fonts:** If you select this setting, the PostScript printer uses its own fonts instead of expecting a translated Type 1 or Type 3 font from Windows. Choose this option only if you are using the basic TrueType fonts that are clones of the basic PostScript fonts. These are Arial (a clone of PostScript's Helvetica), Symbol, and Times New Roman (a Times clone). If you use this option for TrueType fonts that have no PostScript equivalent, your TrueType fonts print in something like Courier or Times instead.

- **Use Substitution Table:** This option lets you tell Windows which PostScript fonts to substitute for TrueType fonts. You specify the substitution fonts in the Substitution dialog box, shown in Figure 3-17. In the figure, the TrueType font Arial is highlighted and *mapped to* (substituted with) the PostScript font Helvetica. Fonts such as Campanile, which have no PostScript equivalent, should be mapped to Download as Soft Font.

- **Use neither option:** If you don't select either of the two preceding options, Windows converts all TrueType fonts to PostScript fonts.

The best options are the second and third, depending on what printing device you select. For 600-dpi or coarser printers, choose Use Substitution Table, because that saves time. The very slight spacing differences between TrueType and PostScript equivalents are not noticeable. For finer printers, don't select Use Substitution Table or Use Printer Fonts. This guarantees good spacing, which is worth the price of extra printing time for high-end work.

Customizing the Windows Environment

You can customize many aspects of Windows, most of which are beyond the scope of this book. But desktop publishers should know at least where to make customizations. The Windows Control Panel, whose default location is in the Main group, contains programs to customize most Windows settings. Figure 3-20 shows the Control Panel.

The Windows Control Panel is similar to the Mac's control panels, although you cannot add your own control panels as you can on the Mac.

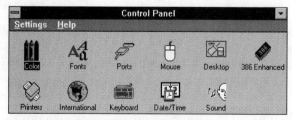

▶ **Figure 3-20:** The Windows Control Panel.

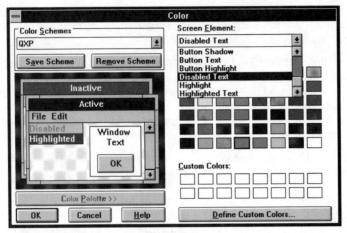

Figure 3-21: The Windows Color dialog box.

Although it's not critical to publishing, you may want to investigate the Color program in the Control Panel. This lets you set up your screen colors — something we all end up doing sooner or later. Figure 3-21 shows the Color dialog box that appears when you select the color icon in the Control Panel. Windows comes with several predefined color combinations, which you can select in the Color Schemes drop-down list. You'll likely want to create your own color scheme and save it, which you do by following these steps.

▶ **Steps: Creating your own color scheme**

Step 1. Select the Color icon in Control Panel. From the Color dialog box that appears, choose Color Palette. This expands the Color dialog box to give you access to a color palette. You can create as many as 16 of your own colors by choosing Define Custom Colors and using the color space and color value controls.

Step 2. Select each interface element one at a time from the miniature Windows screen (in the left part of the dialog box) or from the Screen Element drop-down list in the upper-right corner. Then select the color you want to apply to the element. Repeat this for each element.

Step 3. When you finish selecting all colors, choose Save Scheme and enter a name for the scheme in the Save Scheme dialog box that appears. Choose OK to apply the new scheme to the Windows interface.

Summary

▶ Program and program group windows can be resized, made full-screen, or reduced to icons.

▶ You can put programs from different locations into the same program group, and you can put the same program into more than one group.

▶ The StartUp folder contains programs you want Windows to load immediately after startup. You can set these applications to minimize upon loading.

▶ You can establish a keyboard shortcut for each program item.

▶ To switch between programs, you can use several methods. These include clicking the program windows, using the Task List, or using the keyboard shortcut.

▶ In the File Manager, you can set Windows to load the right program for a particular type of file. You do this by associating a file extension with that program. QuarkXPress does this automatically for QuarkXPress documents.

▶ You can place files in program groups, which is often more convenient than using the File Manager to locate them. Double-clicking the file launches its application and opens the file.

▶ You can use TrueType and PostScript fonts together.

▶ Edit the WIN.INI `softfontx=` settings to control which fonts download to the printer.

▶ Use the Advanced Options dialog box in the Control Panel's Printers dialog box to control how Windows converts TrueType fonts to PostScript format when printing on PostScript printers.

▶ Use the Control Panel to customize the screen environment, including the colors of the Windows interface.

PART II

Document Preparation

No matter how well a publishing program is designed, users always experience an initially steep learning curve. Why? Because publishing is complicated. It's a mix of art and science open to interpretation, experimentation, and boundary-breaking. You can apply a set of publishing tools in many ways, just as you can a set of woodworking tools. And, just as in most professions, no matter how varied the applications, tools are best used after the goal is defined and the approach laid out.

This section explains how to set up QuarkXPress and other tools so that you can take full advantage of QuarkXPress capabilities when creating your documents. By setting up document elements and structure wisely, you save yourself a lot of effort down the road without compromising flexibility.

Keep in mind that preparing a document and its elements requires knowledge of the document as well as of QuarkXPress. For example, to define master pages for layout or to create style sheets for text attributes, you must understand your layout and formatting needs in addition to understanding QuarkXPress. If you're not familiar with QuarkXPress tools, you may want to read Part III, which covers document layout, and Part IV, which covers text issues, before proceeding with Part II. Although you execute the tasks described in Part II in the early stages of document creation, you won't be able to take full advantage of QuarkXPress features until you become more familiar with them.

On the other hand, you may want to read Part II first, to gain a general knowledge of the issues involved in setting up documents, and then move on to Parts III and IV to learn about layout and formatting tools. You can come back later to Part II to find out how to apply your new, detailed knowledge when you set up your documents.

CHAPTER

4

Customizing QuarkXPress

- -

In This Chapter

▶ What program settings QuarkXPress lets you control

▶ How to make your preferences apply to the current document only or to all subsequent documents

▶ Preference options for QuarkXPress's user interface, layout tools, image control, output control, and typography

- -

Why Customize QuarkXPress?

Publishing is a big industry, and one with many variants. For example, one of the authors of this book comes from a newspaper and magazine background, so he is used to working with picas as the basic layout measurement unit, and he calls pull-quotes *decks* and titles *heads*. The other author, however, comes from a technical documentation and corporate communications background, so she is used to working with inches as the basic layout measurement, and she calls pull-quotes *pull-quotes* and titles *titles*. QuarkXPress lets each of us work in our own style, even when working on common projects such as this book. It can do the same for you.

You'll probably set or change most QuarkXPress control settings only occasionally. You'll rarely switch measurement units, for example; after all, QuarkXPress lets you enter any unit you want in dialog boxes, no matter what default settings you establish. But you may change other settings — those aimed at specific documents — more frequently.

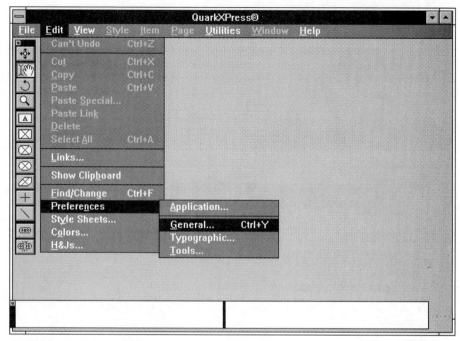

▶ **Figure 4-1:** The Edit Preferences menu.

For example, even if documents are different, chances are that there are commonalities among them, such as certain typefaces that form part of your corporate or public identity. Still, the kind of program settings we discuss in this chapter are meant more to help you use QuarkXPress rather than to establish standards for your document — the subsequent chapters on master pages and style sheets show you how to do that. QuarkXPress offers many controls that enable you to customize the program to the way *you* work.

You establish nearly all QuarkXPress control settings from one menu option: Edit ➪ Preferences. Figure 4-1 shows this menu. You set some document-specific settings by entering values in dialog boxes without having a document open. We cover both types of settings in the following sections, which we divide first by the type of preferences available and then by the dialog boxes that invoke them.

Program Settings

The most important settings — because they affect your everyday work — are those that affect QuarkXPress itself. These also are the least-used settings, because once you set them, you rarely change them. You tell QuarkXPress your preferences for these settings through three options available when you select Edit ➪ Preferences: Application, General, and Tools.

Customizing user interface controls

The Application Preferences dialog box, shown in Figure 4-2, includes two groups of settings: one for the QuarkXPress user interface and one for output. Output is covered in a later section. For the interface, you can control the guide colors, pasteboard width, scroll parameters, image display parameters, screen display parameters, and automatic library saves.

The General Preferences dialog box (accessible via the keyboard shortcut Ctrl+Y) sets controls for default measurement units, placement and use of layout aids, layout controls, and display of text and pictures. You can use the General Preferences dialog box, shown in Figure 4-3, either for the current document or for all new documents. If you change the settings while no document is open, all documents you subsequently create use those settings. If a document is open when you change the settings, only that document is affected.

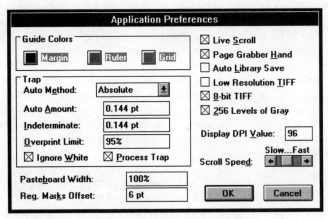

▶ **Figure 4-2:** The Application Preferences dialog box.

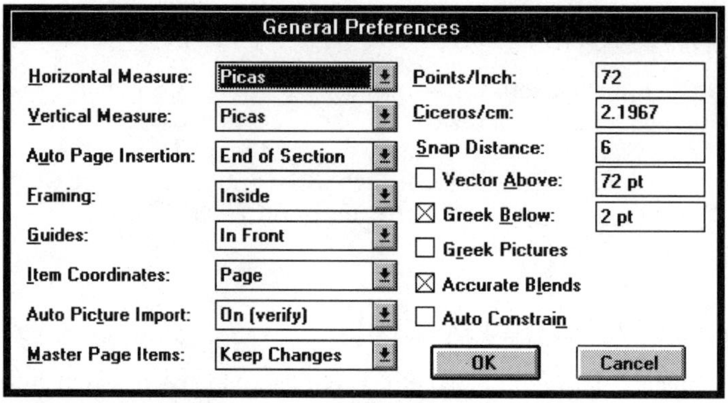

```
┌──────────────────────────────────────────────────────┐
│                    General Preferences                  │
├──────────────────────────────────────────────────────┤
│  Horizontal Measure:  [Picas        ▼]   Points/Inch:  [72    ] │
│  Vertical Measure:    [Picas        ▼]   Ciceros/cm:   [2.1967] │
│  Auto Page Insertion: [End of Section ▼] Snap Distance: [6     ] │
│                                          ☐ Vector Above: [72 pt] │
│  Framing:             [Inside       ▼]   ☒ Greek Below:  [2 pt ] │
│  Guides:              [In Front     ▼]   ☐ Greek Pictures        │
│  Item Coordinates:    [Page         ▼]   ☒ Accurate Blends       │
│  Auto Picture Import: [On (verify)  ▼]   ☐ Auto Constrain        │
│  Master Page Items:   [Keep Changes ▼]    [  OK  ]   [ Cancel ]  │
└──────────────────────────────────────────────────────┘
```

▶ **Figure 4-3:** The General Preferences dialog box.

Guide colors

QuarkXPress provides three types of guides that help you align items: box margins (normally blue), ruler lines (normally green), and the leading grid (normally magenta). The box margin guides show you the column and gutter positions for text boxes, as well as any margins for picture boxes. The ruler lines are lines you drag from the horizontal and vertical rulers so you can tell whether a box lines up to a desired point. The leading grid shows the position of text baselines (defined in the Typographical Preferences menu, described later).

The color of these guides can be important in helping you distinguish them from other lines and boxes in your layout. Figure 4-4 shows all three guides active at the same time. The two lines that cross at the middle left are the ruler guides, and the lighter horizontal lines are the baseline grids.

More often than not, you use margin guides routinely and ruler guides occasionally, particularly when you want to align something within a box to a ruler point. It's easier to use the box coordinates to make sure that boxes or their margins are placed exactly where you want them. But baseline guides help you to estimate column depth and to see if odd text such as a headline causes vertical-alignment problems.

You can change the colors of these guides to any of the 48 colors predefined for you. Or you can select any of 16 colors you can define yourself with the Define Custom Colors option. To set this option, double-click the appropriate button under Guide Colors in the Application Preferences dialog box.

Although you set colors for guides in the Application Preferences dialog box, select the View menu to display the guides. Select Show Guides to display margin guides, and choose Hide Guides to remove them. Likewise, select Show Baseline Grid and Hide Baseline Grid respectively to turn baseline grids on and off.

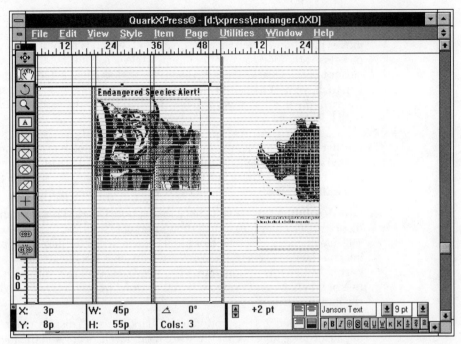

▶ **Figure 4-4:** Box margins, ruler lines, and baseline grid guides.

Ruler lines display whether or not you activate Show Rulers or Hide Rulers. To get rid of a ruler line, select it and drag it back to the ruler.

Image display

QuarkXPress offers several options for global image display, some of which may seem redundant. Three settings in the Application Preferences dialog box affect how you move through your documents: Live Scroll, Page Grabber Hand, and Scroll Speed:

- **Live Scroll:** If you check this box, QuarkXPress automatically scrolls the screen when your cursor moves off the screen. It scrolls the screen until the part of the document you want to access comes into view. Generally, you should check this option.

- **Page Grabber Hand:** If checked, Page Grabber Hand lets you move a graphic in a picture box. When you place the cursor on the graphic, the icon changes to a hand shape. If you press the mouse button and move the mouse, the picture moves within the box, enabling you to crop it as well as reposition it. This option should be checked in most instances.

- **Scroll Speed:** Use this setting to tell QuarkXPress how quickly to scroll through a document. If you set the slider closer to Slow, QuarkXPress moves more slowly across your document, which is helpful if you want to pay close attention to your document while scrolling. If you set the slider closer to Fast, QuarkXPress zips across the document, which might cause you to move past a desired element. Most people prefer a setting somewhere in the middle range. You may have to adjust the setting a few times until it feels right to you.

Three other settings in the Application Preferences dialog box affect how bitmapped images display on-screen: Low Resolution TIFF, 8-bit TIFF, and 256 Levels of Gray. At first, these last two might seem redundant, because an 8-bit image has 256 levels of hue. But there are differences among them:

- **Low Resolution TIFF:** If you check this option, QuarkXPress automatically displays TIFF color files at half their internal resolution. A 256-color (8-bit) TIFF file displays as a 128-color (7-bit) image, which requires less processing and thus displays faster. The actual image is not affected and prints correctly. Use this option unless you need to see images with finer levels of hue or you have a fast video board that won't benefit from displaying low resolution files.

- **8-bit TIFF:** Selecting this option tells QuarkXPress to display color TIFF files at 256 levels of hue, even if there are more levels of color in the file. As with the Low Resolution TIFF option, this does not affect the actual image. If you use video accelerators or video boards designed to display 8-bit images, use this option to get truer layout previews than standard, 4-bit VGA video boards can provide.

  The difference between the Low Resolution TIFF and 8-bit TIFF settings is that the former displays color images at half their internal resolution, no matter what that resolution is, while the latter only affects the display of color TIFF images that have more than 8 bits of color (for example, 16-bit images that have as many as 65,536 colors and 24-bit images that have as many as 16.7 million colors).

These TIFF options do not affect other bitmapped formats, such as PCX, that support different levels of hue. Nor do they affect gray-scale TIFF files.

- **256 Levels of Gray:** Checking this option sets all gray-scale images (in whatever format) to display at 256 levels of gray (as 8-bit images), which is near-photorealistic quality. Otherwise, all gray-scale files display with 16 levels of gray (as 4-bit images). As with the TIFF options, the actual file is unaffected. To use this feature, your monitor must be capable of displaying 256 levels of gray — as most monitors can when using a video board and driver set to display 8-bit images. Unless fast screen display is important, use this option if you have the appropriate display hardware.

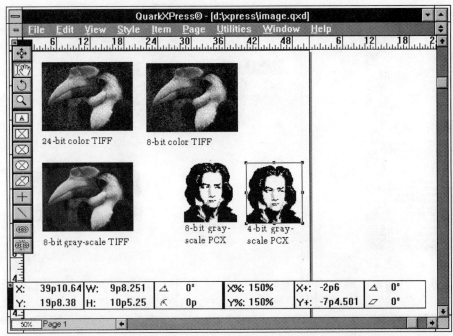

Color monitors, not just monochrome, can display 256 levels of gray if they have an 8-bit video board, although not all programs can mix 256 levels of gray with 256 colors on-screen (paint and image editing programs usually can). QuarkXPress requires the use of a 16- or 24-bit video board to show 256 levels of gray on a color monitor.

Color and gray-scale images are treated separately because color requires more processing. A color file has three constituent colors, compared to one for gray-scale, so color images slow down the system more than gray-scale images.

Figures 4-5 and 4-6 show the differences between images on 8-bit and 4-bit monitors. Figure 4-5 illustrates images on an 8-bit (256-color) Super VGA monitor; Figure 4-6 shows the view on a 4-bit (16-color) VGA monitor. In Figure 4-5, the color images (shown here in gray-scale) appear coarser on-screen than gray-scale images would with the same levels of hue. This is because the levels of hue available are divided into the three colors (red, green, and blue) that make up the color image, while the gray-scale image can use all 256 levels for different shades of gray. Most VGA monitors come with 4-bit (16-color) video boards. As you can see in Figure 4-6, gray-scale images and color images both appear coarse on this type of monitor.

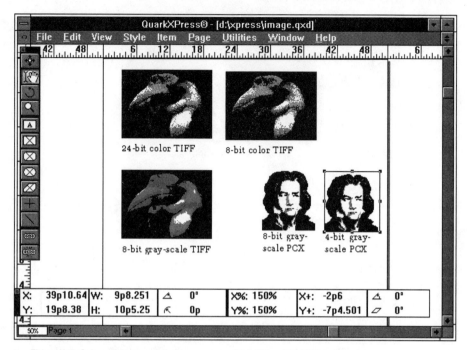

▶ **Figure 4-6:** Color and gray-scale images on a 4-bit (16-color) VGA monitor.

Other display options, available through the General Preferences dialog box, are described later.

Text and picture display

To speed screen display, QuarkXPress offers several options in the General Preferences dialog box (press Ctrl+Y) that control how elements appear on-screen.

■ **Vector Above:** If you select this check box, QuarkXPress uses Windows vector fonts instead of bitmapped fonts when the text is larger than the specified point size (this speeds screen display by reducing the work needed to create bitmaps for large text). The default is 72 points, but you may enter values between 2 and 720 points. This option does not come into play if you use a font scaler such as Adobe Type Manager, Bitstream FaceLift, or Microsoft's built-in TrueType. You use it only when you work with bitmapped fonts, such as those that came with the older version of Windows or were supplied with some printers. Most people can ignore this option and leave the setting at the default. If text appears in a generic-looking, outline form, it is likely due to using a bitmapped font that is larger than the Vector Above setting.

- **Greek Below:** This setting tells QuarkXPress at what size to stop trying to display text and simply use bars of gray to indicate the text instead. The default setting is 7 points, but you can enter values from 2 to 720 points. (This feature is called *greeking* because typographers once used Greek text as placeholder text. The gray bars are in effect placeholder text, so desktop publishing developers adopted the same term.) Greeking small text speeds up screen display, but on faster PCs, the speedup isn't very noticeable. You can turn off greeking altogether by unchecking the box. When you print, text is unaffected by greeking.

- **Greek Pictures:** This setting is similar to Greek Below, except that it applies to images, not text. Checking this option causes all graphics to appear as gray shapes, which speeds up display considerably. This feature is useful after you position and size your images and no longer need to see them to work on your layout. When you print, images are unaffected by greeking.

- **Accurate Blends:** If you check this option, blends between two colors (created via the Colors palette) that you place in a box background appear more accurately on monitors using 8-bit (256-color) video boards. However, it slows down screen redraw on pages with blends. (The default setting has this option checked.) If you have a 24-bit video board, your blends display accurately whether or not you check this option.

Screen display

In the Application Preferences dialog box QuarkXPress lets you set the *dpi* (dots per inch) value for your monitor. Generally, you should leave this setting at the default, because this gives you nearly a 1:1 ratio between images viewed on-screen at 100 percent and their printed size. If you view images at other percentages, they appear about the same size as actual, printed enlargements or reductions of the original.

Different monitors have different dpi settings. Typical settings are: 96 for a 640 × 480-resolution, 13- or 14-inch monitor; 105 for an 800 × 600-resolution, 16- or 17-inch monitor; and 120 for a 1024 × 768, 19-inch monitor. You can change the dpi value in QuarkXPress if you later change monitors; this saves you the effort of reinstalling QuarkXPress.

You also can change dpi settings as a document-independent zoom control. For example, if you want to work on several pages at a time, you can fool Quark-XPress into thinking you have a larger monitor just by making the dpi setting smaller. This causes QuarkXPress to reduce the size of all elements to compensate, letting you see more of the document at once. You can achieve the same effect by changing the view for your document (either through the View menu or by entering a different view percentage in the white box at the document's bottom left), but this view is specific to the current document, so the percentage is saved when you save your document. Using the dpi setting instead lets you change views without affecting the document's view settings. Figures 4-7, 4-8, and 4-9 show how dpi settings affect the view of the same document, which in all cases is set to display at 30 percent of actual size.

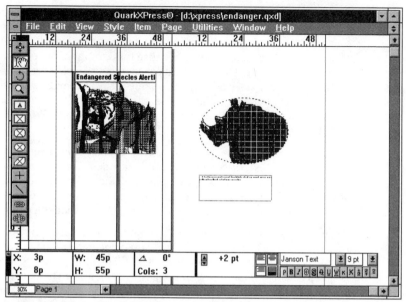

▶ **Figure 4-7:** A document viewed at the standard 96 dpi on a 640 × 480-resolution, 14-inch monitor.

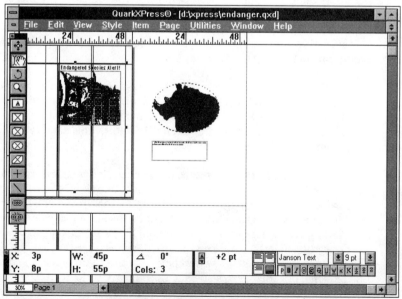

▶ **Figure 4-8:** A document viewed at 72 dpi on a 640 × 480-resolution, 14-inch monitor (normally set at 96 dpi) appears smaller than it really is.

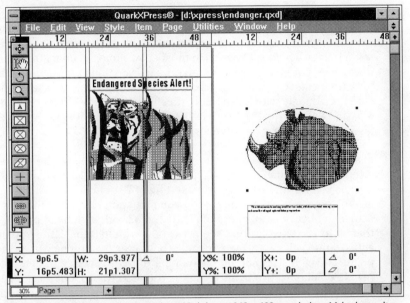

Figure 4-9: A document viewed at 120 dpi on a 640 × 480-resolution, 14-inch monitor (normally set at 96 dpi) appears larger than it really is.

For Macintosh users, 72 dpi results in a 1:1 correspondence between screen image and printed size, so there is a temptation to change the dpi settings to 72. However, in Windows, dpi settings are based on the screen, not on a laser printer, as is the case for the Mac. So leave the dpi settings alone unless you want to follow the preceding tip.

Automatic library save

QuarkXPress's library feature (described fully in Chapter 22) lets you add common elements to a library that is accessible to multiple documents. The default setting saves additions to the library. If you check Auto Library Save in the Application Preferences dialog box, any library additions are automatically added to the current library when you save your document.

Measurement units

Depending on your training, you may be comfortable using a particular measurement unit for layout. Many people measure column width and depth in inches, while others (particularly those with newspaper or magazine backgrounds) use picas. Europeans use centimeters instead of inches and ciceros instead of picas. QuarkXPress supports them all.

Although you can enter any measurement unit in any dialog box by entering the code for the unit after the number (see Chapter 1), you also can set the default units for layout elements. (QuarkXPress assumes that text size and leading is set in points, which is common in most environments, no matter what unit is used for layout elements.) You can set separate units for horizontal and vertical measurements; QuarkXPress offers this flexibility because many people measure horizontally with picas but vertically with inches. Select Horizontal Measure and Vertical Measure in the General Preferences dialog box to set your layout measurement preferences.

In addition, you can set the number of points per inch and the number of ciceros per centimeter through the Points/Inch and Ciceros/cm options, respectively. QuarkXPress uses a default setting of 72 points per inch and 2.1967 ciceros per centimeter. The reason you may want to change these is that the actual number of points per inch is 72.271742, although most people now round that off to 72. (QuarkXPress requires you to round it to 72.27 if you use the actual value.) Likewise, many people (but fewer than those who do so with points and inches) round off the number of ciceros per centimeter to 2.2. Most people don't have problems using the rounded values, but it can make a difference in large documents, such as banners, where registration and tiling of multiple pieces is important.

Customizing tools

QuarkXPress lets you customize how its basic tools work by changing settings in the Tool Preferences dialog box, shown in Figure 4-10. To set the defaults, first select the tool you want to modify. Unavailable options are grayed out, as explained in the following paragraphs. After you make changes, choose Save to record the changes or Cancel to undo them.

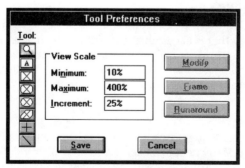

▶ **Figure 4-10:** The Tool Preferences dialog box. Settings for the Zoom tool are shown here.

If you access the Tool Preferences dialog box with no document open, all defaults apply to all subsequently created documents. Otherwise, they apply only to subsequently created boxes and lines for the current document.

The tools you can customize fall into three groups:

- **Zoom tools:** You can change the Minimum and Maximum zoom views to any value from 10 to 400 percent. You also can specify how much QuarkXPress zooms into your document each time you click the document with the Zoom tool active. To do this, enter any value from 10 to 400 percent, in increments of 0.1, into the Increment option box.

- **Box tools:** You can set the item settings for all the box tools: Text Box, Rectangle Picture Box, Rounded-corner Rectangle Picture Box, Oval Picture Box, and Polygon Picture Box. You can establish settings for options normally available for the individual boxes via the Item menu's Modify, Frame, and Runaround options. If you select one of these box tools from the Tool Preferences dialog box, the three buttons corresponding to those Item menu options appear, and you can set them just as you do if you select a box on a document page. The difference is that you are setting them as defaults. Not all Picture Box Specification or Text Box Specification options are available to you; those that affect sizing, for example, are grayed out. But the ability to customize certain settings comes in handy. You can, for example, give oval picture boxes an offset of 1 pica, or set text boxes to have a 3-point frame and a green background. All boxes subsequently created with these tools take on any new preferences you establish in the Tool Preferences dialog box.

- **Drawing tools:** Likewise, you can establish defaults for new lines that you draw with the Orthogonal Line and Diagonal Line tools. You can set most regular-line options that are normally available through the Item menu, but as with the box tools, options that affect position are grayed out. However, you can set other line-specification and runaround options, such as line color and weight. All lines subsequently created with these tools take on any new preferences you establish in the Tool Preferences dialog box.

Layout Settings

In addition to general controls over measurement units and grid colors, QuarkXPress offers other controls over layout through its preferences options. You establish these settings primarily in the default master pages (see the following chapter), the Application Preferences dialog box, and the General Preferences dialog box.

Pasteboard size

The only layout preference set in the Application Preferences dialog box is the pasteboard size, which applies to all documents until you change the setting again.

The pasteboard is a familiar tool to layout artists who are experienced with manual paste-up — the kind you do when you roll strips of type through a waxing machine and then temporarily tack them to the wall or to the outside of your light table until you need them. QuarkXPress supports this metaphor by creating an area to the side of each page that you can use as an electronic scratch pad for picture and text boxes.

If you don't use the pasteboard, you may want to reduce its size. Even if empty, the pasteboard takes up space on your screen that affects scrolling, because the scroll width includes the pasteboard area. Figures 4-11 and 4-12 show the pasteboard set at the default setting of 100 percent and at 50 percent of page size, respectively. At 100 percent, the pasteboard is equal to one page. If you do reduce your pasteboard, items may extend beyond it and appear to be cut off; they in fact remain intact.

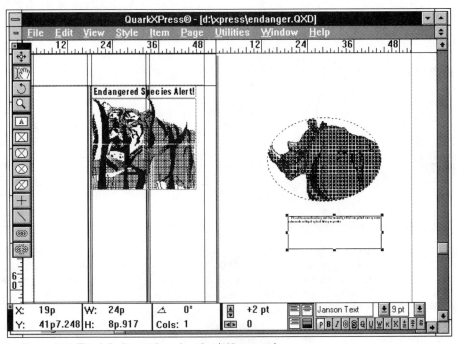

▶ **Figure 4-11:** The default pasteboard setting (100 percent).

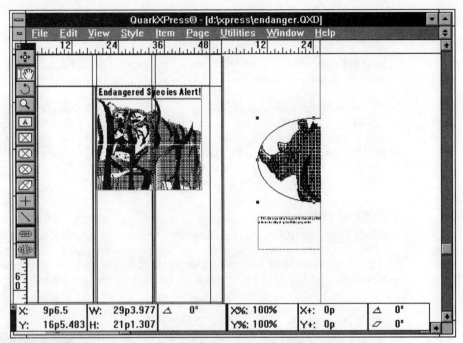

▶ **Figure 4-12:** The pasteboard set at 50 percent of the default size.

Layout aids and controls

Most layout preferences are set through master pages (described in the next chapter) or through the General Preferences dialog box. If a document is open, settings you make in the General Preferences dialog box apply to the current document only; if no document is open, settings apply to all subsequent new documents. The settings you make in the dialog box fall basically into two types: layout aids and layout controls.

Layout aids give you visual feedback from which you can gauge the results of your actions. User-defined preferences for these aids include guide position and page coordinates.

Desktop publishing has long held the promise of automating manual tasks, and *layout controls* are among the QuarkXPress features that do this. In the General Preferences dialog box, you can control how some of these automation features work. User-defined preferences include page insertion, framing position, picture linking, master-page overrides, snap threshold, and box constraints.

Guide position

Select Guides in the General Preferences dialog box to specify whether guides appear in front of boxes (the default setting) or behind them. When guides are behind boxes, it can be easier to see what's in the boxes, but harder to tell if elements within the boxes line up with margins, gutters, or baselines.

 If you select text boxes when guides are set to display behind boxes, the boxes "knock out" the guides. This makes the guides invisible within the box, as Figure 4-13 shows. Boxes stay knocked out even when you select other boxes. But guides overprint the contents of text boxes that are not yet selected. When the screen is redrawn, guides again overprint any text boxes that are not currently selected. (Picture boxes always knock out their guides.)

Page coordinates

Select Item Coordinates in the General Preferences dialog box to tell Quark-XPress whether to base your ruler and frame coordinates on a page or on a spread. If you treat each page as a separate element, keep the option set to Page, the default setting. If you work on a spread as a single unit, change the setting to

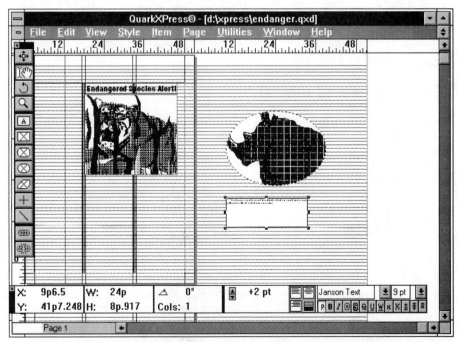

▶ **Figure 4-13:** When guides display behind text boxes, guides within a selected text box become invisible.

Spread. If you choose Spread, the leftmost horizontal coordinate of the right page is the same as the rightmost horizontal coordinate of the left page. If you choose Page, both pages begin at 0.

Page insertion

Auto Page Insertion tells QuarkXPress where to add new pages when all of your text does not fit into a text box you defined in a master page. QuarkXPress creates as many pages as needed to contain all the remaining text. You must define the text box containing the overflow text as an automatic text box in the page's master page. (This is indicated by an unbroken chain icon at the upper left of the master page. Master pages are described in the next chapter.)

Select an Auto Page Insertion setting in the General Preferences dialog box. Your options are:

- **End of Section:** The default setting, this places new pages (which are based on the master page) at the end of the current section (sections are defined via the Page ⇨ Section option, described in Part III, Chapter 11). If no sections are defined, End of Section works the same as the End of Document option.

- **End of Story:** End of Story places new pages (based on the current master page) immediately following the current page.

- **End of Document:** If you select this option, QuarkXPress places new pages at the end of the document (based on the master page used at the end of the document).

- **Off:** If you choose Off, QuarkXPress adds no new pages, leaving you to add pages and text boxes for overflow text wherever you want. The existence of overflow text is indicated by a checked box at the bottom right of the text box.

Framing position

Selecting a Framing setting in the General Preferences dialog box tells QuarkXPress how to draw the ruling lines (frames) around text and picture boxes (done via the Item ⇨ Frame option covered in Part III, Chapter 11). You have two choices: selecting Outside places the frame on the outside of the box; Inside places it inside. Figure 4-14 shows how the two differ. At left, the frame is inside the box, and at right, the frame is outside.

If you change the Framing setting while working on a document, only frames you subsequently create are affected by the change; frames created earlier are unchanged. Thus, you can use both the Inside and Outside settings in the same document.

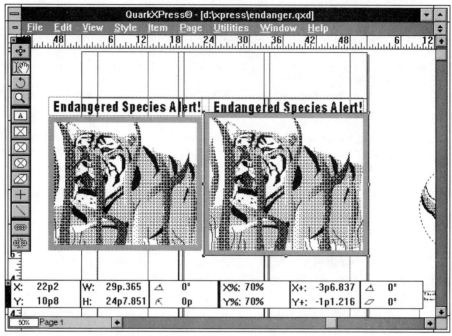

▶ **Figure 4-14:** The Inside framing option (left) and the Outside setting (right).

Picture linking

Auto Picture Import lets you create links to your source images. This is handy if your picture might change frequently and you don't want to forget to update your layout to accommodate it. You can select from three Auto Picture Import settings in the General Preferences dialog box:

- **On (verify):** If you choose this setting, QuarkXPress checks the graphics files to see if they have been modified (by looking at the file's date and time stamp). It then displays a list of all the graphics files in your document so you can decide whether or not to update the layout with the newest version.

- **On:** This setting tells QuarkXPress to automatically import the latest version of changed graphics files.

- **Off:** If you select Off, QuarkXPress does not check to see if the source file has been modified.

In most cases, you should use On (verify) or On, depending on whether you expect graphic files to change much. If files may change size, use On (verify), so you'll know which pictures to check to determine whether layout is affected. If file size is unlikely to change — for example, suppose a logo incorporates the current month but the logo size doesn't change — use the On setting.

Picture linking works only with graphics that have been imported through QuarkXPress's File ➪ Get Picture command. Those pasted into QuarkXPress via the Windows clipboard are not affected. Files pasted through the Windows Object Linking and Embedding (OLE) live-link feature are updated automatically. If you delete or rename a file, the Missing/Modified Picture dialog box appears no matter which automatic import option you select.

Master page overrides

Master Page Items, another setting found in the General Preferences dialog box, lets you control what happens to text and picture boxes that are defined on a master page when you apply a different master page to your document pages. Note that this setting applies only to items used *and* modified on a document page based on a master page's items, not to unmodified items based on a master page. Your options are Keep Changes (the default) and Delete Changes. Figure 4-15 shows an example of how these settings work. In the example:

■ The top two pages are the two master pages. Master Page 1 contains the picture of fruit; Master Page 2, the picture of vegetables.

■ In the second row, Master Page Items is set to Keep Changes. So, when Master Page 2 is applied to the left page, which uses a modified version of the picture box defined in the Master Page 1 (the modified version is

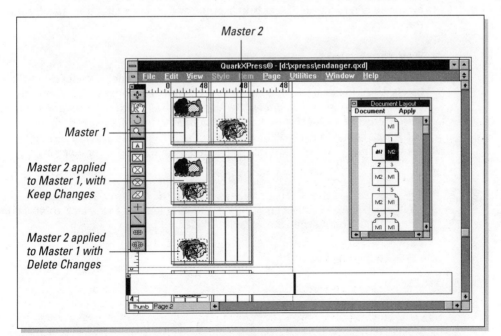

▶ **Figure 4-15:** The Master Page Items setting affects how QuarkXPress treats modified elements.

deeper), the picture box from Master Page 2 is added, resulting in a page with the pictures of fruit and vegetables.

■ When Master Page Items is set to Delete Changes, and Master Page 2 is applied to the right page in row 3, the fruit picture from Master Page 1 is deleted from that page, even though the picture box containing the picture was modified on the document page.

In either row 2 or row 3, if the document page did not use a modified version of the picture box (containing the fruit image) from Master Page 1, the fruit image would be removed no matter which Master Page Items setting was in effect. This is because this setting applies only to elements created in a master page and then modified in the document page to which the new master page is being applied.

Because this can be confusing, follow a simple rule of thumb: leave this setting to Keep Changes. Then, after applying a new master page, manually remove any unwanted elements left behind.

Snap threshold

To set the threshold for when objects snap to guides (assuming Snap to Guides is selected in the View menu), enter a value in the Snap Distance option box, found in the General Preferences dialog box. The default setting is 6 pixels; you can specify any value from 0 to 100 pixels. The larger the number, the further away you can place an object from a guide and still have it automatically snap to the guide.

Box constraints

The last layout control option available through the General Preferences dialog box is Auto Constrain, which controls the behavior of boxes that are created within other boxes. If you check the Auto Constrain option, a box that is created within a text box — a picture box, for example — may not exceed the boundaries of the text box. Nor can you move it outside the text box boundaries. Most people should leave this option unchecked, which is the default setting.

The Item menu offers Constrain and Unconstrain options that can override for any selected box the Auto Constrain setting in the General Preferences dialog box. Constrain appears as an option in the Item menu if the selected box is unconstrained; Unconstrain appears if the selected box is constrained.

Typographic Settings

QuarkXPress lets you define default typographic preferences, which you can then modify for individual styles or for selected text. You specify your preferences in the Typographical Preferences dialog box, shown in Figure 4-16, which you open by choosing Edit ➪ Preferences ➪ Typographic. As with changes you make in the General Preferences dialog box, any changes to the settings in this dialog box affect only the current document. If no document is open, the changes affect all subsequent new documents.

Most of the preferences you define in the Typographical Preferences dialog box need be set only once, although a few are likely to change for different classes of documents. The preferences are described in detail throughout the chapters in Part IV; they are summarized here.

 You cannot set ligatures (combined characters such as fi and fl), as you can in the Macintosh version of QuarkXPress, because Windows does not support ligatures in its character set. To use ligatures, you must use a special typeface, available for some popular typefaces, called an *expert collection*. Expert collections include ligatures, true small caps, and other special characters. These expert collections are described in Part IV, Chapter 14.

Character defaults

Several options affect character defaults. These include the four boxes labeled Superscript, Subscript, Small Caps, and Superior, all found on the left side of the Typographical Preferences dialog box. (Superiors are a special type of superscript that always align along the cap line, which is the height of a capital letter

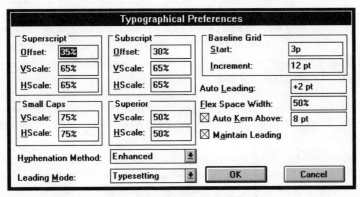

▶ **Figure 4-16:** The Typographical Preferences dialog box.

in the current typeface. They typically are used in footnotes.) These settings define how QuarkXPress creates these attributes. Subscript and Superscript share the same options:

- **Offset:** The Offset option dictates how far below or above the baseline QuarkXPress shifts the subscripted or superscripted character. The default settings are 33 percent for both Subscript and Superscript. We prefer 35 percent for superscripts and 30 percent for subscripts, because those values better take into consideration the effects of leading.

- **VScale and HScale:** These determine scaling for subscript or superscript characters. Although the default is 100 percent, this is useful only for type-written documents; typeset documents typically use a smaller size for subscripts and superscripts — usually between 60 and 80 percent of the text size. The two values should be the same, because subscripts and superscripts are typically not distorted along one dimension.

The options for Small Caps and Superior are similar, even though these are very different attributes:

- **VScale and HScale:** These determine the scaling for small cap or superior characters. The two values should be the same, because small caps and superiors typically are not distorted along one dimension. Usually, a small cap's scale should be between 65 and 80 percent of the normal text, and a superior's scale should be between 50 and 65 percent.

Spacing defaults

The Typographic Preferences dialog box also offers options for vertical and horizontal spacing. There are three vertical-spacing options:

- **Baseline Grid:** These options specify the default positions for lines of text. The Start option indicates where the grid begins (how far from the top of the page), while the Increment setting determines the grid interval. Generally, the grid should start where the basic text box starts, and the interval should be the same as body text leading.

- **Auto Leading:** This determines the default setting for leading in the Paragraph Formats dialog box, through which you establish paragraph settings for styles and selected text. The default is Auto, which sets leading at 120 percent of the current text size. A better option is +2, which sets leading at the current text size plus 2 points — a more typical setting among typographers.

- **Maintain Leading:** If you check this option box, text that falls under an intervening text or picture box snaps to the next baseline grid, rather than falling right after the intervening box's offset. This ensures consistent text alignment across all columns.

There are two horizontal spacing controls:

- **Flex Space Width:** This lets you define the value for a flex space, which is a user-defined space. The default is 50 percent, which is about the width of the letter *t*. A better setting is 200 percent, which is equal to an em space (the width of the letter *M*). An em space is used often in typography but is not directly available in QuarkXPress.

- **Auto Kern Above:** Auto Kern Above enables you to define the point size at which QuarkXPress automatically kerns letter pairs. The default of 10 points is fine for laser-printed documents, but typeset documents should be set at a smaller value, such as 8 points.

Two other options should be left at their defaults:

- **Hyphenation Method:** Keep this option set at Enhanced. Standard exists only to keep the program compatible with earlier Macintosh versions, which had a less-accurate hyphenation algorithm.

- **Leading Mode:** Leave this set at Typesetting. The Word Processing mode exists mainly to enable the program to be backward-compatible with older versions of QuarkXPress. However, some people may want to use Word Processing mode to simulate a typewriter's leading method (in which leading is measured from the top of a capital letter rather than from the text's baseline).

Output Settings

The Application Preferences menu includes several options that affect document output, especially for professional users.

Color trapping

QuarkXPress offers a set of trap options that define how it prints overlapping colors when you use PostScript printers. If you are unfamiliar with color trapping, leave the defaults as they are. The options are:

- **Auto Method:** This setting determines whether QuarkXPress uses the trapping values specified in the Auto Amount option or whether it adjusts the trapping based on the saturation of the abutting colors. If you choose Absolute, the program uses the values as is; if you choose Proportional, QuarkXPress calculates new trapping values based on the value entered in Auto Amount and the relative saturation of the abutting colors. This applies only to colors set at Auto in the Trap Specification dialog box (access this box by choosing Edit ⇨ Colors ⇨ Edit Trap menu). The default is Absolute.

- **Auto Amount:** Select this option to specify the trapping value for which the program calculates automatic trapping, both for the Auto Method option and for the Trap Specification dialog box (accessed via Edit ⇨ Colors ⇨ Edit Trap). You can enter values from 0 to 36 points, in increments of 0.001 points. If you want the amount to be infinite (so colors overprint), enter the word **overprint.** The default setting is 0.144 points.

- **Indeterminate:** The Indeterminate setting tells QuarkXPress how to trap objects that abut multicolored or indeterminate-colored objects, as well as imported color graphics. As with Auto Method, this setting applies only to colors set at Auto in the Trap Specification dialog box. Valid options are 0 to 26 points, in 0.001-point increments, as well as **overprint.** The default is 0.144 points.

- **Overprint Limit:** This value tells QuarkXPress when to overprint a color object. You can specify any percentage from 0 to 100, in increments of 0.1. If you enter 50 percent, QuarkXPress overprints any color whose trap specification is set as Overprint and whose saturation is 50 percent or greater; otherwise, it traps the color based on the Auto Amount and Auto Method settings. This limit affects black objects regardless of whether black is set at Auto or Overprint. The default is 95 percent.

- **Ignore White:** If you check this option box, QuarkXPress traps an object based on all nonwhite objects abutting or behind the object. Otherwise, QuarkXPress calculates a trap based on the smaller of the Indeterminate setting and the trap specification for any other colors abutting or behind the object. This option is checked as a default.

- **Process Trap:** Checking this box tells QuarkXPress to calculate traps for overlapping process colors based on their saturation (for example, it traps 50 percent cyan and 100 percent magenta differently than 80 percent cyan and 100 percent magenta), as well as on all the other trap settings. Otherwise, it uses the same trapping values for all saturation levels. The default setting turns this option on (the box is checked), which makes for smoother trapping.

Trapping is covered in Chapter 21, "Working with Color."

Registration marks

The other output preference set in the Application Preferences dialog box affects the position of registration marks. Choose Reg. Marks Offset to specify the space between the borders of a page and the registration and crop marks. The default is 6 points, which is fine for most printers; you can enter values from 0 to 30 points, in increments of 0.1 points. Unless your printer asks you to change this value, leave it at the default setting.

■ ■

Summary

▶ QuarkXPress allows you to customize layout aids such as guide colors and measurement units to fit your work style.

▶ You can set different view modes for color and gray-scale TIFF images to speed up screen display, as well as hide all images and set text-size display thresholds for faster screen display.

▶ By choosing a setting in the General Preferences dialog box, you can control whether modified elements taken from a master page are retained when you apply a different master page to a document page.

▶ You can specify whether you want boxes that are contained within other boxes to be constrained to the dimensions of the outside box.

▶ You use the Typographical Preferences dialog box to set basic typographic defaults for character attributes (including small cap size and superscript size and position) and for character spacing (including leading).

▶ By making selections in the Application Preferences dialog box, you establish basic trapping values for color elements and specify how you want QuarkXPress to handle different trapping situations.

▶ Specify the position of registration marks by entering a value in the Application Preferences dialog box.

■ ■

Understanding Master Pages

• •

In This Chapter

▶ An introduction to master pages — what they do and what benefits they offer

▶ How to create and modify master pages

▶ How to apply master pages

• •

An Introduction to Master Pages

A *master page* is the basic specification for your document's physical layout. It tells QuarkXPress what model to use when adding new pages. But it's not an overriding specification — you can modify pages slightly or completely after you add them.

When you create a new QuarkXPress document via the File ⇨ New menu option, the main master page is automatically created. QuarkXPress bases the main master page on the settings in the New dialog box, shown in Figure 5-1.

You can establish default settings for the options in the New dialog box by changing the settings and then closing the document (without saving the document).

You also can create new master pages — as many as 127 — for different document elements. For example, you might use the default main masters for your main text, but create three additional master pages for your table of contents, index, and chapter introductions.

New

Page Size
- ⦿ US Letter   ○ A4 Letter   ○ Tabloid
- ○ US Legal   ○ B5 Letter   ○ Other

Width: `8.5"`   Height: `11"`

Column Guides

Columns: `3`

Gutter Width: `1p`

Margin Guides

Top: `8p`   Inside: `3p`

Bottom: `3p`   Outside: `3p`

⊠ Automatic Text Box

⊠ Facing Pages

`OK`   `Cancel`

▶ **Figure 5-1:** The New dialog box, where the basic specifications for the main master page are established.

 If you check the A̲utomatic Text Box option in the New dialog box, all pages you create using this main master page and all pages based on this main master page flow text from a preceding page that has an automatic text box. Likewise, they flow (link) text to the next page with an automatic text box. You can use the link and unlink tools (the chain and broken-chain icons) to change this, as described in Chapter 9, "Working with Text."

The process of creating a new master page can be tricky, so here's a step-by-step guide. As you read, check the figures closely to make sure you're following the process correctly.

▶ Steps: Creating a new master page

Step 1. Display the Document Layout palette by selecting V̲iew ⇨ Show D̲ocument Layout.

Step 2. The Document Layout palette shows your current layout. (If you are working in a new document, you'll have only one or two pages, depending on whether the document is single-sided or double-sided.) The label for each master page appears on the document pages that use it. Pull down the Document menu and select Show Master Pages, as shown in Figure 5-2, to get a list of current master pages.

 The switch icon (the two arrows) below the palette's Control menu lets you quickly jump between Document and Master views. (The Macintosh version of QuarkXPress does not have the switch icon.)

▶ **Figure 5-2:**
Pull down the
Document menu
and select Show
Master Pages to
get a list of
current master
pages.

▶ **Figure 5-3:**
The Document
Layout palette
displays names
of current master
pages.

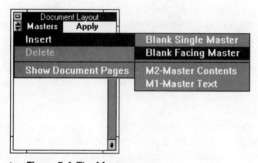

▶ **Figure 5-4:** The Masters menu.

Step 3. The Document menu changes to the Masters menu, and the palette
shows you a list of current master pages, as shown in Figure 5-3. The
names consist of Mx (x stands for the master page number) and a description. (M1 is the main master page.) You can change a name to
make its purpose more apparent, as we have done in the figure. Simply
highlight the name and enter a new one.

Step 4. From the Masters menu, select Insert and then select one of the masters, as shown in Figure 5-4. If you don't want QuarkXPress to use text
or picture boxes from existing master pages when it creates your new
master page — in other words, if you want to create a master page
from scratch — select Blank Single Master for single-sided documents
or Blank Facing Master for double-sided documents. Select an existing
master page if you want to copy its settings and use it as the basis for
your new master page. (You can modify settings you copy; this subject
is covered in the next section.)

 — *Double-sided page pointer*

▶ **Figure 5-5:**
The double-sided page pointer.

Using Blank Facing Master for two-sided documents tells QuarkXPress how to set attributes that alternate between left and right pages, such as inside margins. You can also set left and right pages to have different text boxes and picture boxes. A common example is placing the page number at the bottom right of a right page and at the bottom left of a left page. To accomplish this, you'd need a different text box for left and right page numbers in your facing master page.

Step 5. A page pointer appears to the side of the Document Layout palette, as Figure 5-5 shows. A double-sided page pointer (shown in the figure) has two corners folded down; a single-sided page is simply a rectangle.

Step 6. Move the page pointer into the list of master pages in the Document Layout palette. The pointer changes into an insert pointer, as Figure 5-6 shows. Click the mouse at any location within the palette to add the new master page.

▶ **Figure 5-6:**
The page pointer becomes the insert pointer when you move the page pointer into the list of master pages in the Document Layout palette.

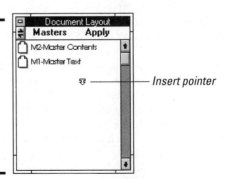

Insert pointer

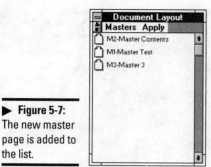

▶ **Figure 5-7:**
The new master
page is added to
the list.

▶ **Figure 5-8:**
Changing the
name of the new
master page.

Step 7. A new master page appears in the list of master pages, as shown in Figure 5-7. Its name and number are based on how many master pages already exist. In the example, the new master page is the third master page, so it is automatically named *M3-Master 3*.

Step 8. You can change the name of the new master page by highlighting it and entering new text. Figure 5-8 shows the new name.

Now, you're ready to actually define your master page. To do this, move to the master page by selecting Page ⇨ Display. Then add, delete, and modify elements by using QuarkXPress layout features, as described in the next section.

Part III covers QuarkXPress layout tools in depth.

How to Modify Master Pages

To change your master page, you must first move to it. Normally, it's not visible in your layout, even in thumbnails view. To move to your master page, select Page ⇨ Display and then select the name of the master page from the menu, as shown in Figure 5-9.

Changing a master page updates all pages in your document that are based on that master page. Change a master page only if you want such global changes to occur. Otherwise, add a new master page and use it for the new layout model you want. You can use the new master page for new pages or apply it to existing ones that you select. (Instructions for creating a new master page are given earlier in this chapter.)

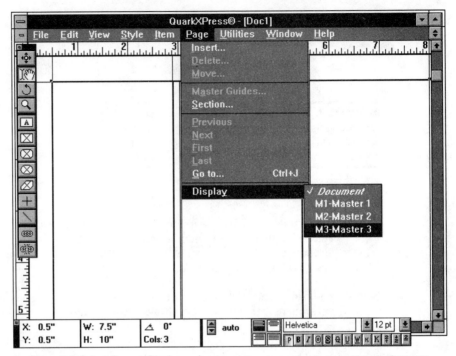

▶ **Figure 5-9:** Select Page ⇨ Display and your master page name to move to a master page.

To edit the main master page settings — which QuarkXPress automatically names *M1-Master 1* when you create a document with File ⇨ New — open the Master Guides dialog box by selecting Page ⇨ Master Guides *after* you move to your main master page. In the Master Guides dialog box, shown in Figure 5-10, you can change the main master page margins and columns originally defined in the New dialog box. You can set these master guides separately for each master page you create.

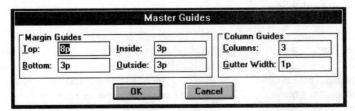

▶ **Figure 5-10:** The Master Guides dialog box.

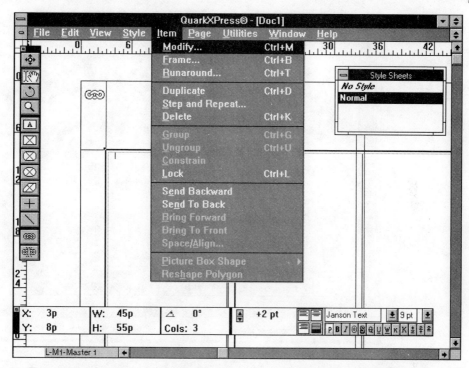

▶ **Figure 5-11:** A sample master page, whose picture and text you modify with the Item menu as you would a normal document page's boxes.

A quick way to jump between master pages (and to jump to regular document pages if the palette is set at Document instead of Master) is to use the Document Layout palette. Double-click the master page name or the regular page icon that represents the page you want to move to.

Double-sided master pages display two pages for you to modify. You can tell which page you're on by looking at the name of the master page, displayed at the bottom left of the screen. If you see the prefix L-, you are working on the left page; likewise, the prefix R- indicates that you are working on the right page. Single-sided master pages have no prefix.

As Figure 5-11 shows, a master page looks like any other page, and you can add, delete, and modify its text and picture boxes as you do for any other page. The only difference is that every element on a master page will exist on every page that is based on that master page. The chain icon at the upper left indicates that text will flow into the automatic text box from the preceding page that uses an automatic text box.

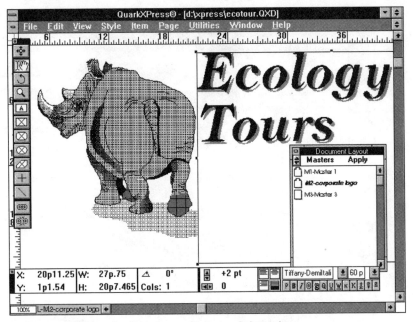

▶ **Figure 5-12:** A sample master page with text and picture boxes.

In Figure 5-12, you see an example master page that includes a picture box of a corporate logo. The ability to add picture and text boxes to your master pages is handy if you want the same elements to appear on several pages of your document. For example, you can put a corporate logo on every page of a brochure without having to place the picture box and graphic on each page by hand.

Use the linking icons — the chain and broken chain — to change link settings for specific master pages. The Link to Current Text Chain option in Page ⇨ Insert also turns on linking when you insert pages whose master pages have automatic text boxes. Chapter 9 covers text linking in more detail.

How to Apply Master Pages

When adding new pages to your document (through the Page ⇨ Insert option), you can specify which master page you want QuarkXPress to use. To do this, make a selection in the Master Page option list, as Figure 5-13 shows. If you select Blank Single Page or Blank Facing Page (available only if your document is set to be two-sided), no text or picture boxes are included in the new pages, so you can make these new pages unique.

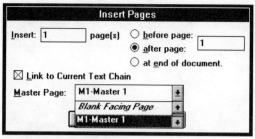

▶ **Figure 5-13:** The Master Page list box contains all available master pages.

You can also apply master pages to existing pages — but be careful, because doing so causes text and layout changes. To apply master pages to existing pages, take the following steps:

▶ Steps: Applying master pages to existing pages

Step 1. Make sure the Document Layout palette is visible (select View ➪ Document Layout). If the left menu says Masters, click it and select Show Document Pages. This brings up a thumbnail view of your pages that shows which master page is applied to each page. Pages without a master page have no label.

Step 2. Select the page to which you want to apply a new master page. You might also display your document in thumbnail view (via View ➪ Thumbnails), as we do in Figure 5-14, so you can readily see which pages are affected.

Step 3. Select Apply. A list of defined master pages and blank masters drops down. Select the master you want to apply to the selected page.

If you apply a different master page to a document page, elements in the document page that are based on the original master page may be deleted, even if modified in the document page. You control whether these modified elements are deleted through the Edit ➪ Preferences ➪ General option, which is covered in Chapter 4. Elements that are based on original master-page elements and have not been modified on the document page are deleted.

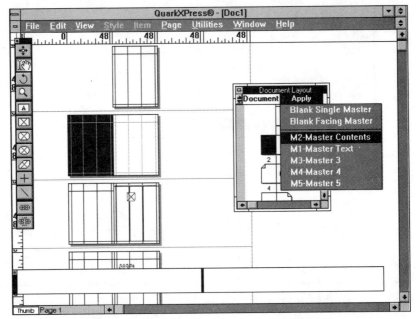

▶ **Figure 5-14:** Display your document in thumbnail view to see which pages are affected.

Overriding Master Pages

Styles and master pages are the two main global settings that you can override locally throughout a document. This is no surprise, since the layout and typographic functions these settings automate are the fundamental components of any document.

The relationship between master pages and locally created layout elements (essentially, picture and text boxes) is similar to that between style sheets and locally applied text formatting: local formatting in a document page overrides any definitions in the master page you apply to that document page. Just as a style sheet is essentially a set of text-formatting macros, master pages are essentially a set of layout-formatting macros.

QuarkXPress offers several ways to override master-page settings; you pick the method you prefer:

Option 1. You can use the Tool Preferences dialog box (see Chapter 4) to set the defaults for many picture-box and text-box attributes, such as background color, frame type, margins, and rotation.

Option 2. You can select the box you want to change the attributes of and then select options from the Item menu. Figure 5-15 shows the Item menu. (The picture-box shape options in the submenu in the figure illustrate that you can change a picture box's shape after creating it, instead of having to delete it and create a new one.) Another way to invoke these menus is to hold Alt and press the underlined letter; for example, Alt+I pulls down the Item menu. Alternatively, you can use the keyboard shortcuts that invoke commonly used dialog boxes and menus. These shortcuts are listed to the right of their menu options. For example, the Frame Specifications dialog box shortcut is Ctrl+B.

Option 3. You can use the QuarkXPress Measurements palette to change box options. (This powerful feature also lets you change text settings. The text settings are on the right side of the palette.) If

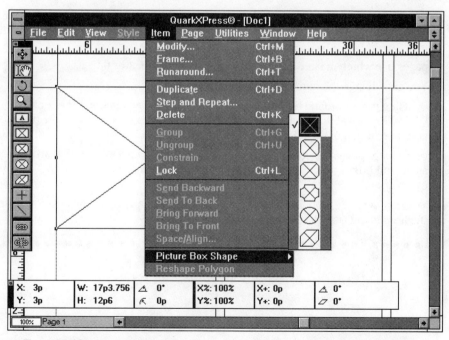

▶ **Figure 5-15:** Picture-box and text-box formatting commands are available through dialog boxes you access from the Item menu.

the palette — a horizontal bar — is missing, use <u>V</u>iew ▷ Show <u>M</u>easurements to display it. Notice that the settings in the palette reflect whatever box is currently selected, providing a handy way to see what your settings are without using menus and dialog boxes.

Option 4. You can create new master pages on-the-fly as you need them. For example, while creating a document you may decide that you want a box for a photograph at the beginning of each section. Create a master page for this section-opening page and then apply it to each section-opening page. If that master page later changes, all documents based on it can also be set to change.

 If you format a document page's boxes locally (through the <u>I</u>tem menu or Measurements palette) rather than through a master page, and if you later apply a master page to that locally formatted document page, the locally created boxes will not change. However, any boxes created by the document page's original master page may be overridden, depending on how your general preferences were set. Chapter 4 covers this process in detail.

Summary

▶ QuarkXPress supports up to 127 master pages. You can apply any of these master pages to any document page to automate the creation and layout of common elements.

▶ You can toggle the Document Layout palette display between a list of which document pages use which master pages and a list of defined master pages.

▶ You can change the names of master pages.

▶ By using the automatic text-box feature in a master page in combination with QuarkXPress's ability to automatically add new pages based on master pages, you can automate much of the layout of long documents.

▶ Use master pages for common elements and formatting. Other global attributes — such as default box settings, measurement preferences, and page numbering — may also be overridden.

▶ You can override global elements by selecting them and applying new formatting through the <u>I</u>tem menu (for picture boxes and text boxes).

CHAPTER **6**

Creating Style Sheets

■■■

In This Chapter

▶ The advantages of using style sheets to create your documents

▶ How to create, modify, and apply styles

▶ How to import word-processor style sheets

■■■

Understanding Style Sheet Basics

Style sheets are similar in purpose to master pages. They define basic specifications for your text: typefaces, type sizes, justification settings, and tab settings. As with master pages, you can override style settings locally whenever you want. (See the section "Overriding Styles" later in this chapter.)

By putting this common text-formatting information into styles — which essentially are macros for text attributes — you can save a lot of effort. Instead of applying each and every attribute individually to text, all you do is tell QuarkXPress that you want certain text to take on all the formatting attributes established in a style tag.

The terminology for styles can be confusing because some programs use them differently, and many people use these terms interchangeably. Here is a run-down of terms as we use them:

■ **Style sheet:** the group of styles in a document. It's called a *sheet* because in preelectronic publishing days, typesetters had typewritten sheets that listed the formatting attributes they were to apply to specific kinds of text, such as body copy and headlines. Some programs, including the DOS version of Microsoft Word, save style sheets as separate files that you attach to specific documents. But QuarkXPress treats style sheets as an integral part of the document (although you can transfer styles among documents), so there is no style sheet per se in QuarkXPress.

■ **Style tag** or **style:** These two terms refer to a group of attributes that you apply to one or more paragraphs. You name the group, or style, so you can apply all the attributes at once. The word *tag* is used because you "tag" selected paragraphs with the style you want to apply. The word *style* also sometimes refers to a character attribute, such as italics or underlining, so many people use *style tag* to refer to the group of attributes. This avoids confusion between the two meanings.

You apply styles to whole paragraphs, not to selected words or sentences. For example, headlines can have a headline style, captions a caption style, bylines a byline style, body text a body text style, and so on. You should create a style for all common paragraph formats. What you call those styles is your business, although using standardized labels can help you and your co-workers apply the right formatting to the right text.

You can use styles in two places: on selected paragraphs in your QuarkXPress document or in the word-processing text you plan to import (either by entering a code to indicate the desired style or by using the word processor's own style sheets, as described in Chapter 6, "Creating Style Sheets"). Which choice you make depends on the type of document you are working on.

 It makes sense to apply styles in your source text for long or routine documents (such as a newsletter, when everyone knows the styles to be used). And it makes sense to apply styles in QuarkXPress for a brochure or other highly designed or nonstandard document.

No matter when you apply styles, you'll find that they are a must for productive publishing of all but a small handful of documents (one-time pieces such as ads are possible exceptions).

Creating Styles

Almost every function you need for defining styles resides in the Style Sheets dialog box, which you access via Edit ➪ Style Sheets, as shown in Figure 6-1.

There are two significant functions you do *not* set in the Style Sheets dialog box:

■ Hyphenation controls are set in the H&Js dialog box (hyphenation and justification), which you access via Edit ➪ H&Js.

■ Character- and space-scaling controls are set in the Typographical Preferences dialog box, accessed via Edit ➪ Preferences ➪ Typographic.

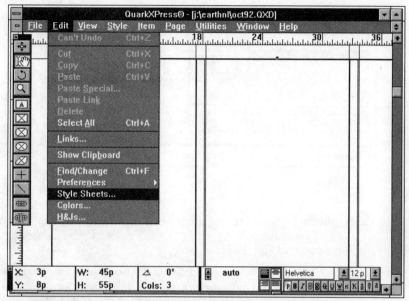

▶ **Figure 6-1:** Select Edit ➪ Style Sheets to open the Style Sheets dialog box.

Both functions are covered in detail in later chapters. See Chapter 12, "Understanding Character Spacing," for information about word and letter spacing; refer to Chapter 13, "Understanding Paragraph Spacing," for more information on hyphenation.

You can create styles without understanding these options and then later retrofit styles to include them. But if you are experienced in typography and somewhat experienced with style sheets (in any program), consider reading those chapters before continuing with this one.

Style Sheets dialog box

The Style Sheets dialog box provides several options for editing style sheets, as Figure 6-2 shows. Your editing choices are as follows:

■ **New** lets you create a new style from scratch or create a new style based on an existing style.

■ **Edit** enables you to edit an existing style. You can also use Edit to create a style by editing an existing style, changing the style name to a new name, and changing whatever attribute settings you want. This has the same effect as the Duplicate option.

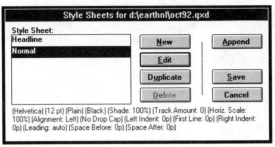

▶ **Figure 6-2:** The Style Sheets dialog box.

- **Duplicate** copies all the attributes of an existing style and gives the duplicate style the name `Copy of style`. You can then change any attribute settings, including the style name.

- **Delete** lets you delete existing styles. This option is grayed out when Normal is selected, because you cannot delete the Normal style. You are asked to confirm the deletion if you applied the style to text in the current document. Any text using a deleted style retains the style's attributes. But the Style Sheet palette and menu show these paragraphs as having `No Style`.

- **Append** enables you to copy a style from another QuarkXPress document.

- **Save** lets you save all the style additions, deletions, and changes you make in the Style Sheets dialog box. You *must* save your styles when leaving the dialog box for changes to take effect.

- **Cancel** instructs QuarkXPress to ignore all style additions, deletions, and changes you made in the Style Sheets dialog box.

If you define text settings through the Style menu or Measurements palette and decide you want to create a style that contains those attributes, just position your text cursor anywhere on the text that has the desired settings. Then choose New in the Style Sheets dialog box. All settings are automatically included in the new style you create. This is handy if you want to experiment with settings on dummy text before creating a style for future use.

Whether you choose New, Edit, or Duplicate when you create a style sheet, the next dialog box to appear is Edit Style Sheet, shown in Figure 6-3. This dialog box is the launching pad for the actual definition of style attributes.

The Name field is not filled in if you selected New. The Based on field reads *No Style* unless you are editing or duplicating a style that uses the based-on option, described later in this chapter. You can enter or change the style name; if you choose the name of an existing style, an error message asking for a new name appears when you choose OK.

Edit Style Sheet

N**a**me:

Caption

Keyboard **E**quivalent:

Based on: *No Style*

(Helvetica) (12 pt) (Plain) (Black) (Shade: 100%) (Track Amount: 0) (Horiz.
Scale: 100%) (Alignment: Left) (No Drop Cap) (Left Indent: 0p) (First Line: 0p)
(Right Indent: 0p) (Leading: auto) (Space Before: 0p) (Space After: 0p)

Character

Formats

Rules

Tabs

OK   Cancel

▶ **Figure 6-3:** The Edit Style Sheet dialog box.

The Keyboard **E**quivalent field lets you set up hotkeys that allow you to apply
styles to text quickly. For example, you can establish F2 as the hotkey for the
Normal style. This tells QuarkXPress to apply that style to currently selected
paragraphs when you press F2. You can use the function keys and the numeric
keypad keys as hotkeys. You also can establish keyboard shortcuts for applying
styles. To enter keyboard shortcuts, press the actual keys you want to use, including combinations with Shift, Alt, and Ctrl, such as Ctrl+Shift+F7.

Don't use Alt with numeric keys, because Windows uses those combinations
to access extended characters such as copyright symbols and foreign letters.

You'll find four buttons along the right side of the Edit Style Sheet dialog box:
Character, **F**ormats, **R**ules, and **T**abs. These invoke the appropriate dialog boxes
for each major part of the style. Select **C**haracter for text attributes such as typeface and size; **F**ormats for paragraph attributes such as leading and indentation;
Rules for ruling lines associated with paragraphs; and **T**abs to define tab stops
and tab types. You can use these in any order and ignore ones that don't apply to
the current style (typically, **R**ules and **T**abs).

The dialog boxes these buttons invoke are identical to the **S**tyle menu dialog
boxes with the same names. The chapters in Part IV cover these dialog boxes
in detail.

A step-by-step guide to creating a style

To create a style, you should have some idea of what basic elements you want in
your document. For example, elements in a newspaper include body text, headlines, bylines, captions, and page numbers (folios). In addition, lead text, pull-
quotes, biographies, subheads, sidebar heads, bulleted lists, and other more
specialized types of formatting may be necessary. Don't worry about knowing in
advance all the types of formatting you need to assign styles to — it's very easy
in QuarkXPress to add a new style at any time.

Start with the body text, because this is the bulk of your document. You can create a style called something like Body Text, or you can modify the Normal style that QuarkXPress defines automatically for each new document and use that as your body text style.

You can create a default Normal style that each new document uses. This is handy if, for example, most of your documents use the same typeface or justification or point size (or any combination of these) for body text. The initial setting for Normal is left-aligned, 12-point Helvetica with automatic leading. To change any attributes of Normal, close all open documents, access the Style Sheets dialog box by selecting Edit ⇨ Style Sheets, and edit the Normal style in the usual way, described next. (Notice that the dialog box says Default Style Sheets rather than the typical Style Sheets for *document name*.) These settings are saved as the new defaults for all future new documents. When creating this default Normal style, you need not use real text, because it is used only to gauge the effects of the style formatting.

In the following example, which illustrates the process of creating styles, we have imported a text file to be used in a newsletter whose style has not yet been defined. When loaded, the text took on the attributes of the Normal style, because we did not use style options in the original word processor. This text has five main elements: the body text, the body lead (which has a drop cap but otherwise is like the body text), the byline, the headline, and the kicker (the small headline above the headline that identifies the type of story — in this case, a commentary). Our newsletter also needs styles for captions, folios (page numbers, the publication name, and the publication date), all of which typically run at the top or bottom of each page. In addition, we need styles for subheads and sidebar heads (for simplicity, we decided that sidebar text will be the same as the body text).

Our first step in defining styles was to invoke the Edit Style Sheets dialog box, as described earlier in this chapter. We then selected the Character button to open the Character Attributes dialog box, shown in Figure 6-4. Then we changed the Font to Janson Text, the Size to 9, and the Track Amount to –2. We left the other attributes alone, because they are appropriate for body text. We clicked OK to return to the Edit Style Sheet dialog box.

Many dialog box options offer drop-down lists to help you make selections faster. For example, in the Character Attributes dialog box, Font, Size, Color, and Shade all offer drop-down lists. You can also enter the value you want in the field directly. In the Font field, QuarkXPress displays the first typeface it finds that begins with the letter you type in. This enables you to jump quickly to or near a particular typeface — convenient if you have a long list to scroll through. Figure 6-5 shows the drop-down list for the Font field.

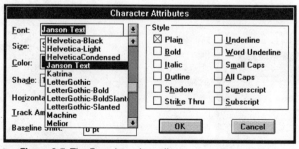

Character Attributes

		Style
Font:	Janson Text	☒ Plain ☐ Underline
Size:	9 pt	☐ Bold ☐ Word Underline
Color:	Black	☐ Italic ☐ Small Caps
Shade:	100%	☐ Outline ☐ All Caps
Horizontal Scale:	100%	☐ Shadow ☐ Superscript
Track Amount:	-2	☐ Strike Thru ☐ Subscript
Baseline Shift:	0 pt	OK Cancel

▶ **Figure 6-4:** The Character Attributes dialog box.

Next, we opened the Paragraph Formats dialog box, shown in Figure 6-6, by selecting the Formats button in the Edit Style Sheet dialog box. We changed the First Line field so the first line of each paragraph is indented 9 points. (See Chapter 15, "Using Special Elements and Effects," for advice on setting indents.) We also changed Alignment to Justified and Leading to +2. (This leading setting tells QuarkXPress to make the leading 2 points more than the point size; the default is Auto, which makes leading 120 percent of the point size.)

In Figure 6-6, you also see the drop-down list for the H&J field; we included this to show where you select hyphenation and justification (H&J) settings. You define H&J sets separately via the Edit ⇨ H&Js menu option, which is fully described in Chapter 13, "Understanding Paragraph Spacing."

We then chose OK to leave the Paragraph Formats dialog box, OK to leave the Edit Style Sheet dialog box, and Save to save all our changes to the Normal style. Figure 6-7 shows this sequence of dialog boxes, numbered in the order in which they occurred. You use this same process to create styles for your documents.

Character Attributes

		Style
Font:	Janson Text	☒ Plain ☐ Underline
Size:	Helvetica-Black	☐ Bold ☐ Word Underline
	Helvetica-Light	
Color:	HelveticaCondensed	☐ Italic ☐ Small Caps
	Janson Text	
Shade:	Katrina	☐ Outline ☐ All Caps
	LetterGothic	
	LetterGothic-Bold	
Horizonta	LetterGothic-BoldSlant	☐ Shadow ☐ Superscript
	LetterGothic-Slanted	
Track Am	Machine	☐ Strike Thru ☐ Subscript
	Melior	
Baseline	0 pt	OK Cancel

▶ **Figure 6-5:** The Font drop-down list.

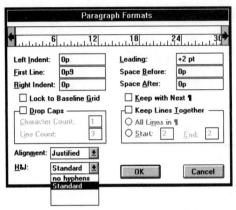

▶ **Figure 6-6:** The Paragraph Formats dialog box.

> At the bottom of the Style Sheets dialog box is a description of the attributes for the selected style. This is a handy way to see what the current settings are, as well as to verify that you set the options you intended.

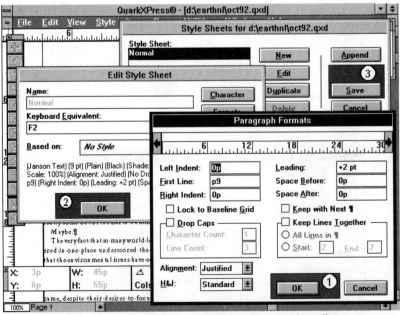

▶ **Figure 6-7:** You move through several dialog boxes to save style attributes.

For details on the options available via the Character Attributes dialog box (accessed via the Character button), the Paragraph Formats dialog box (accessed via the Formats button), the Paragraph Rules dialog box (accessed via the Rules button), and the Paragraph Tabs dialog box (accessed via the Tabs button), see the chapters in Part V. These dialog boxes are identical to those available via the Style menu, because they apply both to whole paragraphs and to selected groups of characters.

Applying Styles

To apply a style, you have three options, as illustrated in Figure 6-8:

- ■ **Option 1:** Use the Style ➪ Style Sheets menu option. This option is the least efficient way to apply styles to text.

- ■ **Option 2:** Use the Style Sheet palette, shown in the upper-right corner of the figure, which you invoke through the View ➪ Show Style Sheets option. (You can resize and move the palette if you want.) This option is the best way to apply styles in most cases.

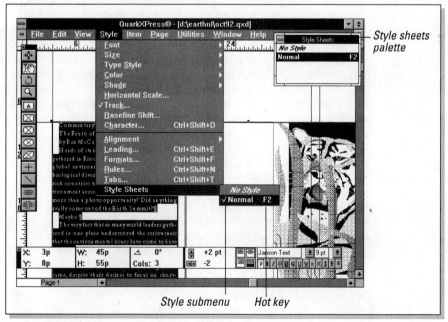

▶ **Figure 6-8:** QuarkXPress offers several avenues for applying styles.

■ **Option 3:** Use the keyboard shortcut, if you defined one in the Edit Style Sheet dialog box. The shortcut key is shown in both the Style Sheet palette and the <u>S</u>tyle ⇨ St<u>y</u>le Sheets menu option (in this example, the shortcut key is F2). This option is the fastest method, but is effective only for very commonly used styles, because it requires memorizing the keyboard shortcuts.

A quick way to select all the text in a document so you can apply the Normal (or other) style to it is to choose Select <u>A</u>ll from the <u>E</u>dit menu. Pressing Ctrl+A achieves the same effect without requiring you to use pull-down menus. To use this feature, you must select a text box containing text with the Text tool. All text in that text box, as well as any text box linked to it, will be selected.

Modifying Styles

To modify styles, you simply open the Style Sheets dialog box and select <u>E</u>dit. You can then change attributes as you want. You can also use this approach to create new styles that are related to current ones.

When you create styles for a document, you'll probably have several similar styles, and some may be variations of others. For example, you might have a body text style plus a style for bulleted lists that is based on the body text style. Fortunately, QuarkXPress uses a technique called "based-on formatting" in its styles. You can tell QuarkXPress to base the Bulleted Text style on the Body Text style, in which you defined typeface, point size, leading, justification, hyphenation, indentation, tabs, and other attributes. You then modify the Bulleted Text style to accommodate bullets — by changing the indentation, for example. The great thing about based-on formatting is that later, if you decide to change the typeface in Body Text, the typeface automatically changes in Bulleted Text and in all other styles based on Body Text — saving you a lot of work in maintaining consistency of styles.

Figure 6-9 shows the Edit Style Sheet dialog box for a style named Caption, which is based on the Normal style. The style description shows what attributes are different from those in the Normal style: the typeface (Rockland is used instead of Normal's Janson Text); the tracking (0 instead of Normal's –2); and first line indent (none instead of Normal's 9 points). Another difference, which is not visible in the dialog box, is that the H&J set is changed to No Hyphens, a previously defined H&J set. If the point size in Normal later changes from its current 9 points to 10 points, Caption's point size changes as well. But if the typeface changes in Normal from Janson Text to Melior, Caption's typeface remains as Rockland because we specified that element explicitly in Caption.

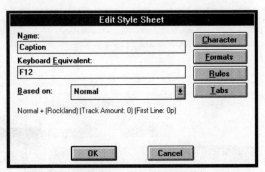

> ▶ **Figure 6-9:** The style description lists differences
> between the Caption style and the style on which it
> is based (Normal).

Another modification technique is simply to duplicate an existing style and then edit the attributes in that duplicate. Alternatively, you can edit an existing style and give it a new name. This is similar to creating a based-on style, except the new style is not automatically updated if the style it is duplicated from is modified — unless the style you duplicated or edited itself is based on another style.

Importing Styles from QuarkXPress Documents

QuarkXPress lets you copy styles from one document to another. You do this by selecting the Append button in the Style Sheets dialog box. When you select Append, you open the Append Style Sheets dialog box, shown in Figure 6-10. This dialog box is similar to the dialog box for opening a QuarkXPress document. You can change drives and directories as needed to select the QuarkXPress document that has the style sheet you want.

You can limit which documents display by using the List Files of Type option at the bottom of the Append Style Sheets dialog box. The default is Files with Style Sheets; your other options are all QuarkXPress documents (those with the extension QXD) or all QuarkXPress templates (those with the extension QXT).

When you select a document and choose OK, QuarkXPress copies all of its styles into your current document. You cannot choose individual styles to import.

If a style in the current document has the same name as a style you are importing, QuarkXPress preserves the current document's style and ignores the style in the other document. The program does not display an error message to tell you that a conflict occurred and was avoided.

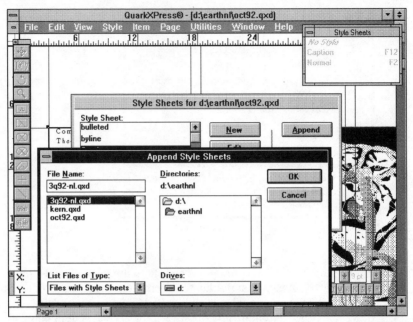

▶ **Figure 6-10:** The Append Style Sheets dialog box, where you select the QuarkXPress document that has the style sheet you want.

 QuarkXPress cannot copy H&J sets associated with imported styles. If imported styles use H&J sets that are undefined in the current document, QuarkXPress displays the error message shown in Figure 6-11. You then have the option to use the Standard H&J set in your current document or to cancel the style import.

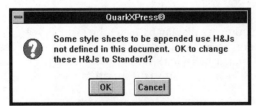

▶ **Figure 6-11:** An error message tells you an imported style uses an H&J set that is undefined in the current document.

Importing Styles from Your Word Processor

QuarkXPress lets you import styles created in several word processors: Microsoft Word for Windows, Lotus Ami Pro, and WordPerfect for Windows are included, as are programs that can save files in Rich Text Format (RTF). Programs that support RTF include Word for Windows and Lotus Ami Pro. When importing files with style sheets, make sure the Include Style Sheets box is checked, as shown in Figure 6-12.

If you are importing text saved in the XPress Tags format (described in the next chapter), use the Include Style Sheets option. Although the purpose of the XPress Tags format is to embed style tags and other formatting information in your text, you still must explicitly tell QuarkXPress to read those tags during import. Otherwise, QuarkXPress imports your text as an ASCII file, and all the embedded tags are treated as regular text and are not acted upon.

If you check the Include Style Sheets check box for formats that have no style sheets, QuarkXPress ignores the setting. Thus, if you typically import style sheets with your text, it's good to get in the habit of always checking this box; doing so causes no trouble when importing other text formats.

Unlike the Convert Quotes check box, the Include Style Sheets check box does not remain checked after you leave the Get Text dialog box. This is another reason to get in the habit of always checking this box if you use word processing style sheets routinely.

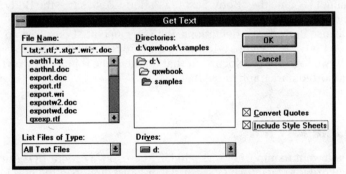

▶ **Figure 6-12:** Check the Include Style Sheets box to have Quark-XPress append your word processor's style sheet to your Quark-XPress document.

Style conflicts

The names of imported style tags are listed in the Style Sheets palette and can be edited like any other style. If the imported style sheet has a style tag that uses a name already in use by the QuarkXPress document, the imported style tag is renamed. The new name takes the form of an asterisk (*) plus the old name.

Although this renaming feature ensures that you don't lose any formatting, what if you want to use an existing QuarkXPress style tag on text that uses a word processor's style tag that is formatted differently? Consider this example:

The QuarkXPress document has a style called Body Text that, among other things, sets the text to 9-point Janson Text with a leading value of +2 points and uses a H&J set called 4 Hyphens Max that limits consecutive hyphens to four and sets the minimum character space to –5 percent.

The text you want to import was created in Word for Windows, and has a style called Body Text that, among other things, sets the text to 12-point Courier and has a leading of 1.5 lines. There is no such thing as additive leading in a word processor, much less an H&J set. Even if the person who created the document could change the other style tag settings to match those in the QuarkXPress style, some tags simply will be different.

When you import your Word text with the Include Style Sheets box checked, QuarkXPress renames the Word style to *Body Text, since QuarkXPress has its own Body Text style defined. But your goal is to have the text that was tagged Body Text in Word take on the attributes of the QuarkXPress tag called Body Text.

You cannot rename the *Body Text tag to Body Text, since the Body Text tag already exists. If you delete the Body Text tag so you can rename *Body Text, you will lose Body Text's definitions. But you can edit *Body Text so that it is *based on* Body Text. Figure 6-13 shows this process. While this means you'll end up with two tags in your document that do the same thing, you won't have to tag each imported paragraph individually.

Miscellaneous import notes

- If you want to import files created in Microsoft Word for DOS (any version) or Word for Macintosh (Version 4.0 or later), first load the files into Micro-soft Word for Windows 2.0 and save them in Word for Windows format. If you want to import files created in WordPerfect for Macintosh (any version) or WordPerfect for DOS (Version 5.0 and earlier), first load them into WordPerfect 5.1 for Windows or DOS and save them in Version 5.1 format. You can load WordPerfect for DOS 5.1 files directly into QuarkXPress, since it uses the same format as WordPerfect for Windows.

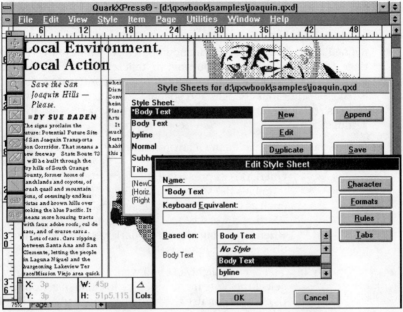

▶ **Figure 6-13:** Use the Based on option to make an imported word-processor style tag take on the attributes of a QuarkXPress style tag.

- For other supported word processors that do not use style sheets, such as Windows Write, formatting applied in the word processor imports into QuarkXPress but is applied directly to the text, as if you had selected the text in Quark and used the Style menu options to directly format the text. The same is true if you import text from word processors that have style sheets but you did not check the Include Style Sheets box; the text formatting is retained, but there are no styles with this formatting.

- You can quickly turn formatted text into styles by selecting any formatted text and using the New button in the Style Sheets dialog box; QuarkXPress transfers that formatting to a style, as described earlier in this chapter.

Overriding Styles

QuarkXPress is designed to give you the maximum control over typography; as a result, there are few global settings but many local settings. You can create several variations on global settings when creating style sheets or H&J sets, and you can override these styles at any time.

Most of your settings are contained in your style sheet, as described earlier in this chapter. Because a style is the publishing equivalent of a macro, all paragraphs tagged with the Headline style, for example, take on the characteristics defined in the Headline style. But sometimes you want to override style settings. One example is when you want to italicize some text for emphasis. You must apply the italics locally to just those words you want italicized. The same is true for other font changes and spacing attributes, as well as special effects such as rotation and color. QuarkXPress offers several ways to override style settings:

Option 1. You can define many font attributes — such as boldface, small caps, underlining, and italics — in your word processor. QuarkXPress preserves this formatting in imported text even as it applies the styles. You can even define much formatting — such as typeface, type size, and justification — in Microsoft Word or a word processor that can save files in RTF format; when importing files into Quark, you check the Include Style Sheets option in the Get Text dialog box.

Option 2. You can highlight text you want to change attributes of and then select the Style menu and pick from its many options. Alternatively, you can use the keyboard shortcuts that invoke commonly used dialog boxes and menus. These shortcuts are listed to the right of menu options that have them. For example, the Character Attributes dialog box shortcut is Ctrl+Shift+D.

Option 3. You can use the QuarkXPress Measurements palette to change text options. (This powerful feature also lets you change text-box and picture-box settings. The box settings are on the left side of the palette.) If the palette is not on-screen, use View ⇨ Show Measurements to turn it on. Notice that the settings in the palette reflect whatever text is currently selected, providing a handy way to see what your settings are without using menus and dialog boxes.

Option 4. You can create new styles on-the-fly as you discover you need them. For example, you may decide while creating a document that you want the first paragraph in each section to have a drop cap (a large letter set in several lines of text) to draw attention to it. Except for the fact that it has a drop cap and the first line is not indented, this lead paragraph is no different than body text. So simply create a new style (under Edit ⇨ Style Sheets ⇨ New) that is based on the body text style rather than the default No Style. Using the Based on option provides another advantage: If you later change the settings for, say, the typeface in your body text, all styles based on body text are instantly updated.

If you format text locally and then decide to create a style from your efforts, you can simply position the text cursor anywhere in the formatted text and use Edit ⇨ Style Sheets ⇨ New. This automatically applies all settings in the selected text to the new style you are creating.

If you format text locally (through the Style menu or Measurements palette) rather than through a style tag, and you later apply a tag to that locally format- ted text, your text may not take on all of the tag's settings. Because local formatting is designed to override global formatting, any formatting applied locally to the text is not overridden by the new style tag, even though that tag was applied after the local formatting. But any formatting not specifically ap- plied locally reflects the style tag's settings. For example, if you apply font attributes locally but do not apply justification settings locally, justification changes when you apply a style tag with different H&J settings, but the font does not.

Summary

▶ Style sheets automate the application of a range of character and formatting attributes.

▶ All but two style sheet controls reside in the Edit ⇨ Style Sheets menu option. Hyphen- ation controls reside in Edit ⇨ H&Js, and character and space defaults are set in Edit ⇨ Preferences ⇨ Typographic.

▶ You can assign keyboard shortcuts for commonly used styles.

▶ The Based on feature lets you create a style that uses attributes defined in another style. If the source style changes, any unmodified attributes in the new style are automatically updated.

▶ QuarkXPress can import styles from other documents. But H&J sets are not copied across documents, and a style whose name is the same in both documents is not overrid- den. QuarkXPress preserves the style in the document to which styles are being imported.

▶ You cannot selectively import styles from a document — all nonduplicate styles are imported.

▶ Be sure to check the Include Style Sheets box in the Get Text dialog box before importing Word for Windows, WordPerfect, or RTF text whose style sheets you want to import. This box must be checked each time you enter the Get Text dialog box.

▶ If an imported word processor style tag has the same name of an existing QuarkXPress style tag, the imported tag is renamed to begin with an asterisk.

▶ By using QuarkXPress's Based on feature, you can have text tagged in a word processor take on the attributes of a QuarkXPress style tag instead of the word processor's style tag. Just edit the imported style tag so it is based on the QuarkXPress style.

▶ You can override global elements by selecting them and applying new formatting through the Style menu (for text) and Item menu (for picture boxes and text boxes).

Preparing Files for Import

Determining Where to do Document Formatting

You can import text and graphics into your QuarkXPress documents in several ways. QuarkXPress is particularly adept at importing documents created in Windows formats. And through the OLE features described in Chapter 23, "Linking to Source Files," you can import file formats not directly supported by QuarkXPress.

QuarkXPress import capabilities may tempt you to do a lot of your text and graphic formatting outside the program; however, it's not always wise to do so.

■ Because a word processor's style sheets won't match all QuarkXPress typo-graphic features, it's often not worthwhile to do extensive coding in your word processor. This is particularly true of layout-oriented formatting. Multiple columns and page numbers, for example, will be of a much higher standard in your final QuarkXPress document than you could hope to create in a word processor. After all, even the sophisticated formatting features in today's word processors don't begin to approach those needed for true publishing. (For more information on this subject, review the preceding chapter.)

■ Similarly, formatting tables in your word processor or spreadsheet is typically a wasted effort, because you have to recreate the tables using QuarkXPress tab settings. If you turn your spreadsheet or chart into a graphic before importing it, you cannot edit the data. Nor can you resize the picture to fit a changing layout without winding up with different-size numbers among at least some charts — a definite no-no.

■ When you work with graphics, however, it does make sense to do extensive work in the originating program. After all, no desktop publishing program offers the kind of graphics tools that an illustration program or photo editor does. Still, some tasks, including setting line screens and other halftone settings, background colors, and frames, are best-suited to QuarkXPress.

Preparing Text Files

What preparation could you possibly need to do for your word processor files? They should just load into QuarkXPress as is, right? Not necessarily, even if your word processor supports one of the QuarkXPress text-import formats. Actually, the key to preparing text files is to not *over*-prepare them.

Most of today's major word processors include basic graphics and layout features to help users format single-document publications. Avoid using these features in files you intend to bring into QuarkXPress. Do your sophisticated formatting in QuarkXPress — that's one of the reasons you invested in such a powerful tool. This approach also enables you to do formatting in the context of your layout, rather than in a vacuum. Much of the graphics and layout formatting you do in a word processor is all for naught anyway, because such non-textual formatting does not import into QuarkXPress. Remember, you're importing text, not documents.

 Limit your word processor formatting to formatting that enhances reader understanding or conveys meaning. Such formatting might include using italics and boldface to emphasize a word, for example, or using style sheets to set headlines and bylines in different sizes and typefaces. (See the preceding chapter for tips on using style sheets in word processor text.) Let your editors focus on the words; leave presentation tasks to your layout artists.

Translating Text Files

One type of file preparation you might need to do is to translate text files into formats supported by QuarkXPress. The following tips can help you work with popular word processors:

- QuarkXPress supports the major Windows word processors — Microsoft Word for Windows 1.*x* and 2.0, Lotus Ami Pro 2.0, and WordPerfect for Windows 5.1.

- Because WordPerfect 5.1 for DOS (the top-selling DOS word processor) uses the same file format as the Windows version, QuarkXPress can read files created in that program, too. At the time we were finishing this book, QuarkXPress did not yet support Microsoft Word, which is the second-best selling DOS word processor, or WordPerfect 4.2, an older and widely used version of WordPerfect.

- If you use WordPerfect 4.2, you must load files into WordPerfect 5.1 and then save them in the newer version's format.

- If you use the Mac version of WordPerfect, you must save files in the DOS/Windows 5.1 format.

- Word for Windows can read Word for DOS files and then save them in Windows format. You (or your layout artist) may need to go through this step to import Word for DOS text. Some versions of Word for DOS have a utility that converts files into Rich Text Format (RTF), which QuarkXPress also supports. In either case, because style information is retained, you can import styles into QuarkXPress along with the text. If you use Version 4.0 or lower of Mac Word, you must save files in the DOS version format, import them into Word for Windows, and then import them into QuarkXPress. If you use Version 5.0 of Mac Word, you must save files in the Windows version format.

- While QuarkXPress can read Ami Pro 2.0 files, it can't read earlier versions. But you can use that program's many export options to save your files in a format QuarkXPress recognizes. These export options include RTF and Word for Windows, both of which retain style sheet information. When you use these options, you can import styles into QuarkXPress along with the text.

- Windows Write, a basic word processor that comes bundled with Windows, imports directly into QuarkXPress. You do not need to do anything special to import files.

- If you want to import a file from WordStar, XyWrite, or MultiMate, you must use a translation program to create a new file in a supported format. Several such programs are available; they're especially handy if you work with outside writers or editors.

Rich Text Format

Microsoft created Rich Text Format (RTF) to serve as a universal file translator. But not all programs create RTF files equally. We have found, for example, that RTF files generated by Ami Pro work with few or no problems in a variety of publishing programs, including QuarkXPress. RTF files generated by Word for Windows are sometimes troublesome, because of extraneous font information. Problems occur particularly in files imported from Word for DOS into Word for Windows, apparently because of differences in font names between the two programs.

RTF has a lot of potential, however, because it can handle in-line graphics, style sheets, and fonts on both Macs and PCs — which is why QuarkXPress supports it. Until software companies write export filters uniformly, there is no guarantee that you can take advantage of the strengths of RTF. But if your word processor creates RTF files that work well in QuarkXPress, by all means, use this format.

ASCII text

Avoid using ASCII text. This format cannot handle any character formatting, so if you use it, you must do a lot of clean-up work in QuarkXPress. Although programs must continue to support ASCII text because it is the only universally supported format, use ASCII as a last resort.

Preserving Special Features in Text Files

Today's word processors let you do much more than enter and edit text. You also can create special characters, tables, headers and footers, and other document elements. Some of these features work when imported into a publishing program, but others don't.

Extended characters

Be careful when using extended keyboard characters, such as the accented letters *é* and *ö*. (You enter extended keyboard characters by holding the Alt key and typing in a three- or four-digit code on the numeric keypad, or by using the Character Map utility in Windows 3.1.) Extended characters do not always translate correctly from DOS-based word processors, because these programs often used their own unique extended-character maps. When you use extended characters, make a note to see which characters survive translation and import.

You'll have the best luck with translating and importing the accented characters and the worst luck with the more exotic symbols. The character-map locations for accented letters are semistandardized, but not all fonts include the more exotic symbols — and if they do, they don't always keep the symbols in the same spaces in their character maps.

Tables

We stated before that you should do table formatting in QuarkXPress, not in your word processor. But there is an exception to the rule: if you use style sheets to format a table with tabs in your word processor, by all means, import the formatted table into QuarkXPress — you then can modify the styles, if necessary, as your layout changes. If, however, you create tables without style sheets, you'll have to do more work than it's worth to undo the formatting from the word processor so that you can redo it in QuarkXPress.

Headers and footers

Headers and footers are a layout issue, not a text issue, so there is no reason to include these elements in your word processor document. Because page numbers will change based on your QuarkXPress layout, there's no point in putting the headers and footers in your word processor document anyway. One word of caution: Some word processors include codes to indicate headers and footers when you save a file in RTF format. These codes appear at the beginning of your imported text, and you must delete them in QuarkXPress.

Footnotes

If you use a word processor's footnote feature and import the text file, the footnotes are placed at the end of the imported text. The superscripted numerals or characters in the footnotes may or may not translate properly.

In-line graphics

Windows word processors typically support in-line graphics, enabling you to import a picture into your word processor document and embed it in text. Word for Windows and WordPerfect for Windows both let you import graphics, and QuarkXPress, in turn, can import the graphics with your text.

Ami Pro and Windows Write let you insert embedded objects, which can include graphics, through OLE links accessed by using the Edit ⇨ Import options in those programs. These embedded objects do not import into QuarkXPress. Instead, you see a series of codes that indicate the links and the filename of each object.

Avoiding Other Text-file Pitfalls

Sometimes, issues not related to the contents of a word processor file can affect how files import into QuarkXPress.

Fast save

Several programs offer a fast-save feature, which adds information to the end of a word processor document. The added information notes what text has been added and deleted and where the changes occurred. You can use this feature to save time, because the program doesn't have to write the entire document to disk when you save the file. When you use the fast-save feature, however, text-import into publishing programs — including QuarkXPress — becomes problematic. We suggest that you turn off fast save, at least for files you import into QuarkXPress. With today's speedy hard drives, the time you gain by using fast save is barely noticeable, anyway.

Figures 7-1 and 7-2 show dialog boxes for WordPerfect 5.1 for Windows (File ⇨ Preferences ⇨ Environment) and Word for Windows 2.0 (Tools ⇨ Options ⇨ Save), respectively. You turn fast save on and off in these dialog boxes. You don't need to worry about whether fast save is enabled if you use Save As or Export options to save the file either in a format other than the word processor's native format or to a different name or location.

In Word for Windows 1.x, you can disable fast save only for a specific document, not as a general option. With the document loaded, use the Save As option on the File menu, choose Options in the dialog box that appears, and then uncheck Fast Save to save the file properly. The next time you save that file, however, Word for Windows uses Fast Save again.

Software versions

Pay attention to the version number of the word processor you use. This caution may seem obvious, but the issue still trips up a lot of people. Usually, old versions (two or more revisions old) or new versions (newer than the publishing

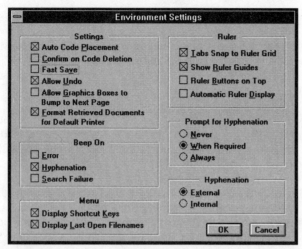

▶ **Figure 7-1:** Uncheck the Fast Save option in WordPerfect 5.1 for Windows for files you import into QuarkXPress.

or other importing program) cause import problems. The import filters either no longer recognize the old format (something has to go to make room for new formats) or were written before the new version of the word processor was released. QuarkXPress is compatible with WordPerfect 5.1 for Windows, Word for Windows 1.*x* and 2.0, Lotus Ami Pro 2.0, and Microsoft Windows Write 3.0 and 3.1.

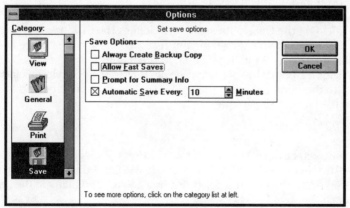

▶ **Figure 7-2:** Uncheck the Allow Fast Saves option in Word for Windows 2.0 (or 1.*x*) for files you import into QuarkXPress.

Using XPress Tags

QuarkXPress offers a file format of its own: XPress Tags, which takes the extension XTG. XPress Tags actually is ASCII text that contains embedded codes to tell QuarkXPress what formatting to apply. You embed these codes, which are similar to macros, as you create files in your word processor.

Most people do not use this option because the coding can be tortuous. You cannot use XPress Tags in conjunction with your word processor's formatting. If you create a file in Microsoft Word, for example, you cannot use XPress Tags to apply a style to a paragraph while using Word's own boldface and italics formatting for text. You either code everything with XPress Tags and save the document as an ASCII file, or you don't use XPress Tags at all. This either-or situation is unfortunate, because the ability to combine a publishing program's formatting codes with a word processor's formatting features adds both power and flexibility — as users of Ventura Publisher and Aldus PageMaker know.

So why have XPress Tags at all? Because this format is the one format sure to support all the formatting you do in QuarkXPress. Its usefulness is not in creating text for import, but in transferring files created in QuarkXPress to another QuarkXPress user or to a word processor for further work. You can export a QuarkXPress story or piece of selected text in the XPress Tags format and then transfer the exported file to another QuarkXPress user or to a word processor for further editing.

Exporting an XPress Tags file into a word processor makes sense if you want to add or delete text without losing special formatting — such as fonts, kerning, or style tags — that your word processor doesn't support. After you edit the text, you can save the altered file (make sure that it is saved as ASCII text) and reimport it into your QuarkXPress layout.

Appendix C of the QuarkXPress manual defines the 61 XPress Tags codes and their variants that you embed in your text file. These codes range from the simple, such as <I> for italicized text, to the moderately complex. The following code is for a 2-point, 100-percent red rule that uses line style 1, is indented 18 points to the right and left of the column, is offset 25 percent, and is placed above the current paragraph:

```
<*ra(02,1,"Red",100,18,18,25%>
```

Basically, you can use as many of the 61 XPress Tags codes as needed, and place them between < and > characters. In the preceding example, we are using the *ra code (which stands for ruling line above) and filling in the parameters it expects.

Some codes are programming-level codes, for which you define the style tags by combining as many of the 61 basic XPress Tags codes as appropriate. The following example defines a style called *Lead* as black, 9.5-point Cheltenham Book Plain with a four-line drop cap, 12 points of leading, a 10-point first-line indent, no left or right indents, no space above, 100-percent shade and scale, full justification, locked to the baseline grid:

```
@Lead=<*J*p(0,10,0,12,0,0,G)*d(1,4)f"Cheltenham
Book"j"black"z9.5s100h100P>
```

The = after @Lead in the preceding example signals QuarkXPress to define the Lead style with the codes between the angle brackets.

To use that style, you type **@Lead:** at the beginning of the paragraph you want to format; the colon tells QuarkXPress to use the style tag. (You can't apply a style tag that you did not define earlier in your text file.)

In practical terms, you might not mind editing XPress Tags slightly or leaving them in a file when you alter its text. But you're not likely to forgo the friendly formatting available in your word processor and in QuarkXPress to apply XPress Tags coding to everything in your text files.

Preparing Tabular Data for Import

QuarkXPress has no filters to accept files in formats such as Lotus 1-2-3, Microsoft Excel, Borland Paradox, or Borland dBASE. That means you have two basic options for preparing files that contain tabular information (usually spreadsheets or databases) for import:

- **Option 1:** Save the files as tab-delimited ASCII text. Then import them and apply the appropriate tab stops (either directly or through styles) to create the desired table.

- **Option 2:** Use the file as a graphic by employing a charting tool (such as Excel, Lotus 1-2-3, Harvard Graphics, or CorelCHART) or by pasting the data into your document through the Windows clipboard. Paste the data as a Windows metafile or bitmap, through the Windows clipboard, or as an OLE link. (See Chapter 23, "Linking to Source Files.")

If you choose the latter option, make sure that you size all charts and tables the same way so that the size of the numbers in them, when imported and placed, is consistent throughout your QuarkXPress document. Try to save your chart in a format that preserves font information, such as EPS or CGM. (Windows metafile also preserves font information.)

Preparing Graphics Files

QuarkXPress offers support for all major formats of graphics files. Some formats are more appropriate than others for certain kinds of tasks. The basic rules are as follows:

- Save line art in a format such as EPS, CGM, or Windows metafile. (These object-oriented formats are called *vector* formats. Vector files are composed of instructions on how to draw various shapes.)

- Save bitmaps (photos and scans) in a format such as TIFF, PCX, or DIB. (These pixel-oriented formats are called *raster* formats. Raster files are composed of a series of dots, or pixels, that make up the image.)

If you output to high-end PostScript systems, make EPS and TIFF formats your standards. EPS files can use PostScript fonts; can be color-separated if produced in a program such as Adobe Illustrator, Aldus FreeHand, or CorelDRAW; and can support an extremely large set of graphical attributes. TIFF files can be color-separated if saved in the CMYK variant of TIFF (which Adobe Photoshop on the Mac can do). You also can manipulate TIFF files in QuarkXPress to apply custom contrasts, line screens, and other photographic effects.

Part V covers issues involving gray-scale (Chapter 20, "Working with Bitmap Images") and color images (Chapter 21, "Working with Color"). Part VII, particularly Chapter 26, "Printing Options," covers issues involving outputting such images.

EPS files

EPS (encapsulated Post Script) files come in several varieties — not every EPS file is the same. You see the most noticeable differences when you import EPS files into QuarkXPress.

Preview headers

The preview header is a displayable copy of the EPS file; because Windows (like the Mac) doesn't use PostScript to display screen images, it can't interpret a PostScript file directly — which is why many programs add a preview header to the EPS files they create.

First, you may not see anything but a big gray rectangle and the words `PostScript Picture` when you import an EPS file. The file either has no preview header or its header is in an unreadable format. This condition is typical for EPS files transferred from the Mac, which uses a different header format. Although the image prints correctly, it's hard to position and crop, because you must repeatedly print your page to see the effects of your work.

If your picture lacks a usable preview header, use this workaround: After you print an EPS graphic, use the Item ⇨ Constrain option to add a polygon picture box inside the picture box containing the EPS file. Edit the polygon so that it becomes an outline of the EPS graphic. (This method ensures both that the outline is the right size and that it moves with the picture box as the layout changes.) Then use this outline as a guide to wrap text around or otherwise manipulate the EPS file. (See Chapter 11, "Additional Layout Features," for details of the Constrain option; Chapter 10, "Working with Picture Boxes," covers picture boxes.)

To generate an acceptable image header in an EPS file created on the Mac, save the file with a PC or DOS header. Adobe Illustrator 3.0 offers this option, but Aldus FreeHand 3.1 does not.

Mac programs are not the only programs that have header problems — CorelDRAW puts no preview header in files exported in Adobe Illustrator format. But if you use the regular EPS format that CorelDRAW exports, a header is provided, provided you check that option before exporting.

A related issue is the header for color EPS images. Most programs create a black-and-white preview header, even for color images. CorelDRAW is an example. But Computer Support Corp.'s Arts & Letters Graphics Editor exports a color preview if you select the Windows metafile option for the preview header; if you select TIFF, you get a black-and-white preview. (A color preview can make the EPS file size very large, which is why most programs create a black-and-white border.)

Color values

To take advantage of QuarkXPress color separation features for imported EPS files, you need to create the colors correctly. (If you intend to print your file on a color printer rather than have it separated, don't worry about the following instructions.)

If you create color images in an illustration program, make sure that you create them using the CMYK color model or using a named spot color. If you use CMYK, the color is, in effect, preseparated. If you use a spot color, define the same color with the same name in QuarkXPress — either as a process color, if you want it separated into cyan, magenta, yellow, and black plates, or as a spot color, if you want it to print on its own plate. (Defining colors is covered in Chapter 26, "Printing Techniques.")

For example, if you use Pantone 111 in a CorelDRAW illustration, shown selected in the drop-down list in Figure 7-3, make sure that you define Pantone 111 in QuarkXPress. (Incidentally, the *CV* after the Pantone color number means *computer video,* which is Pantone's way of warning you that what you see on-screen may not be what you get in print. Because of the different physics underlying monitors and printing presses, colors cannot be matched precisely.)

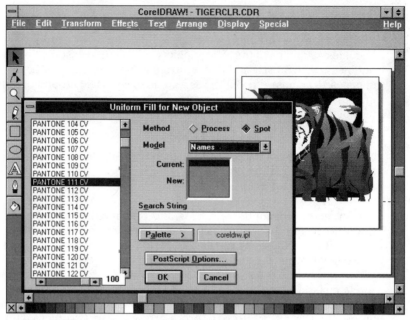

▶ **Figure 7-3:** Selecting a Pantone color in CorelDRAW.

We suggest that you create colors in the CMYK model if you want to color-separate them from QuarkXPress. This way, you don't have to worry about defining the appropriate spot color or setting a process color mix in QuarkXPress.

Most artists use Pantone to specify desired colors, so keep a Pantone swatch book handy to see which CMYK values equal the desired Pantone color. (One of the available Pantone swatch books — *The Pantone Process Color Imaging Guide CMYK Edition* — shows each Pantone color next to the CMYK color build used to simulate it.)

If you don't have the Pantone swatch book, you can define the color in Quark-XPress (by using Edit ⇨ Colors) as a Pantone color and then switch color models to CMYK. QuarkXPress immediately converts the Pantone color to CMYK, and you then know what value to use in your illustration program. Many high-end illustration programs, including CorelDRAW, can do this instant conversion as well.

For more information on defining colors and working with color images, see Chapter 21, "Working with Color," in Part V.

Fonts

When you use fonts in text included in your graphics files, and you export to EPS, you usually have the option to export the text as text or as *curves* (graphics).

If you export text as text, make sure that your printer or service bureau has the fonts used in the graphic. Otherwise, the text does not print in the correct font (you will likely get Courier or Helvetica instead). Remember that QuarkXPress does not show fonts used in graphics in its Font Usage dialog box, so your layout artists and service bureau have no way of knowing which fonts to have available.

An alternative is to export fonts as curves, which translates them into graphics. This option makes your files larger — it takes more commands to describe the curves than it does to specify the font and list the text's characters. But this choice also is safer — especially when you work with files created by other departments or by freelance contractors whose fonts may differ from yours.

Other vector files

Other formats are less complex than EPS, because they usually do not offer the same range of features.

Computer Graphics Metafile (CGM)

The CGM format is perhaps the closest to EPS in artistic possibilities. The major difference is that it does not support color. For black-and-white or gray-scale work, however, CGM may be the better export option, because its files tend to be smaller than EPS files and require less printer memory. If you run into printer memory errors (usually displayed as the `limitcheck` error message on Post-Script printers) when trying to print EPS files with lots of curves, try using a CGM version of the file instead.

Just as EPS does, CGM lets you save text contained in graphics as text or as curves. If your graphics program offers this option, pick the text option if your printer or service bureau has the fonts used in the graphic; otherwise, pick the curves option to ensure that your text prints properly. If you select the text option in your graphics program, or if you don't have the option at all, QuarkXPress prompts you to choose between text and curves when you import the CGM file. (This feature is handy if you or a contractor forgets to convert text curves in the graphics program. But it is better to do conversions in the program that creates the graphic, rather than the one importing it, to minimize the chances of unexpected results.) Figure 7-4 shows this dialog box. The Force Vector Fonts option converts text to curves; Dot Lines ensures that dotted lines remain as dots; Default Color Tables ensures that colors in files created in Harvard Graphics import correctly.

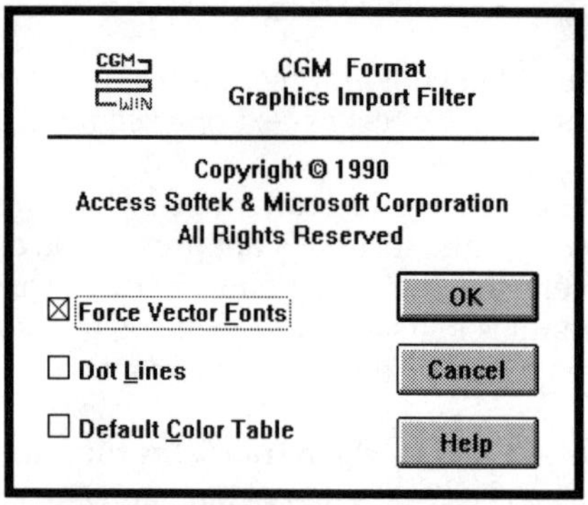

> ▶ **Figure 7-4:** The CGM dialog box. QuarkXPress can convert text in CGM or Micrografx DRW files to curves during import.

Windows metafile

Microsoft created the Windows metafile (WMF) format as its answer to Apple's PICT. Windows metafile is the format all Windows applications can handle for vector art, which means that you can cut a vector image from any Windows program and paste it into any other Windows program, including QuarkXPress.

But the Windows metafile format is not as rich in artistic attributes as EPS or CGM. Don't use the Windows metafile format if you want to color-separate graphics, for example, because the format does not allow named colors, which QuarkXPress requires for color separation of graphics. (Named colors let you associate a label, like *Deep Blue*, with a color and then define how this color is created. QuarkXPress can then control the color separation because it can "read" and modify the definitions for the color. An unnamed color has no similar label that QuarkXPress can use to find out how the color is defined.)

Do use the Windows metafile format to bring simple graphics — such as spreadsheet charts — into your document.

Micrografx DRW

Used in Micrografx's Designer and Windows Draw products, the DRW format falls between CGM and Windows metafile. Files in this format support color, but not named colors; they also give you the option of treating text as text or as curves. Windows metafile supports only unnamed color and cannot convert text to curves; CGM supports text as curves but not named colors.

As with CGM, the Force Vector Fonts option converts text to curves during import with QuarkXPress. The Ignore Background option tells QuarkXPress to ignore the picture background and import only the objects in the graphic.

We found that DRW files do not always import correctly if they contain freehand or Bézier curves — which are translated into flat lines. *Bézier curves* or *splines* are curves that have control handles on each point to let you control the curve arc and angle independently for each point.

PICT

The standard Macintosh format for drawings, PICT (which stands for *Picture*) also supports bitmaps and is the standard format for Macintosh screen-capture utilities. QuarkXPress imports PICT files with no difficulty. (You may have problems with PICT files embedded in a Macintosh QuarkXPress document that is moved to Windows.) Like Windows metafile, PICT does not support named colors, so the colors cannot be color-separated. Because fonts in PICT graphics are translated to curves, you need not worry about whether fonts used in your graphics are resident in your printer or available at your service bureau.

Bitmap formats

Bitmap (also called *raster*) formats are simpler than vector formats, because they are made up of rows of dots (*pixels*), not instructions on how to draw various shapes. But that doesn't mean that all bitmaps are alike.

TIFF

The most popular bitmap format for publishers is TIFF, the *Tagged Image File Format* developed by Aldus Corp. and Microsoft Corp. TIFF supports color up to 24 bits (16.7 million colors) in both RGB and CMYK models, and every major photo-editing program supports TIFF on both the Macintosh and in Windows.

But TIFF comes in several variants, and no program, including QuarkXPress, supports all of them. To ensure compatibility, we recommend that you use uncompressed TIFF files rather than compressed files. That's not to say that compressed TIFF files (especially those using the common LZW compression format) won't work — only that they might not always work.

The biggest advantage to using TIFF files rather than other formats that also support color, such as PCX, is that QuarkXPress is designed to take advantage of TIFF. QuarkXPress can work with the contrast settings in gray-scale TIFF images to make an image clearer or to apply special effects — something

QuarkXPress can't do with any other bitmap format (see Chapter 20, "Working with Bitmap Images"). QuarkXPress also can color-separate TIFF files in the CMYK variant, which Adobe Photoshop can create. No other bitmap format offers this variant; therefore, QuarkXPress cannot color-separate a file in any other bitmap format.

When creating TIFF files, note that not all programs create the image you expect. For example, a photo-editing program such as Image-In, Corel Photo-Paint, or Adobe Photoshop saves your TIFF file in gray-scale or black-and-white — the choice is yours. Ditto for most screen-capture programs. Photoshop also can save in RGB or CMYK color. But if you export a TIFF file from an illustration program such as CorelDRAW, chances are that the result will be a black-and-white TIFF file — colors and grays will be dithered into black-and-white patterns.

PCX

The original PC bitmap format, developed by ZSoft for its PC Paintbrush program, supports color and gray-scale images in its latest version (Version 5). But most programs cannot yet take advantage of this new support, so the PCX format is useful primarily for black-and-white bitmaps. If you want to do color separations of color PCX files or adjust the gray-scale values in a gray-scale PCX file, you're out of luck. (Grays print correctly, though, and color images print correctly on a color printer.)

BMP, DIB, and RLE

The Windows bitmap (BMP) format and its two variants, DIB (Device-Independent Bitmap) and RLE (Run-Length Encoded bitmap), are similar to PCX in that even though they support gray scale and color, QuarkXPress cannot manipulate those attributes. Gray-scale prints properly, as does color on a color printer, but you cannot adjust contrast settings or color-separate images in these formats. BMP is also like Windows metafile in that it is the standard format for Windows bitmaps, a format that can be cut and pasted across Windows applications.

Summary

▶ Don't apply layout-oriented formatting in your word processor document — that's what QuarkXPress is designed to do. Use style sheets if your word processor supports them.

▶ Don't format tables in your word processor unless you do it by defining tab stops in a style sheet that you can import into QuarkXPress and modify further.

▶ Create complex graphics in a graphics program, not in QuarkXPress.

▶ Extended characters may not import correctly, although accented letters usually work.

▶ In-line graphics in your word processor file import into QuarkXPress, but embedded OLE graphics do not.

▶ Use the XPress Tags format to transfer heavily formatted QuarkXPress stories to other QuarkXPress users (Mac or Windows). Also use XPress Tags if you need to edit a heavily formatted story in your word processor and reimport it into QuarkXPress. (You can export stories in the XPress Tags format from your QuarkXPress layout.)

▶ EPS and TIFF are the preferred formats for line art and bitmaps, respectively. If you aren't using a PostScript printer, CGM is the recommended alternative format for line art.

▶ EPS files without a preview header recognizable to QuarkXPress appear on-screen as a gray box, but print correctly.

▶ If you use spot colors in an EPS file, also define those colors in QuarkXPress if you intend to color-separate them. Or, to avoid defining colors in QuarkXPress, define them in your graphics program using the CMYK model.

PART III

Page Layout

Whether consciously or not, the first thing you notice when you look at a document is its layout. Even before you perceive what the publication is all about, assimilate the contents of a graphic, or scan the text, you form an impression of the document based on its construction. Certainly you might make an early assessment based on the quality of the paper and the colors of the ink. But a big part of your initial impression also includes perceptions about the arrangement of text and graphics on the page.

Layout can make the difference between whether people read a document or overlook it. Effective layout is, then, critical to how well readers receive the rest of your document — the text, the typographic effects, the headlines, the photos, the graphics, even the content. More than just a matter of placing text and graphics, layout includes such factors as balance, proportion, and scale. Layout is the process of putting these diverse factors together in such a way that the appearance of a document adds to its content.

Skill with layout takes time, training, and an eye for design. QuarkXPress can't lay out a document for you, nor can it teach you how to do layout. The program also doesn't guarantee that a layout you create will be effective, nor does it prevent you from producing pages that can best be called eyesores. What it can do is to make it relatively easy for you to construct documents that achieve just about any look you have in mind.

If you are concerned about being effective at the layout process, relax. Practice helps, as does allowing yourself enough time to think about what you want the document to accomplish. By taking the time to think through the layout process, you'll continue to improve your skill at designing layouts that complement the document's content and are inviting to the reader.

CHAPTER

8

Getting Started with Layout

■ ■

In This Chapter

▶ Tips on how to design a document layout

▶ How to set measurement preferences

▶ Ways of viewing the document on-screen

▶ How to use guides and rulers

▶ How to group, constrain, and lock layout elements

■ ■

Seven Basic Tips for Good Design

Like other desktop publishing programs, QuarkXPress lets you control how a document will look when you have finished creating it. But to really make the most of this powerful tool, you need to understand some basic ideas about page design. Of course, if you are a trained graphic designer, you already know the basics; you can immediately put QuarkXPress to use, creating effective layouts. But if you are new to the field, try keeping the following Seven Basic Tips in mind as you begin learning about layout:

1. **Keep an idea file.** As you read magazines, books, newspapers, annual reports, ads, and brochures, pick the page layouts you like, and also keep copies of those you dislike. Keep these layouts, good and bad, in a file, along with notes to yourself about which aspects of the layout work well and which work poorly. As you build your layout file, you educate yourself on layout basics.

2. **Plan your document.** It sounds corny, but it's true: Laying out a document is a lot like taking a journey. If you know where you're headed, it's much easier to find your way. Because QuarkXPress makes it easy to experiment as you design a document, it's also easy to end up with a messy conglomeration of text and pictures. You can avoid this pitfall by knowing ahead of time what you are trying to accomplish with the document's layout.

3. **Keep it simple.** When it comes to page layout, simple is better. Even the most experienced, trained graphic designers can tell you that this rule applies at least 99 percent of the time. If you are just beginning to learn how to lay out pages, you'll make far fewer design mistakes if you follow this rule. Regardless of the application, simple layouts are appealing in their crispness, their readability, and their straightforward, no-gimmicks approach.

4. **Leave some white space on the page.** Pages that are crammed full of text and pictures tend to be off-putting — meaning that the average, busy reader is likely to skip them. Keep some space between text columns and headlines and between page edges and layout elements. White space is refreshing and encourages the reader to spend some time on the page. Regardless of the particular document type, readers always appreciate having a place on every page to rest their eyes, a place that offers an "oasis in a sea of ink."

5. **Don't use every bell and whistle.** QuarkXPress is powerful, yes, but that doesn't mean that it is necessarily a good idea to push the program to its limits. You can, for example, lay out a page with 30 columns of text, but would you want to try reading such a page? With QuarkXPress, you can achieve an amazing number of special effects: You can rotate text, skew graphics, make linear blends, add colors, stretch and condense type, and bleed photos or artwork off the edge of the page. But using all of these effects at once can overwhelm readers and cause them to miss any message you are trying to convey. A good rule: Use no more than three special typographic or design effects per two-page spread.

6. **Lay out the document so that someone looking at it can get an idea of what it is.** This sounds like a common-sense rule, but you'd be surprised at how often this rule is broken. If you are laying out an ad for a product, make sure the layout *looks* like an ad, not like a technical brochure.

7. **Don't break rule number 6 unless you know what you are doing.** Creativity is okay, and QuarkXPress helps you express your layout ideas creatively. But don't get carried away. For example, if you are laying out a technical brochure, don't make it look like a display ad unless you understand that this might confuse readers, and you are doing it for a reason.

Figure 8-1 shows two pages that contain the same information but use different layouts. The page on the left has body text set close to the headline. Leading is tight, and except for a spot around the illustration, white space is in short supply. Notice how the page on the right has a lighter look. Which page are you more inclined to read?

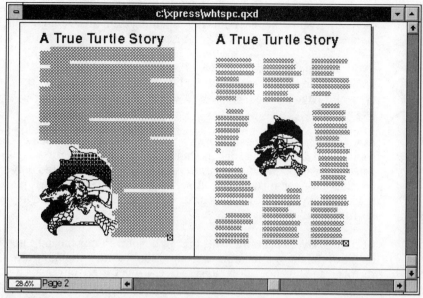

▶ **Figure 8-1:** Including ample white space, as in the example page on the right, makes documents more inviting.

Types of Layouts

Documents come in a variety of shapes and sizes. The most successful documents are those with an appearance that complements their content. In many kinds of documents, you can employ a number of layout styles. Within a multipage document, the layout of any single page typically depends on the overall purpose of the document and on where the individual page appears in relation to other pages.

Some pages have a *stand-alone layout*, because the document itself consists of a single page, or because that particular page falls into a layout type that is either not used elsewhere in the document or is used sparingly. An example of a stand-alone layout is the title page of a book or similar document. Because that page is unique, its layout is not repeated on subsequent pages.

Some pages include elements that are *linked* to other elements on the same page or to elements on other pages in the document. (We'll get to an explanation about how to link text boxes later.) For an example of linked elements, consider a typical magazine article, in which some of the body copy appears within one column or page and the rest appears within another column or page. The two pieces of body copy are linked elements.

Other layout elements, such as headlines, sidebars, and tables, are related to each other. Still other elements are repeating elements; examples include page numbers and folios.

 If your document has a title page or another page with a stand-alone, nonrecurring layout, in the interest of time, you can choose not to develop a style sheet or master page for the page. Master pages and style sheets are covered in Chapters 5 and 6.

As you're beginning to see, there's a lot involved in laying out a document, but sophisticated programs such as QuarkXPress make the process easier. When you lay out a document in QuarkXPress, you really are limited only by your imagination — along with, of course, your budget, QuarkXPress page-size limitations, and any specific design constraints that may be required in your work environment.

Of course, layout requires skills that go beyond simply having a good imagination. Key points to remember: it is important to have enough white space on the page and it is not a good idea to over-use a variety of visual effects. If you are new to layout and do not have the opportunity to take some training courses, you might consider investing in one of the many excellent books available.

Although a full discussion on types of layout is beyond the scope of this book, a brief overview is useful as a background for explaining some of the steps involved in developing layout types. Let's look briefly at some of the most commonly used approaches to layout: horizontal, vertical, facing pages, bleeds, and spreads.

Horizontal layouts

Horizontal layouts often include elements in a variety of widths, with the overall effect being one that moves the reader's eye from left to right. A horizontal layout is often employed in announcements, product flyers, and other marketing collateral pieces. In the example shown in Figure 8-2, the landscape orientation, placement of the columns, and location of the illustration all contribute to draw the eye from left to right.

We devised the layout in Figure 8-2 by first setting up an 8½ × 11-inch page with three columns, and then running the kicker and headline across the width of the columns.

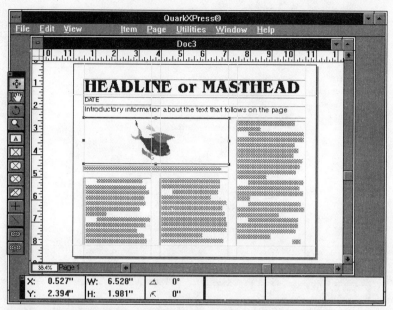

▶ **Figure 8-2:** An example of a horizontal layout.

Vertical layouts

Layouts with a vertical orientation are typical of what you find in most traditional newspapers. The text is presented in long, vertical sections, often with headlines or subheads that are the width of a single column. In addition to newspapers, newsletters and other common corporate documents lend themselves to a vertical orientation. Figure 8-3 shows a type of vertical layout often used for newsletters.

We created the layout in Figure 8-3 by setting up a letter-size page with three columns. The masthead runs across the width of the three columns, one kicker and headline run across the width of the first two columns, and one headline on a secondary article runs across the width of the third column.

Facing pages and spreads

Facing pages are commonly used in multipage documents that have material printed on both sides of the paper, such as newsletters and magazines. Whenever you open a new document, even if you select A̲utomatic Text Box in the New dialog box (F̲ile ⇨ N̲ew), QuarkXPress creates one new master page for the document's right-hand page. If you select A̲utomatic Text Box, QuarkXPress allows you to create master pages in addition to the single new master page.

▶ **Figure 8-3:** Example of a vertical layout, typically used in newspapers, newsletters, and other corporate documents.

If you are creating a facing-pages document that is longer than two pages, it's worth taking the time to set up the master pages for right- and left-side pages. As you read in Chapter 5, "Understanding Master Pages," master pages for facing-pages documents let you specify elements (text, graphics, page numbers, and so on) that you want to repeat on similarly oriented pages throughout the document.

It's easy to find out whether a document has right and left master pages. From the View menu, select Show Document Layout to display the Document Layout palette. Figure 8-4 shows a two-page, facing-pages document and its Document Layout palette.

Documents with facing pages tend to have one or both of the following characteristics:

- Alternating headers and footers on even- and odd-numbered pages. An example of an alternating footer is a page number; if you want the page number to print on the outside bottom corner of the page, the footers on right and left master pages differ from each other.

- An inside margin large enough to accommodate the binding or the spreading of pages as the reader reads the document.

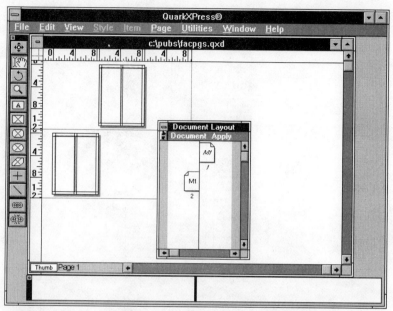

▶ **Figure 8-4:** A Document Layout palette for a facing-pages document.

What happens if you work on a facing-pages document for a while and then decide you want to lay it out single-sided? The answer is easy: Turn off Facing Pages by choosing File ⇨ Document Setup, which displays the Document Setup dialog box. Then click the Facing Pages box to deselect it.

QuarkXPress allows you to create layouts that span two or more side-by-side pages, or *spreads*. Spreads are made up of pages that are adjacent to each other and span a fold in the final document. A set of left- and right-hand facing pages is a spread, as is a set of three or more adjacent pages that appear in a folded brochure.

Refer to Chapter 5, "Understanding Master Pages," for additional information on setting up master pages for documents with facing pages.

Bleeds

A *bleed* consists of a layout element (text, picture, or line) that extends off the edge of the page after the page is trimmed. A bleed can also be a *crossover* — a layout element that spans two or more pages in a document. QuarkXPress easily accommodates bleeds, which can be very effective contributors to page design.

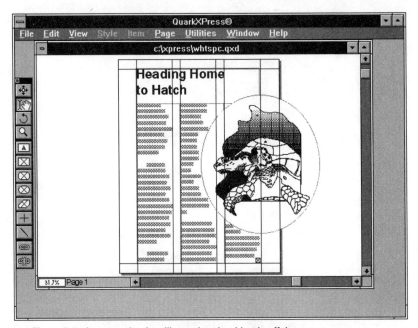

▶ **Figure 8-5:** An example of an illustration that bleeds off the page.

Figure 8-5 shows a page containing an image that bleeds off the page. We created this effect by drawing a picture box, filling it with the turtle illustration, and then using the Item tool to move the box so that part of the illustration extends beyond the page boundary.

Although you can bleed pictures to span the fold between two pages in a document, keep in mind that this sometimes is not a good idea, particularly if you are producing the document without the assistance of a professional printer. The reason? A folded page has to match up with an adjacent page that is physically printed on another sheet. Unless the adjacent pages that hold the bleed form the centerfold of the document, you can end up with a graphic that is misaligned from one page to the next, a problem known as being *out of register*. This registration problem is one that a professional printer can manage during the printing process, but aligning split images is almost impossible in documents that are laser-printed and then photocopied. Unless you are having your document professionally printed, the best advice is to avoid bleeds between pages unless they form a centerfold or fall in a similar setup where the flow of ink is unbroken by a page edge.

QuarkXPress Building Blocks

Layout in QuarkXPress is a matter of arranging the program's basic building blocks, which include boxes that hold text — *text boxes* — and boxes that hold graphics — *picture boxes*. These boxes, along with rules, form the program's primary *layout elements*.

You arrange these elements to produce a layout in QuarkXPress. But before you begin building a page, it's a good idea to understand some components of the document's foundation, including the measurement units you use to position elements on the page and the view format you need to perform various layout tasks.

Measurement systems

To position elements on the page during the layout process, you have to use a measurement system. You need to select a measurement system you feel comfortable with; QuarkXPress lets you select a measurement system for both the horizontal and vertical rulers you employ to lay out a document. The measurement system choices are as follows:

- **Inches:** Inches in typical inch format (¼-inch, ½-inch, and so on).

- **Inches Decimal:** Inches converted to decimal format (.25 inches, .50 inches, and so on).

- **Picas:** One pica is about .166 inches. There are 6 picas in an inch.

- **Points:** One point is approximately ½nd of an inch, or .351 millimeters.

- **Millimeters:** A metric measurement unit — 25.4 millimeters (mm) equals one inch; 1 mm equals 0.03937 inches.

- **Centimeters:** A metric measurement unit — 2.54 centimeters (cm) is an inch; 1 cm equals 0.3937 inches.

- **Ciceros:** This measurement unit is used in most of Europe; one cicero is approximately .01483 inches. This is close in size to a point, which is .01388 inches.

Although most traditional publishing people are in the habit of using picas and points, don't feel that you must conform. There is no "right" or even preferred measurement unit. QuarkXPress offers you this wide range of measurement system choices so that you can select a measurement unit you can relate to. Figure 8-6 shows the General Preferences dialog box, which you open to set or change QuarkXPress's measurement specifications.

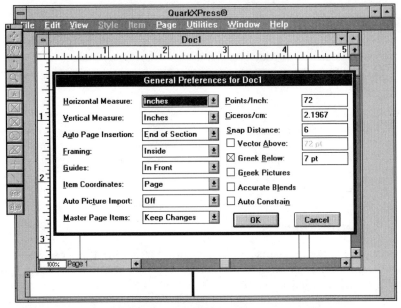

► **Figure 8-6:** The General Preferences dialog box.

If you open the General Preferences dialog box when a document is open and active, your selections affect the settings for just that particular document. If you open the dialog box when no document is open, any selections you make become QuarkXPress's defaults.

To set measurement preferences, select Edit ➪ Preferences ➪ General (Ctrl+Y). Use the Horizontal Measure and Vertical Measure drop-down list boxes to select the measurement unit you want to use. Make any other desired selections in the General Preferences dialog box and choose OK. Preferences are covered in Chapter 4, "Customizing QuarkXPress."

Views

The page view, which you select from the View menu, determines how much of the page you see at one time. The default view, which appears each time you start up the application or open a new document, is Actual 100%.

As you become more accustomed to working with QuarkXPress, you'll find yourself changing the View selection from time to time, based on the specific task you are trying to accomplish. To change the document view, choose View and then select from one of the six available preset view options. You also can change views by a variable amount (between 10 percent and 400 percent) at any time. To do so, enter a percentage value in the box at the corner of the open document window (lower-left side, next to the page number). Preset view options from the View menu are

- **Fit in Window (Ctrl+0):** This view "fits" the page into your computer's screen area.

- **50%:** This view displays the document page at half its actual size.

- **75%:** Choose this setting to display the document page at three-fourths its actual size.

- **Actual (Ctrl+1):** This setting displays the document page at actual size, which may mean that only part of the page is displayed on-screen.

- **200%:** If you choose this setting, QuarkXPress displays the document page at twice its actual size; this view is useful if you are editing text that is 10 points or smaller, or if you are trying to use the visual method to position an item precisely on a page.

- **Thumbnails:** This view displays miniature versions of the document pages. Figure 8-7 shows a thumbnail view, with the third page in the spread selected (highlighted). You can drag a selected page to a position elsewhere in the document by clicking the mouse button and holding it down as you drag the page.

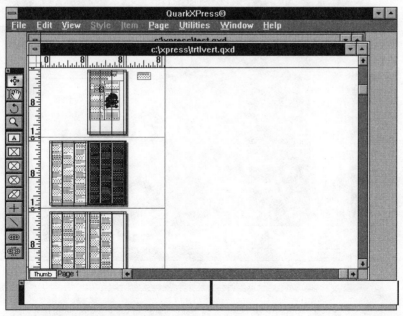

▶ **Figure 8-7:** A thumbnail view of a document.

QuarkXPress offers another way of changing views, and it's one we find particularly useful. To increase the page view in 25-percent increments, select the Zoom tool (it looks like a magnifying glass). When you place the pointer over the document with the Zoom tool selected, the pointer changes to a magnifying glass. Each time you press the mouse button, the view increases in 25-percent increments, up to a maximum of 400 percent. To decrease the page view in 25-percent increments, hold down the Ctrl key as you click the mouse button. You can click the right mouse button to toggle the view between Actual and Fit to Page — no matter what tool is selected. To zoom in on a specific area, you can click the Zoom tool and select a corner of the area you want, hold the mouse button down, drag to the opposite corner of the area, and release the mouse button.

Different views are useful for different tasks. If you are rearranging the order of pages in a document, the Thumbnail view makes it easy to keep track of your actions. If you are doing final copy edits on a block of text you placed into a QuarkXPress document, the 200-percent view setting makes it easier to see your edits, thereby reducing errors. And if you just want to get an overall look at the page to check its balance, the position of graphics in relation to the margins, and so on, the 75-percent and Fit in Window views work well.

The View menu, shown in Figure 8-8, also contains commands that enable you to control the display of other items on-screen. The first section of the menu holds the view option commands. The second section offers commands that control

▶ **Figure 8-8:** Use the View menu to select commands for controlling items on-screen.

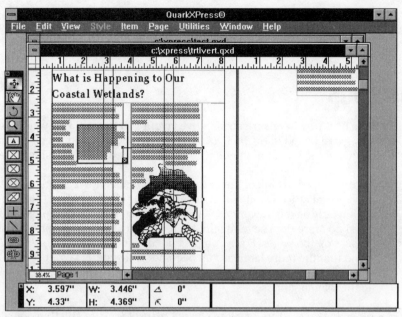

▶ **Figure 8-9:** An example of greeked text.

the display of positioning aids: guides, baseline grid, rulers, and invisibles (tabs, returns, and so on). The third section contains commands that display or hide QuarkXPress palettes. In the second and third sections of the menu, you toggle features on or off; if a command is active, a check appears next to its name.

The Greeking feature

One option closely related to views is *greeking*. When you use greeking, QuarkXPress displays a gray area on-screen to represent text or pictures on the page. Figure 8-9 shows a page with text that is greeked.

Turning on greeking speeds up the screen-refresh time needed to display your QuarkXPress document. In fact, greeking — particularly when used for pictures — is one of the best ways to save screen redraw time.

The General Preferences dialog box (Edit ⇨ Preferences ⇨ General) contains two greeking specifications. One field, Greek Below, tells QuarkXPress to greek the text display when text is a certain point size or smaller. The default value is 7 points, but you can enter a value between 2 and 720 points. If you check the Greek Pictures option, QuarkXPress displays pictures as gray boxes.

For more information on greeking, see the section on text and picture display in Chapter 4, "Customizing QuarkXPress."

Page Setup

The best way to ensure an effective layout is to start with a well-executed plan, always reflected in the final look of the document. If you spend sufficient time planning the layout of the document, you'll need fewer revisions later on.

In other words, think of the first step in layout as the planning phase, or the time you allot to planning and developing your layout ideas. Planning ahead isn't nearly as much work as it sounds. In fact, for most simple documents, you need no more than several minutes to design a basic plan for how elements appear on the pages. For a complex document, you need more time. Keep in mind that the more familiar you become with general layout principles and the more you learn how to best apply QuarkXPress to the task, the quicker you'll be in the planning phase.

How do you start to develop a layout plan? If you are still thinking about what the pages should look like, you can develop some more specific ideas by spending a few minutes sketching out the layout before you sit down to produce the document on the computer. One way to do this is to create a *dummy document*, a valuable layout-planning aid.

Let's say you want to create an eight-page newsletter that has standard, 8½ × 11-inch pages. You can create a dummy by taking two sheets of blank, 8½ × 11-inch paper, aligning one on top of the other, and folding them in half across the width of the paper. This technique gives you a miniature version of your eight-page newsletter.

Next, use a pencil to sketch the dummy's masthead, the cover art and/or stories, and the running headers or footers for each page. Form an idea about how wide you want the top, side, and bottom margins to be, and mark them on the pages. Then indicate which pictures and stories go on each page. Of course, because you will be using QuarkXPress to format the document, you can make changes right up to the point where you produce camera-ready pages.

After you have a general idea of how to structure your document, you can start developing a QuarkXPress style sheet, as described in Chapter 6, "Creating Style Sheets."

You should find all this planning — which actually doesn't take that much time in relation to the other publishing tasks involved — to be time well spent. The process of sketching out the layout helps clarify your thoughts about the basic

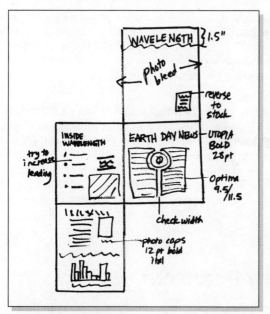

▶ **Figure 8-10:** A rough layout sketch is helpful in planning your document.

layout of your document. You can make preliminary decisions about such things as where to put each illustration and section of text on a page, how many columns of text to use, and whether to use any repeating elements (such as headers and footers). Creating a dummy of your layout, or even a simple rough sketch, is a good way to start formulating ideas. Figure 8-10 shows a typical rough sketch.

If you are already comfortable using QuarkXPress, you may decide to forego the paper-and-pencil sketching of a new document and use QuarkXPress to do the rough design instead. There are some obvious advantages to this approach:

■ When a document has a set number of text and graphic elements, you can use QuarkXPress to make a series of "sketches" of the document. If you like, you can save each sketch as a separate file with a distinct filename. In each sketch, you can use different element positioning, type styles, masthead placement, and so on. Then you can print a copy of each file and use the copies to assist you in finalizing the look of the layout.

- If you are considering many different layout possibilities, you can develop them quickly on QuarkXPress and then print the series in thumbnail (minia-ture) size (choose File ➭ Print ➭ Thumbnails). Seeing the pages in thumb-nail view makes it easier to evaluate the overall balance between page ele-ments, because you are not distracted by the text or the graphics in such a reduced view.

- Printed QuarkXPress copies of rough sketches have a cleaner look, which is especially helpful if you are designing a layout for a client. The advantage to presenting rough sketches that look more "final" is that it tends to make the client approval process go more smoothly, and it can make it easier for you to sell the client on your design. At the same time, slick-looking rough drafts do have a disadvantage: They make it more difficult for clients to understand that what they are seeing is just a rough draft and not a final comp.

How to Start a New Document

After you do your preliminary planning, it's time to begin building the QuarkXPress document. You might have noticed that we keep referring to cre-ating a layout as "building." This is a fair analogy for what's involved in laying out a new document, because document layout encompasses steps similar to those used for building a house. You start with the foundation (the page dimen-sions), build the rooms (the text and picture boxes), and fill the rooms with furniture (the actual text and illustrations or graphics). When the house is built and furnished, you add decorative final touches (lines, frames, color, and other graphic effects).

The first step, then, in laying out a document is to establish the foundation by setting up the basic dimensions of the document page. To do this, make the appropriate selections in the New dialog box to specify page size, margins, number of columns, gutter width between columns, and whether you want QuarkXPress to automatically generate text boxes.

Before you begin setting up a new document, decide on the number of text columns you want to use in all (or most) of the pages in the document. You can always make changes later, but you'll save time if you can decide on the num-ber of columns before you start. For a typical newsletter or magazine, using two, three, or four columns is the norm, but you can certainly vary from this standard if doing so helps you achieve a desired effect.

If you are worried that you have more text than will fit on the document's pages — for example, you want to produce a two-page newsletter but you have two-and-a-half pages' worth of text — consider using one more column than you originally planned. Use three columns instead of two, for instance. Depending on the hyphenation and justification you use, this strategy can make it possible to fit an extra paragraph or two onto the page.

▶ Steps: Setting up a new document

Step 1. Open a new document by selecting <u>F</u>ile ⇨ <u>N</u>ew. This displays the New dialog box, shown in Figure 8-11.

Step 2. In the Page Size area of the dialog box, select the size of your final pages by clicking the button next to your selection. (The size you choose, by the way, need not necessarily be exactly the same size as the paper your printer can hold; we'll discuss this more in Chapter 26, "Printing Techniques.") QuarkXPress offers five standard page size selections in the dialog box and also gives you the opportunity to specify a custom page size. The standard page sizes are as follows:

- **US <u>L</u>etter:** width 8.5 inches, height 11 inches

- **US Le<u>g</u>al:** width 8.5 inches, height 14 inches

- **<u>A</u>4 Letter:** width 8.268 inches, height 11.693 inches

- **<u>B</u>5 Letter:** width 6.929 inches, height 9.843 inches

- **<u>T</u>abloid:** width 11 inches, height 17 inches

QuarkXPress also lets you create custom page sizes. Select <u>O</u>ther and enter any page dimensions ranging from 1 inch × 1 inch to 48 inches × 48 inches.

If you are outputting your document directly to negatives, and you want crop marks to be automatically printed at the page margins for a trimmed page (such as the 8 ⅛ × 10 ⅞-inch page size used by many magazines), select <u>O</u>ther as the page size and enter the page dimensions in the corresponding field.

How do you know which page size is best? The answer to that question is really up to you, but it's useful to note what page sizes are typically used. Many magazines and newsletters use letter size, which is a convenient size for mailing and for fitting into a standard magazine-display rack. Newspapers and larger-format magazines frequently use tabloid size.

▶ **Figure 8-11:** The New dialog box.

If you set the page size in the New dialog box and change your mind later on, you can modify it. Select Document Setup from the File menu and enter the new page dimensions in the appropriate fields in the Document Setup dialog box. Entering the new page dimensions works as long as the new page size is sufficient to accommodate any elements you already placed; if not, a dialog box appears explaining that the page size you are proposing would force some items off the page. To prevent this, you must enter a page size sufficient to hold those items. Move them temporarily from the edge of the current page or onto the pasteboard and then try changing the page size again.

QuarkXPress always displays page width and height in inches, even if you select a different measurement unit in the General Preferences dialog box (which you access when a document is open by selecting Edit ⇨ Preferences ⇨ General). You can specify page dimensions to .001 of any measurement unit, and QuarkXPress automatically makes the conversion to inches in the Page Width and Height fields.

Step 3. In the Margin Guides area of the New dialog box, enter measurement values (to .001 of any unit of measurement) for the top, left, bottom, and right margins of the document. If you are using ragged right text in the document, you can set right margins a bit smaller than you need for justified text. (To create ragged right text, you actually set the text to be left-aligned.)

Keep in mind that once you set up the document specifications in the New dialog box, QuarkXPress gives you no way to redefine the margins other than by manually expanding the boxes on the page. Unless you are sure about the document's margin dimensions, you may want to consider creating and printing a test page (a single, sample page of the document) to verify margins before you invest the effort necessary to lay out the entire document.

Margin measurements determine how far from the outside edges of the paper you can place the document's text and picture boxes. The margins are for the underlying page, but are by no means set in concrete; for example, you can place individual text boxes or picture boxes anywhere on the page, even into these preset margins. One situation in which a page element might cross over into the margin is when you create a bleed, an illustration that ends past the edge of the physical page.

Be careful not to make margins too big, because doing so can give the text and pictures on the page an appearance of insignificance. By the same token, don't make margins too small, which can produce the equally unappealing look that results from having too much information on a page. Also, you might want one margin to be bigger than the margins on the other three sides of a page. For example, if you plan to saddle-stitch or three-hole punch a document, make the inside margin larger so that it can accommodate the staples or holes.

Step 4. In the Margin Guides area of the dialog box, check the Facing Pages option box if the document pages will be printed two-sided, with the right and left pages facing each other when the document is open. Turning on the Facing Pages option tells QuarkXPress to set right and left pages that mirror each other in terms of right and left margins. If you select Facing Pages, consider making inside margins larger than those on the outer edges of the page to allow room for the binding. Margin guides appear as lines on-screen, but the lines do not print.

 You set the measurement unit used for margin and column guides in General Preferences dialog box (Edit ➪ Preferences ➪ General). The default measurement unit is the inch.

Step 5. In the Columns option box (in the Column Guides area of the New dialog box), enter the number of text columns you want to use on most pages. (The reason we say "most" pages is that you can, for example, select three columns in this dialog box, and then, within the document, use two or some other number of columns on a particular page.)

You can specify as many as 30 columns per page, although you won't often need that many, particularly on standard 8½ × 11-inch paper. As with margins, column guides appear as lines on-screen, but the lines do not print.

Step 6. In the Column Guides area of the dialog box, enter a measurement value in the Gutter Width field to specify the amount of space between columns of text. Gutters can be as small as 3 points or as large as 288 points. If you enter a Gutter Width value that is too large or too small, QuarkXPress displays a dialog box showing you the range of values from which you must select. We recommend keeping columns to a reasonable width — generally no wider than 21 picas. Otherwise, the columns may become tiring on the reader's eyes.

 Don't make gutters too small. This causes the columns of text to appear to run together and makes the document difficult to read. A rule of thumb is that the wider the columns, the wider the margins need to be to give the reader a clear visual clue that it's time to move to the next line. If you *must* use narrow gutters (between 0p9 and 2p0, depending on the page width and number of columns), consider adding a thin (0.5 point or smaller) vertical rule in the center of the gutter. To draw the rule, use the Orthogonal Line drawing tool and draw the line from the top of the gutter to the bottom, midway through the gutter width.

Step 7. Activate Automatic Text Box (by placing a check mark in the option box) if you want a text box on the master page that automatically flows text to other pages inserted into the document. If you don't select Automatic Text Box, you must use the Text Box tool to draw text boxes before you place text with the File ⇨ Get Text command.

Step 8. After you finish making selections in the New dialog box, choose OK to open the new page.

Just because you plan to have a certain number of text columns in a document doesn't necessarily mean you should enter that exact number in the Columns field of the New dialog box. Suppose that your publication has three columns, plus pull-quotes that are set out of alignment with the text margins. You may want to try using an 8-column grid and use some of the column grid lines to align the pull-quotes. Of course, if you use this design tip, you don't want text to flow through all columns, so you need to disable (uncheck) Automatic Text Box in the New dialog box.

Figure 8-12 shows a QuarkXPress document that was set up in the New dialog box to have eight columns. We did not select Automatic Text Box, so we used the text box tool to create each of the text boxes. Note how we use the column

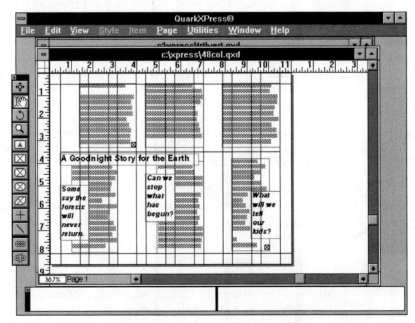

▶ **Figure 8-12:** You can use column markers as alignment guides.

markers as alignment guides in setting up a variety of column treatments, which include pull-quote boxes and columns that vary in width from the top part of the page to the bottom.

QuarkXPress Layout Tools

QuarkXPress offers several layout tools that make it easier for you to produce your document. These tools include guides that help you align text and graphics, a pasteboard area that gives you a convenient way to store document elements until you need them, and a feature that allows you to position elements in layers.

Working with Folded Documents

The folding of pages in a document can be a tricky issue. If you are creating a document that will be folded once or more, here are some factors you need to consider:

■ If you are developing a flyer or brochure that will be folded, choose a page size that allows adequate gutter space. Gutters should be large enough that folds do not occur in the middle of text or pictures. You also need to set an outside margin that is big enough to accommodate any creeping of pages, which can occur in multipage documents that are saddle-stitched (stapled along the fold).

■ If you are creating a trifold brochure — for example, one that is printed on 9 × 12-inch paper and folded into a 4 × 9-inch brochure — setting up the page into even columns with even gutters doesn't work because the space you need to accommodate the folds uses up gutter space. The same is true for any brochure or document that is folded more than two times. If possible, work with your commercial printer to find out what page and column size to use to accommodate the folds. If you are designing a multifold brochure that will not be commercially printed, allow time to experiment with column widths, margins, and folding.

■ The paper on which a folded brochure is printed is a major factor in the success of the document. Your paper choice also plays a large role in how you need to set up the document during layout. Obviously, thick paper reacts differently to folding than thin paper, and thick paper also has a different effect in terms of the amount of page creeping that results in a multipage document. Depending on the weight and texture of the paper, a $\frac{1}{4}$-inch margin set on the first page of a 36-page, saddle-stitched document could be gradually reduced on each page, shrinking to $\frac{1}{16}$th of an inch by the centerfold. We recommend talking with your printer ahead of time if your document has multiple folds or if you are planning a document with 24 or more folded pages and saddle stitching.

Using guides

Laying out a document often means lining up objects with columns, illustrations, headlines, or other objects. Guides are nonprinting lines that make this process easier.

We've already covered two types of guides: margins and columns. And you've seen how you can actually use column guides as alignment aids. QuarkXPress also offers ruler guides, which you "pull out" from the vertical and horizontal document rulers. Of course, you can always use the numeric values displayed in the Measurements palette to precisely position elements, but the ruler guides are handy tools for visually lining up elements on a page. Guides are useful if you want to align an element to another element within a box — such as a part of a picture — and the location is not identified in the Measurements palette (the Measurements palette shows the box's values, not those of its internal elements). You should, however, rely on the numeric values shown in the Measurements palette rather than the pull-out ruler guides when you are concerned about placing boxes and lines precisely on a page.

You can control whether QuarkXPress places ruler and page guides in front of or behind objects on the page. You can select either In Front or Behind in the Guides field of the General Preferences dialog box (to open the dialog box, select Edit ➪ Preferences ➪ General).

The default setting for guide position is Behind, for good reason. If you have many elements on the page, selecting the In Front setting tends to make the guides difficult to locate and control. Placing guides behind other objects becomes more and more important as your document increases in complexity.

Because ruler guides don't print, you can use as many of them as you like. To obtain a ruler guide, simply use the mouse to position the cursor within the vertical or horizontal ruler. Then hold down the mouse button as you pull the ruler guide into place.

Another handy feature for lining up elements on a page is the Snap to Guides feature, which you access through the View menu. When you select this feature, guides have an almost magnetic pull on objects you place on the page, making them "snap" into alignment with the closest guide. You'll appreciate this feature for some layout tasks, but you'll want to disable it for others. Imagine that you are creating a structured document containing illustrations framed with a 0.5-point line and aligned with the left-most margin. In this case, select Snap to Guides so that the illustrations snap into position on the margin. If, on the other hand, you have a document containing design elements that are placed in a variety of locations on the page, you may want to position them visually or by means of the Measurements palette instead of having them automatically snap to the nearest guide line.

You can control the distance within which an item snaps to guides by entering a value in the <u>S</u>nap Distance field in the General Preferences dialog box (<u>E</u>dit ⇨ Prefere<u>n</u>ces ⇨ <u>G</u>eneral). Snap distance is specified in pixels, and the range is 1 to 100. If the Snap distance is set to 6 pixels, any element within 6 or fewer pixels of a guide will "snap" to that guide.

If you have a document open, you can also display another set of grid lines. Selecting <u>V</u>iew ⇨ Show <u>B</u>aseline Grid displays horizontal grid lines that do not print. The actual purpose of these grid lines is to lock the baselines of text onto them, but we find them very useful as positioning guides as well. Chapters 4, 5, and 13 provide more detail on this feature.

You specify the spacing of these grid lines in the Typographical Preferences dialog box (<u>E</u>dit ⇨ Preferences ⇨ T<u>y</u>pographic). In the <u>S</u>tart field of the dialog box, enter a value to tell QuarkXPress how far from the top of the page you want the first line. In the <u>I</u>ncrement field, enter the size of the interval you want between grid lines. Figure 8-13 shows a document page with the baseline grid displayed.

If you want elements to snap to lines in the baseline grid, be sure that the baseline grid is visible (select <u>V</u>iew ⇨ Show <u>B</u>aseline Grid). If the baseline grid is not visible, elements snap to the closest visible guide.

▶ **Figure 8-13:** A document with the baseline grid displayed. Note that text is not aligned with baselines because Lock to Baseline is *not* selected in the Paragraph Formats dialog box (<u>S</u>tyle ⇨ For<u>m</u>ats).

Using the pasteboard

In the old days of publishing, people who composed document pages often worked at a large table — or pasteboard — that held not only the documents on which they were working, but also the odds and ends associated with layout. They might put a headline, a picture, a caption, or a section of text on the pasteboard until they were ready to place the element on the page.

Even though QuarkXPress has automated the page composition process, it includes a tremendously useful pasteboard. You'll find yourself using it all the time. QuarkXPress's pasteboard is an area that surrounds each document spread (one or more pages that are side by side). Each and every spread has its own pasteboard. Figure 8-14 shows the pasteboard, which is holding some layout elements, as it appears around a single-page spread.

The pasteboard appears on the sides of the spread, and you maneuver around the spread and the pasteboard by using the scroll controls. The default size of the pasteboard is the width of the document page, but you can change the pasteboard size if you want it to be larger or smaller.

Usually, the default pasteboard width is sufficient. But you may want to modify it if you need more or less room on-screen. Choose Edit ➪ Preferences ➪ Application to display the Application Preferences dialog box. Enter a percentage

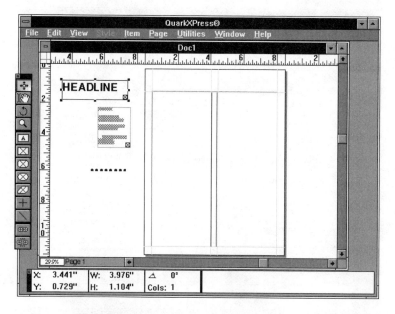

▶ **Figure 8-14:** The QuarkXPress pasteboard holds items for future use.

value in the Pasteboard Width field. A value of 100 percent means that the pasteboard width is equal to — or 100 percent the size of — the width of the document page. When the pasteboard width is to your liking, choose OK to save the change. Keep in mind that the larger the pasteboard, the more memory is required. If you're not short on computer memory, use the default pasteboard width. If you are running short of computer memory, consider reducing the size of the pasteboard to something less than 100 percent.

The maximum width and height of the combined pasteboard and document spread is 48 inches. QuarkXPress reduces the pasteboard size, if necessary, in order to keep the pasteboard and spread at or below the 48-inch maximum width.

Working with layers

QuarkXPress arranges text boxes, picture boxes, and rules in *layers*. You can control the order of these layers, which means you can stack and restack text boxes, picture boxes, and lines on a page, as if each were on its own separate sheet of paper. QuarkXPress does the layering for you, actually placing every element on the page on its own layer.

If your document is fairly simple, and its elements do not overlap, you don't need to be concerned with layers. But if you are laying out complex pages with multiple elements, you need to know how to rearrange the layers.

To rearrange the layers in a document, select the page element you want to shift and locate the appropriate command in the Item menu. The full list of layer commands is available only when the open document contains layout elements in multiple layers. The layer commands include:

- **Send Backward:** Sends the selected element back one layer.

- **Send to Back:** Sends the selected element to the back of the pile.

- **Bring Forward:** Brings the selected element forward one layer.

- **Bring to Front:** Brings the selected element to the front of the pile.

Unless you need them for special effects, avoid overlapping too many elements. If you have more than four or five layers, the screen refresh time (the time it takes to redraw the screen after you make changes) slows down almost exponentially, meaning that you need to allow yourself extra time to sit and wait while the layered page reappears on-screen.

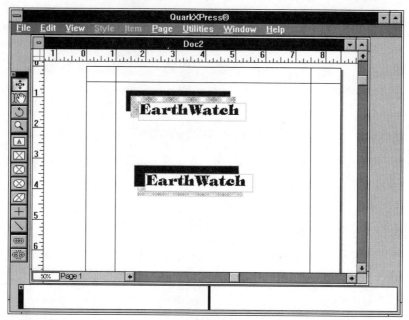

▶ **Figure 8-15:** Examples of layered elements.

Figure 8-15 shows how layers work. In the top example, the text is moved to the front with the Bring to Front command (Item menu), the gray box is brought forward with the Bring Forward command, and the black box is sent to the back of the pile with the Send to Back command. In the bottom example, the order is rearranged. The black box is moved forward one layer with the Bring Forward command.

When you move an element in a layered relationship, it retains its place in the stacking order. In other words, if an element is on a layer third from the top of the stack, it stays on that layer even if you move it. If you need to change the stacking order of elements, use the commands in the Item menu.

As you can see in Figure 8-15, the ability to layer elements can be a powerful layout tool. For example, you can overlap a filled box with another box of text, creating a shadowed or multidimensional effect.

Locking elements in place

Suppose that you've been working on a page layout for some time, and you've positioned an element — for example, the masthead — exactly where you want it to be. Knowing that you still have a number of elements to place on the page,

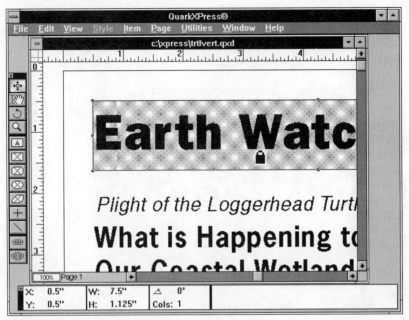

▶ **Figure 8-16:** An example of a locked element.

how can you prevent yourself from accidentally moving or resizing the masthead by means of an errant mouse click?

The answer: Lock the element into position. To lock an element, select it and choose Item ⇨ Lock (Ctrl+L). Figure 8-16 shows a locked masthead. You can tell if an element is locked because the pointer changes to a lock icon when you position it over a locked element.

You can still move and resize a locked element, but you must do so either from the Measurements palette or through options in the Item menu. Essentially, what locking buys you is protection from accidental changes. To unlock a locked element, select the element and choose Item ⇨ Unlock (Ctrl+L).

Grouping and ungrouping layout elements

QuarkXPress offers a feature that is common to drawing programs. The program lets you select two or more elements and *group* them. Grouping means associating multiple items with each other so that QuarkXPress treats the group as a single item during moves, resizing, and edits. Grouping is useful if you want to move related items together while keeping their spatial relationship intact.

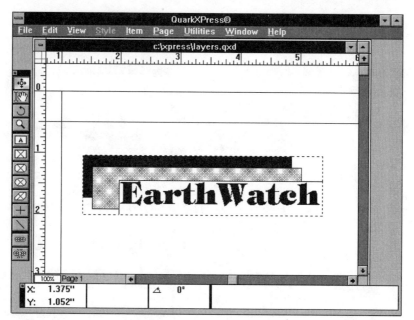

► **Figure 8-17:** A dotted line indicates grouped elements.

To group multiple elements, hold down the Shift key while you use the mouse to select the items to be grouped. Choose Item ⇨ Group. When items are grouped, they are bounded by a dotted line, as shown in Figure 8-17. Note that the Measurements palette for grouped items has only X, Y, and rotation coordinates available, because these are the only Measurements palette controls that can be applied to the entire group.

Just because elements are grouped doesn't mean you can't size or edit them independently. Just select the Content tool and choose the individual element. Then resize the element by dragging its handles, or edit it as you would if it were not part of a group.

You can perform actions (Cut, Copy, Paste, Lock, and so on) on groups that you normally perform on singular elements. You can move an entire group by dragging the mouse as you press and hold the Ctrl key. You also can modify groups of like elements (groups of text boxes, groups of picture boxes, and so on) by using the Item tool and selecting the group, and then choosing Item ⇨ Modify to display the Group Specifications dialog box. To Ungroup previously grouped elements, select the group and choose Item ⇨ Ungroup.

Constraining boxes

Unique to QuarkXPress is the ability to *constrain* a box: you can specify that any new box placed over an existing box cannot be sized or moved beyond the limits of the existing box. Constraining can be considered a subset of grouping, but they differ in that constrained boxes behave in a "parent and child" relationship; the child box is unable to leave the confines of the parent box. In a hierarchy of boxes, the constraining box "parent" is the rear-most box in the hierarchy. It must be large enough to hold all the "child" boxes you want to constrain within it. This relationship is illustrated in Figure 8-18.

Applications that can take advantage of constraining usually are highly structured. One such application is a product catalog. You might set up a large text box that holds descriptive text to constrain a smaller picture box that holds a product illustration. If you develop such a document, and you know ahead of time that you need constrained boxes, you can specify that all boxes in the document are to be constrained. To do this, choose Edit ⇨ Preferences ⇨ General to display the General Preferences dialog box. Check the Auto Constrain box, located just above the OK button.

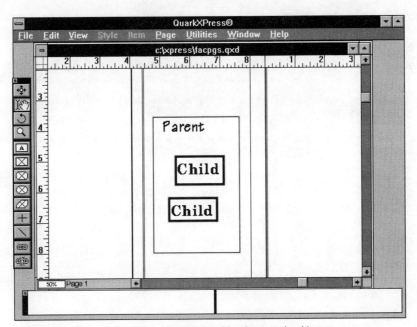

▶ **Figure 8-18:** The parent and child relationship of constrained boxes.

To constrain a particular box, first make sure that all items in a selected group are on a layer in front of the box that is to be the parent in the constraining relationship. With the group selected, choose Item ⇨ Constrain.

After a set of boxes is constrained, you can move and resize individual elements within the constrained group as long as the child elements still fit within the parent box. If you move a constrained box, all elements constrained within it also move.

Summary

▶ Before you begin layout, plan your document by sketching it or by developing a rough version in QuarkXPress.

▶ If you are new to page layout, keep your documents simple, use lots of white space, and keep special effects to a minimum.

▶ The vast majority of documents are printed on 8½ × 11-inch pages, but QuarkXPress lets you create pages as big as 48 inches × 48 inches.

▶ If you create a facing-pages layout, remember to leave enough room on the inside margins to accommodate binding.

▶ QuarkXPress lets you choose from a wide assortment of measurement systems — inches, millimeters, points, and so on. Don't feel pressured to use points and picas if you are more comfortable using inches.

▶ Using guides and grids makes it easier to position elements on the page. And, if you have it selected, Snap to Guides positions elements exactly to the closest guide.

▶ The pasteboard is a handy place for storing elements temporarily until you are ready to use them in the layout.

CHAPTER 9

Working with Text

Creating Text Boxes

To place text on a QuarkXPress page, you need one or more *text boxes*. You can place text boxes on a page in two basic ways: by using the program's automatic text box feature or by drawing one or more text boxes. You can also use a combination of both methods.

To use automatic text boxes, open a new QuarkXPress document. The New dialog box gives you the option of having the program create automatic text boxes in the document. For example, if you specify two columns in the New dialog box and also check Automatic Text Box, text from a text file you place on the page automatically fills two columns and flows into two columns per page as you insert other pages into the document.

The other option is to use the Text Box tool to create the text box, following these steps.

▶ Steps: Using the Text Box tool to create text boxes

Step 1. With the document open to the page on which you want to draw the text box, select the Text Box tool. When you use the mouse to move the pointer onto the page, the pointer changes to look like a cross-hair.

Step 2. Position the cross-hair pointer where you want to locate one corner of the text box.

Step 3. Press and hold the mouse button as you draw the text box to the approximate size you want it to be. Or, if you want to size the box precisely, watch the W (Width) and H (Height) measurements on the Measurements palette, which change to reflect the size of the box as you draw it.

 If you want the text box to be exactly square (instead of rectangular), hold down the Shift key as you draw the box.

Step 4. Release the mouse button.

As we've mentioned, you can see the coordinates change in the Measurements palette as you draw the text box. The X: and Y: numbers display, respectively, the horizontal and vertical coordinates of the text box location. The W: and H: coordinates show the size of the text box. The measurement unit used for all these measurements is whatever unit you select in the Edit ⇨ Preferences ⇨ General dialog box.

Setting Text Box Specifications

After you create a text box, you can set many of its specifications by using the Text Box Specifications dialog box. This dialog box is useful for accomplishing the following tasks:

- Precisely sizing and positioning the text box
- Rotating the text box
- Placing multiple columns within the text box (as opposed to multiple columns within the page)
- Insetting text from the borders of the box
- Setting the parameters for the first baseline

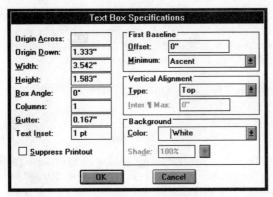

▶ **Figure 9-1:** The Text Box Specifications dialog box.

- Performing vertical alignment
- Adding color to the text box

A number of the specifications you can set within the Text Box Specifications dialog box, such as size and position, can be modified in other ways. For example, to change the text box size or position, you can click and drag the text box or change the settings in the Measurements palette. There is no single "right way" to modify text boxes in QuarkXPress; the program simply gives you a variety of ways to accomplish this task — and many other tasks.

To modify Text Box Specifications, use either the Item tool or the Content tool to select the text box. Then, choose Item ▷ Modify (or press Ctrl+M) to display the Text Box Specifications dialog box shown in Figure 9-1.

Measurement-related specifications in the Text Box Specifications dialog box reflect the measurement preferences you establish in the General Preferences dialog box.

Positioning the text box

After you create and size a text box, you can move it around on the page. If you are concerned with placing a single text box precisely, your best bet is to use the QuarkXPress Measurements palette to fine-tune the box position by following these steps.

▶ **Steps: Fine-tuning a text box position**

Step 1. Create the text box. With the Item tool selected, click the text box to activate it.

Step 2. Enter the X: and Y: coordinate values in the Measurement palette's X: and Y: fields. (X is the horizontal coordinate; changes you make to the X value move the text box side to side. Y is the vertical coordinate; changes you make to the Y value move the text box up and down.)

Step 3. Press Enter or click anywhere outside the Measurements palette to apply the new position coordinates.

You can also use the Text Box Specifications dialog box (choose Item ⇨ Modify to display this dialog box) to position the text box. In the dialog box's Origin Across field, enter the measurement that corresponds to the horizontal position where you want to place the origin (upper-left corner) of the box. In the Origin Down field, enter the measurement that corresponds to the vertical position where you want to place the origin (upper-left corner) of the box. If you want to make other changes to the text box specifications, do so; otherwise, choose OK.

Sizing the text box

QuarkXPress lets you easily change the size of a text box. In addition to setting the box size in the Width and Height fields of the Text Box Specifications dialog box, you can change it in two other ways: by using the mouse to click and drag the "handles" of the text box to size, or by using the Measurements palette to change the size. In Figure 9-2, the handles on the empty text box are the eight small squares on the corners and sides of the box; the Measurements palette is positioned at the bottom of the screen.

Each of these methods carries an advantage. The click-and-drag method is interactive; you watch as the box changes size. This method is useful if you are still figuring out how you want the page to look, because this approach allows for plenty of free-form experimenting.

The Measurements palette method is helpful in that it offers precision, as does the Text Box Specifications dialog box. If, for example, you know that the text box should be precisely 4 inches square, you can enter those coordinates in the W: and H: fields of the Measurements palette.

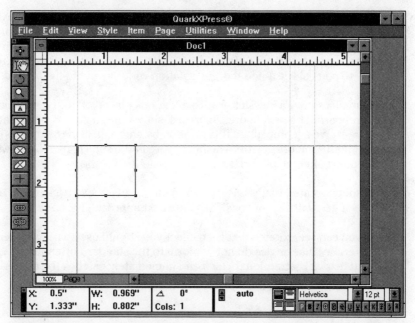

▶ **Figure 9-2:** You can use text box handles or the Measurements palette to resize the box.

Rotating the text box

One of the unique features of QuarkXPress is the way it lets you rotate elements, including text boxes, in precise increments. You can control the amount of rotation in three ways:

■ **Option 1:** Select the text box and choose Item ⇨ Modify (or press Ctrl+M) to display the Text Box Specifications dialog box. You can then enter a rotation amount (between 0 and 360 degrees, in units as small as .001 degrees) in the Box Angle field. If you want to make other changes to the text box specifications, continue; otherwise, choose OK.

To rotate a text box counter-clockwise, use a positive rotation number; use a negative number to rotate a text box clockwise.

■ **Option 2:** You can rotate a text box on-the-fly by using the Rotation tool and selecting the text box. Then drag the box to the rotation angle you want by holding down the mouse button as you move the mouse. Objects rotate around the center of their bounding box (an invisible box that holds objects), which is not always where you think it is.

■ **Option 3:** Enter a rotation degree in the rotation field of the Measurements palette.

Most users find the two numerical methods of rotating text boxes (using the Text Box Specifications dialog box or Measurements palette) to be superior. This is because the on-the-fly method involves more trial-and-error and requires a greater amount of visual skill. Also, it takes a good deal of time to learn how to control the amount of the rotation with the on-the-fly method.

Figure 9-3 shows a newsletter with a text box placed off to the side, on the pasteboard. The next figure, Figure 9-4, shows the same text box rotated 30 degrees. We accomplished this rotation by entering 30 in the rotation field of the Measurements palette. The final figure in the set, Figure 9-5, shows the rotated text after we placed it into the newsletter.

Although rotated text is effective for banners, mastheads, and other display type, it generally is not considered the best approach for body text.

As you can see, rotated text is an effect you should use sparingly because of its power. Because angles do not conform to the standard orientation of text, rotated text calls attention to itself and immediately catches the reader's eye. Reserve rotated text for achieving this effect.

▶ **Figure 9-3:** Plan to rotate the text box on the pasteboard 30 degrees and then place the text box into the newsletter.

▶ **Figure 9-4:** The text box rotated 30 degrees.

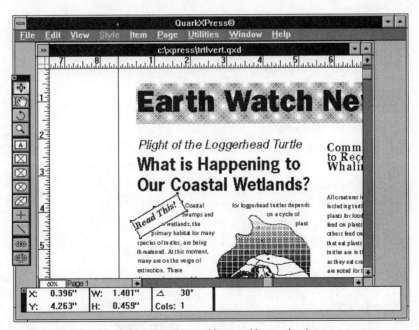

▶ **Figure 9-5:** The rotated text box dragged into position on the document page.

Dividing the text box into columns

On occasion, you may want to vary the number of text columns used within a single page. For example, you may have a document that is set in two columns. For variety's sake, you decide to divide one of two columns on a page into three smaller columns.

Using the Text Box Specifications dialog box, you can do this easily. Select the text box you want to break into more columns. Then choose Item ⇨ Modify (or press Ctrl+M). In the Columns field, enter **3**. This divides the selected text box into three columns. Figure 9-6 shows such a text box. The left-hand column is a text box that is subdivided into three narrower columns.

Setting text inset

The amount of text inset determines the distance between the text and the boundary edges of the text box. Entering a Text Inset value of 1 point (which, by the way, is the default setting) insets the text 1 point from the borders of the box.

For most applications, we see no reason why you need any text inset at all, particularly for text that makes up the body of the document. Text inset comes in handy if you have a text box *within* a text box. Suppose that you have a full page

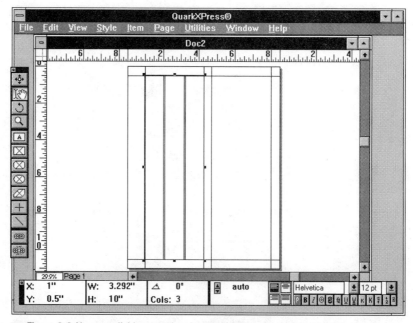

▶ **Figure 9-6:** You can divide a text box into columns.

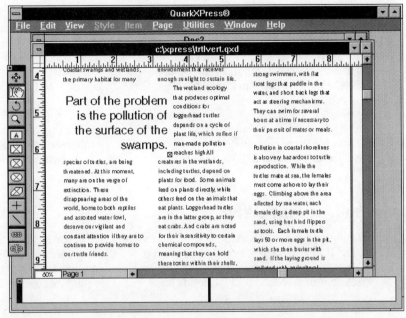

► **Figure 9-7:** A pull-quote with a 10-point text inset that provides white space between the pull-quote and the body text.

of text, and you use a pull-quote (a portion of the text that is copied into a box and enlarged to create a graphic element). Suppose also that you place a frame around the pull-quote. A text inset allows some white space around the pull-quote. Figure 9-7 shows a pull-quote that has text inset of 10 points.

To modify text inset for a text box, select the text box and then choose Item ➪ Modify to display the Text Box Specifications dialog box. Enter the text inset value in the Text Inset field.

As useful as Text Inset is, you might expect that QuarkXPress would give you a number of ways to specify it. But this is one QuarkXPress command you can access in one way only: through the Text Box Specifications dialog box.

Adding Text to Text Boxes

The text portion of your document is important because it conveys the thoughts you are communicating to your audience. The appearance of the text — its type style, size, and so on — can determine how well readers receive your message. The specifics of how to control the characteristics of text are covered in Part IV. This chapter tells you how to get the text into the text boxes.

After you create at least some initial text boxes in your document, it's time to fill them with text. Because QuarkXPress has a built-in text editor, you can, if you like, enter text directly into the text box. The advantage to using the built-in text editor is that you can perform all text-related activities within one program. The disadvantage is that you miss out on using the more sophisticated features of a dedicated word processing program; the text editor built into QuarkXPress is relatively simple.

Even if you do create your text in a separate word processing program, you'll still find plenty of occasions to use QuarkXPress's built-in editor. This feature is useful for creating headlines or shorter pieces such as brochures and ads.

Using the built-in text editor

We definitely recommend using a separate word processor for creating your text, so that you have access to the word processor's greater set of features. If you just have a small amount of text to enter, you can manage with Quark-XPress's built-in text editor, which is basic but does the job. Use the text editor by following these steps.

▶ **Steps: Entering text with the text editor**

Step 1. With the document open, select the Content tool.

Step 2. Use the mouse to place the I-beam pointer at the top of the text box (the I-beam pointer may already be at this location).

Step 3. Click the mouse button. A blinking I-beam cursor appears, which indicates that you can begin typing.

Step 4. Type the text. Figure 9-8 shows how the text box looks when you are typing text into it.

If you use the built-in text editor to enter text, wait until you complete several lines of text before adjusting the font or spacing so that you can better see the effects of any typographical changes you make.

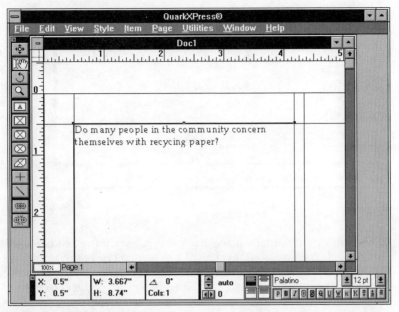

▶ **Figure 9-8:** Typing text into the text box.

Importing text

Instead of using the built-in text editor, you may want to import text from a word processing program. Before importing text into the text box, read about how to prepare your files for import in Chapter 7, "Preparing Files for Import." Then take the following steps to import your text.

▶ **Steps: Importing text into a text box**

Step 1. With the document open, select the Content tool.

Step 2. Use the mouse to place the I-beam pointer at the top of the text box (the I-beam pointer may already be at this location).

Step 3. Choose File ⇨ Get Text to display the Get Text dialog box, shown in Figure 9-9.

Step 4. Use the controls in the dialog box to locate the text file you want to place into the text box.

Step 5. After you locate the text file, choose OK. The text flows into the text box.

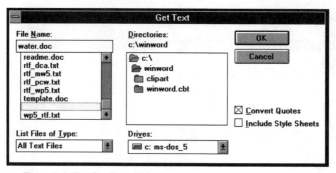

▶ **Figure 9-9:** The Get Text dialog box.

You can import text any place in a text box, even if the text box already contains text. The imported text flows into the text box at the location of the I-beam pointer. Importing text does not remove text that is already in the text box; it just bumps the existing text (following the I-beam pointer) to the end of the inserted text.

Before you import text from a word processor, it's a good idea to open the word-processed file and change the type size to 10 points or smaller. Otherwise, because text typically imports at 12 points, it's likely that you'll need to change it within QuarkXPress. Another reason to make this change is that if you select the Automatic Text box when you create the document, text from the word processor flows in and QuarkXPress automatically adds as many pages as necessary to accommodate the imported text. If the text flows in at 12 points and you actually want to use 10-point type, you must delete the excess pages in the QuarkXPress document later on. Another thing you can do before importing text is to select the font you want to use in the word-processed file so that it imports in the font you want to use in the document.

Linking Text Boxes

Suppose that you have a text box on page 1 of your document. You fill it with text and find that you need to jump the story to (continue it on) page 4. How do you handle it? By linking two text boxes together.

When you think of linking, think of a metal chain with links connected to other links. The only difference is that in QuarkXPress, you are not linking pieces of metal, but boxes that hold text.

Linking is one of the most useful features in QuarkXPress. Use it whenever you want text to flow between text boxes in a continuous stream that is maintained during the edit process. You can unlink boxes when your layout precludes having text flow from one text box to another.

You can always link and unlink boxes after they are filled with text. But linking is easiest when performed at the stage when the text boxes are created but not yet filled with text.

▶ Steps: Linking two text boxes

Step 1. Open the document to the page that contains the first text box you want in the linked chain of text boxes.

Step 2. Click the Linking tool (second tool from the bottom of the Tool palette) to select it.

Step 3. Place the pointer in the text box that is to be the first box in the chain. The pointer changes to look like a chain link. Click the mouse button.

Step 4. Go to the page containing the text box that is to be the next link in the chain. (To go to the page, you can either press Ctrl+J or choose Page ➪ Go to.)

Step 5. Place the pointer in the next text box you want in the chain and click the mouse button. The text box is now linked with the first text box.

Step 6. Repeat steps 2 through 5 until all text boxes you want in the chain are linked.

In Figure 9-10, you see two linked text boxes. Links are indicated by an arrow that shows the end of one link and the beginning of the next link.

On occasion, you may want to unlink text boxes that were previously linked. To split one story that spans two linked text boxes into two separate stories, for example, you use the program's Unlinking tool.

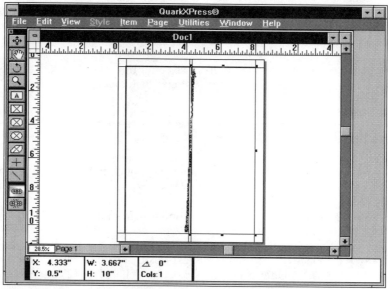

▶ **Figure 9-10:** Two linked text boxes.

▶ Steps: Unlinking two text boxes

Step 1. Open the document to the page that has the first text box in the linked chain.

Step 2. Click the Unlinking tool to select it.

Step 3. Place the pointer in the first text box in the chain. Click the mouse button.

Step 4. Go to the page containing the next text box in the chain. (To go to the page, either press Ctrl+J, or choose Page ⇨ Go to.)

Step 5. Place the pointer in the next text box in the chain and click the mouse button. The text box is now unlinked from the first text box.

Step 6. If you have additional text boxes to unlink, repeat steps 2 through 5.

As a safety feature, the Link and Unlink commands revert to the Content tool to prevent you from linking or unlinking more boxes than you intend to.

Adding Special Effects to Text

We've covered the bread-and-butter basics of how to work with text. Now it's time to explain some of the more creative text effects you can achieve with QuarkXPress, which include effects once created manually and tediously by layout artists.

Text runaround

A *runaround* is an area in a page's layout where you don't want text to flow. *Text runaround* lets you fit copy around an active element (text box, picture box, or line), fitting the text as close to the contours of the element as you want.

Text runaround is an effect often used in advertisements and other design-intensive documents. Like other special effects, text runaround is most effective when not over-used. Done correctly, this technique can add a unique, polished look to a page layout.

To set the specifications for text runaround, select the text box, picture box, or line that holds the contents you want the text to run around. Choose Item ⇨ Runaround (or press Ctrl+T) to display the Runaround Specifications dialog box, shown in Figure 9-11. In the dialog box, you can control the type of run-

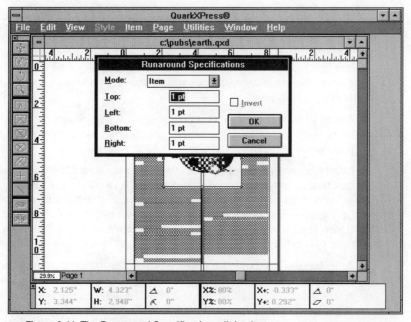

▶ **Figure 9-11:** The Runaround Specifications dialog box.

around as well as the distance between the object and the text running around it. The effects of the options available in the dialog box depend upon the type of element you select.

▶ **Figure 9-12:** Selecting None as the runaround mode creates this overprint.

QuarkXPress offers a variety of runaround options, controlled by the type of element that is active and by what you enter in the <u>M</u>ode field. You have a choice of modes that varies somewhat depending on whether you run text around boxes or lines:

- **None:** This setting causes text behind the active item to flow normally, as if there were no object in the way. Figure 9-12 shows the overprint that happens when you select None.

- **Item:** Choosing Item as the runaround mode causes text to flow around the box that holds the active element. Figure 9-13 shows the effect of Item runaround. This page includes a line, text box, and picture box. Note how the background text flows around the item by a set amount of offset; in this figure, the offset is 1 point. (You usually want a larger offset than this; we tend to use 6 points or more.)

- **Auto Image:** Used only for picture boxes, this mode automatically determines the shape of the image in the picture box and how text flows around it. The runaround follows the shape of the active item, while maintaining the offset that you specify. Figure 9-14 shows how the program flows text around the picture. In this example, we used a 4-point text offset (distance between the text and the picture). This offset is also set in the Runaround Specifications dialog box.

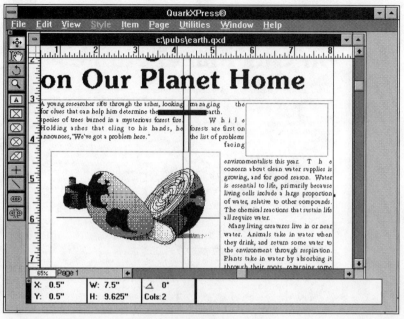

Figure 9-13: An example of an Item runaround.

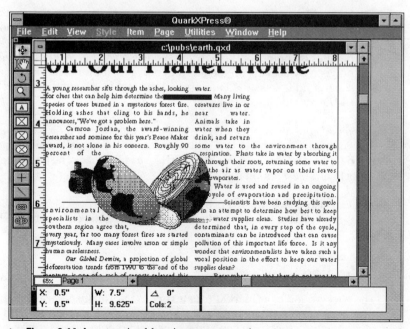

Figure 9-14: An example of Auto Image runaround.

▶ **Figure 9-15:** An example of a Manual Image runaround.

■ **Manual Image:** Also used only for picture boxes, this setting automatically draws a polygon around the active element, but then lets you modify the shape of the polygon by clicking and dragging (with the mouse) the black handles on points of the polygon. You also can move line segments in the polygon by clicking on the line and dragging it into place. In Figure 9-15, the runaround follows the lines around the picture shape that are established by the Manual Image polygon.

When you choose Manual Image, you may want more handles for shaping the polygon than the number QuarkXPress automatically gives you. To add a polygon handle to a line, hold down the Ctrl key as you click the line; a new handle appears at that point on the line.

You can also check the Invert box in the Runaround Specifications dialog box; this option causes the text to fill the picture box and conform to its shape.

Color and shading

The background of a QuarkXPress text box is normally neutral, meaning that when you print your document, the background is the same color as the color of your paper stock. You can add a background color to a text box, and you can specify the percent shade of the color.

Even if the document is to be printed in a single ink color, you can still add texture to a text box by applying a color (including black) and then specifying a light shade of the color — in the 10- to 40-percent range. We have found many occasions where this technique added to the appearance of a newsletter masthead or a sidebar in a magazine article, even though the pages were printed in black.

▶ **Steps: Applying color and shading to a text box background**

Step 1. Select the text box and choose Item ⇨ Modify to display the Text Box Specifications dialog box.

Step 2. In the Background Color field, select a color from the list box.

Step 3. In the Shade field, select a shade percentage from the list box. Or enter a shade percentage in the field (you can specify this value to three decimal places and choose any value between 0 and 100 percent).

Step 4. Choose OK to close the dialog box.

When you shade a picture box, check the shading level by printing the page. How dark the shading appears on the printout depends on the printer device and its resolution.

You also can add color to the text itself. Use the Content tool to select the text and then choose Style ⇨ Color. Select a shade percentage for the text color by choosing Style ⇨ Shade. Another way is to use the Colors palette described in Chapter 21, "Working with Color."

For more information on applying color to text, refer to Chapter 15, "Using Special Elements and Effects."

Vertical alignment

You can align text within text boxes with the top, bottom, or middle of the text box. Or you can space it evenly between the top and the bottom of the text box. Figure 9-16 shows four different ways of vertically aligning text in text boxes. From left to right, the vertical alignments shown in the figure are: top, centered, bottom, and justified.

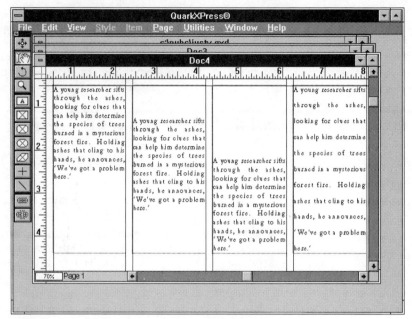

▶ **Figure 9-16:** Four ways of vertically aligning text in text boxes.

To change the vertical alignment of text, select the text box and choose Item ⇨ Modify to display the Text Box Specifications dialog box. Choose an alignment type from the list box in the Vertical Alignment section of the dialog box.

If you plan to use justified vertical alignment, keep in mind that you need to place any pictures outside the text box that holds the vertically justified text. The presence of a picture disables vertical justification.

Vertical justification spaces text evenly between the first baseline and the bottom of the text box. As long as there are no hard returns in the text, leading adjusts to make each line space the same size as the others in the box. However, if text contains a hard return, you need to specify an inter-paragraph spacing value in the Inter (¶) Max field. This value tells QuarkXPress the maximum amount of space it can insert between vertically justified paragraphs. If you want the leading to remain constant between paragraphs, set Inter (¶) Max to 0.

Summary

▶ You can choose whether a document has automatic text boxes.

▶ QuarkXPress offers a variety of methods for sizing and positioning text boxes.

▶ Positive rotation values, which you specify in degrees, rotate a text box counter-clockwise; negative rotation figures rotate the box clockwise.

▶ Rotated text is effective, but only if it is not overused in a document.

▶ Not all pages need to have the same number of columns. To vary the page layout in a document, you can vary the number and width of text columns on a page.

▶ Text inset is useful if you are setting a text box near or within another text box and you want some space between them. It is also a good idea to use text inset for text boxes that have frames around them.

▶ You'll want to use a separate word processor for creating text to be placed in text columns. But in a pinch, the built-in QuarkXPress text editor can handle simple jobs.

▶ QuarkXPress's linking feature is helpful if you have text that starts on one page and continues on another.

CHAPTER

10

Working with Picture Boxes

In This Chapter

▶ Creating picture boxes

▶ Sizing, positioning, and rotating picture boxes

▶ Adding pictures to picture boxes

▶ Suppressing picture printout

▶ Adding background color to picture boxes

Creating Picture Boxes

One of the best features of QuarkXPress is the way it allows you to place a variety of layout elements on the page. In the preceding chapter, you learned how to place, size, and position text boxes. Now it's time to learn to do the same with picture boxes. In this chapter, we cover the mechanics of the picture box. Later in the book (in Part V), you learn more about modifying the graphics that you place into picture boxes and about how to create simple graphics.

When you create text boxes in QuarkXPress, you are limited to a rectangular shape. When creating picture boxes, you have more choices.

To create a picture box in one of four shapes — rectangle, rounded-corner rectangle, oval, or polygon — you "draw" it using one of four picture box tools in the Tool palette. Figure 10-1 shows picture boxes created with the four tools. Note the "handles" on the polygon picture box in Figure 10-1; picture boxes created with the polygon or oval tool have handles in a rectangle surrounding

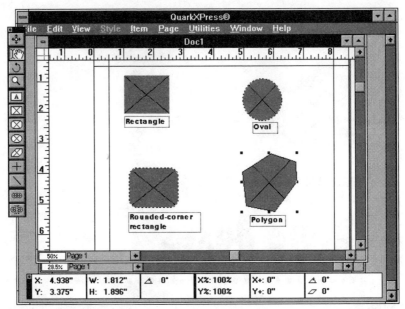

▶ **Figure 10-1:** Four types of picture boxes.

the picture box. The handles around the polygon are always in a rectangular pattern, regardless of the shape of the polygon. The following steps guide you in the process of drawing picture boxes.

▶ Steps: Drawing a picture box

Step 1. Open the document to the page on which you want to draw the picture box; then click one of the Picture Box tools. When you use the mouse to move the pointer onto the page, the pointer changes to look like a cross-hair.

Step 2. Place the cross-hair pointer at the location where you want to position one of the corners of the picture box.

Step 3. Press and hold the mouse button as you draw the picture box to the approximate size you want it to be. Or, if you want to be precise about it, watch the W (Width) and H (Height) measurements on the Measurements palette change to reflect the size of the box as you draw it. As you draw the picture box, the X: and Y: coordinates in the Measurements palette display, respectively, the vertical and horizontal coordinates of the text box location. The W: and H: coordinates show the size of the picture box.

If you want the picture box to be perfectly square, hold down the Shift key as you draw the box with the Rectangle Picture Box tool. If you want the picture box to be a perfect circle, hold down the Shift key as you draw the box with the Oval Picture Box tool.

Polygon picture boxes are useful if you are importing a picture that has an irregular shape. Experienced designers sometimes use polygon picture boxes to create unique effects, such as placing a picture into an unusually shaped box.

When you draw a polygon picture box, as shown in Figure 10-2, position your mouse at the point where you want to begin the polygon. Click and hold the mouse button as you draw the first line of the polygon. When you release the mouse button, QuarkXPress interprets that as the end of the first line segment in the polygon. Click and hold the mouse button again to draw the next line, and continue until you complete the polygon. You can tell when the polygon is completed because the pointer changes from a cross-hair to an open square. Polygon picture boxes must have at least three sides.

Step 4. When you finish drawing the box, release the mouse button.

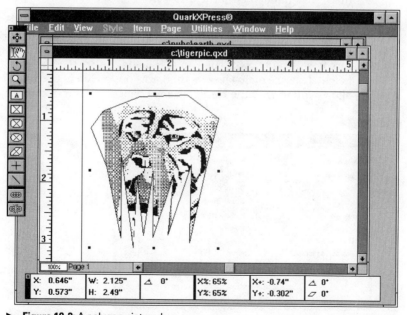

▶ **Figure 10-2:** A polygon picture box.

Setting Picture Box Specifications

As with text boxes, you can establish a number of specifications for picture boxes. For picture boxes, you use the Picture Box Specifications dialog box, shown in Figure 10-3. This dialog box is useful for precisely sizing and positioning a picture box, rotating it, scaling it, and adding color to the picture's background.

Part V of this book, Graphics, covers many of the options available in the Picture Box Specifications dialog box. The following section explains those options that deal with sizing and positioning the picture box and with keeping pictures from printing.

Sizing and positioning picture boxes

You can control the size and position of a picture box in a number of ways:

- **Option 1:** Enter numerical values in the Picture Box Specifications dialog box (select Item ⇨ Modify). The Origin Across and Origin Down fields control the placement of the box, and the Width and Height fields control its size (the origin is the upper-left corner of the box). This option is great for placing and sizing picture boxes precisely, but it has one drawback: the dialog box blocks your view of the actions you take so that you can't see the results until you exit the dialog box.

- **Option 2:** Change the settings in the Measurements palette. X is the horizontal coordinate; changes you make to the X value move the picture side to side. Y is the vertical coordinate; changes to the Y value move the picture box up and down. The W and H fields control the box's width and height. Like the dialog box method, this option offers precision and also allows you to view the results of any changes as they occur.

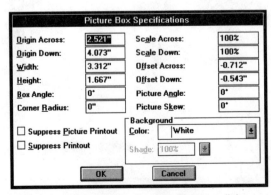

▶ **Figure 10-3:** The Picture Box Specifications dialog box.

■ **Option 3:** Use the Item tool to drag the entire box into position or to resize the box by clicking and dragging on the box handles. You also can use the Content tool (which, for pictures, becomes a grabber hand) to move the picture within the box. Again, you can see your actions on-screen.

The easiest way to resize polygon picture boxes is to click and drag the box handles, which appear in a rectangle around the polygon shape. Holding down Alt+Shift as you resize a box, resizes it proportionally. Press Ctrl+Shift to keep a rectangular box square or an oval box circular as you resize it. Press Ctrl+Alt+Shift to keep the picture and its box in proportion as you resize it.

It's nice that QuarkXPress gives you such a variety of ways to modify picture boxes. You'll probably use all of them at some point.

The measurement units used for specifications in the Picture Box Specifications dialog box reflect the settings you establish in the General Preferences dialog box.

Changing the shape of the picture box

After working on a layout for a while, you may decide that the shape of a particular picture box is not right. You might be tempted to just delete the picture box, along with its contents, and start again. But that isn't necessary, because QuarkXPress offers a couple of ways to change the shape of the picture box, even if it already contains the picture.

If you created the picture box with the rectangular tool or the rounded-rectangular tool, you can change its shape by modifying its corner radius. The corner radius is the radius of an invisible circle inside the corner of the picture box. The sides of the invisible circle touch the sides of the picture box.

Rectangular picture boxes have a corner radius of 0 (zero), and if you change the corner radius enough, you can turn rectangular boxes into rounded rectangles or ovals. In fact, a rounded-corner picture box actually is a rectangular box that has a corner radius of 0.25 inches. Figure 10-4 shows the effect of an enlargement to the corner radius of a rounded-rectangular picture box. The larger the corner radius number, the closer the box gets to becoming an oval.

Another way of changing the shape of a picture box is to select the picture box and choose the Item menu. As you can see in Figure 10-5, the last section of the Item menu has a Picture Box Shape command, which in turn offers a list box that lets you select a new shape for the picture box.

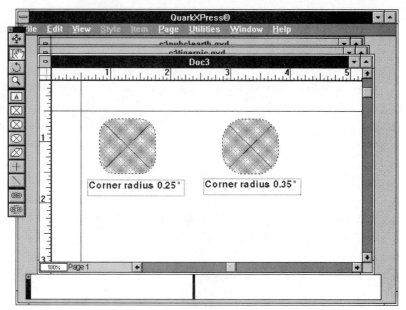

▶ **Figure 10-4:** The corner radius affects the shape of the picture box.

If you want to change the shape of a polygon picture box, select the box and choose Reshape Polygon from the Item menu. You then can change the shape of the polygon by clicking and dragging its handles and lines.

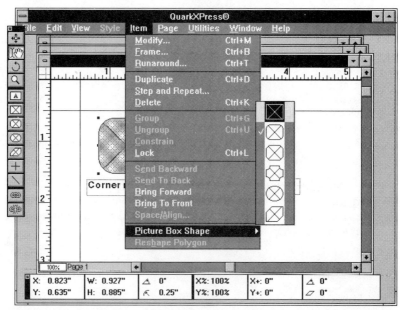

▶ **Figure 10-5:** The Picture Box Shape list box

Rotating the Picture Box

QuarkXPress lets you rotate picture boxes in precise increments of .001 degrees. You can control the amount of rotation in three ways:

- **Option 1:** Select the picture box and choose Item ⇨ Modify to display the Picture Box Specifications box. Then enter a rotation amount (between 0 and 360 degrees, in increments of .001 degrees) in the Box Angle field. If you want to make other changes to the picture box specifications, do so. Otherwise, choose OK.

To rotate a picture box counter-clockwise, use a positive rotation value; use a negative value to rotate it clockwise. Figure 10-6 shows a picture box that is rotated 30 degrees. (Because the Runaround mode for the box is set to Item, the text automatically runs around the picture box. See Chapter 9, "Working with Text," for details.)

- **Option 2:** You also can rotate a picture box on-the-fly. To do this, use the Rotation tool. Select the picture box and rotate it by dragging it and holding down the mouse button as you move the mouse.

- **Option 3:** Use the Measurements palette to rotate the text box. Simply enter a rotation degree in the rotation field.

▶ **Figure 10-6:** A picture box rotated 30 degrees.

▶ **Figure 10-7:** You can rotate picture boxes independently of the pictures inside them.

You might want to rotate the picture box but keep the picture itself at its original orientation. To do so, rotate the picture box and then open the Picture Box Specifications dialog box. In the Picture Angle field, enter the reverse value of the picture box's rotation angle. For example, if the picture box is rotated 33 degrees, set the Picture Angle at -33 degrees. Figure 10-7 shows a picture box with these rotation settings.

Suppressing Picture Printout

As you develop a document layout, you may want to print rough-draft copies of it from time to time. Consider printing them without the contents of any picture boxes. Suppressing picture printout saves considerable printing time.

QuarkXPress gives you two options for suppressing picture printout. The first, Suppress Picture Printout, prevents the picture from printing, but prints any frame or background color for the box. The second — and quickest — option, Suppress Printout, prevents the picture *and* its background from printing. To choose either option, take the following steps.

▶ **Steps: Suppressing picture printout**

Step 1. Select the picture box to make it active.

Step 2. Choose Item ⇨ Modify to display the Picture Box Specifications dialog box.

Step 3. Select Suppress Picture Printout box or Suppress Printout by putting a check mark in the box next to the option.

Step 4. Choose OK to close the dialog box.

If you select one of these options, remember to go back into the Picture Box Specifications dialog box and uncheck the box before printing final copies of the document.

Adding Pictures to Picture Boxes

After you create a picture box, you're ready to fill it with a picture. The following steps show you how.

▶ **Steps: Placing pictures in picture boxes**

Step 1. With the document open and the picture box selected, click the Content tool.

Step 2. Choose File ⇨ Get Text to display the Get Picture dialog box.

Step 3. Use the controls in the dialog box to locate the picture file you want to put into the picture box.

Step 4. After you locate the picture file, choose OK. The picture appears in the picture box.

After you import the picture, you probably will need to make some modifications to it. Figure 10-8 shows an example of how an imported picture first appeared. As you can see, the picture is both too big for the picture box and is off center. We'll explain how you can change the size of the picture in Part V, which covers the details of working with graphics.

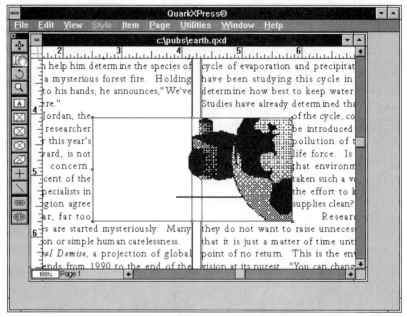

▶ **Figure 10-8:** How an imported picture first appears.

To move the graphic around so that it is positioned where you want it to be, click the Content tool. When you position the pointer over the picture box, it becomes a grabber hand (it actually looks like a little hand). Click the mouse button again and keep it pressed as you drag the picture into position.

If you want to center the graphic in the picture box, let QuarkXPress center it, precisely, for you. All you have to do is press Ctrl+Shift+M. Pressing Ctrl+Shift+F fits the graphic to the box's dimensions, distorting the graphic if necessary. Press Ctrl+Shift+Alt+F to fit the graphic to the box, keeping the aspect ratio of the graphic.

When you open a document, you can tell QuarkXPress to automatically replace any pictures that were changed in another program since the last time you opened the document. Choose Edit ➪ Preferences ➪ General to display the General Preferences dialog box. In the Auto Picture Import field, choose On. If you prefer to have QuarkXPress notify you before it imports pictures that were modified, choose the On (verify) option. The default setting for Auto Picture Import is Off, meaning that pictures are not automatically updated to the latest version (see Chapter 4, "Customizing QuarkXPress," and Chapter 23, "Linking to Source Files").

Adding Background Color and Shade

As with text boxes, you can add a background color to a picture box, and you can specify the percent shade of the color. To apply color and shade to a picture box background, take the following steps.

▶ **Steps: Adding background color to picture boxes**

Step 1. Select the picture box and choose Item ⇨ Modify to display the Picture Box Specifications dialog box.

Step 2. In the Background Color field, select a color from the list box.

Step 3. In the Shade field, select a percentage from the list box or enter a percentage. You can specify a value between 0 and 100 percent, in increments as small as .001 percent.

Step 4. Choose OK to close the dialog box.

You can also add color and shade by using the Colors palette (see Chapter 21, "Working with Color").

Using Picture Boxes to Mark Halftones

Here's an application where the ability to add color and shade to a picture box really comes in handy. If your document will include halftone photos to be stripped in by the printer, you can draw a picture box to mark the position where a halftone will be placed. Then you can fill the picture box with 100-percent black, creating a black box that marks the spot where your printer is to strip in a photographic halftone.

■ ■

Summary

▶ QuarkXPress lets you draw picture boxes in a variety of shapes, including the versatile polygon.

▶ After you create and fill a picture box, you can easily change the box's shape, even if it is a polygon.

▶ To create a perfect square or circle picture box, hold down the Shift key as you draw with the rectangular picture box tool or the oval picture box tool.

▶ Resize picture boxes by using the Measurements palette or by dragging their sizing handles.

▶ You can rotate a picture box one direction and its contents another.

▶ To save time when printing rough drafts of your document, suppress the printout of pictures.

▶ QuarkXPress can automatically use the most current version of a picture created in another program, but only if you so specify.

■ ■

CHAPTER

11

Additional Layout Features

- -

In This Chapter

▶ Aligning and spacing layout elements

▶ Adding rules or arrows to the layout

▶ Adding decorative frames to text and picture boxes

▶ Copying elements and pages from one document to another

▶ Saving pages as EPS files

- -

Aligning Multiple Elements

It's not at all uncommon to have a set of two or more layout elements that you want to line up to a certain X or Y coordinate, or space a certain distance apart, or both. QuarkXPress lets you align items according to their left, right, top, or bottom edges, or their centers. You also can control the amount of space between multiple items and specify whether they are evenly spread across the page or staggered horizontally or vertically.

Space/Align

The Space/Align Items dialog box is a powerful feature that allows you to control the spacing and alignment of elements in your layout.

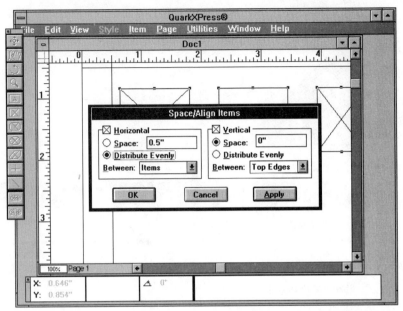

▶ **Figure 11-1:** The Space/Align Items dialog box with settings for aligning items on a page.

How does Space/Align work? Showing an example is the best way to illustrate it. Let's say you have three boxes on a page, and you want the boxes to be precisely aligned by their top edges with one-half inch between the boxes. Figure 11-1 shows the settings you make in the Space/Align Items dialog box to accomplish this layout. To establish a layout like the one shown in the example, follow these steps.

▶ Steps: Setting up the sample layout

Step 1. With the Item tool selected, hold down the Shift key and click each of the three boxes to select them.

Step 2. Choose Item ⇨ Space/Align to display the Space/Align Items dialog box.

Step 3. Click the Horizontal box to select it. Choose Space, below the Horizontal box, and enter **0.5"** in the Space field.

Step 4. Select Distribute Evenly and then Items from the Between list box.

Step 5. Click the Vertical box to select it. Choose Space, below the Horizontal box, and enter **0"** in the Space field.

Step 6. Select Apply to apply the changes without saving them, and then choose OK to save the changes.

If you are new to QuarkXPress and want to increase your layout expertise, do some experimenting. Draw a few text boxes and apply different X and Y coordinates to them in the Measurements palette. Also, try using different settings in the Space/Align Items dialog box. This is a great way to learn how these features work.

Step and Repeat

Whenever you can, it's a good idea to let the computer do the work for you. And QuarkXPress makes it easy for the computer to do extra work. As an example, the program has the ability to create multiple copies of selected elements and to space them horizontally or vertically at regular intervals. This powerful feature is called *Step and Repeat*.

Suppose that you want to create a page that contains a section of lines on which readers write answers to questions. Step and Repeat lets you use one of the QuarkXPress line drawing tools to draw a line and then repeat it at regular vertical intervals.

Figure 11-2 shows an example of this type of form. A text box is at the top of the page. Note the single, solid, 1-point line drawn with the orthogonal line tool just below the dotted line. You can tell that the line is active because of the sizing handles on each end.

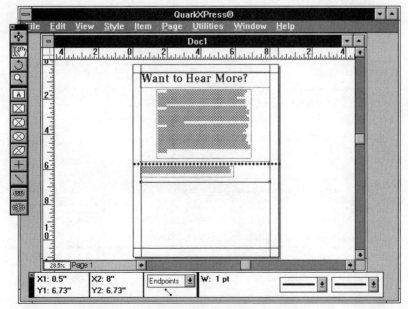

▶ **Figure 11-2:** A questionnaire created using Step and Repeat.

Figure 11-3 shows the Step and Repeat dialog box, which you access by choosing Item ➪ Step and Repeat.

To duplicate the solid line in the sample questionnaire and repeat it at even intervals, we established the following settings in the dialog box:

■ In the Repeat Count field, we entered the number 10, indicating that we wanted 10 repeats of the line.

■ In the Horizontal Offset field, we entered 0", meaning that we do not want each repeated line to shift sideways.

■ In the Vertical Offset field, we entered 0.25" to vertically space each repeated line one-quarter inch from the previous line.

We chose OK after making these settings changes, and the result was the lined-paper effect at the bottom of the page, shown in Figure 11-4. As you can see by this example, Step and Repeat is useful for creating forms, tables, and other similar documents that have a design element reproduced multiple times and spaced at regular intervals.

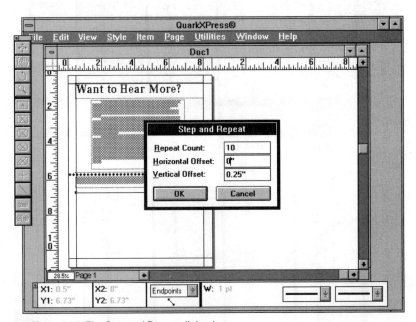

▶ **Figure 11-3:** The Step and Repeat dialog box.

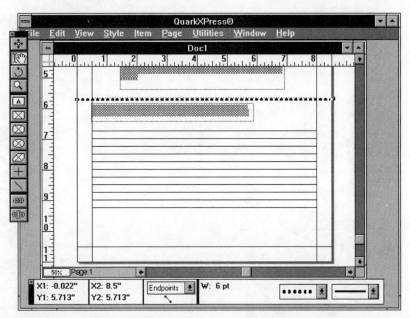

▶ **Figure 11-4:** A few quick changes in the Step and Repeat dialog box produced these lines for the questionnaire.

Entering a positive Horizontal Offset value places repeated elements to the right of the original; a negative value places them to the left. Likewise, a positive Vertical Offset value, like the one we used in our example, places repeated elements below the original element.

Adding Rules and Arrows

Rules (lines) often add a nice finishing touch to a document page. You can use rules to make a headline more interesting, to mark where one section of text ends and another begins, or to separate parts of a page. In a multicolumn spread that includes separate pieces of information, rules added over the heads of each piece help to clearly delineate where one piece ends and another begins.

In QuarkXPress, you create, size, and position rules much the same way you do text and picture boxes. Here are some steps to follow in creating rules:

■ **To create a rule:** Select either of the two line drawing tools, the Orthogonal Line tool or the Diagonal Line tool. The first draws lines that are horizontal and vertical only, while the second can draw lines in any direction. (The

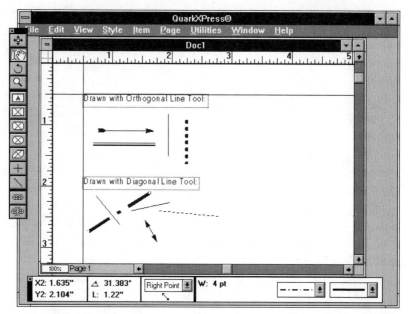

▶ **Figure 11-5:** Examples of rules drawn with the Orthogonal Line and Diagonal Line tools.

Diagonal Line tool can also draw a horizontal or vertical line if you hold down the Shift key as you draw.) Figure 11-5 shows some examples of rules drawn using each of the two line drawing tools.

■ **To size a rule:** Use the Measurements palette to select the rule's width and length. Or drag the rule's sizing handles until the rule is the desired length.

■ **To select a rule type and line end:** To select a rule type (dotted, doubled, solid, and so on) and line end (arrow point, and so on), select the rule to make it active. Choose Item ⇨ Modify to display the Line Specifications dialog box (shown in Figure 11-6) and make the selections you want. Another way of selecting a rule type is to choose one of the line selections in the Measurements palette, as shown in Figure 11-7. This palette also offers a drop-down list box that lets you pick from a variety of line endings, including arrows. If you select a rule composed of two or more lines, keep in mind that the multiple lines may not appear if the line weight is too small. This is because the line weight you specify is the *total* line weight for the double or triple line. A line weight of 1 point for a double or triple line is so small that the line appears as a single, 1-point line.

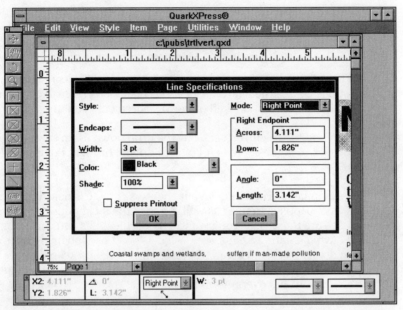

▶ **Figure 11-6:** The Line Specifications dialog box.

▶ **Figure 11-7:** You can select a line type and ending from the Measurements palette.

- **To reposition a line:** Select the line and then drag it into position. You also can reposition a line by entering new X and Y coordinates in the Measurements palette or by entering position coordinates in the Line Specifications dialog box (choose Item ⇨ Modify to display the dialog box).

- **To rotate a line:** Enter a value (in degrees, in .001-degree increments) in the Angle field of the Line Specifications dialog box (Item ⇨ Modify). Or enter a value in the rotation field of the Measurements palette.

The line mode, which you set using the drop-down list in the Line Specifications dialog box, must be set to Left Point, Midpoint, or Right Point in order to rotate a line.

As we emphasized in earlier layout chapters, simple is nearly always better. This axiom applies to rules as well. Some of the most obnoxious layouts you'll ever see are those that employ a variety of rule types and widths on the same page. Avoid creating a bad page design — don't use too many rules and arrows. If you do use rules and arrows, keep them simple and keep their weights on the light side. Even for a double or triple line, anything more than about 8 points is just too heavy and overpowers the page.

Framing Text or Picture Boxes

Framing is a QuarkXPress option that lets you add a plain or fancy line around the edge of a box or, if you have a group of boxes, around every box in the group. Most of the time, the text and picture boxes you use to lay out a page will be unadorned, but you may occasionally want to add a frame. Figure 11-8 shows a text box surrounded by a double-lined frame. Notice that we kept the line type simple and the line weight light to create a better visual effect.

Just because you create a frame around a box, it doesn't necessarily follow that you want the frame to appear on the final, printed document. For one of our applications, a newsletter, we use a 0.5-point frame as a keyline to indicate to our commercial printer which boxes we want to be screened. During the actual printing process, the frame line drops out, and all that's left is the screen.

Sometimes you might want to draw the frame inside the margins of the box, and other times you might want it outside the margins. To control whether the frame is inside or outside the box, choose Edit ⇨ Preferences ⇨ General to display the General Preferences dialog box. In the Framing field, select either Inside or Outside. Here are the steps to follow when adding a frame to a box. You can use the same steps to add a frame to all the boxes in a group.

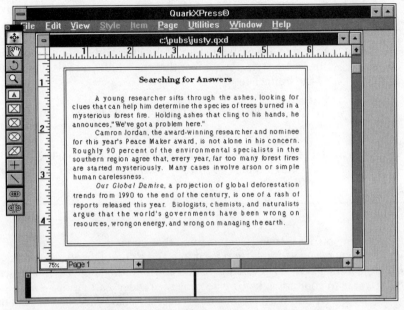

Searching for Answers

A young researcher sifts through the ashes, looking for clues that can help him determine the species of trees burned in a mysterious forest fire. Holding ashes that cling to his hands, he announces, "We've got a problem here."

Camron Jordan, the award-winning researcher and nominee for this year's Peace Maker award, is not alone in his concern. Roughly 90 percent of the environmental specialists in the southern region agree that, every year, far too many forest fires are started mysteriously. Many cases involve arson or simple human carelessness.

Our Global Demise, a projection of global deforestation trends from 1990 to the end of the century, is one of a rash of reports released this year. Biologists, chemists, and naturalists argue that the world's governments have been wrong on resources, wrong on energy, and wrong on managing the earth.

▶ **Figure 11-8:** An example of a framed box.

▶ Steps: Framing a box

Step 1. Use the Item tool to select the box or group and then choose Item ⇨ Frame to display the Frame Specifications dialog box, shown in Figure 11-9.

Step 2. From the Style list box, select one of the seven available frame styles. To give you a preview of what the frame style looks like, QuarkXPress displays the style you select on a box beneath the title of the dialog box.

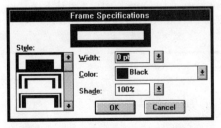

▶ **Figure 11-9:** The Frame Specifications dialog box.

Step 3. In the Width field, enter a line width for the frame line. You can make the frame as wide as you want, as long as it is not too big to fit the bounds of the box. If you choose one of the frame styles that has more than one line, you must make the lines wide enough to accommodate the frame style. Remember that the width you select is the total width of the frame line.

Step 4. In the Color field, select a color from the list box; the default setting is black.

Step 5. In the Shade field, select a shade percentage from the list box or type a percentage value (up to 100 percent, in 0.1-percent increments) in the field.

When you use framing, keep in mind that understatement is an art. The difference between a simple, narrow frame and a complicated, large one often is the difference between speaking quietly and shouting. Realize that understatement works to your advantage by keeping the reader's attention — as opposed to losing it by bombarding the poor reader's visual senses. Be careful not to make the frame line too wide or complex, which can overpower the balance of a page. For simple framing, we prefer using a single-line frame between 0.5 and 2 points.

Anchoring Boxes

QuarkXPress lets you select a text box or a picture box and anchor it — attach it — to the text that surrounds it. You might want to do this to keep a graphic with a certain passage of text. Anchored items "flow" with the text to which they are anchored, even during the most massive of edits. One common application of anchored boxes is to create a page that incorporates icons as small graphic elements in a stream of text.

QuarkXPress treats anchored elements as individual characters of text. After you anchor them, you can cut, copy, paste, and delete these items just as if they were single characters of text. To anchor a text box or a picture box, just follow these steps.

▶ Steps: Anchoring a text or picture box

Step 1. Using the Item tool, select the box.

Step 2. Cut or copy the box in the same way you cut or copy any single text character (use Edit ➪ Cut or Edit ➪ Copy).

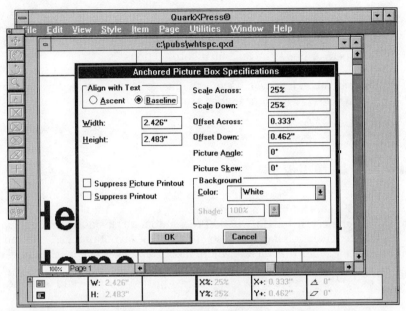

Figure 11-10: The Anchored Picture Box Specifications dialog box.

Step 3. Using the Content tool, position the cursor at the location where you want to anchor the box and paste in the box (select Edit ⇨ Paste).

After the box becomes an anchored box, you can modify it by selecting it and then choosing Item ⇨ Modify to display the Anchored Text Box or Anchored Picture Box Specifications dialog box, shown in Figure 11-10. Because the anchored box is considered a text character, you can also modify it using the Measurements palette.

Note that handles on an anchored box are different along certain edges because of how the box is anchored; you can use the sizing handles to make the box bigger in one direction but not in others.

If you anchor a polygon picture box, the box itself takes on the rectangular shape of the polygon's sizing handles.

Managing the Layout

Sometime during the layout process or after you place all the text boxes, picture boxes, and rules, you may want to make some structural changes to the document. For example, you might decide that an element on page three should be moved to page six. You might edit the copy so that what initially occupied nine pages fits on an eight-page spread. Or you might realize that, because the document has "grown" larger than you first anticipated, you need to add page numbers or break the document into sections.

We call this category of document changes *managing the layout.* QuarkXPress has a full set of features that let you easily handle the tasks associated with managing the layout.

Adding and deleting pages

In the early stages of the document layout process, you don't need to think much about adding pages, provided you enable Auto Page Insertion in General Preferences. If you do, QuarkXPress automatically inserts enough pages to hold the text files you import. At any point in the layout process, you can change the specifications that dictate where those new pages occur. The initial default location is the end of the document, but you may prefer to change it to the end of the story (current set of linked text boxes) or to the end of the section.

To change the location where pages are automatically inserted, choose Edit ➪ Preferences ➪ General to display the General Preferences dialog box. Choose End of Story, End of Section, or End of Document and then choose OK to close the dialog box.

If you include a prefix in the document page numbers (an example of a prefix is the 20- in page 20-1), be sure to include the prefix when you specify pages to insert, delete, or move. You can also specify absolute page numbers by using a plus sign (+) before the absolute page number. For example, if the page you want to move is numbered 20-1, but is actually the 30th page in the document, you can use either 20-1 or +30.

After you place most of the text and pictures in a document, you might decide to insert one or more additional pages. To do this, choose Page ➪ Insert to display the Insert Pages dialog box, shown in Figure 11-11. In the Insert field, enter the number of pages to insert. Then click the button that corresponds to the location where you want the pages to be inserted. QuarkXPress automatically renumbers the inserted pages and those that follow.

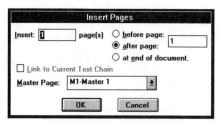

▶ **Figure 11-11:** The Insert Pages dialog box.

To delete one or more pages, choose Page ➩ Delete to display the Delete Pages dialog box and then enter the numbers of the pages to be deleted. After the deletion, QuarkXPress automatically renumbers the pages.

Rearranging pages

Rearranging pages involves moving them to different locations in the document. One way to move pages is to choose Page ➩ Move to display the Move Pages dialog box shown in Figure 11-12. If you want to move just one page, enter its page number in the Move page(s) field. If you want to move a range of pages, enter the first page in the range in the Move page(s) field and the last page in the thru field. The buttons in the dialog box let you select where you want the pages to end up; your choices are: before a specified page, after a specified page, or at the end of the document.

You can also rearrange pages by reducing the document to thumbnail view (choose View ➩ Thumbnails) and then dragging the thumbnails into the new page order. After the document is displayed in thumbnail mode, select the page you want to move and then drag it to its new place in the document. When the pointer changes to an arrow, you can release the mouse button to finalize the placement of the page.

One advantage to the thumbnail method is that you can more easily visualize the effects of your page moves; you can actually see them occurring in thumbnail view. Another advantage is that during a page move, the pointer indicates how the move affects other pages in the document. If the pointer looks like a miniature page, it means that the move does not change the placement of other pages in the document. If the pointer looks like a left-pointing or right-pointing arrow, it means that moving that particular page "bumps" pages to the left or to the right. If the pointer looks like a down-pointing arrow, as it does when the document does not have facing pages, it means that succeeding pages will be moved.

 If you want to move a set of adjacent pages (for example, pages three through six) in thumbnail view, hold down the Shift key while you select the first and last pages in the range.

Move Pages		
Move page(s): 2 thru: 3	○ before page:	
	● after page: 1	
OK Cancel	○ to end of document.	

▶ **Figure 11-12:** The Move Pages dialog box.

Numbering sections and pages

Sometimes you may want to number pages in a QuarkXPress document consecutively, from first page to last. Other times, such as when the document grows to an unwieldy size or when you are required to do so because of prescribed formatting standards, you may want to break the document into sections. Technical manuals or books with chapters are often broken into sections to make it easier for the reader to locate information.

If the document is divided into sections, you generally want the page numbers to reflect the document's structure. For example, give the 11th page in section 5 the page number *5-11* so that readers can easily determine where their place in the document is in relation to the rest of the publication.

Breaking the document into sections

To break a document into sections, open it to your intended first page in a section. Choose Page ⇨ Section to display the Section dialog box, shown in Figure 11-13. Check the button next to Section Start to make the current page the first page of the section.

You can then select the numbering format you want applied to the section. You can enter a prefix (in the page number 5-1, the prefix is 5-) up to four characters long in the Prefix field. In the Number field, enter the number you want assigned to the first page in the section. The default Number setting is 1, but you may want to change it to a different number. For example, if you are producing a book that already has pages 1 and 2 preprinted, you want your QuarkXPress pages to begin with a page number of 3. The Format field offers a list box showing the possible formats for automatic page numbering. These include: Arabic numerals (1, 2, 3); uppercase or lowercase Roman numerals (I, II, III or i, ii, iii); and uppercase or lowercase letters (A, B, C or a, b, c). The format you select applies to all page numbers that are automatically generated in this section of the document.

Automatically numbering the pages

The typical way of instructing QuarkXPress to automatically number all pages in a document is to place the Current Text Box Page Number character on the master page (see Chapter 5, "Understanding Master Pages"). But, particularly if the document is divided into sections, you may want to add automatic page numbers on regular pages.

To enter the Current Text Box Page Number character, create a text box of the approximate size necessary to

▶ **Figure 11-13:** The Section dialog box.

hold the page number. Position the text box where you want the page number to appear. Using the Content tool, select the text box and hold down the Ctrl key while you press the 3 key. You can then modify the font, size, and attributes of the page-number character. Automatic page numbers take on the modified attributes.

Creating automatic *Continued on . . .* markers

Whenever your document contains a *jump* (where text that cannot fit entirely on one page is continued on another, linked page), consider adding automatically generated *Continued on . . .* and *Continued from . . .* markers to the document.

To use this feature, draw a text box at the location in the document where you want the *Continued on . . .* or *Continued from . . .* markers to appear. Press Ctrl+2 to have the page number for the previous box holding the story to automatically appear, and press Ctrl+4 to place the marker for the next text box page-number character. Figure 11-14 shows the *Continued on . . .* marker, which says *None* because we haven't yet added pages to hold the overflow text. After we do, the marker will automatically reflect the continued-on page number.

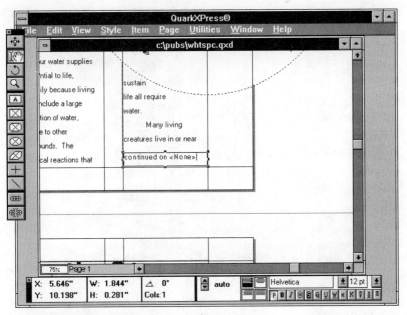

▶ **Figure 11-14:** The *Continued on . . .* marker.

Copying Elements from One Document to Another

One of our favorite QuarkXPress features enables copying layout elements or even entire pages from one document to another. To use this feature, open both documents and then drag-copy the item from one document to another by using the following methods:

- To copy a layout element from one document to another, open both documents. Display them next to each other by choosing Window ▷ Tile. Make sure that the view you select for both documents is any view *except* thumbnail. Select the item you want to copy in the source document and hold the mouse button as you drag the element to the destination document. You must use the Item tool to select the item.

- To copy a page from one document to another, open both documents. Display them next to each other by choosing Window ▷ Tile. This time, make sure that the View of both documents *is* thumbnail, as shown in Figure 11-15. Select the page you want to copy in the source document and hold the mouse button as you drag the page to the destination document.

Drag-copying layout elements or entire pages from a source document to a destination document has no effect on the source document.

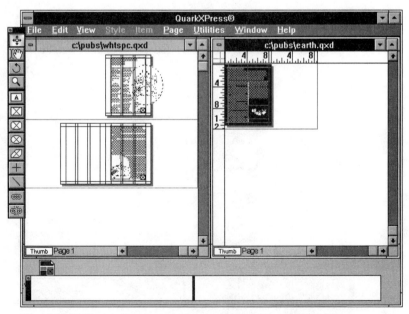

▶ **Figure 11-15:** Display documents in thumbnail view to copy a page from one document to the other.

Saving a Page as an EPS File

QuarkXPress has a nifty feature that lets you, in effect, take a picture of a page in a document and turn the picture into an EPS file. You can then use the EPS file as an illustration for another document. A catalog of brochures is a good examples of an application of this feature. You might create several brochures, make an EPS file of each brochure cover, and then create a marketing piece that shows all the brochure covers.

▶ **Steps: Saving a page as an EPS file**

Step 1. Open the document that contains the page you want to save.

Step 2. Choose File ➪ Save Page as EPS to display the Save Page as EPS dialog box, shown in Figure 11-16.

Step 3. Enter a name for the new EPS file in the File Name text box.

Step 4. Click the B&W radio button to save the page in black and white, or click the Color button to save the page as a color file.

Step 5. In the Page text box, enter the page number of the page you want to save as an EPS file.

Step 6. If you want to modify the scale of the page as you save it, enter a percentage value in the Scale text box; 50% (which is the default) reduces the page to half its original size.

Step 7. If you want to be able to view the EPS file on-screen before you place it in a picture box, click on the Include TIFF Preview box.

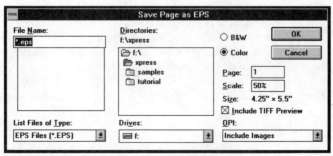

▶ **Figure 11-16:** The Save Page as EPS dialog box.

▶ **Figure 11-17:** An example of page saved as an EPS file and used as an illustration in another document.

Step 8. If you are using Open Prepress Interface, choose one of the following options in the OPI drop-down list. Your selection determines how pictures and comments are included with a page saved as an EPS file. (If you're not using OPI, don't worry about this step.)

■ **Include Images** includes pictures in TIFF and EPS formats and substitutes the low-resolution TIFF if the higher-resolution printing file for the pictures cannot be found. This option is the one used most often.

■ **Omit TIFF & EPS** omits both TIFF and EPS pictures in the file but includes OPI comments in the file for both types of pictures. If you are printing to an OPI prepress system that replaces TIFF and EPS pictures, choose this option.

The picture on the page in Figure 11-17 is a page saved as an EPS file.

■ ■

Summary

▶ Whenever you can, let the computer do the work for you, as it does when you use the Step and Repeat feature.

▶ If you add arrows or rules to a layout, keep them simple — light in line weight and plain in line type.

▶ Framing is useful for indicating keylines that a commercial printer uses when placing screens and halftones.

▶ As with rules, the best frames are simple. Understated rules work best.

▶ Anchoring text or picture boxes makes them behave the same as individual characters of text.

▶ Consider breaking a document into sections if it gets too long. When you do break it into sections, use the Section feature in the Page menu to apply section references to page numbers.

■ ■

PART IV

Typography and Text

Typographic treatment of text can be a subtle, yet powerful, part of your presentation. Although you define the basic look of your document with layout and styles, you give it texture and richness through the way you handle text. Until desktop publishing nearly eliminated the profession, typographers were artists who determined the details of how words looked on a printed page. They dealt with color, weight, and other subtleties that made text inviting and gave it added meaning.

QuarkXPress gives desktop publishers the tools that typographers used to enhance document aesthetics and content. With a little experimentation and a few guiding principles, you too can use these typographic tools to improve the aesthetic appeal and clarity of your documents.

CHAPTER

12

Understanding Character Spacing

- -

In This Chapter

▶ How to use tracking and kerning features

▶ Ways to alter word and letter spacing to change the appearance of text

▶ When and how to use character scaling and special fixed spaces

- -

Why Worry about Spacing?

Often ignored by novice publishers, *character spacing* is one of the fundamental tools you can use to enhance the look of a document. Character spacing encompasses several aspects: kerning, tracking, scale, and hyphenation. As a group, these four aspects determine what typographers call *color*.

Color essentially refers to how uniformly a block of text appears when you view it slightly out of focus. Look at several magazines that have a fair amount of text on a page. Then focus your vision on a spot between you and the page, causing the text to blur. The resulting gray level and consistency is color.

Color affects the readability and overall feel of a document. Generally speaking, a light to medium color is preferable, because it is easier on the eye.

Several factors influence color, the most fundamental being the typeface. An airy, light typeface such as New Baskerville has a light color, while an earthy, heavy typeface such as Tiffany Heavy has a dark color. Figure 12-1 shows the same text in these two typefaces. Notice how the text on the left, shown in New Baskerville, looks lighter than the Tiffany Heavy text on the right.

▶ **Figure 12-1:** Different typefaces produce different color.

How to Adjust Character Spacing

Regardless of a typeface's intrinsic weight, you can affect its color by adjusting character spacing. QuarkXPress gives you several different tools to accomplish this.

Tracking

Tracking has the greatest effect on color. Also called *letter spacing*, tracking is a setting for each tag that defines how much space is between individual letters in a document. The more space between letters — the looser the tracking — the lighter the color. When tracking is taken to an extreme, text begins to break up and lose color, because it no longer has consistency.

QuarkXPress sets the defaults for tracking at 0. This tells the program to use the letter spacing that the typeface's font file dictates in its width table.

In QuarkXPress, you can set tracking for each style and override tracking for any selected text.

▶ Steps: Setting tracking in a style sheet

Step 1. Access the Edit Style Sheet dialog box by selecting Edit ➪ Style Sheets ➪ New or Edit ➪ Style Sheets ➪ Edit, depending on whether you are creating a new style or editing an existing one.

Step 2. Select Character in the Edit Style Sheet dialog box to access the Character Attributes dialog box.

Step 3. Enter the tracking amount (in units from –100 to 100) in the Tracking blank. Use a minus sign (–) to reduce spacing (for tighter tracking).

QuarkXPress sets tracking in increments of 200ths (one-half percent) of an *em*, a measurement unit not known to most people. An em is the width of a capital letter *M* in the current type size. In most typefaces (decorative and symbol fonts are the main exceptions), an em is the same width as the current point size. So in 10-point Avant Garde or 10-point Times New Roman, an em is 10 points wide. Thus, reducing tracking by 20 units (or 10 percent) makes 10-point type 1 point closer together, 9-point type 0.9 points closer, 25-point type 2.5 points closer, and so on.

You'll rarely increase tracking, but doing so makes particularly good sense in two situations. One is in headlines that use heavy fonts. Text can look crowded unless you give it some typographical breathing room — known as *air* in typographers' parlance. You may also want to increase tracking to achieve a special effect that is increasingly popular: spreading out letters in a word or title so that letters are more than one character apart. This usually is used with all-caps text that is short, all on one line, and used as a kicker or other secondary label. Figure 12-2 shows an example of such a type treatment. Tracking in the highlighted text is set at 100 units, a very loose tracking setting.

If you're using small type (12 points or smaller) and placing it in narrow columns (16 picas or narrower), you'll probably want tighter tracking, because the eye more readily sees gaps between small forms and in narrow columns than it does between large forms and in wide columns. Settings from –2 to –10 should work for most common typefaces. Remember that the "best" amount of tracking is a decision based not on "right" or "wrong," but on personal aesthetics and the intended overall feel of the document.

Editing tracking tables

Although you can set tracking values in your style sheets, if you find yourself constantly applying tracking values to certain fonts, you may find it more convenient to alter the fonts' tracking tables. QuarkXPress provides an XTension to edit tracking values for TrueType and Adobe Type 1 PostScript typefaces. The tracking editor appears under the Utilities menu as Tracking Edit.

▶ **Figure 12-2:** The highlighted text, *GUEST EDITORIAL,* is an example of loose tracking.

With the tracking editor, you edit a line that defines the relationship between point size and tracking value. When you click on a point in the line, you create a turn point at which the direction of the line can change. Figure 12-3 shows a typical setting that tightens tracking for body text and small headline text (any text below 24 points in this example) to –10 units. Tracking for text 42 points and larger is left alone, while tracking for text between 42 and 24 points gets tighter as the point size decreases, changing gradually from 0 to –10 units.

The tracking editor treats each face of a typeface — such as plain, bold, italic, and bold italic — separately, so make sure you make tracking adjustments in all faces of the typefaces you alter. And keep in mind that the appropriate tracking values may be different for each face, especially for heavier faces like bold and ultra.

If you decide that your tracking table edits were misguided, you can reset them to the default setting, which is defined in the typeface's font files (it is usually 0), by selecting the Reset button. This works even if you already saved your settings and exited the tracking editor.

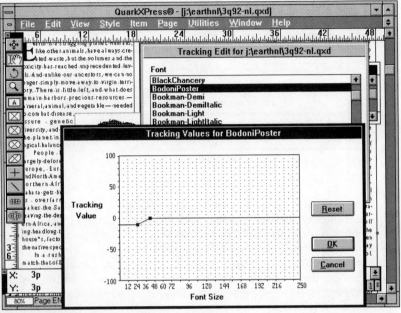

▶ **Figure 12-3:** The tracking editor.

 QuarkXPress associates an edited tracking table with the document that was active when you invoked the tracking editor. This means that if you give a service bureau your QuarkXPress document to output to negatives on an imagesetter, your tracking changes remain intact. If you want tracking changes to affect all your documents, invoke the tracking editor with no document selected. Any future document uses the new settings.

To apply the default values to a document in which you have changed spacing settings (including tracking), open the document. QuarkXPress automatically detects whether a document's settings match the defaults for that copy of QuarkXPress, and displays the dialog box shown in Figure 12-4. The dialog box also shows you which settings differ. Select Use XPress Preferences to apply the default settings.

Changing tracking on-the-fly

You can use the tracking editor to set tracking values permanently or use QuarkXPress style sheets to establish values for all text that uses a particular style. But there are several situations in which you may want to apply tracking on a case-by-case basis:

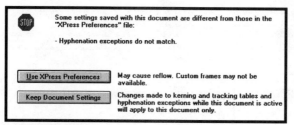

▶ **Figure 12-4:** Select default tracking values or retain document settings in this dialog box.

Copy fitting: Squeezing or, occasionally, stretching text to make it fit into a fixed amount of space is called *copy fitting.* You can do this to an entire story, but it is more common to retrack widows and any lines that have only a few characters (fewer than six or so), because you gain a whole line by forcing those characters to move into previous lines. You can also copy-fit by cutting out some text, but this requires the involvement of an editor, not just a production person, because meaning might be affected. Generally, you highlight one or two lines that seem to have excess space and reduce the tracking settings.

Removing widows and orphans: Even if fitting text within a certain space is not an issue, widows and orphans are frowned upon in serious publishing because they can look awkward.

When the last line of a paragraph consists of only a few characters, it is called a *widow.* This is considered typographically unsightly, particularly on a line that begins a column. How many characters constitutes a widow is personal judgment. We tend to consider anything shorter than a third of a line a widow. An *orphan* refers to the first line of a paragraph (which is indented) that begins at the bottom of a column. Orphans are less taboo than widows. We tend to not worry about them.

Creating special effects: You may want to stretch out certain words, such as *Note* or *Warning,* to create a special effect. Generally, stretched-out text is formatted in all caps or small caps. If you use this effect in labels or kickers that comprise a self-contained paragraph, it's better to create a style with these settings rather than apply the tracking manually.

Altering ellipses (. . .): Many people find the ellipsis character (generally available as Alt+0133 from the numeric keypad) too tightly spaced and so use three periods instead. If you don't like the amount of spacing QuarkXPress provides when you type three periods with default tracking settings, you can change the spacing through tracking. You cannot retrack the ellipsis character itself — spacing within the character doesn't change — so if you want to define the ellipsis via tracking, use three periods instead of the ellipsis character.

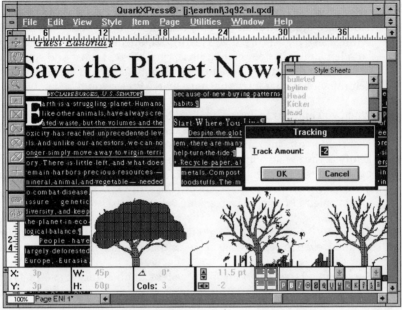

▶ **Figure 12-5:** The Tracking dialog box.

To apply new tracking values, select the text you want to retrack. (If you want to retrack all text in a story, use Edit ⇨ Select All to select all the text, rather than highlighting it with the mouse.) After you select the text, you can change the tracking values in three ways:

- **Option 1:** Select Style ⇨ Track and enter the tracking value in the Tracking dialog box, shown in Figure 12-5.

- **Option 2:** A faster way to change tracking values is to use the Measurements palette, which is also shown in Figure 12-5, at the bottom of the screen. The number to the right of the left and right triangles shows the current tracking value (–2). Highlight that number and enter a new value. Or click the triangles to change the values incrementally. Clicking the left-pointing triangle decreases the value, while clicking the right-pointing triangle increases the value. The triangles work only in multiples of 10 units.

- **Option 3:** The fastest method is to use the appropriate keyboard shortcut. Press Ctrl+Alt+Shift+} to increase tracking by one unit; press Ctrl+Alt+Shift+{ to decrease it by one unit. Pressing Ctrl+Shift+} increases tracking by 10 units; pressing Ctrl+Shift+{ decreases it by 10 units.

Applying tracking to justified text

Tracking settings are not the only influence on character spacing. Justification settings also play a role. If you justify document margins (aligning text against both left and right column margins), QuarkXPress must add space between words and characters to create that alignment. If tracking settings were the sole determinant of character spacing, QuarkXPress would be unable to justify text.

When you apply tracking to justified text, QuarkXPress applies tracking after the justification. That means if you specify tracking of –10 (equivalent to 5 percent tighter spacing) and QuarkXPress adds 2 percent more space on a line to justify it, the net spacing on that line is 3.1 percent (102 percent width for justification times 95 percent tracking: $1.02 \times .95 = 96.9$ — $100 – 96.9 = 3.1$ percent), or a tracking value of about –6. Nonetheless, the Tracking menu and the Measurements palette both show a tracking value of –10.

This is not a bug, but simply a reflection of how justified text has always been handled, even in typesetting systems that predate desktop publishing.

Keep in mind that any publishing system ignores tracking settings if that's the only way to justify a line.

You should realize that justification settings influence actual tracking, so set them to work in conjunction with tracking settings to meet your overall spacing goals.

To select justification spacing options, use the Edit Hyphenation and Justification dialog box, as described in the next section and in Chapter 13 in the section, "Hyphenation and Justification."

Word and letter spacing

In addition to overall space between characters, you should consider the space between words. Word spacing can be critical in helping readers separate words in text that would otherwise be confusing.

A good rule of thumb: The wider the column, the more space you should put between words. This is why books tend to have more word spacing than magazines. Like all other typographic issues, there's a subjective component to picking good word spacing. Experiment to see what works best in your documents.

QuarkXPress puts its word spacing features in its Edit Hyphenation and Justification menu, not with its other character spacing options. You access this menu through the Edit ➪ H&Js menu option. The default settings are stored as Standard. Make sure you modify Standard with your preferred word-spacing settings (called *H&J sets*) before creating other H&J sets, because they are based on Standard's settings.

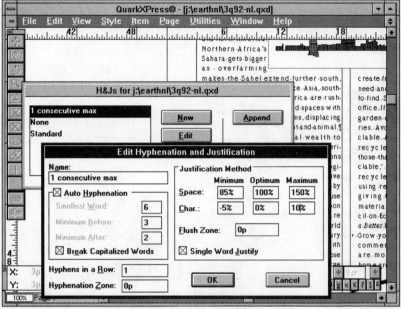

▶ **Figure 12-6:** The Edit Hyphenation and Justification dialog box.

Figure 12-6 shows the Edit Hyphenation and Justification dialog box. The Space and Char settings let you control how QuarkXPress adds spacing between characters and words to justify text. Space settings control word spacing; Char settings control letter spacing. The QuarkXPress default establishes the same value for the minimum and optimum settings, but they do not have to remain the same. However, you cannot set the optimum setting at less than the minimum or more than the maximum.

The *minimum* setting tells QuarkXPress the smallest amount of space allowed between words or characters. The *optimum* setting tells QuarkXPress the amount of space you want between words and characters, and QuarkXPress sets spacing as close to that setting as possible. The *maximum* setting tells QuarkXPress the upper limit on space between words or characters.

If your text is justified, QuarkXPress never places characters closer together than the minimum setting. But it may exceed the maximum setting if that's the only way to make the line fit. If your text is not justified (if it is left-aligned, right-aligned, or centered), QuarkXPress uses the optimum settings for all text.

▶ **Figure 12-7:** Default word-spacing settings (left) vs. the authors' recommended settings (right).

We prefer minimum settings that are less than the optimum, because that helps text fit more easily in narrow columns. Also, we have found that desktop publishing programs tend to add more space than we prefer, so we typically tighten the word and letter spacing to compensate. At the same time, we usually leave the maximum word spacing at 150 percent. Figure 12-7 compares the default settings to our preferences. The paragraph on the left uses QuarkXPress default settings; the one on the right uses the settings we recommend. As you can see, the paragraph on the right has fewer awkward gaps and takes up one less line of page space.

The settings shown in Figure 12-6 — 85 percent minimum, 100 percent optimum, and 150 percent maximum for word spacing and –5 percent minimum, 0 percent optimum, and 10 percent maximum for letter spacing — work well for most newsletters and magazines output on an imagesetter. For material destined for final output on a 300-dpi laser printer, you may want to keep the defaults, because laser printers have coarser resolution and thus cannot make some of the fine positioning adjustments our settings impose. In some cases, laser printers move characters closer together than desired, even when the same settings work fine on a higher resolution imagesetter.

The "Hyphenation and Justification" chapter later in this section describes how to use hyphenation settings in concert with letter and word spacing.

Kerning

Kerning tells the output device — such as a laser printer, typesetter, monitor, or film recorder — to add or, more typically, subtract, a certain amount of space between specific pairs of letters any time those pairs occur in a document, so that their spacing seems natural. The information on what pairs of letters to kern and how much to kern them by is stored in the font file as a *kerning table*.

Without kerning, some letters may appear to be farther apart than other letters in the same word, tricking the eye into thinking they are in fact in different words. You can see an example of this in Figure 12-8. On the top line of the figure, the unkerned letter pairs *AV* and *to* appear far enough apart that the eye may perceive them as belonging to separate words. Kerning adjusts the spacing to prevent this problem, as shown in the bottom line of the figure.

Kerning is important for all large type. The larger the characters, the larger the space between them, and thus any awkward spacing becomes more noticeable. For smaller type, kerning is often not noticeable, because the space between letters is already so small.

Because kerning requires QuarkXPress to look at every pair of letters to see whether they have special kerning values, turning on this feature for all text can slow down screen display considerably. To get around this problem, QuarkXPress offers the Auto Kern Above feature, which you turn on and off through the Edit ⇨ Preferences ⇨ Typographic dialog box. This option tells QuarkXPress to stop kerning when text reaches a certain size. Any text at or below the size you specify is not kerned.

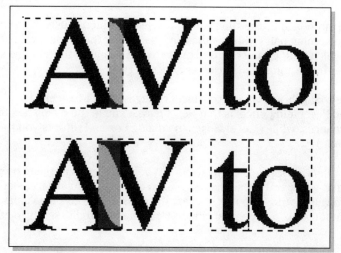

▶ **Figure 12-8:** Unkerned letter pairs (top) and kerned pairs (bottom).

The cut-off size you choose for Auto Kern Above is both a personal choice, based on aesthetic judgment, and a technical choice, based on the output device. The relatively low resolution on a 300-dpi laser printer limits how fine you can adjust spacing between characters. But on a 1270- or 2540-dpi imagesetter, there is practically no limit to how much control you have over spacing, so you should take advantage of it.

A rule of thumb is to set Auto Kern Above between 8 and 12 points. It makes sense to set Auto Kern Above to your basic body text size, and for most people, basic body text size falls between 8 and 12 points. If your base text is 9 points, set Auto Kern Above to 9 points. However, use a small value (8 or 9) for any text you output to a 600-dpi or finer device, regardless of the size of your body text.

Editing kerning tables

Often, the kerning table for a font may not match your preferences for some letter pairs. In some cases, the table may not include kerning information for certain letter pairs that cause you trouble. Quark bundles an XTension with Quark-XPress so you can edit kerning information for any TrueType or Adobe Type 1 PostScript typeface. It appears under the Utilities menu as Kerning Table Edit. You can modify existing settings, add new pairs, or remove existing pairs.

Figure 12-9 shows the kerning editor. Predefined kerning values display in the Kerning Values window, through which you can scroll to select pairs whose values you want to change. To add your own pairs, enter the two letters at the Pair prompt. In either case, enter the kerning value at the Value prompt. If you are modifying existing kerning values, select Replace; if you are adding a kerning pair, the button will be labeled Add. As with tracking, the unit of measurement is ¹⁄₂₀₀ of an em, or roughly one-half percent of the current point size. Negative values decrease space between the letters, positive numbers add space.

Related options in the kerning editor are Delete, which is used to delete the selected kerning pair (which is the same as setting the kerning value to 0), and Reset, which undoes any changes made to the kerning values in this session (changes made and saved earlier are *not* reset).

To save changes, select OK. To cancel changes, select Cancel. (The difference between Reset and Cancel is that Reset leaves you in the dialog box to make other changes, while Cancel closes the dialog box and returns you to your document.)

The kerning editor treats each face of a typeface — such as plain, bold, italic, and bold italic — separately, so make kerning adjustments in all faces of the typefaces you alter. And keep in mind that the appropriate kerning values are different for each face because characters are shaped differently in each face.

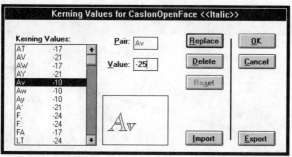

▶ **Figure 12-9:** The kerning table editor.

QuarkXPress associates an edited kerning table with the document that was active when you invoked the kerning editor. This means that if you give your QuarkXPress document to a service bureau to output to negatives on an imagesetter, your kerning changes remain intact.

If you want kerning changes to affect all documents, invoke the kerning editor with no document selected. Any future document uses the new settings.

To apply your default settings to a document with altered preferences (including kerning), open the document and select Use XPress Preferences when QuarkXPress asks whether to use the default settings or the document's settings. QuarkXPress automatically detects whether a document's settings matches the defaults for that copy of QuarkXPress.

The kerning editor also has options to import and export kerning tables, through the Import and Export buttons. Kerning tables have the KRN filename extension and may be saved on any drive or directory. This is valuable if you want to ensure that all PCs (and Macs) in your office use the same kerning information or that clients or service bureaus use the same kerning values you do.

Changing kerning on-the-fly

At times, you may want to manually kern specific letter pairs. Your document may incorporate typefaces you use so rarely that it's not worthwhile to modify the kerning table, for example. QuarkXPress enables you to modify kerning on the fly for any letter pairs you select. Put your text cursor between the two letters. You now have three ways to change the kerning values:

■ **Option 1:** Select Style ➪ Kern and enter the kerning value in the Kerning dialog box, shown in Figure 12-10.

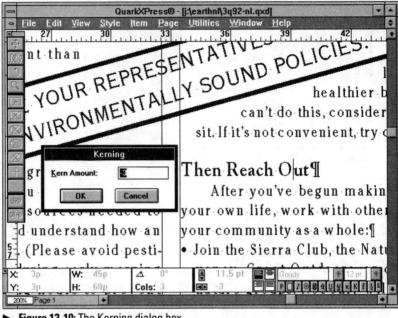

▶ **Figure 12-10:** The Kerning dialog box.

■ **Option 2:** A faster method is to use the Measurements palette. The number to the right of the left and right triangles shows the current kerning value (–3). Highlight that number and enter a new value. Or click the triangles to change the values incrementally: The left-pointing triangle decreases the value while the right-pointing one increases the value. Both triangles work only in multiples of ten units.

■ **Option 3:** The fastest way to change kerning values, especially when you want to experiment, is to use the keyboard shortcuts. Pressing Ctrl+Alt+Shift+} increases kerning by one unit; Ctrl+Alt+Shift+{ decreases it by one unit. Ctrl+Shift+} increases kerning by ten units; Ctrl+Shift+{ decreases it by ten units.

If you highlight characters rather than place the text cursor between the two characters you want to kern, QuarkXPress displays Track instead of Kern in dialog boxes and menus. Tracking is discussed in detail earlier in this chapter.

Horizontal scale

One unusual but occasionally effective way to influence typographic color is to change the typeface's horizontal scale. This compresses or expands the actual characters (rather than the space between the characters) to a percentage,

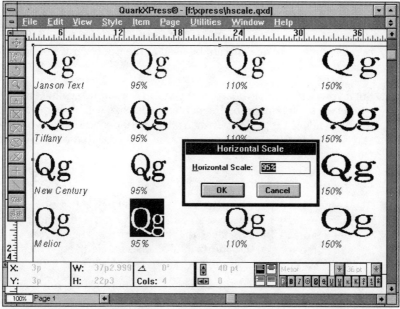

▶ **Figure 12-11:** The Horizontal Scale dialog box.

ranging from 25 to 400 percent, in 0.1 percent increments. The Horizontal Scale option is available from the Style menu. Figure 12-11 shows the dialog box that appears when you choose Horizontal Scale.

You do not need to enter the percent symbol (%) when you enter the scaling value. QuarkXPress automatically assumes the value is a percentage.

Scaled text can be useful in several applications:

■ To fit text in the available space.

■ To call attention to display type, such as drop caps, headlines, or other type-as-design elements.

■ To create a different feel for an existing typeface that might otherwise not be appropriate for the use intended. An example is compressing wide typefaces for use as body text.

A traditional typographer would blanche at the thought of scaling type, because each typeface is designed to be displayed optimally at a certain weight and size. (That's why the *hinting* pioneered by Adobe in its Type1 PostScript fonts, as well as in TrueType fonts, was such a breakthrough: it automatically adjusts the typeface's characteristics for various sizes. And that's why boldface is more than just fatter characters and italics is more than just slanted characters.)

When you change a typeface's scale, you distort the design that was so carefully crafted. Instead, a traditional typographer would argue, use existing expanded or compressed (also called condensed) versions of the typeface, because they were designed to be used at their percentage of horizontal scaling.

But if you don't go overboard, you can use horizontal scaling effectively. Scaling a typeface to 50 percent or 150 percent of its size will likely destroy its character. But scaling a typeface between 90 and 110 percent often works well, and staying between 95 and 105 percent results in type that is not noticeably different, yet distinct.

Pay attention to the kind of typeface you scale:

- A sans serif typeface such as Eurostile, Helvetica, or Univers works best, because its generally even shape has fewer intricate elements that might get distorted. But typefaces that have darker vertical strokes (the constituent components) than horizontal strokes can look odd when expanded much. Optima is an example of such a typeface.

- Many serif typefaces work fine if horizontally scaled only slightly. Squarer typefaces such as Melior and New Century Schoolbook lend themselves best to scaling without perceived distortion. When you slightly compress wide typefaces such as Tiffany, which are normally used for headlines and other display type, they can acquire a new feel that makes them usable as body text. Finer typefaces such as Janson Text more quickly become distorted, because the differences between the characters' already shallow horizontal strokes and already thicker vertical strokes become more noticeable — especially when expanded.

- Avoid scaling decorative typefaces such as Brush Script, Dom Casual, and Park Avenue. However, Zapf Chancery can be scaled slightly without looking distorted.

Figure 12-12 shows sample scaling on four common typefaces. For more dramatic scaling effects, use a typeface editing program such as Altsys's Fontographer or ZSoft's SoftType. These programs enable you to edit the actual shapes of each character, so you can create a more heavily compressed or expanded variant of the typeface that does not look distorted.

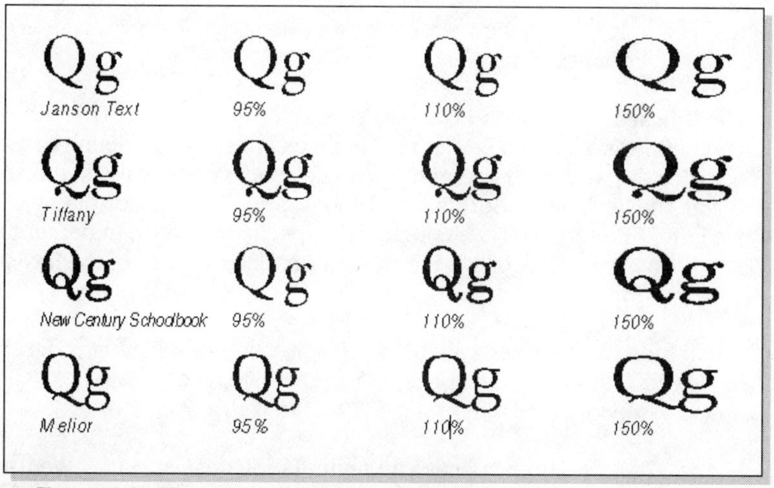

▶ **Figure 12-12:** Effects of scaling on four typefaces.

Special Spaces

In some cases, you may want to impose specific kinds of spacing, rather than rely on the normal spaces, whose width is affected by tracking and justification settings. QuarkXPress provides several special space options:

Nonbreaking space: This space ensures that a line does not wrap between two words if you do not want it to. The command is Ctrl+spacebar.

En space: An en space (press Ctrl+Shift+6) is typically used in numbered lists after the period following the numeral. An en space makes a number more visible, because the number is separated more from the following text than words in the text are separated from each other. En spaces also are used before single-digit numerals when a numbered list includes both single- and double-digit numerals. (In most typefaces, a numeral occupies the width of an en space. So putting an en space before numerals 1 through 9 aligns them with the 0 in the number 10.) A variation of the en space is the *nonbreaking en space*, accessed by pressing Ctrl+Alt+Shift+6.

Punctuation space: A punctuation space, accessed via Shift+spacebar, is the width of a period or comma. It is typically used to ensure alignment of numerals when some numbers have commas and others don't — as in 1,083 and 612. To align the last three digits of both numbers, you place an en space and a punctuation space before 612. A variation is the *nonbreaking punctuation space*, accessed via Ctrl+Shift+spacebar.

Some people call a punctuation space a thin space; regardless, it is generally half the width of an en space.

Flexible space: Unique to QuarkXPress, a flexible space (Ctrl+Shift+5) is a space you define as a certain percentage of an en space. If you define a flexible space as twice the width (200 percent) of an en space, you create an em space. You define the flex space width in the Typographic Preferences dialog box, accessed via Edit ⇨ Preferences ⇨ Typographic. Specify the width in percentages from 0 to 400, in increments of 0.1. For the nonbreaking variant of the flex space, press Ctrl+Alt+Shift+5.

A common fixed space available in most desktop publishing programs, but not in QuarkXPress, is an em space. You can create an em space by using two en spaces or by defining a flex space to be the width of an em.

Figure 12-13 shows en spaces and punctuation spaces in use. We used en spaces and punctuation spaces to align the numbers in the first column of numbers (under *"Trees planted"*). We also used an en space before the "9" in the top paragraph so that it right-aligned with the "10" in the following paragraph, and we used an en space after the numbers in those two paragraphs to make the numbers in the list more visible.

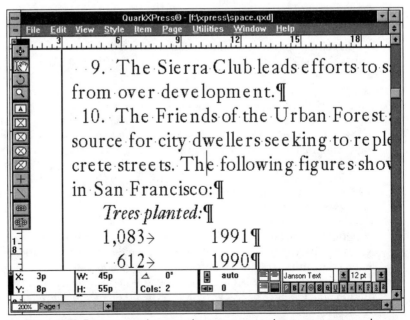

▶ **Figure 12-13:** En spaces and punctuation spaces control text appearance and alignment.

■ ■

Summary

▶ Typographic attributes can be set both in style sheets and on selected text. Attributes set on selected text override any attributes set via a previously selected style sheet item.

▶ Tracking determines spacing between all characters to optimize overall appearance. Kerning determines spacing between two specific characters to optimize their appearance. QuarkXPress uses the same menu option for both, although the label changes depending on whether multiple characters are highlighted (tracking) or the text cursor is between two characters (kerning).

▶ Use tighter tracking for small text in narrow columns as opposed to wide columns. Use loose tracking for large text set in dark or heavy typefaces.

▶ Use more word spacing for wide columns, less for narrow columns. Set the minimum word spacing to be less than the optimum word spacing, giving QuarkXPress sufficient flexibility when justifying text.

▶ Use Utilities ➪ Tracking Edit to globally change tracking for a particular typeface throughout a document, regardless of which style tag is applied. You can set the typeface's tracking to be different for different text sizes. Tracking settings in style tags and those applied locally will augment global tracking settings, not replace them.

▶ Use Utilities ➪ Kerning Table Edit to permanently change kerning-pair values for a particular typeface in your document. These values may be exported for use in other documents.

▶ Use interactive tracking as the first option to fix widows and orphans.

▶ If necessary to properly justify text, QuarkXPress will override maximum word-spacing and tracking settings by adding more space. But, in an effort to justify text, it will not bring text closer together by overriding minimum word-spacing settings.

▶ Set automatic kerning to 8 points if you intend to typeset your document; leave it at 10 points if you intend to use a 300-dpi laser printer.

▶ Use horizontal scaling judiciously and sparingly.

▶ An en space is usually the same as the width of a numeral, so it makes a good placeholder when aligning numbers. Likewise, a punctuation space makes a good placeholder when aligning numbers that contain commas or decimal points.

▶ By defining a flex space to be 200 percent, you create an em space, which is often used as the paragraph indent value in multicolumn layouts.

■ ■

CHAPTER

13

Understanding Paragraph Spacing

- -

In This Chapter

▶ How to use leading in your documents

▶ Techniques to ensure consistent vertical alignment

▶ When and how to use other vertical spacing features

▶ How hyphenation and justification affect paragraph spacing, and how to set them

- -

The Many Aspects of Paragraph Spacing

Paragraph spacing plays an important role in determining how accessible text appears column after column, page after page. Even if character spacing creates blocks of text that have good color, bad paragraph spacing can keep readers from committing to reading that well-colored text.

Effective paragraph spacing takes into account many factors, from the length of paragraphs — make them too deep and readers skip them — to the justification method. Balancing these attributes is critical to deriving good overall spacing. But no matter what techniques you use, keep in mind that the overall goal is to move the reader through the text, using contrast to create visual divisions and using uniformity to create cohesion.

The Importance of Leading

Tracking, kerning, and word spacing let you establish good typographic color horizontally. *Leading* lets you do the same vertically. Named for the bits of lead that printers used to separate metal type in early printing presses, leading varies based on several elements: column width, type size, whether text is justified or ragged, and total amount of text, as explained later.

Determining leading settings

There are several ways to set leading. One is in the Paragraph Formats dialog box of the Edit ➪ Style Sheet option. Another is through the Style ➪ Leading menu (the shortcut is Ctrl+Shift+E). A third is through the Measurements palette. The number to the right of the up and down triangles reflects the current leading setting, which you can highlight and change or raise or lower incrementally by clicking on the up or down triangles.

The most important factor affecting good leading is column width. The wider the column, the more space you need between lines to keep the reader's eye from accidentally jumping to a different line. That's why books have noticeable space between lines while newspapers and magazines, which use thin columns, have what seems to be no space at all.

A related concern is whether type is justified or ragged-right. Justified text usually requires more leading than nonjustified text, because the ragged margin gives the eye a distinct anchor point for each line.

For multicolumn text, a good rule of thumb is to set leading at the current point size plus 2 points for text 9 points and larger. For text 8 points and smaller, a standard measurement is the current point size plus 1 point. Add another 1 point or half point, respectively, if your column width is greater than 16 picas but less than 27 picas; add at least 2 more points if your text is wider than 27 picas.

You can alter the feeling of text by making small changes in leading and point size, as you can see in Figure 13-1. Even though the typeface and justification are the same, the text on the left, set at 9.5-point Janson Text with 11-point leading, has a very different texture than the text on the right, set at 9-point Janson Text with 11.5-point leading. This creative use of leading lets you subtly but effectively differentiate between sections or elements without resorting to extreme use of typefaces or layout variations.

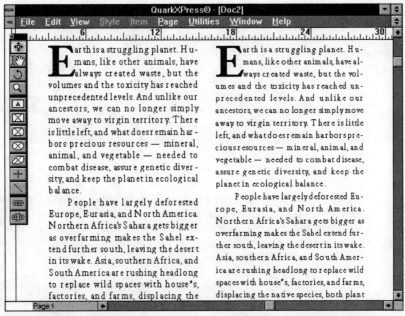

▶ **Figure 13-1:** Small changes in leading and point size make a dramatic difference.

Most programs, including QuarkXPress, offer an automatic leading option, which usually sets leading at 120 percent of text size. This is fine for 10-point type, because it results in 12-point leading. But for 9-point type, it results in 10.8-point leading, which is an awkward size on which to base a layout grid. And at larger type sizes, leading becomes too large; for example, 43.2-point leading is set for 36-point text.

Although it provides an auto leading option (enter **0** or **auto** as the leading value), QuarkXPress also offers a better alternative. You can set leading to be a certain number of points more than the current type size, no matter what the type size. Enter **+2**, for example, for leading 2 points more than the current type size. This *additive leading* option also ensures that any line that has larger-than-normal type (such as a drop cap) won't overprint other lines.

Additive leading has a drawback. If you use superscripts (perhaps for footnotes), subscripts, or special text or symbols that extend beyond the body text's height or depth, you get uneven spacing. This is because some lines have more leading than others to accommodate the outsized or outpositioned characters. QuarkXPress bases the additive leading on the highest and lowest character in a line, not on the body text's normal position. If you can't alter your text so that none of it extends beyond the body text range, don't use this option. Instead, specify the actual leading you want in each style tag.

Maintaining consistent vertical alignment

As important as using appropriate leading values is ensuring that vertical alignment is consistent. (Although the goal is to ensure that lines in a column align
horizontally, this method is called *vertical* alignment, because layout artists
must move the text in the columns vertically to ensure correct alignment.) Before desktop publishing, it was not uncommon for columns to be slightly out of
alignment horizontally, because lining up strips of text by hand is nearly impossible to do precisely. (This is still the case in many newspapers and in some
magazines produced with old-fashioned techniques.) Being within a point or
two was considered adequate. No longer. Uneven type columns today smack of
amateurism.

QuarkXPress offers two settings in the Typographic Preferences dialog box to
prevent this problem. If set properly, QuarkXPress's Baseline Grid Increment
and Maintain Leading controls eliminate such slight misalignments. You access
these settings through the Typographic Preferences dialog box, shown in Figure
13-2 (select Edit ➪ Preferences ➪ Typographic).

Used with the Lock to Baseline Grid option in the Paragraph Formats dialog box
(accessed by selecting Style ➪ Formats), the Baseline Grid Increment feature
enables you to ensure that the baselines — the bottoms of your letters — lock
onto the grid lines you set for a document. Any text tagged with a style that has
the baseline grid locked is automatically positioned to align with the document
grid, ensuring that text aligns across columns.

Misalignment is most noticeable in body text, which is your most common text.
So set your baseline grid to be the same as the leading for body text, and make
sure to check the Lock to Baseline Grid option in the paragraph style for that
body text (usually called *Normal*).

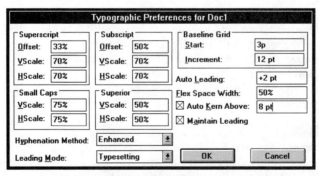

▶ **Figure 13-2:** Establish global leading control settings in the
Typographic Preferences dialog box.

Do *not* use the Lock to Baseline <u>G</u>rid option on text whose style has different leading settings, as this could result in awkward spacing between lines in text of that style. For example, if your body text has 11-point leading but your sub-heads have 15-point leading, turning on the baseline lock option forces Quark-XPress to move the subhead to the next grid point, which is either 11 or 22 points below the previous line of body text. This occurs even though you set the leading for the subhead style to place the subhead 15 points after the previ-ous line of body text.

You can ensure consistent vertical alignment by putting some thought into your styles when you create them. If you do this, you don't have to use the Lock to Baseline <u>G</u>rid option and can avoid some of the problems associated with it. You won't have to worry if you have styles with different leading amounts or if additive leading causes some lines to have different leading than others.

For example, when you pick 11.5 points as body-text leading, make sure other text elements add up to multiples of 11.5. If subheads are 14 points, give them 16-point leading and put 7 points of space above them (a total of 23 points, or two body-text lines) or 18.5 points of space above (a total of 34.5 points, or three body-text lines). If the byline is 8 points, give it a leading of 9.5 with 2 points of space above or below it. In both cases, make sure that these other ele-ments do not take more than one line. Otherwise, the leading from the second line means that their total vertical space is no longer a multiple of 11.5. If you cannot ensure this, create a tag with the same leading but different space above (and maybe below) to use when the text in these paragraphs takes two lines.

The M<u>a</u>intain Leading option in the Typographic Preferences dialog box main-tains proper leading for text that falls under an intervening text box, such as one that contains a sidebar, picture, or pull-quote. If you check this option, the line following a text box is positioned an even multiple of lines under the last line above the text box, ensuring vertical alignment across all columns. If you turn this option off, text is positioned immediately after the text box, which may not be the right position to align it with other columns.

Choosing the correct leading mode

A global setting related to leading control is Leading <u>M</u>ode. With very few ex-ceptions, you should set this at Typesetting, which measures leading from baseline to baseline. The first version of QuarkXPress measured leading from top of text to top of text, which Quark calls Word Processing mode. This mode is not used in professional publishing, and even many old word-processing tem-plates were based on measuring leading from the baseline. Unless you have a specific reason to select Word Processing mode, leave this setting at the default Typesetting mode.

Additional Paragraph Spacing

In addition to leading, you can also specify the amount of space above or below paragraphs, as well as indents from the right and left margins. You do this in the Paragraph Formats dialog box, shown in Figure 13-3. To access the dialog box for individual paragraphs, select Style ➪ Formats (the keyboard shortcut is Ctrl+Shift+F). For styles, access the dialog box via the Formats button in the Edit Style Sheet dialog box (accessed via Edit ➪ Style Sheets).

By using the indent and space options, you can call attention to a paragraph by offsetting it from surrounding paragraphs. In Figure 13-3, we selected Left Indent, Right Indent, Space Before, and Space After to frame the paragraph with extra space on all four sides.

Don't overdo extra paragraph spacing. The effect's success depends on its being used rarely. Common uses include indenting a long quotation or highlighting a recommendation. You need not alter all four options as we did in the example in Figure 13-3; typically, a left indent is sufficient to offset a paragraph from surrounding text.

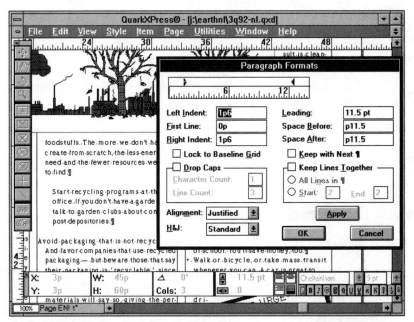

▶ **Figure 13-3:** The Paragraph Formats dialog box.

The Space Before and Space After options are also useful in positioning elements such as bylines, pull-quotes, and subheads that don't follow the same leading grid as the body text. In addition, you can use these options to ensure that the grid is maintained despite the use of larger or smaller type sizes for these elements, as discussed in "Maintaining consistent vertical alignment," earlier in this chapter.

Hyphenation and Justification

Hyphenation and justification are not always thought of as influencing typographic color, but they do. Both have a great impact on the shape of text, which is an important part of the impression the text conveys.

QuarkXPress treats these features as related. Although you set justification for individual styles through the Edit Style Sheet dialog box, you set the justification method in a more basic setting, through H&J sets defined in the Edit Hyphenation and Justification dialog box, accessed via Edit ⇨ H&Js.

In the Edit Hyphenation and Justification dialog box, shown in Figure 13-4, you set up H&J sets that control hyphenation and justification parameters for any styles based on them. A document can have different H&J sets, which lets you combine several typographic and layout approaches in the same document.

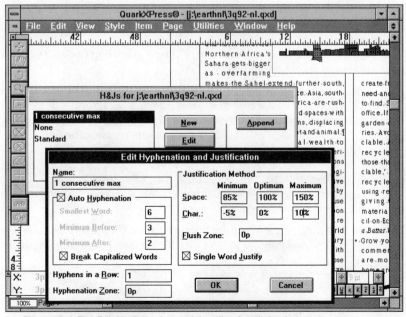

▶ **Figure 13-4:** The Edit Hyphenation and Justification dialog box.

If you want to use H&J sets from another document in your current document, select the Append option in the H&Js dialog box. Also choose this option if you establish master settings when no document is open. This lets you append (copy) all the H&J sets from existing documents and templates. Note that any H&J sets in the current document (or master settings) that have the same name as sets you append from the other document are not altered.

You can tell you are editing master H&J sets when the dialog box title is `Default H&Js` instead of `H&Js for filename`.

Justification methods

The two main justification methods — Space and Char — control how QuarkXPress spaces words and letters to align text against both margins of a column. Because justification requires QuarkXPress to figure out where and how much space to add line by line, it needs some guidance on how to do so. That's where the three options — *minimum, optimum,* and *maximum* — or the two justification methods come into play.

Essentially, *minimum* justification settings tell QuarkXPress how much it can squeeze text to make it fit in a justified line, while the *maximum* settings tell the program how much it can stretch text to make it fit. QuarkXPress does not squeeze text more than the minimum settings allow, but it does exceed the maximum settings if it has no other choice. If text is not justified, QuarkXPress uses the *optimum* settings for all text. The Space and Char. options that control these settings are discussed in more detail in Chapter 12, "Understanding Character Spacing."

When you use justified text, QuarkXPress gives you two more options: Flush Zone and Single Word Justify.

- The Flush Zone setting, measured from the right margin, tells QuarkXPress when to take the text in the last line of a paragraph and force it to justify against both margins. (Normally, the last line of a justified paragraph is aligned to the left.) If text in the last line reaches the *flush zone,* it is justified; otherwise it remains left-aligned.

We recommend that you do not use the Flush Zone feature. When the last line in a justified paragraph is left-aligned, it gives the reader a needed clue that the paragraph is complete.

- Selecting Single Word Justify tells QuarkXPress it is OK to space out a word that is long enough to take up a single line if needed to justify that line.

We recommend that you always turn on Single Word Justify, even though words that take up a full line are rare. When they do occur, having them left-aligned (which is what happens if this option is not selected) in a paragraph that is otherwise justified is confusing, because readers might misinterpret them as the end of the paragraph.

Hyphenation settings

Hyphenation settings determine the "raggedness" of nonjustified text (text that is left-aligned, right-aligned, or centered) and the size of gaps in justified text (where text is aligned against both the left and right margins of a column). By varying the hyphenation settings, you can achieve a significantly different feel, as illustrated in Figure 13-5.

In the figure, the two left columns are identical, even though the leftmost is set at unlimited hyphenations and the second is set at three consecutive hyphens maximum, because there are not enough long words in the text to force many consecutive hyphenations. But the third column, where hyphenation is turned off, has several awkward gaps and takes an extra line of page space. The right–most column is set as justified text with unlimited hyphenation, showing the difference between left-aligned and justified text.

To turn hyphenation on, make sure the Auto Hyphenation box is checked. We also recommend turning on Break Capitalized Words. Although some traditionalists argue against hyphenating proper names, and some pragmatists do not use this feature because most hyphenation dictionaries make mistakes with many proper names, there is no compelling reason not to treat proper names

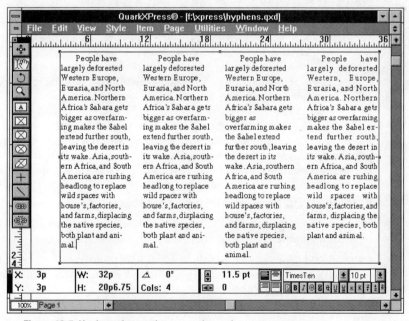

▶ **Figure 13-5:** Hyphenation settings can alter column appearance.

as you do any other text. If the program improperly hyphenates proper names, add them to your document's exception dictionary (described in Chapter 17) rather than prohibiting their hyphenation.

Controlling the hyphenation zone

Generally, you want a consistent variation in nonjustified text. In traditional typography, this *rag*, as uneven line endings are called, is manually modified to give it a pleasing shape. This is done by retracking some lines or manually inserting hyphens. A "pleasing shape" is usually defined as one that undulates and has few consecutive lines of roughly the same width.

QuarkXPress lets you partially control the rag of nonjustified text through Hyphenation Zone control, found in the Edit Hyphenation and Justification dialog box. A setting of 0 tells QuarkXPress to hyphenate whenever it can. Any other setting specifies the range in which a hyphen can occur; this number is measured from the right margin. You won't often need this feature, because QuarkXPress does a decent job of ragging text on its own. But if you do use it, a setting no more than 20 percent of the column width usually works best. No matter what settings you use, expect to occasionally override QuarkXPress through manual hyphenation to make the rag match your preferences.

Limiting the number of consecutive hyphens

The more hyphens you allow, the more easily QuarkXPress can break lines to avoid awkward gaps (in justified text) or awkward line endings (in nonjustified text). But too many hyphens in a row results in text that is hard to read. The eye gets confused about which line it is on, because it loses track of which hyphen represents which line. You control the number of consecutive hyphens by selecting a setting in the Hyphens In A Row option box.

A good setting for Hyphens In A Row is 3 consecutive hyphens. This gives the eye enough context to keep lines in sequence without unduly constraining the publishing program. Avoid having fewer than two consecutive hyphens as your maximum, because that typically results in awkward spacing.

Setting word hyphenation parameters

How a publishing program hyphenates is determined in large part by *word hyphenation parameters*. There are three such parameters:

- Smallest Word determines how small a word must be before QuarkXPress hyphenates it. The default of six letters is a reasonable default, although five is acceptable as well.

■ Minimum <u>B</u>efore determines how many characters must precede a hyphen in a hyphenated word. The default of three characters is a typical typog–rapher's threshold. Consider changing the setting to 2 if you have narrow columns or large text. While many typographers object to two-letter hy-phenation — as in *Af- rica* or *ra- dar* — it often looks better than text with large gaps caused by the reluctance to hyphenate such words. It also makes sense for many words that use two-letter prefixes such as *in-* , *re-* , and *co-* .

■ Minimum <u>A</u>fter determines how many characters must follow a hyphen in a hyphenated word. The default setting of two characters is common for newspapers and is most often seen in words ending in *-ed*, such as *edit- ed*. Although it may seem to contradict our rationale for advocating two-letter hyphenation at the beginning of a word, we prefer three-letter hyphenation at the end. Except for words ending in *-ed* and sometimes *-al,* most words don't lend themselves to two-letter hyphenation at the end of the word. Part of this is functional — it's easy for readers to lose two letters beginning a line. We prefer two-letter hyphenations at the end of a word only when the alternative is awkward spacing. As with all typography, this ultimately is a personal choice.

Never use a minimum setting of 1 for Minimum <u>B</u>efore. If you do, you get hy-phenations such as *A- sia, a- synchronous* and *u- nique* that simply look terrible in print. They also don't provide enough context for the reader to anticipate the rest of the word. Likewise, never use a minimum of 1 for Minimum <u>A</u>fter, be-cause you get hyphenations such as *radi- o*. Again, words broken in this manner look awful in print. They also go against reader expectations, because the norm is to have several letters after a hyphen.

Hyphenation overrides

To override hyphenation settings for a paragraph, use the Paragraph Formats dialog box, shown in Figure 13-6. You can apply a different H&J set to the cur-rently selected paragraphs by selecting a new set in the dialog box. This comes in handy if, for example, you want to disallow hyphenation in a particular para-graph without affecting the rest of the text.

To access the dialog box, select <u>S</u>tyle ➪ For<u>m</u>ats or press the keyboard short-cut Ctrl+Shift+F, and then change the H&J setting to an appropriate H&J set (de-fined in the <u>E</u>dit ➪ <u>H</u>&Js dialog box). If you want to disallow hyphenation for a specific paragraph, insert your text cursor anywhere on the paragraph and go to the Paragraph Formats dialog box. Select None (or whatever you named the H&J set that disallows hyphenation) as the new H&J setting. Other paragraphs using the same style are unaffected by this local override.

Paragraph Formats

| 3 | 6 | 9 |

Left Indent: `0p`   Leading: `11.5 pt`
First Line: `1p6`   Space Before: `0p`
Right Indent: `0p`   Space After: `0p`
☐ Lock to Baseline Grid   ☐ Keep with Next ¶
☐ Drop Caps   ☐ Keep Lines Together
 Character Count: `1`   ○ All Lines in ¶
 Line Count: `3`   ○ Start: `2` End: `2`

Alignment: `Justified`   **Apply**
H&J: `Standard`
  1 consecutive
  None
  Standard

OK   **Cancel**

▶ **Figure 13-6:** Choose hyphenation settings through the Paragraph Formats dialog box.

Most of the time, you want to change the place in a particular word where QuarkXPress inserts the hyphen rather than to override the style settings for a particular paragraph. QuarkXPress lets you do this through its soft hyphen feature.

To manually insert a soft hyphen, type Ctrl+- between the letters you want the hyphen to separate. This soft hyphen "disappears" if the word moves (due to the addition or deletion of text, for example) to a place where a hyphen is not appropriate. Should the word and its soft hyphen move to a spot where a word break is appropriate, the hyphen reappears.

The only way to locate a soft hyphen is to use the arrow keys to move your text cursor through a word. When the tracking/kerning display (the left and right triangles with a number to their right) disappear from the Measurements palette, your cursor is on a soft hyphen.

If a word is already hyphenated, the soft hyphen overrides QuarkXPress's hyphenation of the word. The program uses the soft hyphen rather than the setting in the hyphenation dictionary. You can prevent hyphenation altogether by putting a soft hyphen at the beginning of a word.

If you are not sure how to properly hyphenate a word, QuarkXPress's Suggested Hyphenation feature can help. To access the Suggested Hyphenation dialog box, shown in Figure 13-7, select Utilities ⇨ Suggested Hyphenation or use the keyboard shortcut Ctrl+H. QuarkXPress shows the recommended hyphenation settings for the current word (or, if more than one word is selected, for the first word in the selection).

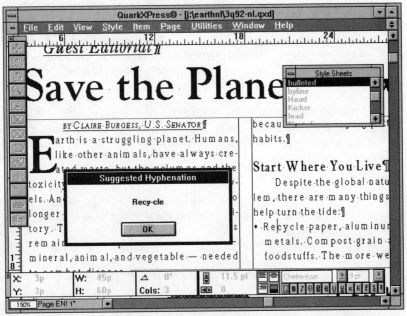

► **Figure 13-7:** The Suggested Hyphenation dialog box.

 The Suggested Hyphenation feature takes into account the current H&J set. If the set specifies that no hyphen may be inserted until after the first three letters of a word, the Suggested Hyphenation dialog box does not show any legal hyphenations that may exist after the second letter in the word. While handy, this feature does not replace a dictionary as the final authority.

Inserting manual hyphens repeatedly into the same words is more work than necessary. Instead, add your own hyphenation preferences to QuarkXPress through the hyphenation-exception dictionary feature. You do this through the Hyphenation Exceptions dialog box, shown in Figure 13-8. To access the dialog box, select Utilities ➪ Hyphenation Exceptions.

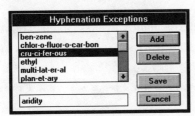

► **Figure 13-8:** The Hyphenation Exceptions dialog box.

By adding words to the hyphenation dictionary, you can give QuarkXPress hyphenation instructions for words the program does not know, hyphenates incorrectly, or hyphenates differently than your stylebook specifies. Additionally, you can prevent hyphenation of specific words by adding them to the dictionary. This dictionary can be global, affecting all documents, or local, affecting only the current document.

As you add words, indicate allowable hyphenation points by inserting hyphens. To prevent a word from hyphenating, type it in without hyphens. You can change existing hyphenation exceptions by clicking on the word you want to change. The Add button is replaced by the Replace button, and whatever word you type in replaces the one highlighted.

If you are in a document that does not use the standard QuarkXPress preferences, any hyphenation exceptions you enter affect only that document. To define hyphenation exceptions you want to use globally, close all active documents (to be sure that your changes are saved in the standard preferences file). Part VI, "Document Management," describes how to manage preferences in more detail, particularly in chapter 24, "Using QuarkXPress in a Workgroup Environment."

With the *nonbreaking hyphen character*, you can tell QuarkXPress to prevent a line of text from wrapping after a hyphen. Enter Ctrl+Shift+- to create this character. It is generally used when the text following a hyphen is short, as in words such as *follow-up*.

Summary

▶ The wider the column width, the more leading you should have, to help the eye find the beginning of the next line when moving from the end of one line to the beginning of the next.

▶ Use the additive leading option rather than the Auto leading option; this avoids fractional point sizes for leading. An exception is if your subscripts or other nonbaseline characters extend beyond the leading's setting.

▶ Use the Space Before and Space After options to highlight elements like bylines and subheads by giving them enough space to be visually separate from surrounding elements.

▶ For most text, keep the maximum number of consecutive hyphens between 2 and 4.

▶ Create different H&J sets; have at least one with standard hyphenation settings and another with hyphenation turned off (for elements like headlines, bylines, and pull-quotes).

▶ Use the Utilities ⇨ Hyphenation Exceptions feature to add specialized words to the hyphenation dictionary.

14

Working with Typefaces

In This Chapter

▶ How typefaces differ and how those differences affect document creation in QuarkXPress

▶ Effective ways to use type styles and type variants

▶ How to use ruling lines

▶ How to access and use special symbols and characters

Type Variations

A typeface usually has several variations, the most common of which are: *roman, italic, boldface,* and *boldface italic* for serif typefaces; and *medium, oblique, boldface,* and *boldface oblique* for sans serif typefaces. Other variations include *thin, light, book, demibold, heavy, ultrabold,* and *black*, which refer to type weight, and *compressed, condensed, expanded,* and *wide*, which describe type scale.

Each of these variants, as well as each available combination of variants (for example, compressed light oblique), is called a *face.* Some typefaces have no variants; these are typically *calligraphic typefaces,* such as Park Avenue and Zapf Chancery, and *symbol typefaces,* such as Zapf Dingbats and Sonata. In Figure 14-1, you see samples of several typefaces and their variants. By using typeface variants wisely, you can improve reader understanding of document content and also present that content more attractively.

Serif Typefaces:	Sans Serif Typefaces:	Calligraphic/Decorative:
Times Ten roman	Univers medium	*Zapf Chancery*
Times Ten italic	*Univers oblique*	*Brush Script*
Times Ten boldface	**Univers boldface**	**Dom Casual**
Times Ten boldface italic	***Univers boldface oblique***	*Park Avenue*
Tiffany demibold	Univers light	*Shelley Allegro Script*
Tiffany heavy	**Univers black**	Architect
Cheltenham light	Univers Condensed Light	COPPERPLATE 29AB
Cheltenham book	Univers Condensed	POSTCRYPT
Cheltenham boldface		
Cheltenham ultrabold	Avant Garde book	Symbol:
Bodoni poster	**Avant Garde demibold**	⬛✦⊙♒♈♐☀♒ (Carta)
Caslon 224 book	Eras light	✳❀☐✳ ✦✳■✳ (Zapf Dingbats)
Caslon 224 medium	Eras book	♪♩♫ ♪♩♪ (Sonata)
Caslon 224 black	Eras medium	✚✘■Ⅴ⃝♌✘■Ⅴ⃝✦ (Wingdings)
Bookman light	**Eras demibold**	ΣψℲ~∀⊥μβολ γρεεκ (Symbol)
Bookman demibold	**Eras boldface**	
	Eras ultrabold	

▶ **Figure 14-1:** Samples of typefaces and their variants.

The name game

The many variants of a typeface confuse many users, especially because most programs use only the terms *normal* (or *plain*), *italic*, *bold*, and *bold italic* to describe available variations. When a typeface has more than these basic variations, the programs usually split it into several typefaces.

For example, in some programs, Helvetica comes as Helvetica, with medium, oblique, boldface, and boldface oblique faces; Helvetica Light/Black, with light, light oblique, black, and black oblique faces; Helvetica Light/Black Condensed, with condensed light, condensed light oblique, condensed black, and condensed black oblique faces; Helvetica Condensed, with condensed medium, condensed oblique, condensed boldface, and condensed boldface oblique faces; and Helvetica Compressed, with compressed medium and condensed oblique faces. When there are this many variations, you have to know that, for example, selecting bold for Helvetica Condensed results in Helvetica Condensed Bold type.

Fortunately, the issue of what face a program designates as plain, italic, and the rest rarely comes into play. You usually encounter it in one of the following situations:

■ When exchanging files between PCs and Macs — because some vendors use slightly different names for their typefaces on different platforms. The Utilities ⇨ Font Usage option enables you to correct this problem by replacing one typeface name with another.

■ When working with a service bureau whose typeface names are different or whose staff uses the traditional names rather than the desktop-publishing names.

■ When working with artists or typesetters to match a typeface. The best way to reach a common understanding is to look at a sample of the typefaces being discussed.

Desktop publishing programs popularized the use of the term *font* to describe what traditionally was called a *typeface*. In traditional terms, a typeface refers to a set of variants for one style of text, such as Palatino. A *face* is one of those variants, such as Palatino Italic. A font, in traditional terms, is a face at a specific point size, such as 12-point Palatino Italic. (Until electronic typesetting was developed, printers set type using metal blocks that were available only in a limited range of sizes.) Throughout this book, we use the traditional terms.

How to Mix and Match Typefaces

There are thousands of typefaces, and each has a different feel. Matching the typeface's feel to the effect you want for your document is a trial-and-error process. Until you are experienced at using a wide variety of typefaces (and even then), experiment with different typefaces on a mock-up of your document to see what works best.

It is a good idea to define a standard set of typefaces for each group of publications. You may want all employee-benefit newsletters to have a similar feel, which you can enforce by using common body text and headline typefaces, even if layout and paragraph settings differ. The key to working with a standard set of typefaces is to avoid limiting the set to only a few typefaces. Select more typefaces than any one document might use; this gives you enough flexibility to be creative while providing an obviously standard appearance. You also can use the same typeface for different purposes. For example, you might use a newsletter's headline typeface as a kicker in an advertisement. A consistent — but not constrained — appearance is a good way to establish an identity for your company.

It is common to use serif typefaces for body copy and sans serif typefaces for headlines, pull-quotes, and other elements. But there is no rule you should worry about following. You can easily create engaging documents that use serif typefaces for every element. You also can create all–sans-serif documents, although this is rarely done, because sans serif typefaces often are hard to read when used in many pages of text. (Exceptions include typefaces such as News Gothic and Franklin Gothic, which were designed for use as body text.) No matter what typefaces you use, the key is ensuring that each element calls an appropriate amount of attention to itself.

Here are some basic guidelines:

- Use a roman, medium, or book-weight typeface for body text. In some cases, a light weight works well, especially for typefaces such as Bookman and Souvenir, which tend to be heavy in the medium weights.

Make sure you output samples before deciding on a light typeface for body text, because many light typefaces are hard to read when used extensively. Also, if you intend to output publications on an image setter (at 1200 dpi or finer resolution), make sure you output samples on that image setter, because a light font may be readable on a 300- or 600-dpi laser printer but too light on a higher resolution printer that can reproduce thin characters more faithfully than a laser printer. (The laser printer may actually print a light typeface as something a bit heavier; because the width of the text's stroke is not an even multiple of the laser printer's dots, the printer has no choice but to make the stroke thicker than it should be.)

- Use a heavier typeface for headlines and subheads. A demibold or bold usually works well. Avoid using the same typeface for headlines and body text, even if it is a bolder variant. On the other hand, using the same typeface for subheads and headlines, even if in a different variant, helps ensure a common identity. (And if you mix typefaces, use those that have similar appearances; for example, use round typefaces with other round typefaces and squared-off typefaces with other squared-off typefaces.)

- If captions are long (more than three lines), use a typeface with the same weight as body text. If you use the same typeface as body text, differentiate the caption visually from body text. Using a boldface caption lead-in (the first words are boldface and act as a title for the caption) or putting the caption in italics distinguishes the caption from body text without being distracting. If captions are short (three lines or fewer), consider using a heavier face than body text or a typeface that is readily distinguished from your body text.

- Avoid using more than three typefaces (not including variants) in the main document elements (headlines, body text, captions, pull-quotes, and other elements that appear on most pages). However, some typefaces are very similar, so you can use them as a group as if they were one. Examples include Helvetica, Univers, and Arial; Futura and Avant Garde; Times and its many relatives (including Times New Roman and Times Ten); Galliard and New Baskerville; Souvenir and Korinna; and Goudy Old Style and Century Old Style. You can treat these almost as variants of one another, especially if you use one of the pair in limited-length elements such as kickers, pull-quotes, and bylines.

- Italics are particularly appropriate for kickers, bylines, sidebar headlines, and pull-quotes.

Type Styles

Typefaces have several faces — such as boldface and italics — to give publishers visual variety and content guides. Publishing programs (as well as some word processors) also offer special *typeface attributes*, such as small caps, shadows, and underlines, to provide even more design and content tools.

How to change typeface attributes

QuarkXPress lets you change typeface attributes in several ways:

- **Option 1:** Use the Measurements palette (this is the easiest method). To select a typeface quickly, click the typeface list in the palette and enter the first letter of the typeface's name. The list jumps to the first typeface that begins with that letter. This is faster than scrolling if you have many type-faces available. Below the typeface list is a row of type-style attributes: plain, boldface, italics, outline, shadow, strikethrough, underline all, word underline, small caps, all caps, superscript, subscript, and superior. Any current style settings for the selected text are highlighted.

Figure 14-2 shows the Measurements palette, from which you can control almost every typographic specification, including leading, tracking, para-graph alignment, typefaces, type size, and type style. (Settings for the current text box appear on the left side of the palette.)

X:	3p	W:	45p	△	0°		11.5 pt		Cheltenham		9 pt	
Y:	3p	H:	60p	Cols:	3		0		P B I O S U W K H 0 9 V			

▶ **Figure 14-2:** The Measurements palette.

- **Option 2:** Use the Style menu. Options available in this menu include Font, Size, Type Style, Color, Shade, Horizontal Scale, Kern or Track (depending on whether text is selected), Baseline Shift, and Character (which lets you define several attributes at once). You can see the menu in Figure 14-3.

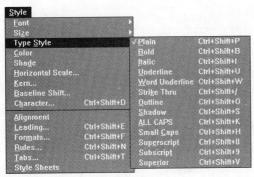

▶ **Figure 14-3:** The Style menu.

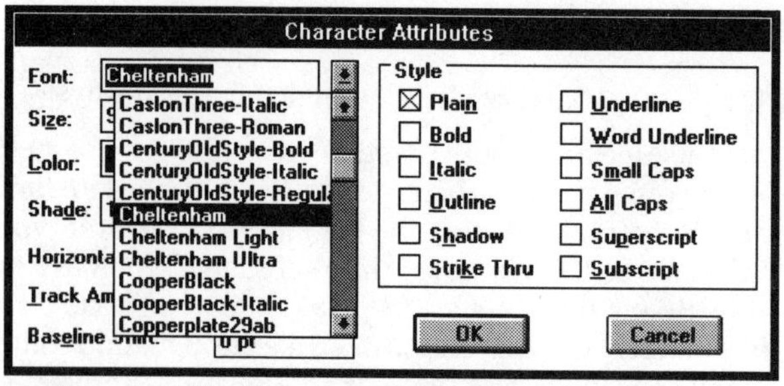

▶ **Figure 14-4:** The Character Attributes dialog box.

■ **Option 3:** Use the Character Attributes dialog box, which you access with the shortcut key Ctrl+Shift+D. Figure 14-4 shows the dialog box. You can set several type settings at once.

■ **Option 4:** Use keyboard shortcuts. Use the codes in Table 14-1 in combination with Ctrl+Shift. For example, for plain text, press Ctrl+Shift+P.

Table 14-1:	Shortcut Keys for Typeface Attributes
Use these shortcut keys in combination with Ctrl+Shift.	
Attribute	*Shortcut Key*
Plain	P
Bold	B
Italic	I
<u>Underline all</u>	U
<u>Word</u> <u>underline</u>	W
~~Strikethrough~~	/ (slash)
Outline	O (letter O)
Shadow	S
ALL CAPS	K
SMALL CAPS	H
Superscript	0 (zero)
Subscript	9
Superior	V

Plain refers to the basic style for the selected typeface. Most commercial typefaces come with a roman or medium face as the basic style. But many typefaces created by do-it-yourselfers or converted via programs such as Altsys's Fontographer, Ares Software Corp.'s FontMonger, and Atech Software's AllType come with each face as a separate typeface. So, for example, you may have Magazine Roman, Magazine Italic, Magazine Bold, and Magazine Bold Italic as separate typefaces in your fonts menu. If you select Magazine Bold Italic, QuarkXPress's palettes and dialog boxes show its style as plain, but it appears and prints as bold italic. This is not a bug in QuarkXPress, but simply a reflection of the fact that the basic style for any typeface is called "plain," no matter what the style actually looks like. In some programs, like FontMonger, you can set a typeface such as Magazine Bold Italic so it is listed as bold italic in QuarkXPress's palettes and dialog boxes.

QuarkXPress cannot apply a bold style to a typeface that does not have one. If the typeface has a bolder face, QuarkXPress is likely to use that, assuming the typeface uses the correct internal label so QuarkXPress knows to do this. Similarly, QuarkXPress cannot apply an italic style to a typeface that does not have one. But it does recognize that when you select italics for a sans serif typeface, oblique face is what you want.

If you change the face of selected text to a face (boldface or italics) not supported by the text's typeface, QuarkXPress may appear to have applied that face successfully. However, when you print, you will see that the face has not really been changed (although the spacing has changed to accommodate the new face). What has happened is that QuarkXPress and the Windows type scaler (such as TrueType or Adobe Type Manager) mistakenly create a screen font based on your request for a face change. When the text with the nonexistent face is printed, Windows finds no printer file for that face and uses the closest face it has for the typeface used.

Basic text styles

Most people are familiar with basic text styles such as boldface and italics — after all, we see them routinely in newspapers, magazines, ads, and television. Despite that familiarity, these styles can be misused, especially by people experienced in producing reports on typewriters and word processors, where these basic styles are used differently than in published (typeset-quality) documents.

The following is a primer on the use of basic text attributes in body text. (Other effects are covered later in this chapter.) "How to Mix and Match Typefaces," earlier in this chapter, offers guidelines on using these attributes in other types of text elements. As always, these and other guidelines are meant to be ignored by those purposely trying to create a special effect.

Italics

Italics are generally used to emphasize a word or phrase in body text. For example: "We *must* do what we can to clean up the environment." Italics are also used to identify titles of books, movies, television and radio series, magazines, and newspapers: "Public TV's *Nova* series had an excellent show about endangered species last night." Italics can also be applied to lead-in words of subsections or in lists (these are described in the "Special Elements and Effects" chapter later in this section).

In typewritten text, people often use underlines or uppercase as a substitute for italics, but do not substitute these effects in published text.

Boldface

Boldface is rarely used in body text because it is too distracting. When boldface is used, it is typically applied to the lead-in words in subsections. As a rule, do not use it for emphasis — use italics instead. However, when you have a lot of text and you want people to easily pick out names within it, boldfacing the names may be appropriate. If, for example, you create a story listing winners of a series of awards or publish a gossip column that mentions various celebrities, you may want to boldface people's names in order to highlight them.

Small caps and all caps

Capital letters have both functional and decorative uses. Functionally, they start sentences and identify proper names. Decoratively, they add emphasis or stateliness.

Capital letters have a more stately appearance than lowercase letters most likely because of the influence of Roman monuments, which are decorated with inscribed text in uppercase letters (the Romans didn't use lowercase much). These monuments and the Roman style have come to symbolize authority and officialism. Most government centers have a very Roman appearance, as a visit to Washington, D.C., quickly confirms.

Using all capital letters has two major drawbacks:

■ Text in all caps can be overwhelming, because uppercase characters are both taller and wider than lowercase. In typeset materials, as opposed to typewritten, all caps loom even larger, because the size difference between a capital letter and its lowercase version is greater than it is in typewriter characters, which are all designed to fit in the same space. All caps can be thought of as the typographic equivalent of yelling: "READ THIS SENTENCE!" Now, read this sentence.

- People read not by analyzing every letter and constructing words but by recognizing the shapes of words. In all caps, words have the same rectangular shape — only the width changes — so this reading aid is lost. All caps is harder to read than regular text.

The use of small caps can result in elegant, stately text that is not overwhelming. The smaller size of the caps overcomes the "yelling" problem of all caps. Figure 14-5 shows an example of effective use of small caps. In the example, the kicker and byline are set in small caps.

The key to using small caps is to limit them to short amounts of text, where it's OK not to give readers the aid of recognizable word shapes. Small caps are effective in kickers, bylines, and labels (see the section "Organizational aids" in Chapter 15, "Using Special Elements and Effects").

QuarkXPress lets you set the proportional size of small caps (compared to regular caps) in the Typographic Preferences dialog box, shown in Figure 14-6. (You can also set the relative size and position of superscripts, subscripts, and superiors in this dialog box.) To access the dialog box, select Edit ⇨ Preferences ⇨ Typographic. You can set the horizontal and vertical proportions separately, although they are usually the same. QuarkXPress's default setting is 75 percent, and most small caps should be set between 70 and 80 percent.

▶ **Figure 14-5:** Small caps are used for the kicker and byline in this example.

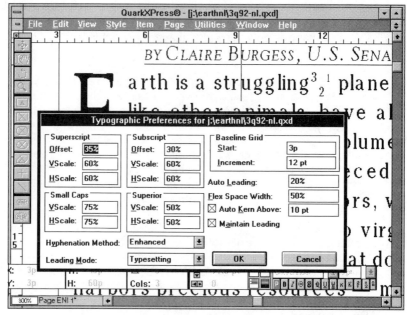

▶ **Figure 14-6:** Set the size of small caps in the Typographic Preferences dialog box.

If you want typographic settings to affect all documents, invoke the preferences dialog box with no document selected. Any future documents use the new settings.

To apply default settings to a document with altered preferences (including typographic settings), open the document and select Use XPress Preferences when QuarkXPress asks whether to use the default settings or the document's settings. (QuarkXPress automatically detects whether a document's settings match the defaults for that copy of QuarkXPress.)

Some typefaces have a version — sometimes called an *expert collection* — that includes specially designed small caps. These caps are not merely proportionally scaled; their strokes are also modified to make them a bit darker. When you scale a character to be smaller, you make its strokes smaller, which makes the character lighter than the equivalent lowercase letter. Figure 14-7 compares small caps generated by QuarkXPress (top) with the true small caps (bottom) for the Garamond typeface. Simulated small caps can look weaker than true small caps. This is usually not a problem, but for design-intensive work such as advertising, the quality difference often makes it worthwhile to get the expert-collection typeface. Keep in mind that using the small caps option in Quark-XPress does not access the expert-collection typeface; you must explicitly apply that typeface to the characters in question.

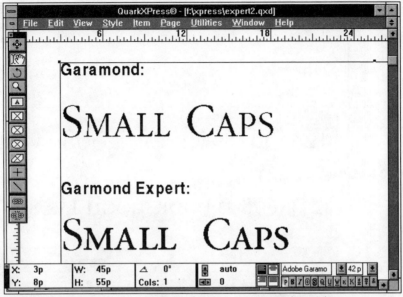

▶ **Figure 14-7:** Simulated small caps (top) and true small caps (bottom).

Traditional numerals

If you look at books published early in this century or in previous eras, you'll notice that the numerals look very different than the ones you see today in books, magazines, and newspapers. Numerals used to be treated as lowercase letters, so some, such as the number 9, had *descenders*, just as lowercase letters such as *g* and *p* do. Others, such as the number 6, had *ascenders*, as do lowercase letters such as *b* and *d*. But this changed, and most modern typefaces treat numerals like capital letters: no descenders and no ascenders. This keeps numerals from sticking out in headlines, but it also can make numerals too prominent in some text, especially in type-intensive documents such as ads, where individual character shapes are important to the overall look.

Adobe and other type foundries resurrected the old-fashioned numerals as part of expert-collection typefaces. As you can see in Figure 14-8, which shows the two types of numerals for the Garamond typeface, the traditional numerals are more stylized and have the typographic feel of lowercase letters. The surrounding text includes parentheses and letters with ascenders and descenders to better show how the two types of numerals look with mixed text.

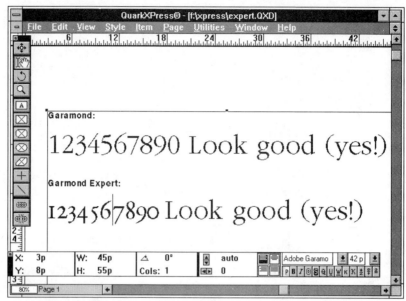

► **Figure 14-8:** Modern numerals (top) and traditional numerals (bottom).

Although they often look more elegant, old-fashioned numerals have three drawbacks you should consider before using them routinely:

■ They reside in a separate font, so you must change the font for each and every numeral (or groups of numerals). Even if you code this in your word processor, it can be a lot of extra work. In tables and other numerals-only text, this is less of an issue, because you can have a separate style for text that uses the expert font.

■ They do not have the same width. Modern numerals are almost always the same width (that of an en space), so typographers and publishers don't have to worry about whether columns of numbers align. (Because all numerals are the same width, they align naturally.) But the old-fashioned numerals in expert fonts have variable widths, just like most characters, so they can look awkward in columns of numbers even if you use decimal or comma alignment.

■ They are unusual in modern typography, so they can call more attention to themselves than is appropriate. For design-intensive work, this is usually not an issue, but in commonplace documents such as reports and newsletters, they can look out of place. As their popularity grows, this may change.

Superscripts, subscripts, and superiors

Superscripts, subscripts, and superiors let you indicate notes in your text and set some mathematical notations. While numerals are typically used for these notes, you can also use special symbols such as asterisks and daggers. These notes are in a smaller size than the rest of the text and are positioned above or below the regular baseline.

Superscripts and subscripts are typically used in math and other sciences. A superscript can indicate an exponent, such as a^2 for *a squared,* or a notation, such as U^{235} for *uranium-235.*

Superscripts are commonly used for footnotes, too, but QuarkXPress also offers *superiors,* the traditional typographic method of indicating footnotes. A superior is similar to a superscript, except that the top of a superior always aligns with the top of the text's cap height. A superscript, by contrast, need not align with anything. The advantage to using a superior is that you don't have to worry about the footnote (or whatever) bumping into the text in the line above. This problem is particularly acute if you have tight leading and the superscript is positioned below a character that has a descender (such as a *g* or *p.*) Another potential problem is uneven leading, which is explained later.

Footnotes set via your word processor to be superscripted import as superscripts. If you want to use superiors, you must manually change superscripts to superiors. You cannot use the Edit ➪ Find/Change option to search for superscripts and replace them with superiors, because superiors is not an option in the Find/Change dialog box.

As it does for small caps, QuarkXPress lets you set the relative size and spacing for superscripts, subscripts, and superiors. You do this in the Typographic Preferences dialog box, accessed via Edit ➪ Preferences ➪ Typographic. You may need to experiment to derive a setting that works for all paragraph styles.

We prefer the following settings: superscripts offset 35 percent and scaled 60 percent; subscripts offset 30 percent and scaled 60 percent; and superiors scaled 50 percent. If you refer back to Figure 14-6, you can see these settings; the text behind the Typographic Preferences dialog box illustrates how these settings place superscripts, subscripts, and superiors into actual text.

If you use additive leading (see explanation in the previous chapter, "Understanding Paragraph Spacing") and your superscript or subscript settings cause the superscripts or subscripts to extend beyond the text's height or depth, you get uneven spacing. This is because some lines have more leading than others to accommodate the outsized or outpositioned characters. (QuarkXPress bases the additive leading on the highest and lowest character in a line, not on the text's normal position.) If you can't alter your text — by changing either its leading or the subscript and superscript settings — so that none of it extends beyond the text's range, don't use the additive-leading option.

If you want typographic settings to affect all documents, invoke the Typographic Preferences dialog box with no document selected. Any future document uses these new settings.

To apply default settings to a document with altered preferences (including typographic settings), open the document and select Use XPress Preferences when QuarkXPress asks whether to use the default settings or the document's settings. (QuarkXPress automatically detects whether a document's settings match the defaults for that copy of QuarkXPress.)

Baseline Shift

A feature similar to superscripting and subscripting is Baseline Shift, which lets you move text up or down relative to other text on the line. The biggest difference is that the text size does not change. This effect is rarely needed, although it can come in handy when you position text for ads and other design-intensive text or when you use it with effects such as ruling lines to create reverse text (see the next section, "Underlines and rules").

If you need to do so, you change baseline shift through the Baseline Shift dialog box, shown in Figure 14-9, which you access via Style ⇨ Baseline Shift. Entering a positive number moves the text up; a negative number moves it down.

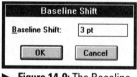

▶ **Figure 14-9:** The Baseline Shift dialog box.

You can use the Baseline Shift feature and change the text size to create superscripts or subscripts that differ from the normal settings in a document. Most people won't need to do this; among those who may are scientists and engineers whose documents require several levels of subscripting or superscripting.

Unlike superscripts and subscripts, baseline shifts do not cause uneven leading when used with additive leading. Instead, QuarkXPress lets text overprint lines the text shifts into.

Underlines and rules

Underlines and rules are not typically used in body text in published documents. In fact, underlines are used in typewritten text as a substitute for italics. But underlines do have a place in published materials: as a visual element in kickers, subheads, bylines, and tables. When used in such short elements, underlines add a definitive, authoritative feel.

Using underlines

QuarkXPress offers two types of underlines: *regular underline* (Ctrl+Shift+U), which affects all characters, including spaces; and *word underline* (Ctrl+Shift+W), which underlines only nonspace characters (letters, numerals, symbols, and punctuation). When choosing which underline type to use, there is no "right" or "wrong" — let the aesthetics of the document be the determining factor.

Using ruling lines

Underlines are limited in line size and position — all underlines are fixed by QuarkXPress. But you can create underlines and other types of lines meant to enhance text with the ruling line feature. QuarkXPress offers a wide range of ruling lines through the Paragraph Rules dialog box, which you access via the keyboard shortcut Ctrl+Shift+N or by selecting Style ⇨ Rules. When this dialog box first appears, it has only two options: Rule Above and Rule Below. If you check either (or both) of these options, the dialog box expands to offer more choices. Figure 14-10 shows the dialog box with both Rule Above and Rule Below checked and with the Style option selected for Rule Below.

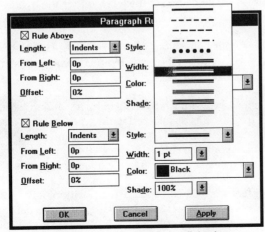

▶ **Figure 14-10:** The Paragraph Rules dialog box.

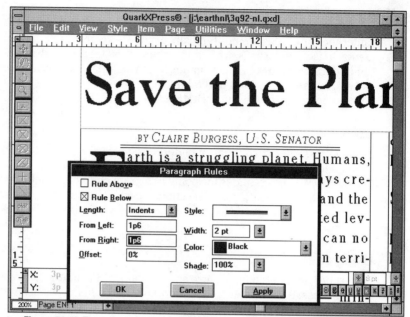

▶ **Figure 14-11:** The rule underneath the byline is an example of a rule with the L<u>e</u>ngth option set at Indents.

The first option available for the Rule Abo<u>v</u>e and Rule <u>B</u>elow is the L<u>e</u>ngth option. You have two choices: Indents and Text. Selecting Indents makes the rule the width of the current column, minus the settings in From <u>L</u>eft and From <u>R</u>ight. Figure 14-11 shows a ruling line set this way, under the byline of the sample article.

When you select Text as your L<u>e</u>ngth option, the rule is the width of the text it is applied to. In Figure 14-12, you see how the byline rule now appears when you choose Text instead of Indents.

You typically use Indents when you want a rule to be a standard width no matter what the length of the text it is associated with. An example is a series of centered labels in a menu — *Seafood, Vegetarian, Pasta,* and so on — whose lengths vary greatly. By making the rules the same width, you call more attention to the rules and to the fact that they indicate a major heading.

By selecting the <u>O</u>ffset feature, you can specify the position of the rule relative to the text in the paragraph above it (for Rule Abo<u>v</u>e) or in the paragraph below it (for Rule <u>B</u>elow). You can use percentages from 0 to 100, or you can use units of your default absolute measurement (picas, inches, centimeters, etc.) from a negative value of half the rule's width to 15 inches (90 picas or 38.1 cm).

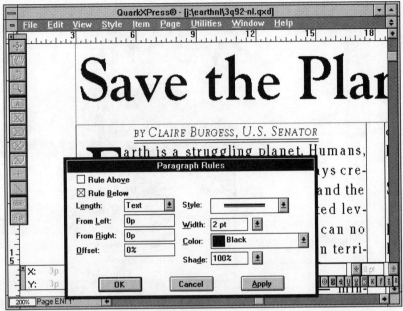

▶ **Figure 14-12:** The rule underneath the byline is an example of a rule with the Length option set at Text.

Moving a rule up or down via the Offset feature does not affect leading, so QuarkXPress may move the rule into unrelated text. If you want a 2-point ruling line to be 6 points below the text associated with it, and you want the next paragraph to be another 6 points below that, you must set the leading on the paragraph with the ruling line at 14 points (6+2+6).

You can use the Offset feature to create reversed type, as illustrated in the byline treatment in Figure 14-13. To do this, you essentially move the rule into the text line associated with it. The key is to make the rule larger than the text. In Figure 14-13, the text is 8 points, so we set the rule (shaded at 40 percent black) to be 12 points, which provides a margin above and below the text. (Make your rule at least 2 points larger than text to get an adequate margin.) We then offset the rule by –6 points (the maximum allowed, or half the rule size). That was not enough, so we selected the text and used the Baseline Shift feature (described earlier in this chapter) to shift the text down 2 points, which centered it in the gray rule. We also changed the text color to white via Style ⇨ Color (described in the next chapter, "Using Special Elements and Effects"). Last, by selecting the Style ⇨ Formats dialog box, we added 6 points of space below the byline so the gray rule does not touch the text below it.

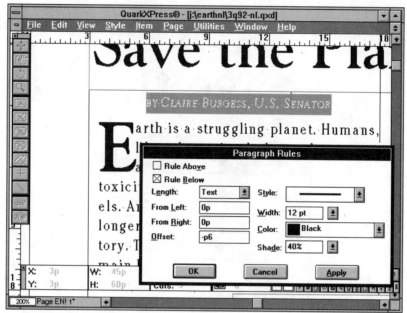

▶ **Figure 14-13:** The byline in this figure is an example of how you can create reversed type with the Offset feature.

Typographic Characters and Symbols

Several characters that are not used in traditionally typed business documents are used routinely in typeset documents. Do not ignore these symbols, because readers expect to see them in anything that appears to be published, whether on the desktop or via traditional means. If you're used to working only with typewritten or word-processed documents, pay careful attention to the proper use of these characters.

Quotes and dashes

The most common of these characters are *true quotation marks* and *em dashes* (so called because they are the width of a capital *M* when typeset). The typewriter uses the same character (") to indicate both open and close quotation marks, and most people use two hyphens (- -) to indicate an em dash when typing. Using these marks in a published document is a sign of amateurism. Figure 14-14 shows what typographical dashes and quotes look like.

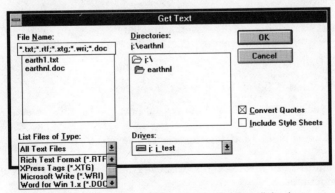

> ▶ **Figure 14-14:** True quotations marks and an em dash.

Fortunately, QuarkXPress offers an option during text import that automatically changes typewriter dashes and quotes to their typographic equivalents. When you get text, make sure that you check the Convert Quotes box (it also handles em dashes) in the Get Text dialog box, as shown in Figure 14-15.

Do not use the keyboard apostrophe (') as an open single quote — use the open single quote key (`) instead. QuarkXPress does not translate apostrophes that begin a word into open single quotes. This is not a bug: English allows contractions to begin a word — such as "'tis the season" — so automatic translation would create errors.

> ▶ **Figure 14-15:** Select Convert Quotes in the Get Text dialog box when you import text.

When you type text in QuarkXPress, however, you must type in a command to get typographic quote marks, because they are not available on a standard keyboard. The commands are:

" (open quote)	Alt+Shift+[
" (close quote)	Alt+Shift+]
' (open single quote)	Alt+[
' (close single quote)	Alt+]

Punctuating text with quotes confuses many people, but the rules are not complicated:

- Periods and commas always go inside the quotation.

- Semicolons and colons always go outside the quotation.

- Question marks and exclamation marks go inside if they are part of the quote, outside if not. When the main clause is a question, but the quote is a declaration, the question mark takes precedence over the period, so it goes outside the quotes. When the main clause is a question, and the quote is an exclamation, the exclamation takes precedence, and it goes within the quotation. For example:

  Did he really say, "I am too busy"?

  She asked, "Do you have time to help?"

  I can't believe she asked, "Do you have time to help?"

  He really did yell, "I am too busy!"

- When a single quote is followed immediately by a double quote, separate the two with a nonbreaking punctuation space (Ctrl+Shift+spacebar):

  He told me, "She asked, 'Do you have time to help?' "

  He told me, "Bob heard him say, 'I am too busy.' "

  She asked me, "Can you believe that he said, 'I am too busy'?"

For more information on these rules, refer to a grammar guide.

If you want to enter dashes in text while in QuarkXPress, you must also use special commands:

— (em dash)	Ctrl+Shift+=
— (nonbreaking em dash)	Ctrl+Alt+Shift+=
– (en dash)	Ctrl+=

Typographers are divided over whether you should put spaces around em dashes — like this — or not—like this. Traditionally, there is no space. But having space lets the publishing program treat the dash as a word, so there is even space around all words in a line. Not having a space around dashes means the publishing program sees the two words connected by the em dash as one big word, so the spacing added to justify a line between all other words on the line may be awkwardly large, since the program doesn't know to break a line after or before an em dash that doesn't have space on either side. Still, whether to surround a dash with space is a decision in which personal preferences should prevail.

A nonbreaking em dash does not let text following it wrap to a new line. Instead, the break must occur at a spot preceding or following the dash.

The en dash, so called because it is the width of a capital *N,* is a nonbreaking character, so QuarkXPress does not let a line break after it. Traditionally, an en dash is used to:

■ Separate numerals, as in a range of values (*14–16 entries*).

■ Label a figure (*Figure 4–6*).

■ Indicate a multiple-word hyphenation (*Civil War–era*).

Symbols and special characters

A typeface comes with dozens of special symbols ranging from bullets to copyright symbols. The most common ones are accessible from QuarkXPress through the following commands:

- **En bullet:** Press Alt+Shift+8. A bullet is an effective way to call attention to issues being raised. Typically, bullets are used at the beginning of each element in a list. If the sequence of the elements is important, as in a series of steps, use numerals instead of bullets.

  Keep in mind that you have many alternatives to using the regular en bullet (so called because it is the width of a lowercase *n).* Using special characters such as boxes, check marks, triangles, and arrows, you can create attractive bulleted lists that stand out from the crowd. More information on how to select such characters is provided later in this chapter.

© **Copyright:** Press Alt+Shift+C. A copyright symbol signifies who owns text or other visual media. The standard format is *Copyright © 1992 IDG Books Worldwide. All rights reserved.* For text, you must include at least the © symbol, the word *Copyright,* or the abbreviation *Copr,* as well as the year first published and the name of the copyright holder. (Note that only the © symbol is valid for international copyright.) Works need not be registered to be copyrighted — the notice is sufficient.

® **Registered trademark:** Press Alt+Shift+R. This is usually used in advertising, packaging, marketing, and public relations to indicate that a product or service name is exclusively owned by a company. The mark follows the name. You may use the ® symbol only with names registered with the U.S. Patent and Trademark Office. For works whose trademark registration is pending, use the ™ symbol. Use Alt+Shift+2.

§ **Section:** Press Alt+Shift+6. This symbol is typically used in legal and scholarly documents to refer to sections of laws or research papers.

¶ **Paragraph:** Press Alt+Shift+7. Like the section symbol, the paragraph symbol is typically used for legal and scholarly documents.

† **Dagger:** Press Alt+Shift+T. This is often used as a footnote character.

When you want a long portion of text to run so that it appears as one visual block — a tactic often used for article openers in highly designed magazines — consider using symbols such as § and ¶ as paragraph-break indicators. (Frequently, they are set in larger or bolder type when used in this manner.) The symbols alert readers to paragraph shifts. *Rolling Stone* magazine is particularly partial to this effect. Figure 14-16 shows an example of how it can be used.

The Macintosh version of QuarkXPress offers a wider selection of symbols accessed via codes. Those listed in the preceding list match the codes for the Mac version (if you consider Alt as the equivalent of the Mac's Option key). You must access other symbols offered by the Mac through the standard Windows methods, described next.

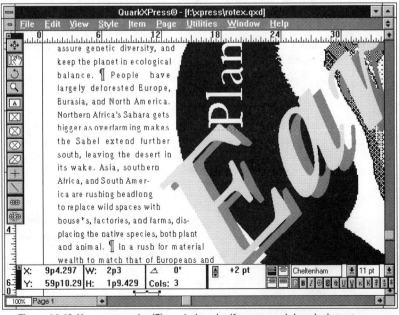

▶ **Figure 14-16:** You can use the (¶) symbol to signify paragraph breaks in text.

Character Map

In addition to the symbols covered in the preceding section, other symbols — including foreign-language characters — are accessible if you know the four-digit Windows code for them. You enter the four-digit code (which begins with a zero) by holding the Alt key and typing in the four digits. You must enter the four digits using the numeric keypad rather than the numbers above the letters on the main keyboard.

You can find these four-digit codes in the Windows manual. But the codes may differ from typeface to typeface, so the manual may not always be accurate. A simpler solution is to use the Character Map program that comes with Windows 3.1. Figure 14-17 shows the program in use.

You cannot switch to Character Map (or any other application) if you are in a dialog box that does not have a close handle in the upper-left corner. So if you want to paste a special character into a dialog box's option field (such as for a tab leader), get the character from Character Map before invoking the dialog box. Note that the character may not appear properly in the option field, although it appears correctly in your document.

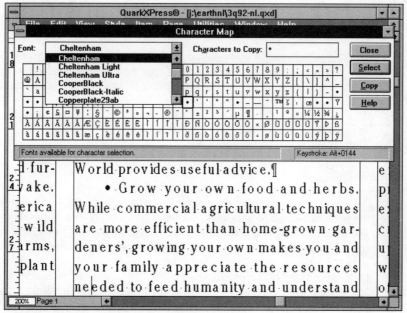

▶ **Figure 14-17:** Using Windows 3.1 Character Map.

▶ Steps: Using Character Map

Step 1. Single-click the Windows control button (at the upper left of the screen) and select the S̲witch To option. (Or use the keyboard shortcut Ctrl+Esc.)

Step 2. From the Task List, select Character Map if it is running. Otherwise, select Program Manager and find the Character Map program (it is most likely in the Accessories group if you did not move it).

Step 3. Make sure the typeface you are using or want to use (perhaps you want to use a symbol typeface) is selected in the F̲ont option.

Step 4. In the character map that appears, find the character you want. If you hold down the mouse button while scrolling through the map, an enlarged character appears to help you better identify what you are seeking.

Step 5. When you find the character, double-click it (or single-click it and then choose S̲elect). The character appears in the Ch̲aracters To Copy option. (You can select several characters, one after another.)

Step 6. After you select all the characters you want, click the C̲opy button to put them on the Windows Clipboard.

Step 7. Return to QuarkXPress via the Task Manager (as in Steps 1 and 2) and move your text cursor to the spot where you want to insert the character(s). Or, if the QuarkXPress window is visible, single-click anywhere in it.

Step 8. Paste the character(s) in by pressing Ctrl+V or by selecting E̲dit ⇨ P̲aste.

As you select characters, Character Map displays in the lower-right corner the keypad code used to access each character. This comes in handy if you find yourself selecting the same character repeatedly; you can use the keypad code instead of switching to Character Map to access the character.

Make sure you don't close Character Map or QuarkXPress. Instead, use the Minimize handle or the Task List to move to other applications. Otherwise, you have to relaunch the closed application.

If you use special symbols or characters fairly often (whether in QuarkXPress or any Windows program), move the Character Map application to the StartUp group, so it is available each time you run Windows.

Do not change the typeface while in Character Map unless you want all selected characters to be in the newly selected typeface. You cannot mix typefaces in one Character Map session.

Summary

▶ Keep in mind that some typefaces come with groups of faces — usually normal (plain), italic, boldface, and boldface italic — while others come as separate typefaces for each face. For the former, such as Times, you can change the face by using the style options in the Measurements palette or the Style menu options. For the latter, you must change the typeface (for example, from Tiffany Bold to Tiffany Bold Italic).

▶ The Utilities ➪ Font Usage option lets you replace typefaces with new ones. This is especially handy when moving documents from computers with different sets of typefaces.

▶ The Measurements palette is usually the fastest way to change type attributes.

▶ Use italics for emphasis and titles of intellectual works (like books, movies, and plays). Use boldface as lead-in labels or, less frequently, for special emphasis.

▶ Avoid using all capital letters. Consider using boldface or small caps instead.

▶ Superiors are often better for use with footnotes, but all word processors use superscripts instead, and QuarkXPress offers no way to search and replace superscripts with superiors.

▶ Use a combination of baseline shifting and point-size changes to create multiple levels of superscripts and subscripts.

▶ QuarkXPress offers two underline options — one that underlines all text, including spaces, and one that underlines only nonspace characters. The first option is usually preferred.

▶ You can define your own ruling lines and associate them with paragraphs; this is particularly helpful when used for headings and other design-oriented display text.

▶ Make sure you use typographic quotes and dashes, not the typewriter equivalents. (QuarkXPress can be set to convert these when importing documents, but not when entering text within QuarkXPress.)

▶ QuarkXPress offers access to several special characters directly from the keyboard. Others can be accessed by their Windows ANSI code from the numeric keypad or via the Windows 3.1 Character Map utility.

15

Using Special Elements and Effects

In This Chapter

▶ When and how to use indentation, bulleted lists, and other types of lists

▶ Typographic techniques that aid text organization

▶ How to enhance text with drop caps and related effects

▶ How to apply effects such as rotation, shadows, and outlines

In addition to the space-oriented typographic controls that help determine a document's overall "color," you can use several typographic features to enhance your presentation. These features include drop caps and other attention-grabbers, organizational aids such as bulleted lists, and visual labels such as small caps. What all these effects have in common is that they enable you to add meaning or provide reader guidance by changing the appearance of individual characters or small groups of characters.

Organizational Tools

One of the most important uses of typographic effects is to create visual signposts that guide the reader through a document. The effects most commonly used for this purpose fall into four basic groups: indents and outdents, bullets and lists, visual labels, and dingbats.

Indents and outdents

Despite their many variations, all indents and outdents share one goal: to break up a document's solid left margin. These breaks give the reader variances to notice — variances that signify a change in elements. It's less important to break up the right margin of a document, because people read from left to right and thus pay most attention to the left margin. In languages that are read from right to left, such as Hebrew and Arabic, the opposite is true.

To set indents, either for a selected paragraph or when defining styles, use the Paragraph Formats dialog box, shown in Figure 15-1. To open the dialog box, select Edit ⇨ Style Sheets to access the Edit Style Sheet dialog box, and then select the Formats button. Or select Style ⇨ Formats (keyboard shortcut is Ctrl+Shift+F).

The most basic use of an indent is to offset the first line in a paragraph. This is particularly true in multicolumn publications that use first-line indents rather than blank lines between paragraphs to indicate the start of a new paragraph.

 Make sure your first-line indents aren't too small. Usually, indents should be between one and two ems in size. An em is as wide as your current point size, so if text is 9 points, the first-line indent should be between 9 and 18 points. If columns are thin (more than three columns to a standard page), make indents closer to 9 points than 18 points. This avoids gaping indents or awkward justification in the first line of a paragraph.

An outdent, also called an *exdent* or a *hanging indent,* achieves the same function as a first-line indent, but moves the first line out into the margin, rather than indenting it. It usually is reserved for bulleted lists, because it takes a lot of

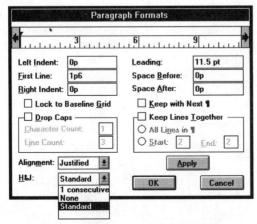

▶ **Figure 15-1:** Set indents in the Paragraph Formats dialog box.

space that otherwise might be used for text. Some people use outdents for sidebars to provide a visual counterpoint to standard text; this works if the sidebars are not too long.

Another form of indenting is called *block indenting*. In a block indent, the entire paragraph is indented from the left margin, right margin, or both. A typical use of block-indenting — usually from the left, but sometimes also from the right — is to indicate extended quotations. Typically, these are also set in a smaller type size. Use the Left Indent and Right Indent fields to set block indents.

You can indent text other than body text. For example, you might indent bylines or credit lines. You can indent headlines, so that the kickers overhang a little bit, or you can indent subheads. As long as you don't go overboard and end up with a seesaw pattern, using indents on a variety of elements helps keep a page visually active, even when it is filled primarily with text.

If you indent several elements in the same document, use only a few different levels of indentation — two or three at most. For example, it works well to use the same amount of indentation on bylines and kickers, even if the indentation amount differs from the amount used for the first line of body-text paragraphs. If you have too many levels of indentation, there is no pattern to help guide the reader's eye, and the resulting document appears jumbled.

Bullets and lists

Lists are an effective way to organize information so that discrete elements are treated individually, with each clearly visible as a separate entity and yet obviously part of a bigger grouping. The two most popular ways to indicate lists are to use bullets or sequential labels (either numerals or letters).

Depending on the length of list items and the width of columns on the page, you may be content simply putting a bullet or label at the beginning of each item. This works best when your itemized text takes many lines (more than five or six) in multicolumn text. Otherwise, you'll probably want to have a hanging indent in itemized paragraphs, with the bullet or label hanging over the text's left margin, which is itself brought in from the column's left margin. The two right columns in Figure 15-2 show examples of hanging-indent lists, while the left-hand column shows a list that uses only first-line indents.

QuarkXPress does not offer a feature that automates the creation of bulleted or labeled lists, but you can cut out most of the work involved by creating a style with the proper settings. After you create the style, all you have to do is apply it to the appropriate paragraphs and add the bullets or labels to the text. Figure 15-3 shows the settings for a bulleted list style. These settings create the proper indentation for a hanging-indent bulleted list. (We also could have applied these settings directly to a single paragraph through Style ⇨ Formats; the dialog box is the same.)

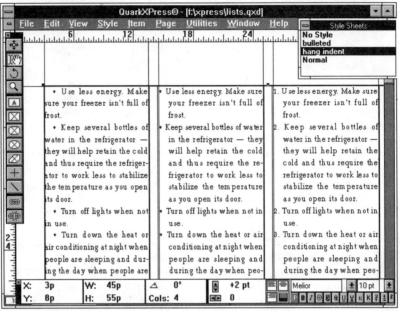

▶ **Figure 15-2:** Different types of indented lists.

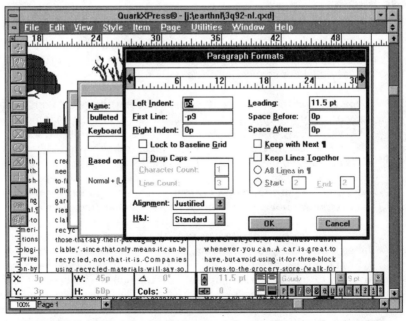

▶ **Figure 15-3:** Example settings in the Paragraph Formats dialog box for a hanging-indent, bulleted list style.

The key to creating a hanging-indent bulleted list is to make the left indent and the first-line indent the same amount, but in different directions. Use a positive setting for the left indent and a negative setting for the first-line indent. The negative setting creates an outdent. Using the same setting for the outdent as for the left indent ensures that the bullet starts at the column margin, since the two values in essence cancel each other out for the first line. The indent amount should equal the space needed for the bullet or label character.

Here is how we determined the settings:

1. We decided to use a regular en bullet as the text character, rather than a square or other shape.

2. We created a new style called *Bulleted*. We based the style on the Normal style used for the body text, so our typeface, leading, size, and other settings were already set for the bulleted text.

3. We opened the Paragraph Formats dialog box by selecting Edit ➪ Style Sheets and then selecting the Formats button. We changed the settings in the Paragraph Formats dialog box so that the left indent is 9 points (0p9, or 0 picas and 9 points), which is the width of an en bullet and its trailing space — the 0 before the *p* is optional. That shifts the entire paragraph margin in from the left margin 9 points.

An en bullet and its trailing space usually take as much room as the current point size, which makes it easy to figure out the indentation settings needed to achieve the correct alignment for the hanging indent.

4. We set the first line's indent at –0p9. Using a negative number as the First Line setting moves the first line *out*, creating an outdent instead of an indent. The left indent and first-line indent settings cancel each other out, ensuring proper alignment of the bullets, as explained earlier.

If you want to use other characters as bullets, you must experiment with left-indent and first-line-indent values to get the right settings.

5. We saved the style and applied it to the paragraphs we wanted bulleted.

6. The last step was to enter the bullets, which we did by using the shortcut Alt+Shift+8. Another option would have been to use a placeholder character (such as an asterisk) in our original text file, and then use the find-and-replace feature to change the placeholder to a bullet after importing the text file into QuarkXPress. (Find and replace techniques are covered in Chapter 17, "Editing Text.")

If we wanted to use numerals instead of bullets in the list, we would first determine whether there would be one or two digits in the numerals. In most typefaces, a numeral is the width of an en, which is half the current point size. After factoring in the space taken by the period and the trailing space, you typically need 1.2 ems of space for a hanging indent. An em space is equivalent to the current point size. If we needed two digits, that space would be 1.2 ems (one digit, the period, and the trailing space) plus an en (0.5 ems), or 1.7 times the current point size. Note that the amount of space taken by the period and the trailing space will vary based on the typeface and whether the text is justified, so you will have to experiment with settings for your own text.

To ensure proper alignment of the single-digit numerals in a list that contains some two-digit numerals, put a leading en space (Ctrl+Shift+6 or Ctrl+Alt+Shift+6) before the single-digit numerals.

How to Choose a Bullet

Although the en bullet (•) is the most popular bullet character, there is no reason to use only this character.

A solid square makes the bullet appear bolder and more authoritative. A hollow square gives a "strong but silent" feel. A triangle appears more distinct without being as heavy as a solid square. Arrows reinforce the bullet's basic message of "Look here!" Geometric shapes are great alternatives to the traditional bullet, and typefaces such as Zapf Dingbats and Wingdings offer several. (Wingdings comes with Windows 3.1, and Zapf Dingbats comes with some type-scaling programs and typeface packages.)

Several typefaces offer whimsical characters that can work as bullets in the right context. Another possibility is to use symbols with specific meanings: You can use astrological signs for a horoscope column, religious symbols for a church or temple newsletter, or check marks and check boxes for election materials.

It's likely that your typeface has special symbols or diacritical marks (language symbols) that may work as bullets. You also can use a

logo as a symbol if you create a typeface that uses it. (You can do this with such programs as Altsys's Fontographer or ZSoft's SoftType. CorelDRAW also lets you create typefaces, but most Windows programs, including QuarkXPress, often cannot read the typeface properly if it was created in Version 2.0; Version 3.0 fixed this problem.) Using a logo is particularly effective if it is simple and readily identified with your organization.

The accompanying figure shows a sampling of potential bullet characters.

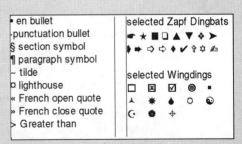

▶ A sampling of characters to use in place of the traditional en bullet.

Consider using a fixed space (described in Chapter 12, "Understanding Character Spacing") after a bullet or label to ensure that text always starts in the same position on each line with such a label. If your text is not justified, the normal space will always be the same width, so alignment will not be a problem, but you may want to use an en space anyhow so there is a bit more space after the bullet or label than there is between words in the text; this will help set the bullet or label off a bit from the rest of the text.

Visual labels

Another variety of list uses in-text labels that highlight the first few words of each new element. These highlighted words might be a few words that act as a mini-headline, or they may simply be the first few words of the paragraph.

You can use any of several type attributes to define in-text labels. To help you see how each looks, we've used the attributes within the following descriptions. Unless otherwise noted, these effects are available from both the Style menu and the Measurements palette. You also can access many of them by using the keyboard shortcuts listed in Chapter 14, "Working with Typefaces."

- **Boldface:** The "strongest" attribute, boldface often is used as a second-level subhead when the first-level subhead is a stand-alone headline set in a larger size and perhaps in a different typeface. It also can be used to indicate a first-level subhead in reports or newsletters when strong design is not a priority.

- *Italics:* This is a favorite choice. If you use boldface as a second-level subhead, italics is a natural option for third-level subheads. It also can be used after a bullet when each bulleted item contains a narrative description that benefits from a label summarizing its content.

- Underlines or rules: A common choice for documents that are meant to look like word-processed or typewritten documents, underlines or rules convey a "no frills" feel. They fall between boldface and italics in terms of visual impact. If you use rules, avoid using rules thicker than 2 points (anywhere from 0.5 to 1.5 is usually sufficient), and stay away from special rules such as dotted or thick-and-thin rules. Stick with single or double rules so that you don't distract readers from the text you're trying to emphasize.

- SMALL CAPS: This is a classy choice for text that doesn't need a strong visual label. Small caps appear no stronger visually than regular text, so they are not effective if you want to make labels more visible than the surrounding text (for example, so a reader can scan the labels to see which text is relevant). But small caps provide a way to add text labels that summarize content without interfering with the overall look of the document. As with italics, small caps work well in conjunction with bullets. Combining small caps with italics or boldface is an effective way to create labels that have more impact and yet retain the classy look of small caps.

- ■ Typeface change: By changing to a typeface that is distinctly different from the current text, you can highlight labels very effectively. If you choose this option, try to pick a typeface used elsewhere in the document, so you avoid the ransom-note look. When body text is set in a serif typeface, it's typical and appealing to use a sans serif typeface for the label, but the reverse is often less effective. We used Univers as the typeface for the label of this paragraph instead of the typeface we normally use.

- ■ Scaled text: By scaling text wider, you can create a subtle label that has more visual impact than small caps and about the same impact as italics. (To access scaling features, select Style ⇨ Horizontal Scale. You cannot select this effect from the Measurements palette.) Be careful not to scale text too much (we used 125 percent here), or it will look distorted. A less-effective variation is to scale down the label text, so that it is narrower. This technique can work if you combine it with another attribute — for example, small caps and/or boldface — to counteract the reduced visual impact of the condensed text.

- ■ Size change: By making text a few points larger, you can subtly call attention to labels without being too explicit about it. Don't set the label size more than a few points more than the size of the body text, and never make label text smaller than body text. (We made the label text 2 points larger than body text here.) As with scaling text, this technique can be combined with other techniques to work more effectively.

Changing the horizontal scale and text size generally are the least effective of the methods used to indicate labels, and they can easily be misused. If you do decide to scale text or change its size, consider carefully the settings you choose.

Dingbats

A *dingbat* is a special character used as a visual marker, most typically to indicate the end of a story in a multistory document like a magazine. A dingbat is especially useful if you have many stories on a page or many stories that "jump to" (continue on) later pages, because it may not be readily apparent to readers whether a story has ended or has jumped elsewhere.

As with bullets, you can use almost any character as a dingbat. Squares and other geometric shapes are popular choices, as are logos or stylized letters based on the name of the publication or organization.

The easiest way to create a dingbat is to set a tab in your body-text paragraph style (or in whatever style you use for the last paragraph in a story). Set this tab to be right-aligned to the column's right margin; this is usually where dingbats are placed. If columns are 14 picas wide, set the tab at 14 picas, as shown in Figure 15-4. After you set the tab, go to the final paragraph in the story and add a tab after the last letter. Then add your dingbat character (and change its type-face, if necessary).

If you define the dingbat tab in the style used for your body text, you don't have to worry about remembering to apply the right style to the final paragraph after the layout has been completed and text edited, added, or cut to fit the layout.

A dingbat need not be aligned against the right margin. You may want to place it one em space after the last character in the paragraph, in which case you simply add two nonbreaking en spaces (Ctrl+Alt+Shift+6) before the dingbat. Or you can use the flex space feature explained in Chapter 12, "Understanding Character Spacing."

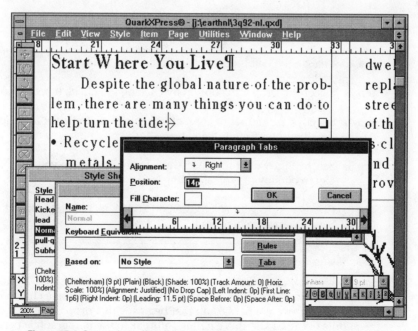

▶ **Figure 15-4:** Set a tab to align dingbats to the column margin.

Drop Caps

Using *drop caps* (a large letter set into several lines of normal-size text) is a popular way to guide readers through changes in topics. Drop caps also are frequently used to identify the introduction and conclusion of a story. When drop caps are used in this manner, the introduction and conclusion usually do not have subheads, although the sections between may have subheads.

QuarkXPress automates most of the steps involved in creating a drop cap. To set a drop cap, open the Paragraph Formats dialog box by selecting the Formats button in the Edit Style Sheet dialog box or by choosing the Formats option in the Style menu (the keyboard shortcut is Ctrl+Shift+F).

Because you are likely to use this effect more than once, it is best to create a style for any paragraphs that use it. In most cases, the settings for a drop-cap paragraph are the same as those for body text, except that the paragraph's first line is not indented and a drop cap is defined. Rather than repeat all the settings for the body text when creating a drop cap style, you can simply follow these steps.

▶ **Steps: Creating a drop cap style sheet item**

Step 1. Select Based On from the Edit Style Sheet dialog box and select the body text style as the basis for the new style.

Step 2. Change the Left Indent setting to 0.

Step 3. Select the Drop Caps option by clicking the check box next to it.

Step 4. Specify the number of characters (usually 1) to be set as drop caps in the Character Count dialog box.

Step 5. Set the Line Count to specify how many lines deep you want the drop cap to occupy (a typical setting is 3).

Step 6. Choose OK to get back to the Edit Style Sheet dialog box and select Save to store the new style.

Figure 15-5 shows the settings described in the preceding steps. By also selecting the Keep Lines Together option, as is done in the example shown in Figure 15-5, you can prevent a paragraph that begins with a drop cap from breaking in the middle of the cap. In this example, a break in the paragraph is permitted, but only after four lines of text, which ensures that at least one line of full-length text follows the drop cap. (If you decide to set a one-time drop cap by choosing Style ⇨ Formats instead of creating a style, the Paragraph Formats dialog box you see is identical to that in the figure.)

▶ **Figure 15-5:** Sample settings used to create a style for a paragraph beginning with a drop cap.

After you create the drop-cap style, you can apply it easily. Position your cursor anywhere on the appropriate text. Then select the new style from either the Style ⇨ Style Sheets option or the Style Sheets palette (if the palette is not visible, use View ⇨ Show Style Sheets to turn it on).

A final step is to change the drop cap's typeface. This is optional — there is no reason that a drop cap can't have the same typeface as the rest of the paragraph. But typically, a drop cap is either set in boldface or in a completely different typeface, which gives the drop cap higher visibility and usually results in a more interesting design. It's common for drop caps to be set in the same typeface as the headline or subhead. To change the drop cap's typeface, select it with the mouse and use the Measurements palette's font list or the Style ⇨ Fonts menu. In the example shown in Figure 15-6, Goudy Bold is selected as the drop-cap typeface.

A common question related to the use of drop caps arises when a paragraph begins with a quotation: Should you use the open quotation character ("), the open single-quote character ('), or no character at all to indicate the start of a quote? Most typographers choose the last option to avoid having overly big quotation marks, and traditionalist stylebooks agree. (Do, however, use the close-quotation mark (") at the end of the quotation.) Although this is an

▶ **Figure 15.6:** Selecting a typeface for a drop cap.

accepted practice, some people find it confusing, because they don't realize they've been reading a quote until they get to the end of it. If you insist on indicating an open quote, use the single quote (') — it distracts the eye from the actual first letter less than the double quote ("). Be sure to set the drop cap's Character Count setting to 2, not 1. Otherwise, you wind up with a large quotation mark only!

A similar effect to a drop cap is a *raised cap,* which is simply a large first letter on the first line of a paragraph. A raised cap does not drop into the surrounding paragraph but rises above it instead. To create this effect, simply select the first character and change its point size and, optionally, its typeface.

You also can create a hybrid between a drop cap and a raised cap. For example, you can add a drop cap that is four lines tall and drops in two lines of text. To do this, make the drop cap's line count 2, select the drop-cap character, and then change its size. Note that when you do this, the Measurements palette options change from displaying actual point sizes to percentages, such as 200%. You are not limited to the choices you see on-screen; you can highlight a percentage shown and type in your own number. Alternatively, you can use the Style ⇨ Size menu to accomplish the same thing (select Other to get the percentage options). If you are comfortable using keyboard shortcuts, the fastest method is to press Ctrl+Shift+\, which opens the Font Size dialog box.

When you use a larger point size for a raised cap or a hybrid drop cap, the cap may extend into the text above. It's likely that you will need to insert extra returns above the cap to keep text from overprinting. One way to avoid this is to use additive or automatic leading options in your style tag. For information on these leading options, see Chapter 13, "Understanding Paragraph Spacing."

You can create yet another variation of a drop cap by moving the drop cap away from the text to make it more pronounced. Use the Style ⇨ Kern menu or enter a kerning value in the Measurements palette to move the drop cap. In addition, you can compress or expand the drop cap with the Style ⇨ Horizontal Scale menu option.

Figure 15-7 shows several variations of drop caps. Reading from the top of the figure to the bottom and starting at the left column, you see: a traditional three-line drop cap; a three-line raised cap (the point size is three times the leading); a three-line drop cap in a typeface different from body text; a three-line drop cap that has both a different typeface and extra kerning; and a combination raised/drop cap that has a different typeface and is set to print as outline text.

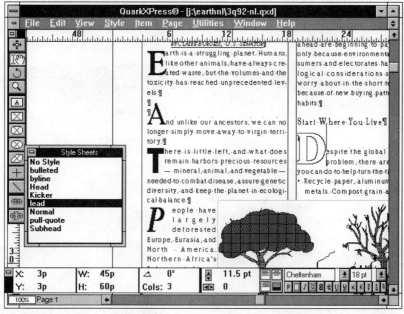

▶ **Figure 15-7:** Drop cap variations.

Text Rotation

Text rotation is a popular and effective way to treat *display type,* or type used as art. Some people consider drop caps and titles to be display type, while others consider them to be merely body type. How you treat them depends on how design-intensive your publication is. If all your titles and drop caps follow the same format, you're treating them as body type. But if you make the title of each chapter or story distinct, and perhaps make the drop caps for opening pages different as well, you're treating those elements as display type.

Instead of limiting you to display-type treatments that involve changes in font and size only, desktop publishing lets you also move type to different angles of rotation, adding another weapon to your design arsenal. QuarkXPress offers rotation in any angle, giving you maximum flexibility.

In addition to being used for story titles, rotated text is sometimes used to create angled pull-quotes, banners and flags on ads and covers, and identifiers at the outside of a page. Figure 15-8 offers examples that illustrate some of the potential of this design tool.

To rotate text, you must first put it in its own text box. QuarkXPress actually rotates the text box, not the text within it. After you put the elements to be rotated in their own text boxes and switch to the Item tool, you can rotate them in any of three ways:

▶ **Figure 15-8:** Examples of rotated text.

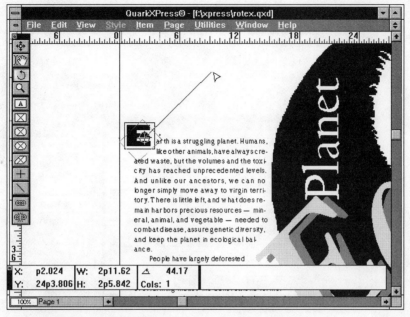

► **Figure 15-9:** Using the Rotation tool.

■ **Option 1:** Use the Measurements palette to enter the rotation amount (the top option on the third column, indicated by a geometric-angle symbol). This is the simplest method, especially if you know what angle of rotation you want in advance.

■ **Option 2:** Use the Rotation tool (the curved arrow), as shown in Figure 15-9. The advantage to this tool is that it is free-form, letting you eyeball the angle as you turn the text. This comes in handy when, for example, you want to match the text's rotation to a graphic element. The disadvantage is that it takes time to learn to control the rotation tool accurately. You can always fine-tune the angle later through the Measurements palette, however.

■ **Option 3:** Use the B̲ox Angle option in the Text Box Specifications dialog box, shown in Figure 15-10. To open the box, select I̲tem ➪ M̲odify or use the keyboard shortcut Ctrl+M. This is the most cumbersome approach, but it is the fastest method if you also want to modify other settings, such as background color and text-frame position.

It's likely that you will need to set runarounds for rotated text boxes so they don't interfere with other text and graphics. You also may need to reposition the rotated text box so its new angle works with other elements on the page. This requires using the Item tool, as described in Chapter 9, "Working with Text," in Part III, "Page Layout." (Remember, you are in effect treating text as graphics, so layout and graphics techniques now come into play.)

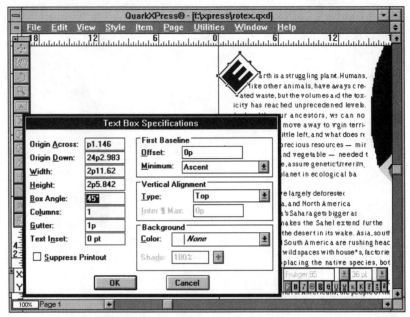

▶ **Figure 15-10:** Using the Box Angle option to rotate text.

Text rotation works well when combined with other features. For example, in Figure 15-8, the drop cap's font is changed to match that of the *How to Save* part of the headline. It is also scaled horizontally 120 percent so it stretches over the three lines of text it drops into. And it is set at the same angle as the word *Earth* to help tie the text to the title treatment. On the right page, rotated text for the page number is set in a white color, set against a black background, and placed in a text box set flush against the page edge. This is a graphic way to make page numbers visible in a highly visual layout while keeping them from distracting from the story.

Fancier rotation techniques, such as having text follow an arc, can also be effective. To use them, however, you need a graphics program that can manipulate text as part of a graphic, such as CorelDRAW, Adobe Illustrator, and Aldus Free-Hand, or a program that lets you manipulate text and export it as a graphic, such as ZSoft's SoftType.

Colored and Shaded Text

As with most special effects, apply color or shading to text sparingly, and reserve these treatments for elements that serve as text-as-art. Good places to use color or shading include titles, bylines, pull-quotes, and ancillary elements such as page numbers.

QuarkXPress lets you apply color or shading (or both) to any selected text or to any paragraph whose style uses color or shading settings. You can access these effects in several ways:

- **Option 1:** Make selections in the Style ➪ Color and Style ➪ Shade menus.

- **Option 2:** Select a color through the color palette (made visible by choosing View ➪ Show Colors and invisible by choosing View ➪ Hide Colors).

- **Option 3:** Make a selection in the Character Attributes dialog box. To apply effects to selected text, open the dialog box by selecting Style ➪ Character or by using the keyboard shortcut Ctrl+Shift+D. To apply effects to a style, select Edit ➪ Style Sheets and then select the Character button.

Figure 15-11 shows examples of both shading and color. The byline is shaded at 20-percent black, which contrasts well with the drop shadow, whose preset value is 50 percent. The word *Earth* in the title is set at 100-percent yellow so it pops out from the background illustration of the pelican. The drop shadow also helps lift the word from the illustration.

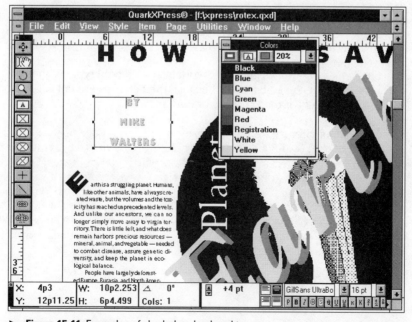

▶ **Figure 15-11:** Examples of shaded and colored type.

As Figure 15-11 shows, light colors and shades are best used with bold, large type, because this keeps them from getting lost in the layout. They also work well when combined with other effects, as is done in the example.

Darker colors, such as blues and reds, work well in borders or as the colors of large outlined text.

The Colors palette has three icons at the top. In the example shown in Figure 15-11, the Text icon is depressed, indicating that color is being applied to text. The Frame icon indicates whether color is applied to the border, or frame, of the text box, if one has been defined; the Background icon signals whether color is applied to the text-box background. Chapters in Part III, "Page Layout," and in Part V, "Graphics," cover the use and creation of color in more detail.

Shadows and Outlines

Desktop publishing made it easy to create shadowed and outlined text — tasks that were difficult in traditional typesetting because they required manual intervention (through darkroom or paste-up techniques). In the early days of desktop publishing, you could identify most desktop-published work because it usually used one or both of these effects. Unfortunately, the effects were so overused that many professionals sneered at the "ransom note" look produced by computer-based publishing novices.

QuarkXPress offers options to create shadows or outlines from any typeface. Figure 15-12 shows a sample of text that incorporates these effects. Note that the Measurements palette shows the current text settings (bold italic shadow).

Shadows and outlines generally work best with bold type. With lighter type, the characters become obscured, because their strokes are not wide enough to be distinguished from the shadow or outline.

You cannot alter the shadow's position and percentage of gray. If you want a different type of shadow, you must create your own in a program such as ZSoft's SoftType. An alternative method, which you can use in QuarkXPress, is to duplicate the text box that contains your text, turn off text runaround, and apply the color or shade you want to the duplicate text box. Place the duplicate text box under the original text box. The original text box acts as the "non-shadow" text, while the duplicated text box becomes the "shadow." You can position the shadow wherever you prefer to create the effect you want. Figure 15-13 shows this technique.

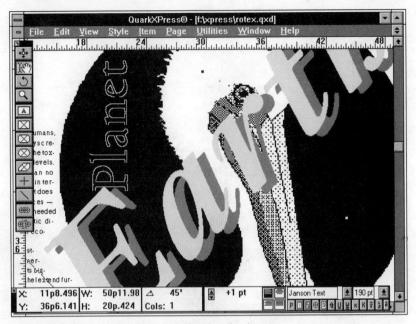

▶ **Figure 15-12:** Examples of shadowed and outlined text.

A particularly stylish effect that uses shadows is to make the text the same color as the background (usually white) and apply a shadow to the text. This effect simulates raised lettering, as the phrase "HOW TO SAVE" in Figure 15-14 illustrates.

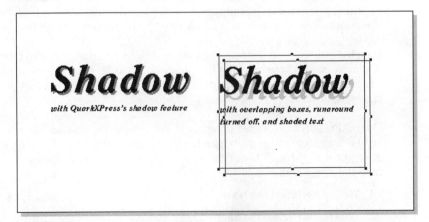

▶ **Figure 15-13:** You can use QuarkXPress's default shadows (left) or create your own by overlapping text boxes (right).

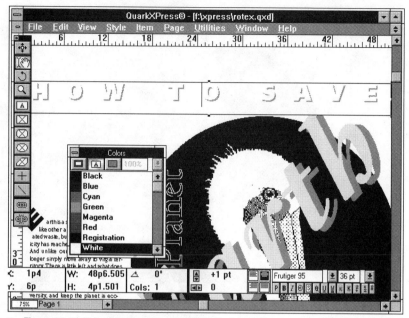

▶ **Figure 15-14:** Using shadows to simulate raised lettering.

Hanging Punctuation

A technique used often in advertising is *hanging punctuation,* in which periods, commas, hyphens, and other punctuation marks fall outside the right margin. This technique is used in text that is either aligned right or justified — it does not make sense to hang punctuation in centered or left-aligned text, because the punctuation would be too far away from the accompanying text.

Hanging punctuation keeps letters aligned along the right margin, but gives the text some visual flow by using the punctuation as an exterior decoration. Figure 15-15 shows an example of right-aligned text in which the punctuation hangs off the margin.

QuarkXPress (or any other program) offers no tool to handle this effect. For right-aligned text, you can create hanging punctuation by using tabs, either in a style sheet or through the style menu for the selected text. Here is how we created the hanging punctuation shown in Figure 15-15:

1. We right-aligned the text.

2. We created a tab that aligned right at 43 picas, 3 points. This tab was used at the beginning of each line. For text that took more than one line, we used a line break (Shift+Enter) instead of a normal paragraph (Enter) so that all

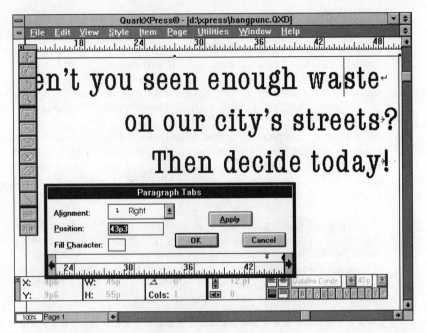

▶ **Figure 15-15:** An example of hanging punctuation.

lines of text aligned together. We chose an alignment value that placed the tab far enough from the text box's right margin (here, 45 picas) that any punctuation character would fit between that tab and the text box's right margin. (A rule of thumb is to use between one-third and one-half of the current point size, because the biggest punctuation symbol — the question mark — usually is about that size.)

3. We added a second tab that aligned right at 43 picas, 4 points. (This value could have been anything more than the first tab's value of 43 picas, 3 points. At the current point size, 1 point was comparable to the natural letter spacing. Print out sample text at various tab settings before determining a final value.) We used this tab between the text and the punctuation. If there is no punctuation on a particular line, no tab is needed.

When setting tabs, use the ruler in the Paragraph Tabs dialog box, not the document ruler at the top of the screen.

The advantage to this approach is that you can use the same tab settings (usually through a style sheet) for all text in which you want this effect. The disadvantage is that it does not work on justified text.

The other method of accomplishing this effect — and the method you must use if text is justified — is to create two text boxes, one for the text and one for any punctuation marks that end a line. You'll probably need two styles as well: one for the text (either right-aligned or justified) and one for the punctuation (left-aligned). The simplest way to handle this is to create a style for the punctuation based on the style for the text, so that if the style for text changes, so does the punctuation style. You can then change the alignment in the punctuation style.

After creating the two text boxes, align them so that the punctuation appears properly spaced after its corresponding text. Then use QuarkXPress's lock feature (Item ⇨ Lock or Ctrl+L) to prevent the two boxes from moving accidentally. You can also group the boxes so they keep the same relationship if moved (use Item ⇨ Group or Ctrl+6).

 Regardless of which approach you use to create hanging punctuation, if your text changes, you must manually change the line endings or punctuation positions. But because hanging punctuation is used only in small amounts of text, this is not a terrible burden. Also make sure that you turn off hyphenation, so you don't get double hyphenation (one from the hyphenation feature and one from the punctuation you enter manually).

Summary

▶ A rule of thumb for proper first-line indentation value is to keep the indent between one and two ems — or between the text point size and twice that size. Use smaller values in this range for narrower columns than for wider columns.

▶ Keep the total number of indentation levels to a maximum of three for most documents.

▶ Use a style tag to ease the creation of bulleted lists.

▶ Consider using bullet characters other than the standard en bullets.

▶ When using enumerated lists that have ten or more items, be sure to precede single-digit numbers with an en space so all the numbers align on the decimal.

▶ Use typeface attributes, such as boldface and small caps, and typeface changes, as visual labels.

▶ By using dingbats to end stories in multistory documents like newsletters, you let the reader know for sure whether a story has ended or continues elsewhere.

▶ Drop caps can come in several forms. Don't lock yourself into only one drop-cap format.

▶ Rotated text must be in its own text box.

▶ Use light colors only on bold, large text. Dark colors can also be used on small, thin text and as text outlines.

▶ QuarkXPress's shadows cannot be altered. But you can create your own shadow effects by having text boxes that overlap slightly (runaround must be turned off).

▶ You can create effects like hanging punctuation through tab settings or by having two independent text boxes locked or grouped together.

CHAPTER

16

Using Tabs

Reviewing Your Options: Tab Styles

Tab stops make it possible to align text within columns, which is handy for lists, tables, and other columnar data. You can also use tabs to align single characters, such as dingbats, which are described in Chapter 15, "Using Special Elements and Effects." Tabs can be tricky, because there are so many tab options and because it is often hard to predict how much space you need between tabs to make the tab fit nicely.

Typewriters usually offer left-aligned tabs only: You press the tab key and that moves the carriage to a new left "margin." But QuarkXPress offers a wide variety of tab alignments, which are available through the Paragraph Tabs dialog box, shown in Figure 16-1. Each type of tab has its own tab mark on the tab ruler to help you remember which tab is set which way.

You have the following tab options:

- **Left:** Text typed after the tab aligns to the tab as if the tab were a left margin. This is the most popular alignment for text.

- **Center:** Text typed in after the tab is centered, with the tab location serving as the center mark. This is almost as popular as left alignment for text and symbols (such as check boxes in a features table).

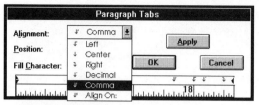

▶ **Figure 16-1:** Tab styles available through the
Paragraph Tabs dialog box.

■ **Right:** Text typed in after the tab aligns to the tab as if the tab were a right
margin. This alignment is typically used with tables of numbers, because
regardless of the number of digits, you want the ones digit (the rightmost
digit) in all numbers to align with each other, the tens digit (the next digit to
the left) in all numbers to align with each other, and so on.

■ **Decimal:** Numbers with a decimal (.) that are typed in after the tab align on
the period. This is handy if you have data with varying numbers of decimal
places, such as 10.2 and 40.41. If there are no decimals in a number, the
number aligns as if there were a decimal *after* the number. When the data is
a mix of numerals and text, it aligns at the first numeral. If the data consists
of text only, with no numerals at all, the text aligns left. (See Figure 16-2 for
examples.)

■ **Comma:** Numbers with a comma (,) that are typed in after the tab align on
the comma. This is convenient if you have some data with decimal places,
such as 5,210.2, and some without, such as 10,240. If the data is a mix of
numerals and letters, it aligns at the first numeral. If there are no numerals in
the data, the text right-aligns to the tab location.

If a number does not contain commas, it aligns as if a comma followed the
number, which is usually not what you want. (See Figure 16-2 for examples;
the positioning of 789.99 clearly shows this counterintuitive positioning.) A
decimal tab is usually a better option, unless you are using numbers that
have no decimals but do have commas.

■ **Align On:** With this option, you specify which character the text aligns on.
You can specify any letter, number, punctuation, or symbol in the current
typeface (use Alt+keypad codes to get special characters not available from
the keyboard). The align-on tab handles mixed text (in which some text has
the alignment character and some does not) in the same manner as the
comma tab.

Figure 16-2 shows how the decimal, comma, and align-on tabs work when used in
a variety of text. As the figure illustrates, the QuarkXPress decimal alignment
feature is smart enough to handle any kind of number, but the comma alignment
can deliver unwanted alignments when numbers don't have commas.

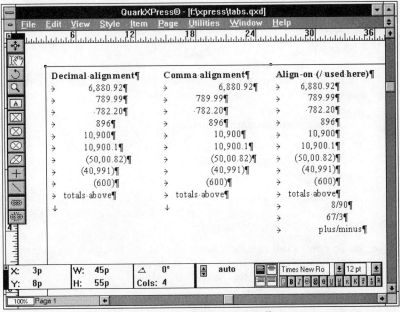

Setting Up Tabs

The default tab settings in QuarkXPress place a left tab every half inch. To set up other tabs, you use the Paragraph Tabs dialog box.

If you want to create or modify a style that has tab settings so you can use them throughout a document, select the Tabs button in the Edit Style Sheet dialog box (select Edit ⇨ Style Sheets). If you are working only on a specific paragraph or want to override a style locally, select Style ⇨ Tabs or use the keyboard shortcut Ctrl+Shift+T to access the Paragraph Tabs dialog box.

You may set as many as 20 tab stops for a paragraph. Once in the dialog box, set tabs as follows:

▶ **Steps: Setting your own tabs**

Step 1. Select the alignment you want from the Alignment option.

Step 2. Either type in the position in the Position text box or move your mouse to the tab ruler and click the location of the tab. If you click the tab with the mouse and keep the mouse button pressed, you can move the tab.

All measurements in the tab ruler are relative to the text's left margin, not to the absolute page or text-box coordinates. That way, in multicolumn text, tabs in each column appear as you would expect. For example, when a tab stop is defined at 3 picas, a tab used in column 1 will occur at 3 picas from column 1's left margin, while a tab used in column 3 will occur at 3 picas from column 3's left margin. Thus, when figuring out where tab stops should be, be sure to use the tab ruler, not the document ruler.

It's just as easy to change tab settings:

- **To change a tab's alignment:** Single-click the tab (its position shows up in the <u>P</u>osition option) and then move to the A<u>l</u>ignments option and select a new alignment.

- **To change a tab's position:** Single-click the tab (its position shows up in the <u>P</u>osition option) and then hold the mouse button down and slide the tab to a new position on the tab ruler.

- **To copy a tab to a new location:** Single-click the tab (its position shows up in the <u>P</u>osition option) and then move your cursor to the <u>P</u>osition option and enter a new tab-stop location. When you choose OK to exit the dialog box, you set both tabs.

- **To delete a tab:** Single-click the tab, keep the mouse button pressed, and lift the tab up out of the tab ruler.

- **To remove all tabs:** Hold Ctrl and click the tab ruler. Tab settings revert to the style's settings if you are working locally. If you are working in a style definition, tab settings revert to QuarkXPress's defaults.

Using Leaders

A *tab leader* is a series of characters that runs from text to text within tabular material. Usually, a period is used as the tab leader character. A leader's purpose is to guide the reader's eye, especially across wide distances. For an example, look at the tables of contents in this book: A dot leader appears between the section and chapter names and their page numbers.

QuarkXPress calls a tab leader a *fill character*. To define a leader, enter a character in the Fill <u>C</u>haracter text box, which you find in the Paragraph Tabs dialog box. In Figure 16-3, a period is selected as the Fill <u>C</u>haracter. You can enter nonkeyboard characters by typing in their Alt+keypad Windows code or by using Character Map (as described in Chapter 14, "Working with Typefaces").

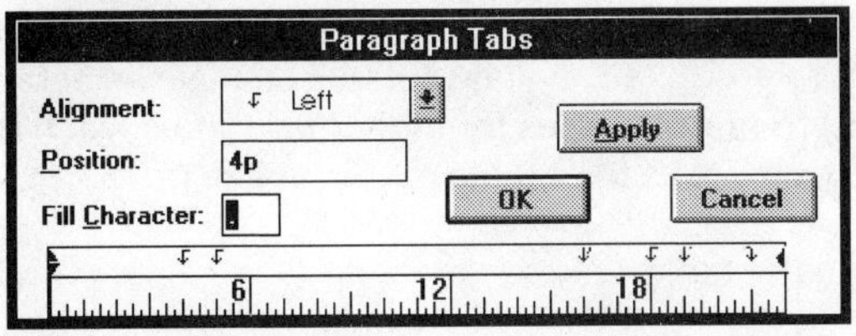

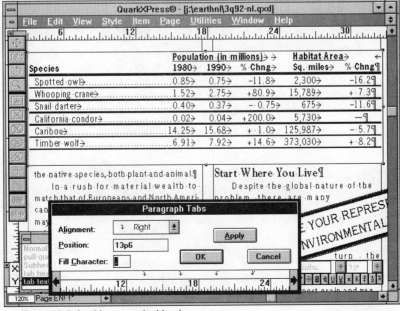

Figure 16-3: Select a tab leader character in the Fill Character text box.

Creating Tables with Tabs

By combining various tab settings with other typographic features — and by first thinking through the look you want for your table — you can create sophisticated tables in QuarkXPress. Figure 16-4 shows an example table.

The table incorporates a mix of tab settings defined in two styles, one for the table text and one for the table headline. (The Paragraph Tabs dialog box shown in the figure gives the settings for the table text.) The table's styles also include ruling lines and indentation settings.

Figure 16-4: A table created with tabs.

To avoid creating separate styles for each table, consider deriving standard tab settings that apply to groups of similar tables. Then use local tab settings (through Style ⇨ Tabs) to modify styles for individual tables when necessary or to create completely new tabs for a table that is unlike others.

Here is how we created the table:

1. We typed in a sample line of text, placing tabs between each column.

2. We used the Style ⇨ Tabs feature to define tab stops. We determined tab stops by guessing where columns should be, based on text length for each column. We determined alignment based on the type of data: We chose left alignment for regular text; decimal alignment for numbers with decimals; and right alignment for numbers without decimals. After making educated guesses, we chose Apply to see the result. We moved our tab stops and selected Apply until we were satisfied.

When planning a table, set tabs to accommodate the longest text you expect to include in each column, so the tabs work with all rows in your table.

3. We wrote down the tab stops and repeated step 2 for the table's title row. The tabs stops for the title row are different than those of the table body. All tabs in the title row align left, because the titles do not contain any numbers with decimals or commas to align elements on. The tab stops for the years in the title are different than the tab stops for the population figures in the table body because the numerals in the year must start to the left of the decimal point in the figures. Otherwise, the title would appear out of alignment.

4. We chose Cancel so none of our locally set tabs would take effect.

5. We created two new styles — Table Body and Table Title — that used the tab stop settings we determined earlier. We also set our typeface, size, and ruling-line settings. The ruling line below the title here is 2 points; the ruling line between the rows is 1 point. (Chapter 6, "Creating Style Sheets," covers styles in detail.)

6. We applied the new styles to the table text as we entered the rest of the table.

If you want vertical lines between table columns, create a picture box for them the size of the table. Then turn off text wrap for the text box and use the Line tool to draw the lines. (How to set text boxes is covered in Chapter 9, "Working with Text," in Part III, "Page Layout.") Next, select the text box containing the text and the picture box containing the lines (hold down Shift when clicking the second box, so the first one remains selected). From the Item menu, select Group, so the two boxes stay together if the layout later changes. Keep in mind, however, that if the text reflows, the lines do not move with the table text unless the table is in its own text box, independent of the rest of the story.

Summary

▶ Tabs set with comma alignment or with alignment on a user-defined character will not work as expected for text that does not contain the alignment character. But tabs set with decimal alignment will work as expected in these cases.

▶ Tab stops are relative to the text box's left margin, not to the page's ruler.

▶ Tab stops are limited to 20 per paragraph.

▶ Nonkeyboard characters may be used as tab leaders. Use the Windows ANSI code or the Windows 3.1 Character Map utility to access them.

▶ You can create tables by defining tab stops for tabular text. If tables share common formats, you can define a style tag for tables and then locally override it for tables that need fine-tuning.

CHAPTER 17

Editing Text

● ●

In This Chapter

▶ How to insert, delete, and move text

▶ Ways to search and replace text and text attributes

▶ How to use the spell checker and modify the spelling dictionary

▶ How to apply the techniques described in previous chapters in Part IV, "Typography and Text," to make text fit your layout

● ●

Using Basic Editing Techniques

Like all publishing programs, QuarkXPress assumes you do the bulk of your text editing in a word processor, so it does not provide word-processor–level editing tools. But it's a fact of life that you will do at least minor editing in your layout, either to correct mistakes that slip through in the word-processed version or to make changes related to the needs of the document layout, such as removing or adding text to make copy fit. (See the "Copy Fitting" section later in this chapter for copy-fitting techniques).

The most basic level of editing involves adding or deleting text. To do this, position your text cursor (which appears if you are using the Content tool) at the spot where you want to make changes and click the mouse button. You then can start typing or deleting text.

If you want to delete blocks of text, select them before cutting or deleting. To select a block of text, position the text cursor at one end, hold the mouse button down, and move the cursor to the other end, releasing the button when you reach the end of the text you want to select. The selected text is highlighted.

To select all text in a text box (as well as in linked text boxes), select any text in the box and choose Edit ➪ Select All (keyboard shortcut is Ctrl+A).

You can also replace text by selecting it and typing in new text or pasting in text from the Clipboard (via Edit ➪ Paste or the keyboard shortcut Crtl+V). The new text takes the place of the old and can be from another part of your document, from another QuarkXPress document, or from another Windows program. The new text can be a copy of text (use the Edit ➪ Copy command or the keyboard shortcut Crtl+C from the source program), or it can be text cut from another document (use the Edit ➪ Cut command or the keyboard shortcut Crtl+X).

Cut text and *deleted* text are different. QuarkXPress inserts cut text automatically into the Clipboard, but does not do this with deleted text. (You delete text by using the Delete key or Backspace key.) The only way to recover deleted text is via Edit ➪ Undo Typing. Cut text remains in the Clipboard until you cut or copy other text.

You move text by cutting it from one location and pasting it into another. You duplicate text by copying it at one location and pasting it into another.

All Windows programs do not use the same shortcuts for copy, paste, and cut. QuarkXPress for Windows uses Ctrl+C for copy, Ctrl+V for paste, and Ctrl+X for cut, just as in the Macintosh version (if you equate the Mac's command key (⌘) with the PC's Ctrl key). But WordPerfect for Windows 5.1 and Lotus 1-2-3 for Windows 1.0 use Ctrl+Insert, Shift+Insert, and Shift+Delete, respectively, which were Windows standards until recently. Applications from the same vendors may not use the same shortcuts: For example, Microsoft Word for Windows 2.0 uses the standard Macintosh shortcuts (as does QuarkXPress), but Microsoft Excel 3.0a uses the old Windows standards (the new Excel 4.0 follows the new Windows standards). Some applications support both sets of shortcuts.

Replacing Text and Text Attributes

Basic editing tools are fine for doing simple editing, but you may want to replace one piece of text with another throughout your document. Suppose, for example, that you create a product manual, and you need to change the product's version number throughout the manual. You can make the changes in the original word-processor document and then replace the text in your QuarkXPress document with the updated text. Or you can use QuarkXPress's built-in replace function, which you access through the Find/Change dialog box, shown in Figure 17-1.

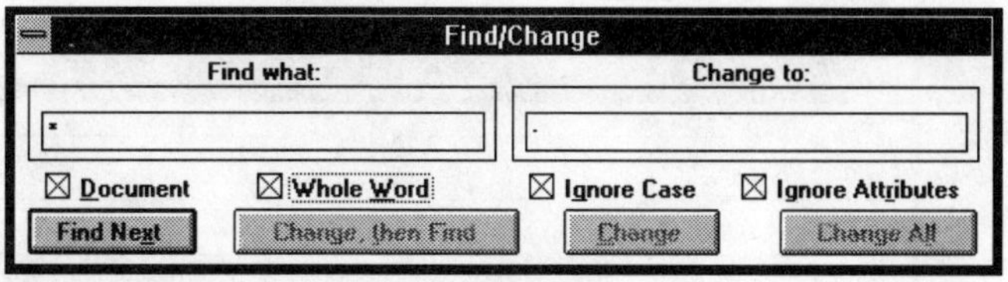

▶ **Figure 17-1:** The Find/Change dialog box.

Replacing text

The Find/Change dialog box (accessed via Edit ⇨ Find/Change or the shortcut Ctrl+F) lets you replace text throughout the current story, which is defined as text in the currently selected text box plus all those linked to it. You also can replace text throughout the entire current document. The QuarkXPress replace function works like the standard search and replace tool found in word processing programs. You can search for whole words or for words whose capitalization matches the words or characters you type in the Find what field. In Figure 17-1, QuarkXPress is instructed to replace asterisks with bullet characters.

You can tell Quark to search for and replace a word regardless of capitalization by selecting Ignore Case. If the Document box is checked, the replace affects all stories and text in your document. The other buttons, such as Find Next, work as they do in word processors.

Changing attributes

Find/Change lets you replace more than text. You can replace text attributes, typefaces, and sizes as well. To access these options, deselect the Ignore Attributes check box. This expands the Find/Change dialog box and offers you attribute replacement options, as Figure 17-2 shows.

In the example shown in the figure, we replace any asterisks set in 9-point Cheltenham with solid square boxes set in 10-point Zapf Dingbats (that's what typing a lowercase *r* generates in that typeface). We want QuarkXPress to replace any asterisks in the document that are not part of a word. To do this, we select the Document option and the Whole Word option. (Choosing Whole Word tells QuarkXPress to search for any asterisk that has a space on either side — the program regards such a character as a "whole word.") We also left Ignore Case checked, although it has no function for symbols such as asterisks that have no case.

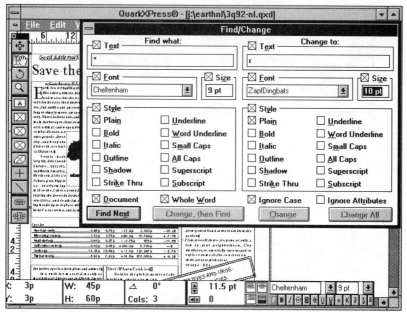

Figure 17-2: Search and replace typeface attributes through the Find/Change dialog box.

You can combine various options to tailor your search. In the example, we select specific text, typeface, and styles for both the search and replace functions. We do this by checking the Text, Font, Size, and Style check boxes in the Find what: and Change to: columns of the dialog box.

If you leave an option unchecked in the Find what: column, QuarkXPress includes any variant (such as style) in the search. If we did not check Size in the Find what: column but did check it in the Change to: column, QuarkXPress would change a Cheltenham Plain asterisk of any size to a 10-point Zapf Dingbats solid square.

If you leave an option unchecked in the Change to: column, QuarkXPress applies the formatting of the text that was searched to the replacement text. If we did not check Size in the Change to: column, the size of the bullet replacing the asterisk would be the same size as the asterisk.

When you leave Text unchecked in the Find what: column, you replace attributes only. You might do this to change all underlined text to word-underlined text, bold text to small cap text, News Gothic bold text to News Gothic bold italic, or 8-point text to 8.5-point text.

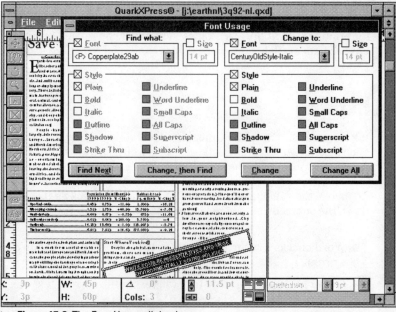

Figure 17-3: The Font Usage dialog box.

Check an attribute box in the Style section of the dialog box if you want to use an attribute. Remove the check mark if you don't want to use an attribute (such as bold) in your search and replace, and make the box gray to tell QuarkXPress to retain whatever attribute is set. (Clicking a box once unchecks it if checked or checks it if unchecked. Clicking it twice makes it gray.) In the example shown in Figure 17-3, the replacement text will be plain but not bold or italic, but any text that is in outline, shadow, strikethrough, underline, word underline, small caps, all caps, superscript, or subscripts will retain those attributes.

You can search and replace all character attributes available in the Measurements palette except for superiors.

Using the Font Usage utility

You also can replace text attributes by using a QuarkXPress utility called Font Usage. Available through Utilities ⇨ Font Usage, this utility lists text style and typeface combinations used in the current document. In the example shown in Figure 17-3, we search for Copperplate 29ab Plain, and Font Usage highlights where this type style appears in the document. We can now replace it with another typeface and/or style attribute.

Font Usage is designed primarily to help you determine what typefaces are used in a document so you or your typesetter know what typefaces you need for printing. The utility also comes in handy if you open a document that uses a typeface not available on your PC; you can replace that typeface with another.

Spell Checking

When you edit text, spelling mistakes invariably crop up. QuarkXPress offers a spelling checker to catch such errors, as well as a tool that enables you to specify the proper spelling of words the program does not recognize.

To invoke the spelling checker, select Utilities ⇨ Check Spelling. This drops down the submenu shown in Figure 17-4, which offers you three spell-checking choices:

- **Word** checks the current word (or the first word in a group of selected words).

- **Story** checks the current story (all text in the current text box, as well as any text in text boxes linked to it).

- **Document** checks every word in the current QuarkXPress document.

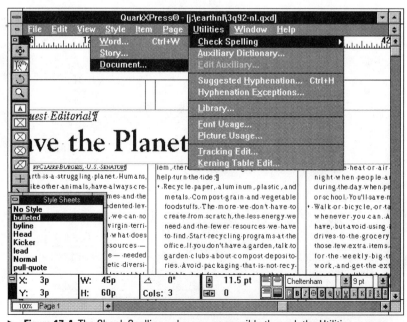

▶ **Figure 17-4:** The Check Spelling submenu, accessible through the Utilities menu.

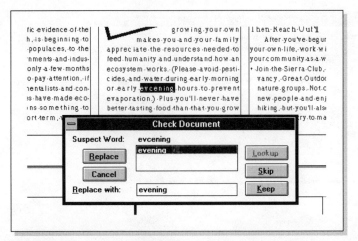

▶ **Figure 17-5:** Choose the correct spelling of a word in the Check Document dialog box.

You can quickly check spelling for the current word by pressing the shortcut keys Ctrl+W.

The spelling checker displays words it does not recognize one at a time, giving you an opportunity to correct or ignore (skip) the word. The spelling checker can suggest correct spellings for words it believes are misspelled. Figure 17-5 shows the spelling checker displaying a suggested correction. To ask Quark-XPress to suggest a word, click the Lookup button. To accept a suggested replacement, click the word and the Replace button. You also can type in the correct word yourself, whether or not you use Lookup.

You can add words that QuarkXPress does not know (most common for specialty words or proper names) to an auxiliary dictionary. If an auxiliary dictionary is open, you can add a word while in the spelling checker by selecting Keep when QuarkXPress displays a word unknown to it.

Creating auxiliary spelling dictionaries

You can create a common auxiliary dictionary to be shared by multiple documents, or you can establish a dictionary specific to a particular document. Use Utilities ➪ Auxiliary Dictionary to invoke the Auxiliary Dictionary dialog box, shown in Figure 17-6. Through this dialog box, you can create a new dictionary or open an existing one. You can also detach a dictionary from a document, which means that QuarkXPress uses its permanent dictionary only.

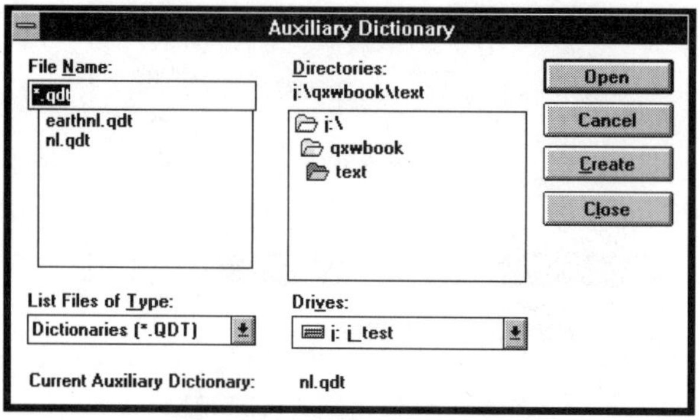

▶ **Figure 17-6:** The Auxiliary Dictionary dialog box.

Auxiliary dictionaries can reside on any drive in any directory (folder), and they do not have to reside in the same place as the document(s) using them. Dictionary files have the extension QDT. In the example shown in Figure 17-6, the current document is using a dictionary called NL.QDT that resides on drive J: in the QXWBOOK\TEXT directory.

- **To create an auxiliary dictionary for a specific document:** Open the document and access the Auxiliary Dictionary dialog box. Enter a filename in the File Name field (the current name will be *.QDT, which indicates there is no current directory open). Any existing dictionaries in the current drive and directory are listed below the File Name field. If you create a dictionary with the same name as any dictionary listed, you are asked whether you want to replace the existing dictionary with a new one.

- **To create a default auxiliary dictionary for all new documents:** Make sure no documents are open before invoking the Auxiliary Dictionary dialog box. Enter a filename as described in the instructions for creating an auxiliary dictionary for a specific document.

- **To use an existing dictionary for the current document:** Open your document and then open an existing dictionary from the Auxiliary Dictionary dialog box.

- **To use an existing dictionary as the default for all new documents:** Make sure no documents are open and then open an existing dictionary from the Auxiliary Dictionary dialog box.

- **To detach an auxiliary dictionary from a current document:** Open the document and select Close in the Auxiliary Dictionary dialog box.

- **To detach an auxiliary dictionary as the default dictionary for all new documents:** Make sure no documents are open. Select Close in the Auxiliary Dictionary dialog box.

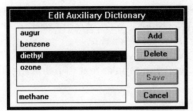

▶ **Figure 17-7:** The Edit Auxiliary Dictionary dialog box.

If a dictionary is associated with the current document or selected as the default auxiliary dictionary, its name appears at the bottom of the Auxiliary Dictionary dialog box as Current Auxiliary Dictionary.

Editing an auxiliary dictionary

After your document has an auxiliary dictionary, you can add or remove words from the dictionary through the Edit Auxiliary Dictionary dialog box (accessed via Utilities ⇨ Edit Auxiliary), shown in Figure 17-7. QuarkXPress displays any existing entries alphabetically.

- **To add a word:** Simply type the word in the field below the list of current words and choose Add.

- **To delete a word:** Select the word with the mouse or enter it in the field below the current list of words (this highlights it in the list). Choose Delete.

No changes to the dictionary take effect unless you choose Save and exit the Edit Auxiliary Dictionary dialog box. If you do not want to save your changes, choose Cancel.

Copy Fitting

Copy fitting is the process of making text fit the layout, often by altering the spacing. Rarely does your original, unmodified text fit the layout! Copy fitting is a concern particularly in magazines, newsletters, and newspapers, where the number of pages is set in advance, and you don't have the option of adding or removing a couple of pages because you have more or less text.

Copy fitting requires you to juggle several spacing factors, so you should understand the techniques described in Chapters 12 and 13 before applying the techniques outlined here.

You typically must take several actions, often in concert, to make text fit in the available space. Because the usual problem is having more text than space, the following tips assume the goal is to shorten text. But you can use the same procedures in reverse to expand text. Note that we give these tips in order of preference; use the last tips only if you can't make text fit using the first few suggestions.

■ Edit text to remove extra lines. Be on the lookout for lines at the end of a paragraph that have only a few characters. Getting rid of a few characters somewhere else in the paragraph may eliminate these short lines, reducing the amount of page space needed while keeping the amount of text removed to a minimum.

■ Track text so that it occupies less space and especially so that short lines are eliminated. Chapter 12, "Understanding Character Spacing," describes several ways to track text.

■ Tighten the leading by a half or quarter point. This is not noticeable in many cases and may save you a few lines per column, which can add up quickly. The section on leading in Chapter 13, "Understanding Paragraph Spacing," describes several methods to do this.

■ Reduce the point size by a half point. This saves more space than is first apparent, because it allows you to place a few more lines on the page and put a bit more text in each line. Change point size in the style sheet or select text and use the Measurements palette or the Style ⇨ Size menu (accessible by the keyboard shortcut Ctrl+Shift+\).

■ Set the horizontal scale of text to a slightly smaller percentage (perhaps 95 percent) to squeeze more text in each line. The section on horizontal scale in Chapter 12, "Understanding Character Spacing," explains how to do this.

■ Set slightly narrower column gutters or slightly wider margins.

If you use these methods, apply them globally to avoid a patchwork appearance. The only exception is changing tracking on individual lines; if you limit tracking changes to no more than 20 units, it won't be obviously different to a reader.

Summary

▶ Cut and paste works with individual QuarkXPress documents, across multiple QuarkXPress documents, and across Windows applications. However, formatting information usually does not copy between applications.

▶ The Find/Change dialog box lets you search and replace not just text but text attributes. You can replace just text, just attributes, or just text with certain attributes.

▶ The Font Usage dialog box shows you which typefaces are used in your documents and moves you to the first part of the document that uses a particular typeface.

▶ You can create auxiliary dictionaries that contain special words the basic spelling checker does not know, and you can have multiple documents share an auxiliary dictionary.

PART V

Graphics

Whether drawn with QuarkXPress tools, created electronically in separate illustration programs, or captured electronically with scanners, graphics are a vital part of page design. Often the most glamorous parts of a document, pictures and other graphics, add an important visual element and play a major role in attracting the reader's eye.

QuarkXPress has a solid set of graphics tools that enable you to import, create, and modify pictures. It lets you meld your visual skills — or those of a professional designer — with your verbal skills to create a unified product.

The examples in the chapters that follow show some of the effects you can achieve using the graphics features in QuarkXPress.

CHAPTER 18

Modifying Graphics

- -

In This Chapter

▶ Using the Measurements palette to make changes to a picture box

▶ Modifying the contents of a picture box by using the Picture Box Specifications dialog box

▶ Sizing and positioning a picture correctly within a picture box

▶ Speeding up the printing of review pages that contain graphics

- -

In Part III, "Page Layout," we discussed how to create a picture box and fill it with an imported picture. We also talked about how to make changes to the size and position of a picture box.

After you create, position, and size a picture box, you may want to make some changes to the contents of the box: the picture itself. You can alter the contents of an active picture box by using the Style menu, by changing the values in the Measurements palette, or by changing the controls in the Picture Box Specifications dialog box (which you open by selecting Item ⇨ Modify). This chapter shows you how to use the Measurements palette and the Picture Box Specifications dialog box to modify graphics; you learn how to use the Style menu options in Chapter 20, "Working with Bitmap Images."

Using the Measurements Palette to Modify Graphics

To use the Measurements palette to modify the contents of a picture box, you must first make the picture box active. (If the box is active, its sizing handles are visible around the edge of the box.) You also must display the Measurements palette (if the palette is not displayed, choose View ▷ Show Measurements).

In Figure 18-1, you see a page containing a picture box. The figure shows the page just after we filled the picture box with a picture. We used the Rectangular Picture Box tool to draw the picture box, and we filled the box with the picture by choosing File ▷ Get Picture (the shortcut method is to press Ctrl+E). Note the sizing handles on the borders of the box; these indicate that the box is active.

The Measurements palette appears at the bottom of the screen in Figure 18-1. You can make several changes to the box through the Measurements palette:

- Entering new values in the X and Y fields changes the distance of the picture box border from the page edge. The boundaries of the picture box shown in Figure 18-1 are ½-inch from both the top and left sides of the page.

- Entering new values in the W and H fields changes the width and height of the picture box. In the figure, the current dimensions are 7.5×8.661 inches.

- Entering a value in the ◿ field rotates the picture box. Because the box in Figure 18-1 is not rotated, the value in the field is 0 (zero) degrees.

- Entering a value in the ◜ field changes the shape of the picture box corners. For example, entering a value of 0.25 inches causes the picture box corners to become rounded.

- The setting in the X% and Y% fields in Figure 18-1 is 100 percent. Changing the percentage values in the X% and Y% fields reduces or enlarges the picture in the picture box. To keep the proportions of the picture the same, enter the same value in the X field as you enter in the Y field.

- Entering any value except zero in the ◿ field located at the right side of the palette rotates the picture *within* the picture box. (The ◿ field on the left side of the palette rotates the entire picture box.) The current value for the picture box in Figure 18-1 is zero, which means the box is not rotated.

- Entering any value except zero in the ▱ field slants the contents of the picture box. In Figure 18-1, the picture-box contents are not slanted.

After you use the Measurements palette to make changes to the picture box, press Ctrl, or move the cursor somewhere else on the screen, to apply the changes.

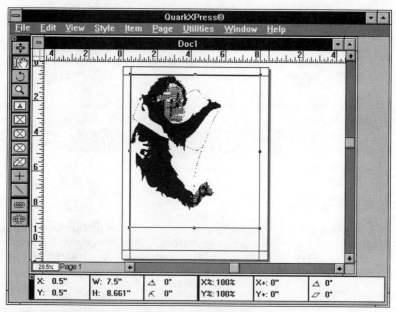

▶ **Figure 18-1:** An active picture box filled with a graphic.

Using the Picture Box Specifications Dialog Box

You also can make a number of modifications to a picture contained in an active picture box by using the Picture Box Specifications dialog box, shown in Figure 18-2. To display the dialog box, select the picture box to make it active and then choose Item ▷ Modify (or use the shortcut key combination Ctrl+M).

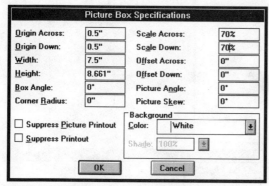

▶ **Figure 18-2:** The Picture Box Specifications dialog box.

Values in the Origin Across, Origin Down, Width, and Height fields control the position and size of the picture box. You can specify these values in units as small as .001 of any measurement system. In Figure 18-2, the origin (the upper-left corner of the picture box) is 0.5 inches from the top and left edges of the page. The picture box width is 7.5 inches and the height is 8.661 inches.

The following sections describe the remaining fields in the Picture Box Specifications dialog box and explain how to apply them to an active picture box. You can make changes in one or all of these fields. When you finish making selections in the dialog box, choose OK to save your changes.

Box Angle

Entering a value in the Box Angle field rotates the picture box around the center of the box. Box angle values range from -360 to 360 degrees, in increments as small as .001 degrees. Figure 18-3 shows the effect of rotating the picture box 5 degrees.

 Figure 18-3 is shown for example purposes only. If you actually use a rotated picture box in a document, you typically size the picture box so that it is small enough to fit within the margins of the page.

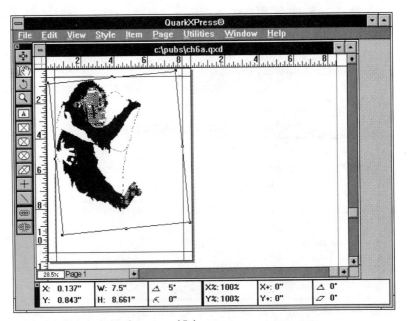

▶ **Figure 18-3:** A picture box rotated 5 degrees.

Corner Radius

Entering a value in the Corner Radius field changes the shape of a picture box's corners. The reason this field contains the word *radius* is that invisible circles exist in the corners of boxes drawn in QuarkXPress. These circles are located within the bounds of the box corners and touch the two sides of the box next to them. The radius is the size of the circle used to form rounded edges to the box.

The Corner Radius field is not available when the picture box is an oval or polygon.

When you first create a rectangular picture box, its corner radius values are 0 (zero). You can enter a measurement value from 0 to 2 inches, in .001 increments of any measurement system. Figure 18-4 shows the effect of selecting a corner radius of .25 inches.

We don't recommend changing the corner radius of a picture box unless you are certain it adds to the design of the page. Rounded-corner picture boxes typically are not effective and can make a layout appear amateurish.

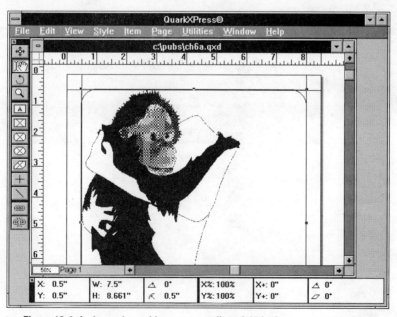

▶ **Figure 18-4:** A picture box with a corner radius of .25 inches.

Scale Across and Scale Down

As you work with QuarkXPress, you'll probably use the Scale Across and Scale Down feature frequently. In fact, it's one of the handiest items in the entire program, especially if you create documents that include graphics.

When you first fill a picture box with a picture (by choosing File ⊃ Get Picture or by using the shortcut Ctrl+E), QuarkXPress places the picture in the text box at 100-percent scale. It's not at all uncommon for the picture to be larger or smaller than you would like, and you can change its size by entering new values in the Scale Across and Scale Down fields. You can specify a size from 10 to 1,000 percent of the picture's original size. You can enter scale values in increments as small as .1 percent. You don't have to enter the same values for Scale Across and Scale Down; you can enter different values for these two to distort the picture.

In the first figure illustrations presented in this chapter, we used a picture at its original size, or 100-percent scale across and down. Figure 18-5 shows the same illustration scaled across and down 70 percent.

You can use keyboard shortcuts to increase or decrease Scale Across and Scale Down values:

■ Press Ctrl+Alt+Shift+< to decrease Scale Across and Scale Down values by 5 percent.

■ Press Ctrl+Alt+Shift+> to increase Scale Across and Scale Down values by 5 percent.

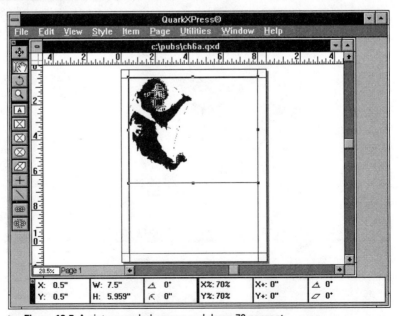

▶ **Figure 18-5:** A picture scaled across and down 70 percent.

Offset Across and Offset Down

Often, imported pictures are not positioned within the box as you want them to be. A picture might be too far to the left, too far to the right, or too high or low within the box.

One easy way to position a picture within the picture box is to use the Content tool. First, select the Content tool. If you then place the cursor over the active picture box, it turns into a grabber hand that lets you shift the picture into place.

You can do the same thing — but in a more precise, numerical fashion — by entering values in the Offset Across and Offset Down fields in the Picture Box Specifications dialog box. Figure 18-5 shows the picture box with the picture offset as it was for the original import. In Figure 18-6, we adjust the offset to the right by entering an Offset Across value of 2.5 inches. This moves the content 2.5 inches to the right. (A negative number would move it to the left.)

The change we made in Figure 18-6 improved the "across," or horizontal, placement of the picture within the picture box, but the top of the picture still touches the top edge of the box. To fix this, we enter an Offset Down value of 0.6 inches. You see the result in Figure 18-7. A negative number would move the picture up.

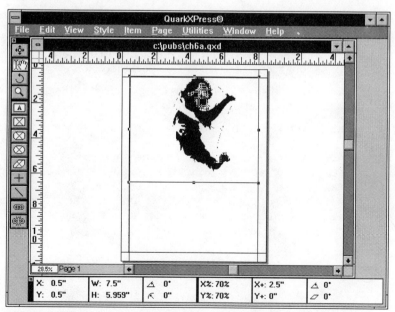

▶ **Figure 18-6:** Adjusting the Offset Across value to 2.5 inches shifts the picture toward the center of the picture box.

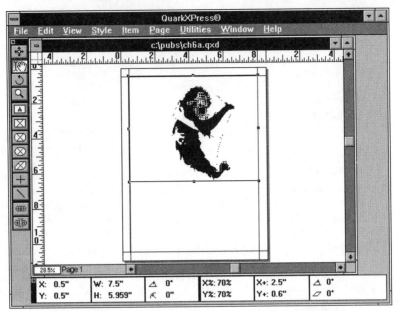

▶ **Figure 18-7:** Adjusting the Offset Down value to 0.6 inches moves the picture down from the top of the box.

Keyboard methods for positioning a picture within a picture box include the following:

■ Ctrl+Shift+F stretches or shrinks the picture to the borders of the picture box without keeping the picture's aspect ratio.

■ Ctrl+Alt+Shift+F fits the picture as close as it can to the picture box but maintains the picture's aspect ratio.

■ Ctrl+Shift+M centers the picture in the middle of the picture box.

If you keep a picture's aspect ratio, it means you keep its proportions the same as you enlarge it or reduce it. Keeping aspect ratio means keeping equal scale-across and scale-down percentages, such as 50%, 50%, and so on. Sometimes you want to place a graphic but you aren't sure what shape the picture box should take. So you create the picture box, import the picture, and then resize the picture box to fit the graphic.

Picture Angle

When you first place a picture into a picture box, it is oriented in the same angle it had in its source graphics program. Occasionally, you may want to change the angle of the picture without changing the angle of the picture box itself.

Entering a value in the Picture Angle field of the Picture Box Specifications dialog box rotates the picture within the box. The picture is rotated around the center of the picture as it was created in the original graphics program. The angle of the box stays the same; only the contents rotate.

You can enter Picture Angle values from –360 to 360 degrees, in increments as small as .001 degrees. Figure 18-8 shows the effect of changing the Picture Angle from 0 degrees to 40 degrees.

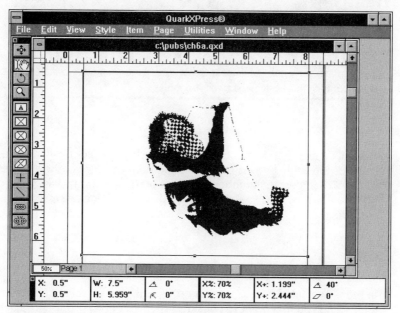

▶ **Figure 18-8:** The picture box contents are rotated 40 degrees; the box itself is not rotated.

Picture Skew

Another special effect you can try with QuarkXPress is *skewing,* or slanting, a picture within its box. You do this by entering a value in the Picture Skew field of the Picture Box Specifications dialog box. You can enter values from –75 to 75 degrees, in increments as small as .001 degrees. If you enter a positive value, the picture skews to the right; if you enter a negative value, the picture skews to

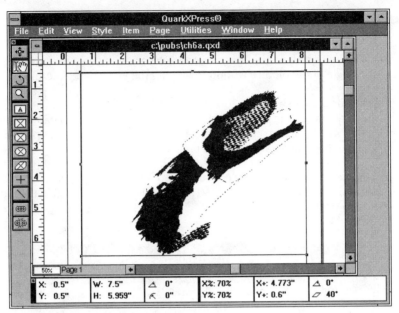

▶ **Figure 18-9:** This picture is skewed 40 degrees.

the left. Figure 18-9 shows the effect of skewing our picture 40 degrees. Skewing changes the angle formed by the left and bottom edges of the picture; normally it is at 90 degrees; the number you enter is the amount by which this 90 degrees is changed (thus 25 degrees makes it 115 degrees clockwise, or an acute angle of 65 degrees).

Suppress Picture Printout and Suppress Printout

In these two fields, you can select options that speed document printing — something you may want to consider when you print proof or rough copies. If you select Suppress Picture Printout, the frames or backgrounds of picture boxes print, but the contents of the picture boxes do not. Selecting Suppress Printout takes this option one step further. It prevents picture box frames, backgrounds, and contents from printing.

To choose either option, check the box next to the option label. If you select one of these options, remember to go back into the Picture Box Specifications dialog box and uncheck the box before printing final copies of the document.

If you use frames around picture boxes, we recommend that you print review copies with Suppress Picture Printout selected. This enables you to see the size and placement of the frames.

Background Color

QuarkXPress lets you add color to the background of a picture box and control the depth (*saturation*) of the color. To add color to the background of an active picture box or to change an existing background color, select a color from the Color list box in the Picture Box Specifications dialog box.

If you don't find the background color you want in the Color list box, you can create it. Choose Edit ⇨ Colors and use the color selection screen that appears to create the color you want. See Chapter 21, "Working with Color," for more on creating custom colors.

One of the selections available in the Color list box is None. If you select None, the picture box background is transparent.

After you select the background color (Item ⇨ Modify) you want to apply to the picture box — if you select a color other than None or White — you can specify the saturation level of the color. Select a predefined shade (0 to 100 percent) in the Shade list box or enter a custom shade value (in increments as small as 0.1 percent) in the Shade field.

Keyboard Shortcuts for Modifying Graphics

Here is a summary of some keyboard shortcuts you can use to modify graphics within active picture boxes:

- Ctrl+M opens the Picture Box Specifications dialog box.
- Ctrl+Shift+F fits the picture to the picture box (this shortcut does not keep the picture's aspect ratio).
- Ctrl+Alt+Shift+F fits the picture to the picture box, maintaining aspect ratio.
- Ctrl+Shift+M centers the picture in the picture box.
- Ctrl+Alt+Shift+< decreases the Scale Across and Scale Down values by 5 percent.
- Ctrl+Alt+Shift+> increases the Scale Across and Scale Down values by 5 percent.

■ ■

Summary

▶ You can modify the contents of a picture box by using the Measurements palette, by entering values in the Picture Box Specifications dialog box, or by using certain keyboard shortcuts.

▶ QuarkXPress lets you change the corner radius of a picture box to round the box corners. We recommend avoiding this unless you need to do so for some specific design requirement.

▶ If you print review or rough-draft copies of your document, consider using Suppress Picture Printout or Suppress Printout. These options prevent graphics from printing and speed up printing time. If you use frames around picture boxes, print the review pages with Suppress Picture Printout selected, so you can see the size and position of the box frames.

■ ■

19

Creating Graphics in QuarkXPress

In This Chapter

▶ Using QuarkXPress tools to create simple graphics

▶ Creating a basic organization chart

▶ Creating a bar chart

Why create graphics in QuarkXPress? That's a good question. True, this powerful program lets you accomplish amazing feats with documents. But let's face it, QuarkXPress is not — nor does it claim to be — a graphics program. Given the choice and sufficient resources, you most likely will use a separate graphics program to create graphics and then import those graphics into QuarkXPress picture boxes.

On the other hand, you may not have the budget for a separate graphics program. Or if your graphics needs are on the order of simple boxes, shades, and lines, a graphics program would be overkill. If you fall into this category, you'll be pleased to know that, given some patience and ingenuity, you can create a decent range of simple graphics within QuarkXPress. In fact, the program is really quite adept at handling bar charts, organizational charts, and simple flow diagrams:

- With the assorted picture box tools (rectangular, rounded rectangular, oval, and polygon), you can create a range of simple shapes.

- You can add background color and shade (saturation) to a text or picture box to add color or texture to the shapes you create.

- Using the Frame feature, you can add one of seven possible frame patterns to the boundaries of a picture box, and you can specify the width of the frame. Chapter 11, "Additional Layout Features," has more information on frames.

- You can create a variety of lines and arrows, and you can specify the width of the lines.

- Because QuarkXPress places every layout element on its own layer, you can arrange all of the items in this list by bringing them forward or sending them backward in a stack of elements.

In short, although QuarkXPress is not a bona fide graphics program, it offers a satisfying set of tools you can use to create simple graphics.

Creating a Simple Organizational Chart

The process of producing a basic organizational chart shows you how you can put some QuarkXPress tools to use in creating simple graphics. The following section details a step-by-step process we used to create an organizational chart.

Step 1: Drawing a text box

First, we opened a new document (File ➪ New). Using the Text Box tool, we drew the text box shown in Figure 19-1. We then adjusted the size of the text box by selecting and then dragging the box's sizing handles. Another way of sizing the text box is to enter values in the W and H fields (Width and Height) in the Measurements palette.

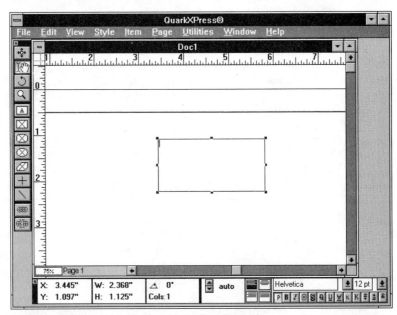

▶ **Figure 19-1:** A text box drawn with the Text Box tool.

Step 2: Entering and formatting text

With the text box still active, we selected the Content tool and typed the text into the first text box, as shown in Figure 19-2. We used the Measurements palette to select the font, boldface the name, and center the text.

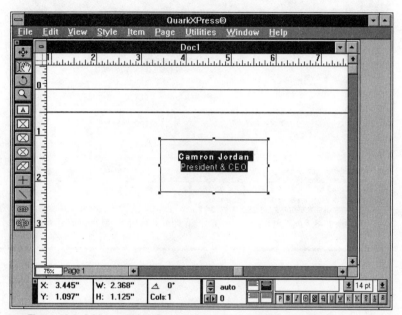

▶ **Figure 19-2:** Add text to the text box after selecting the Content tool.

Step 3: Duplicating the text box

To add the other two boxes for the chart, we could have drawn them to match the size and style of the first box. Instead, we made two copies of the first text box. To do this, we chose the Item tool, selected the text box to make it active, and selected Edit ▷ Copy (the shortcut is Ctrl+C). We then pasted the copied box twice by choosing Edit ▷ Paste (the shortcut is Ctrl+V).

Next, we positioned the two new text boxes, as shown in Figure 19-3. We used the Item tool to drag them into their approximate positions and then refined their positions by entering values in the X and Y fields in the Measurements palette.

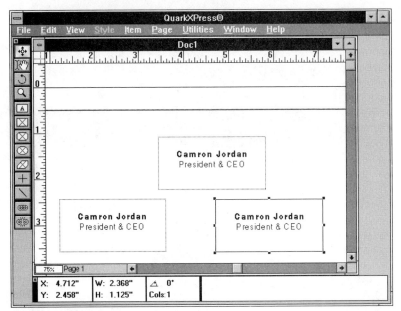

▶ **Figure 19-3:** Position the text boxes using the Item tool and the Measurements palette.

Step 4: Changing text in copied text boxes

Our next step was to replace the text in the two new text boxes, which was duplicated from the first text box. We used the Content tool to select the duplicated text and typed in the correct names in each text box. By doing this one line at a time (name line and then title line), we were able to maintain the type attributes we established in the first text box. Figure 19-4 shows the three boxes positioned correctly and containing the proper text.

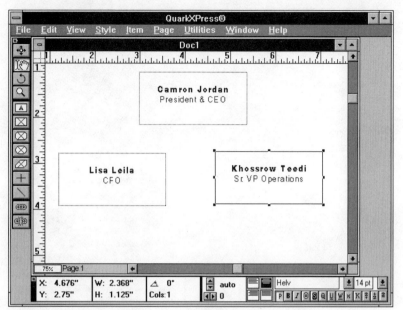

▶ **Figure 19-4:** Replace the text in the two new text boxes with the correct names and titles.

Step 5: Adding circles to the chart

To indicate the next level of subordinates in the organizational chart, we chose to use circles instead of rectangles, as you can see in Figure 19-5. To draw a circle, we used the Oval Picture Box tool. To create a true circle instead of an oval, we held down the Shift key while we drew the shape. After we made the initial circle the correct size, we duplicated it three times. We did this by selecting the Item tool, clicking the circle to make it active, and choosing Edit ▷ Copy (the shortcut is Ctrl+C). Then we pasted the copies by choosing Edit ▷ Paste (the shortcut is Ctrl+V).

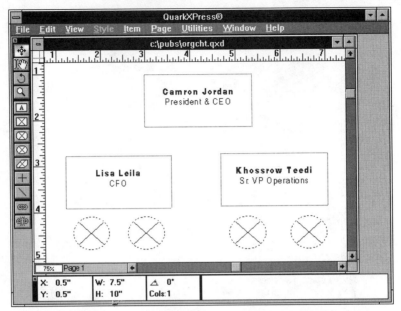

▶ **Figure 19-5:** The circles on the chart indicate the next level of organization.

Step 6: Adding drop shadows for effect

To create a shadowed effect behind the text boxes, we drew a picture box and used the W and H fields in the Measurements palette to make the picture box the exact size of the text boxes. The picture box is shown in Figure 19-6. We then filled the picture box with 100-percent black by choosing Item ⇨ Modify (the keyboard shortcut is Ctrl+M) to open the Picture Box Specifications dialog box, where we selected a Background Color of Black and a Shade of 100 percent.

Next, we duplicated the filled picture box three times. We selected the Item tool, clicked the picture box to make it active, and chose Edit ⇨ Copy (the shortcut is Ctrl+C). Then we pasted the copies by choosing Edit ⇨ Paste (the shortcut is Ctrl+V). We used the Item tool to drag the filled picture boxes on top of, but slightly offset from, the text boxes. Then we sent the filled picture boxes to the back of the layered stack by choosing Item ⇨ Send to Back. In Figure 19-7, one of the filled picture boxes has been placed behind the text box on the left. The other two picture boxes are still in front of the their respective text boxes, ready to be sent to the back of the layer.

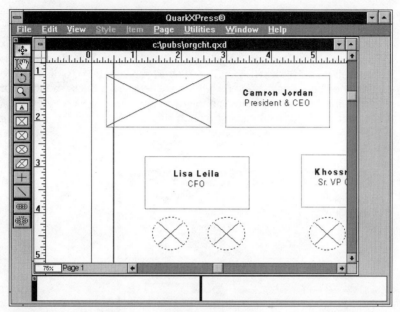

▶ **Figure 19-6:** To add shadows to text boxes, first create a picture box the same size as the text boxes.

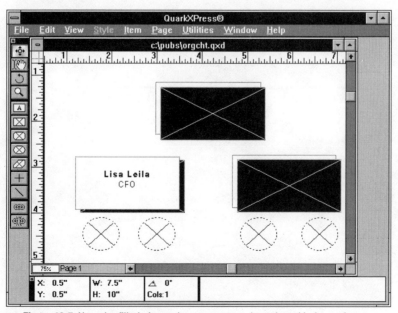

▶ **Figure 19-7:** How the filled picture boxes appear when placed in front of text boxes (top and right) and behind text boxes (left).

Step 7: Shading the circles for effect

To give the circles a more distinctive appearance, we added a 20-percent black shade to them. To do this, we used the Item tool to select a circle. Then we chose Item ➪ Modify (the keyboard shortcut is Ctrl+M) to display the Picture Box Specifications dialog box, where we selected a Background Color of Black and a Shade of 20 percent, as shown in Figure 19-8. We repeated this process for each circle. The results are shown in Figure 19-9.

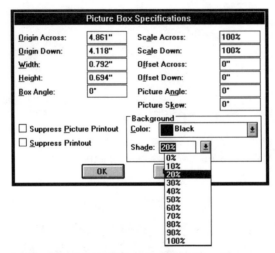

▶ **Figure 19-8:** Add shade to the circles by making selections in the Picture Box Specifications dialog box.

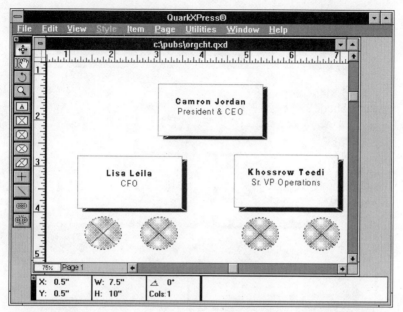

▶ **Figure 19-9:** The results of the background color and shade values entered in Figure 19-8.

Step 8: Connecting elements with arrows and lines

To finish our simple organizational chart, we needed to add lines and arrows, as shown in Figure 19-10. To add the arrows and lines that connect the top box with its two subordinate boxes, we first used the Orthogonal Line tool to draw the horizontal sections of the lines. Then we drew the vertical sections. (We used the line-sizing handles to drag the lines to the correct size.) Finally, we used the line settings in the Measurements palette to set the line widths at 1 point and to add the arrowheads to the vertical sections of both lines.

To connect the elements in our simple organizational chart, we used the Diagonal Line drawing tool to draw the slanted lines. We then used the line settings in the Measurements palette to select a dotted line type and a width of 4 points.

If you use QuarkXPress to create simple graphics, you will find instances when you want to group boxes and lines so you can move them around on the page without altering their arrangement. To temporarily group items, hold down the Shift key and select the items you want to activate. This groups them together. To keep the multiple-selected items grouped, choose Item ⇨ Group.

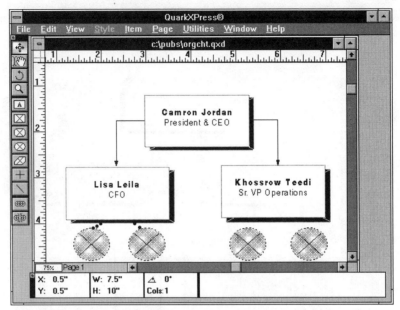

▶ **Figure 19-10:** Adding lines and arrows completes the chart.

Creating a Bar Chart

With some of the same tools used to create the organizational chart in the preceding example, you also can create a bar chart. To create the bar chart shown in Figure 19-11, we used vertical guides that we dragged out one at a time from the ruler. (To do this, position the cursor in the vertical ruler and hold down the mouse button as you pull the guide into place.)

To create the rest of the chart, we drew individual text boxes to hold the years (1988, 1989, and so on), and we rotated the text boxes 35 degrees before dragging them into position. For each bar in the bar chart, we drew a picture box and filled each with a different shade percentage, from 20 to 100 percent.

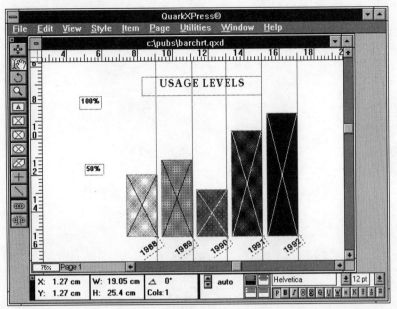

▶ **Figure 19-11:** A simple bar chart created in QuarkXPress.

Summary

▶ You can create simple shapes using the QuarkXPress picture box tools (rectangular, rounded rectangular, oval, and polygon).

▶ Use Background Color and Shade settings in the Picture Box Specifications dialog box to add color or texture to shapes.

▶ You can create lines and arrows, and you can specify the width and pattern of the lines.

▶ You can arrange elements in a layered stack and then bring elements forward or backward in the stack.

CHAPTER

20

Working with Bitmap Images

Choosing Acceptable File Formats

QuarkXPress offers sophisticated controls over bitmap images. This is particularly true for gray-scale images, which usually are scanned photographs but also can include original artwork created by a paint program. Gray-scale images have long been an important part of traditional publishing.

Through the Style menu, QuarkXPress offers the full controls over gray-scale images that traditional publishers expect. But there's a catch: QuarkXPress offers these controls only for image files in the TIFF format (Tagged Image File Format, originally developed by Aldus and Microsoft for Aldus's PageMaker product), and then only for files with at least 8 bits of color depth (256 gray levels).

For more information on TIFF and other file formats, see Chapter 4, "Customizing QuarkXPress," and Chapter 7, "Preparing Files for Import."

Files in vector formats, such as CGM and EPS, can also contain bitmap images. These files print to the best resolution of the printer. You must control output resolution and effects in the original illustration program, because the publishing program cannot control these attributes for bitmaps embedded in vector files.

Non-TIFF gray-scale images

When you work with gray-scale PCX (PC Paintbrush) or BMP (Microsoft Windows bitmap) files, convert them or save them in 8-bit TIFF format before bringing them into QuarkXPress if you want to use any of QuarkXPress's image controls. Otherwise, non-TIFF gray-scale files print at the defaults for your printer. Figure 20-1 shows the limited options available for non-TIFF gray-scale images. Negative is the only option available in the Style menu for gray-scale PCX and BMP files and for color files in any format.

TIFF files come in many varieties. For best results, use an uncompressed TIFF format if it is available in your scanning or paint application. Some programs use data compression (LZW is a common method), which QuarkXPress does not always read reliably, leading to low-resolution or poor-resolution images.

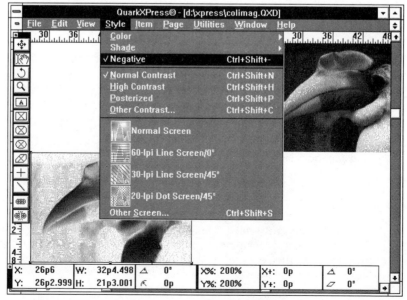

▶ **Figure 20-1:** Image-control options for non-TIFF gray-scale images.

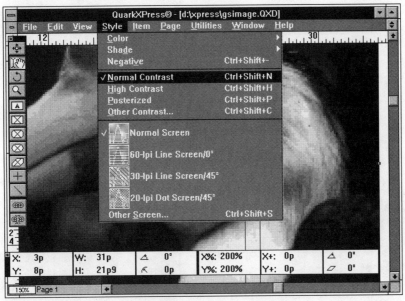

▶ **Figure 20-2:** Image-control options for gray-scale TIFF files.

Gray-scale TIFF files

When you work with gray-scale TIFF files, you can apply any of several filters that affect the levels of gray in the image. You also can create your own filter effects. In addition, you can control the output line screen, screen angle, and screen element (described in detail later in this chapter). You can apply colors and shades to your image, exchanging black for another color or shade. Figure 20-2 shows the options available for a gray-scale TIFF file. The Style menu has a separate set of options for bitmap images when the Content tool is active and a picture box containing an image is selected.

Black-and-white and color bitmap files

With black-and-white bitmap files (including those in TIFF and PCX formats), you have no control over gray levels — because there aren't any. You do have the ability to create a negative image (exchange black for white and vice versa), but you cannot alter contrast. Other controls — including line screen, colors, and shades — are available, however. Figure 20-3 shows the image-control options available for black-and-white bitmap images. When you use color TIFF files, only one control is available, as with non-TIFF gray-scale images: You can create a negative image.

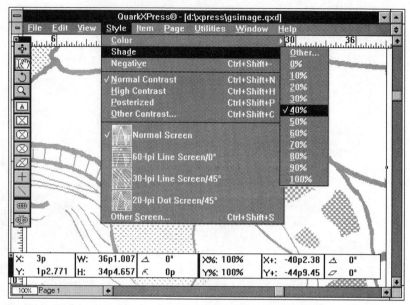

▶ **Figure 20-3:** Image-control options for black-and-white bitmap files.

Color files in other bitmap formats, such as BMP and PCX, are not supported. QuarkXPress may lock up if you try to import such an image.

Save bitmap files — whether gray-scale, color, or black-and-white — in the size you intend to use for layout. Enlarging a bitmap more than 20 to 50 percent can result in a blocky-looking image, as illustrated in Figure 20-4, which shows a cameo image enlarged 300 percent. The poor image results because the pixels that make up the image are enlarged along with the image itself. Reducing a bitmap doesn't cause such problems, although it can waste disk space and processing time, because the file contains more information than is used.

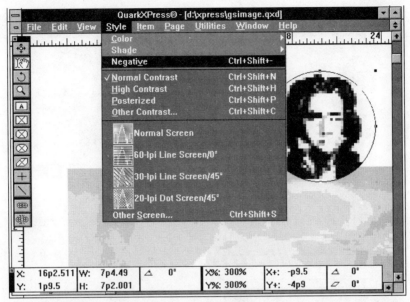

▶ **Figure 20-4:** This bitmapped cameo image, enlarged to 300 percent, looks blocky because the pixels that make up the image are enlarged along with the image itself.

Setting Gray-Level Controls

All controls over bitmap images reside in the Style menu. To access these options, activate the Content tool, select the picture box containing the image you want to alter, and then select Style. The Style menu displays a different set of options when a picture box is selected than it does when a text box is selected (described in Chapters 12 through 17).

The Style menu offers five controls — called *contrast filters* — over gray levels. In all the following examples, the figures display both the image and the Picture Contrast Specifications dialog box. In reality, this dialog box appears only if you select Other Contrast. We included the dialog box in all the figures to show you the actual settings used for each filter and to make it clearer how to create or modify a filter.

■ **Negative (Ctrl+Shift+–):** This swaps black with white, causing a photographic-negative effect. Figure 20-5 shows how an image appears with the Negative filter applied.

■ **Normal Contrast (Ctrl+Shift+N):** Selecting this setting returns an image to the original settings defined in the source file. Figure 20-6 shows how the image in Figure 20-5 appears normally. Use this option if you changed the settings and decide you don't like the results.

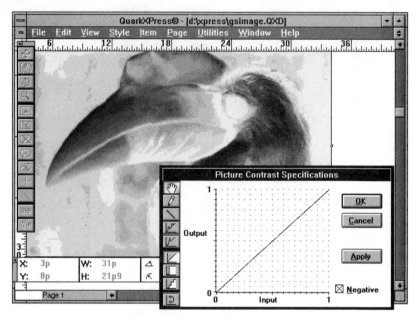

▶ **Figure 20-5:** A gray-scale image with the Negative filter applied.

■ **High Contrast (Ctrl+Shift+H):** If you choose the High Contrast setting, QuarkXPress turns any part of the image that is 30-percent gray or darker into 100-percent black. It makes anything lighter than 30-percent gray into 0-percent black — in other words, it makes that part of the image transparent (it usually appears as white unless the picture box has a background color). Figure 20-7 shows how the image shown in Figure 20-6 appears with the High Contrast filter applied.

■ **Posterized (Ctrl+Shift+P):** This setting gathers groups of gray levels and makes them all the same level. In effect, this reduces the number of different gray levels and creates a banding effect. Figure 20-8 shows how the original image shown in Figure 20-6 appears with the posterization filter applied.

■ **Other Contrast (Ctrl+Shift+C):** The Other Contrast setting lets you create your own filter or modify one of the previously mentioned filters. When you use this setting, the Picture Contrast Specifications dialog box appears.

Make sure the Context tool is selected; otherwise, these filter options will be grayed out.

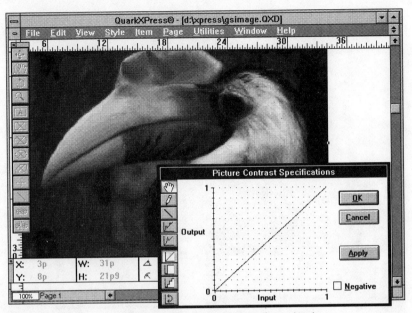

▶ **Figure 20-6:** A gray-scale image at its normal (original) gray levels.

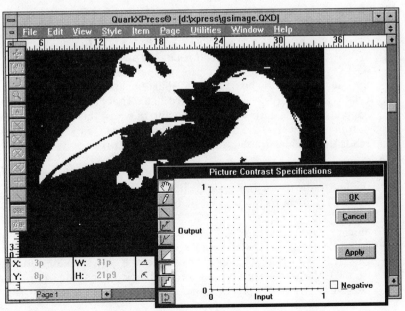

▶ **Figure 20-7:** A gray-scale image with the High Contrast filter applied.

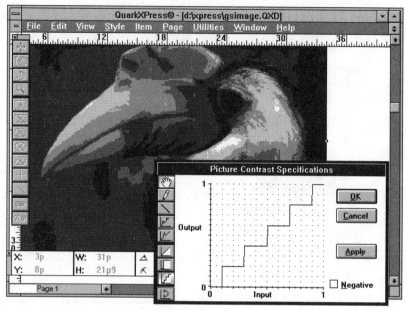

▶ **Figure 20-8:** A gray-scale image with the posterization filter applied.

How filters work

Essentially, a contrast filter tells QuarkXPress how to print each level of gray. When you set the gray-level control to Normal Contrast, the program prints each level of gray as it exists in the original graphic. In the Picture Contrast Specifications dialog box, you see a diagonal line when you choose the Normal Contrast setting (refer back to Figure 20-6). That line, technically called a *gamma curve,* describes the relationship between the input gray level and the output gray level — the difference between what QuarkXPress "sees" when it reads the original graphic and what it actually prints.

If you refer again to Figure 20-7, you see that when you choose High Contrast, the line in the dialog box goes abruptly from 0-percent black for all gray values up to 30 percent to 100-percent black for all values greater than 30 percent.

Similarly, when you choose Posterized (see Figure 20-8), the line appears as a series of steps. These steps correspond to the banding that results when QuarkXPress groups a range of grays into one gray level for output (everything from 0 to 10 percent prints as 0-percent black, everything from 10 percent to 30 percent prints as 20 percent, and so on).

The line for the Negative filter (see Figure 20-5) appears to be the same as for the Normal Contrast filter. The difference is that the Negative box (at the bottom right of the Picture Contrast Specifications dialog box) is checked. Selecting the Negative box tells QuarkXPress to reverse the gray-scale relationships — to use the opposite, or negative, of the line displayed in the picture box. You can achieve the same effect by drawing the gamma curve line from the upper left of the grid to the bottom right and deselecting the Negative box.

Custom gray-level settings

The Picture Contrast Specifications dialog box, which you open by selecting Style ⇨ Other Contrast, includes several icons along its left side. Using these icons, you can establish custom gray-level settings by drawing your own gamma curve line. From top to bottom, the icons and their uses are as follows:

- The hand icon lets you move the entire line in any direction, which is useful for shifting all gray-level mappings at once. For example, shifting the line upward darkens the entire image, because lighter input values are mapped to darker output values. Moving the line in this way results in a consistent image, even though gray levels are shifted.

- The pencil icon lets you draw your own line, which is handy if you want to experiment.

- The line icon causes points on the line to appear so you can move them. It works similarly to an arrow tool applied to points on a polygon or curve in a graphic program. This is useful for editing existing lines, especially those that have discontinuities between points (such as in the high-contrast filter).

- The modify-line icon lets you select any point on the line and move it. Like the line icon, this icon is helpful for editing existing lines, particularly if the changes are not discontinuous.

- The modify-step icon lets you select increments on the line and move them as a group. The selected segment between two points on the line moves. This is most helpful when editing posterization settings.

Normal

High

Posterized

- The Normal, High Contrast, and Posterized line icons all reset the gray-level settings to the defaults for those standard options.

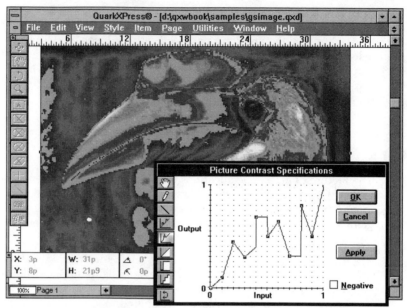

▶ **Figure 20-9:** Use the Apply button to preview changes to the gray-level map.

 ■ The swap-axis icon lets you put the input axis at the left of the grid and the output axis at the bottom. This is beneficial if you are used to editing gamma curves oriented in the transverse direction of QuarkXPress's default orientation.

You can use several different tools to edit the same line. You also can use the Negative check box with any kind of line. Checking the box has the effect of flipping the gray-level map horizontally (so that left and right are swapped), although the line appears the same on-screen.

Because you can fundamentally alter the character of an image by editing its gray-level map, QuarkXPress lets you preview the effects of your edits via the Apply button. Figure 20-9 is an example of using several effects, mostly by modifying the gamma curve with the modify-line and modify-step tools at various points on the curve. We used the Apply button to preview our changes before deciding whether to implement them by choosing OK. QuarkXPress actually implements your changes only if you choose OK.

 If, after editing a gray-level map, you want to return the image to a more common gray-level map, you can use the standard options on the Style menu or reenter the dialog box and use one of the default-setting icons (like Normal, Posterized, or High Contrast).

Using Line-Screen Controls

Most people never worry about line screens — in fact, many desktop publishers don't know what they are — although they can have a profound effect on how your bitmap images print. Many artists use line-screen controls to add a whole new feel to an image.

In traditional printing, a line screen is an acetate mask covered with a grid of spots; printers use such a device to convert a continuous-tone image like a photograph into the series of spots, called a *halftone*, which is required to reproduce such an image on a printing press. (Color images use four sets of spots, one each for cyan, magenta, yellow, and black; the process of filtering out each of these colors is called *four-color separation,* which is described more fully in Chapters 21, "Working with Color," and 26, "Printing Techniques"). Take a magnifying glass to a photo — either color or black-and-white — in a newspaper or magazine, and you'll see the spots that the photo is made of. These spots are usually dots, but they can be any of several shapes.

When making a halftone the traditional way, a line-screen mask is placed on top of a piece of photographic paper (such as Kodak's RC paper, used for decades in traditional photography); the continuous-tone original is then illuminated in a camera so the image is projected through the mask onto the photographic paper. The photographic paper is exposed only where the mask is transparent (in the grid holes, or spots), producing the spots that make up the image to be printed. The size of each spot depends on how much light is passed through, which in turn depends on how dark or light each area of the original image is. Think of a window screen through which you spray water: the stronger the spray, the bigger the spots behind the screen's holes.

The spots that make up the image are arranged in a series of lines, usually at a 45-degree angle (this angle helps the eye blend the individual spots to simulate a continuous tone). The number of lines per inch (or *halftone frequency*) determines the maximum dot size as well as the coarseness (*halftone density*) of the image (thus the term *line screen*). The spots in the mask need not be circular — they can be ellipses, squares, lines, or more esoteric shapes like stars. These shapes are called *screen elements*. Circular dots are the most common type, because they result in the least distortion of the image.

When your source image is electronic, how do you create the series of black spots needed to mimic continuous gray tones? Desktop publishing programs use mathematical algorithms that simulate the traditional piece of photographic line screen. Because the process is controlled by a set of equations, desktop publishing programs such as QuarkXPress offer more options than traditional line screens, which come in a fixed set of halftone frequencies and with a limited set of elements.

Understanding lpi

Lines per inch (lpi) and dots per inch (dpi) are not related, because the spots in a line screen are variable-sized, while dots in a laser printer are fixed-sized. (Because newer printers using Hewlett-Packard's Resolution Enhancement Technology or Apple Computer's PhotoGrade use variable-sized dots, the distinction may disappear one day.) Lines per inch specifies, in essence, the grid through which an image is filtered, not the size of the spots that make it up. Dots per inch specifies the number of ink dots per inch produced by the laser printer. These dots are typically the same size; therefore, a 100-lpi image will appear finer than a 100-dpi image.

Depending upon the size of the line-screen spot, several of a printer's fixed-sized dots may be required to simulate one line-screen spot. For this reason, a printer's or image setter's lpi is far less than its dpi. For example, a 300-dpi laser printer can achieve about 60-lpi resolution, while a 1270-dpi image setter can achieve about 120-lpi resolution and a 2540-dpi image setter about 200-lpi resolution. Resolutions of less than 100 lpi are considered coarse, while resolutions of more than 120 lpi are considered fine.

But there's more to choosing an lpi setting than knowing your output device's top resolution. An often overlooked issue is the type of paper the material is printed on. Smoother paper (such as *glossy-coated* or *super-calendared*) can handle finer halftone spots because the paper's coating (also called its *finish*) minimizes ink bleeding.

Standard office paper, such as that used in photocopiers and laser printers, is rougher and has some bleed that is usually noticeable only if you write on it with markers. Newsprint is very rough and has a heavy bleed. Typically, newspaper images are printed at 85 – 90 lpi, newsletter images are printed on standard office paper at 100 – 110 lpi, magazine images are printed at 120 – 150 lpi, and calendars and coffee-table art books are printed at 150 – 200 lpi.

Other factors affecting lpi include the type of printing press and the type of ink used. Your printer representative should advise you on preferred settings.

If you output your document from your computer directly to film negatives (rather than to photographic paper that is then "shot" to create negatives), inform your printer representative. Outputting to negatives allows a higher lpi than outputting to paper, because negatives created photographically cannot accurately reproduce the fine resolution that negatives output directly on an image setter have. (If, for example, you output to 120 lpi on paper and then create a photographic negative, even the slightest change in the camera's focus will make the fine dots blurry. Outputting straight to negatives avoids this problem.) Printer representatives often assume you are outputting to paper and base their advised lpi settings on this assumption.

Effects of line-screen settings

Seeing is believing when it comes to special graphics effects, so you'll want to experiment with line-screen settings before going to press with your document.

Special graphics effects are available only for PostScript printers, because other types of printers do not have the correct controls in their circuit boards to do the calculations required to achieve these effects.

In most cases, you should use Normal Screen, which is the default for all imported images. The default line-screen frequency for Normal Screen is set in the File menu's Printer Setup dialog box, through the Halftone Frequency option. The default screen angle is 45 degrees, and the default screen element is a dot; neither of these defaults can be changed.

But when you want to do something special, you can. As a rule, most people using line-screen effects prefer coarser halftone frequencies to make the image coarser but bolder; they usually simultaneously change the screen element to a line or other shape to change the image's character. In acknowledgment of this tendency, QuarkXPress predefines three line-screen settings that you can apply directly from the Style menu:

- **Normal Screen:** This setting uses the defaults defined via File ⇨ Printer Setup (see Chapter 26, "Printing Techniques").

- **60-lpi Line Screen/0 (°):** This setting creates a 60-line-per-inch (lpi) halftone frequency, using lines aligned at 0 degrees (horizontal) as the screen element.

- **30-lpi Line Screen/45 (°):** This sets a 30-lpi halftone frequency using lines aligned at 45 degrees as the screen element.

- **20-lpi Dot Screen/45 (°):** This sets a 20-line-per-inch halftone frequency using dots aligned at 45 degrees.

The icons accompanying the descriptions show what the effects look like. None of these options has a keyboard shortcut.

If one of the line-screen settings has already been applied to an image, a check mark appears to the left of the appropriate icon.

The last option available from the Style menu is Other Screen, which lets you define any combination of frequency, element, and angle you want. Selecting this option (also available via the shortcut Ctrl+Shift+S) opens the Picture Screening Specifications dialog box. Figure 20-10 shows this dialog box; behind it is a view of an image set at 30 lpi with a dot-screen element at 45 degrees. (You cannot preview your settings; here we applied the settings and reinvoked the dialog box to show the settings and their effects simultaneously.)

If a user-defined screening specification is applied to an image, a check mark appears to the left of the Other Screen option in the Style menu.

You can see on-screen the effects of the settings you make. If you check the Display Halftoning box in the Picture Screening Specifications dialog box, QuarkXPress displays the image with the screening specifications applied. This helps you see how your settings affect the image, and it also helps you remember which images have special screening affects applied to them. If this box is unchecked, the image will not change on-screen, although it will print with the new screening specifications.

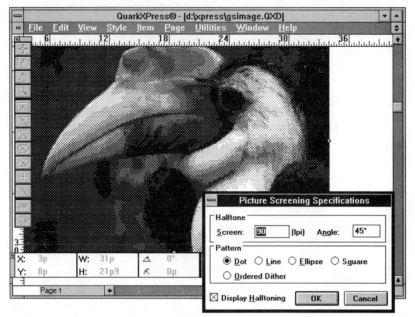

▶ **Figure 20-10:** The Picture Screening Specifications dialog box lets you set all screen controls.

Because of limits in monitor resolutions, QuarkXPress cannot display halftone frequencies finer than 60 lpi, which is the default setting for 300-dpi laser printers. If you use a finer halftone frequency, QuarkXPress displays the image at the best resolution available for your monitor. You can tell if a special line screen is applied, even if you can't exactly determine the setting.

To gauge the effects of different line-screen elements, compare Figures 20-11 through 20-14. Figure 20-11 shows the effects of a line screen set at 30 lpi, using dots as the screen element. Figure 20-12 shows a line screen with the same 30 lpi, but with ellipses as the screen element. In Figure 20-13, squares are used as the screen element, and in Figure 20-14, lines are used as the screen element. In all four figures, the screen elements are arranged at a 45-degree angle.

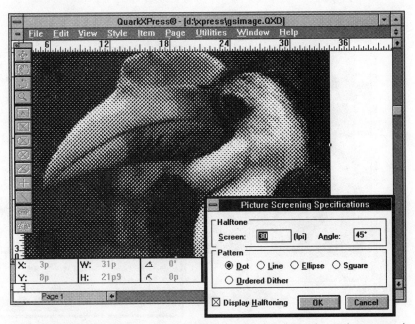

▶ **Figure 20-11:** A gray-scale image set at 30 lpi, with dots arranged at 45 degrees used as the screen element.

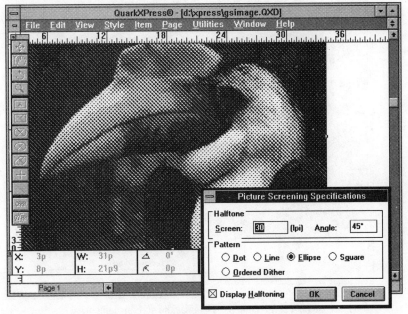

▶ **Figure 20-12:** A screen that uses ellipses as the screen element.

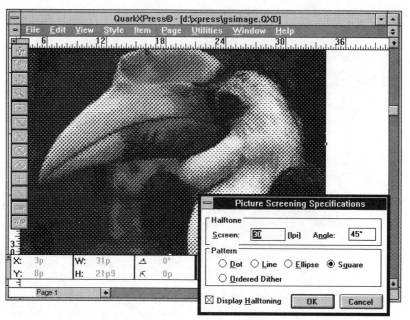

▶ **Figure 20-13:** A screen that uses squares as the screen element.

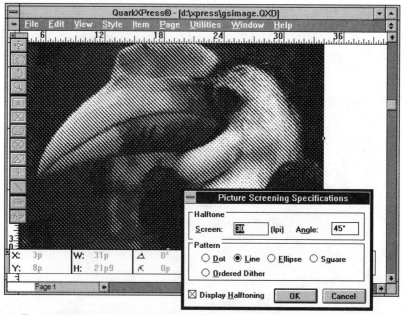

▶ **Figure 20-14:** A screen that uses lines as the screen element.

We recommend that you create a sample page that has a series of strips set for different line screens and line elements. You can accomplish this by taking the following steps.

▶ Steps: Creating a sample page of line screens and elements

Step 1. In an image-editing program, create a gray-scale TIFF file that has a smooth gradient from white to black. The image in this file should be shaped like a long rectangle, either horizontal or vertical, with the gradient going from one end to the other, along the longest axis.

Step 2. Import this object into a QuarkXPress document's picture box and then duplicate that box several times, placing each duplicate next to the previous one. You now have a series of gradient strips.

Step 3. Use the Style ⇨ Other Screen option to set each strip at a different line-screen setting. We recommend you do this at least for common line-screen frequency settings (such as 20, 30, 60, 85, 110, 120, 133, and 150). You can then copy all these picture boxes to a new page and change the screen element for each (which you must do one at a time). Likewise, you can do the same for different screen angles.

Step 4. Output these pages on a 2540-dpi image setter.

You can use the resulting guide to see the effects of various line-screen settings on the entire range of gray values, from white to black. You can also create a similar guide using a sample gray-scale photo.

Dithering

An effect related to halftone screening is called *dithering*. Dithering means to replace gray levels with a varying pattern of black and white. This pattern does not attempt to simulate grays; instead, it merely tries to retain some distinction between shades in an image when the image is output to a printer that does not have fine enough resolution to reproduce grays (through the fine grid of dots used in screening to reproduce each gray shade). In other words, dithering uses coarse patterns of dots and lines to represent the basic details in a gray-scale image. A set of mathematical equations determines how the dithered pattern appears for each image; the basic technique is to replace dark shades with all black, medium shades with alternating black and white dots or lines, and light shades with a sparse pattern of dots or lines.

There are many such sets of equations; QuarkXPress uses one called *ordered dithering*, which you select by choosing Ordered Dither in the Picture Screening

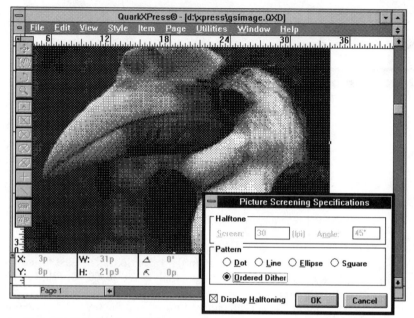

▶ **Figure 20-15:** The Ordered Dither option converts gray-scale images into course black-and-white images for output to low-resolution printers.

Specifications dialog box. Figure 20-15 shows the dialog box and an image to which ordered dithering is applied. This image is a dithered version of the original image in Figure 20-6. To apply other dithering equations, you must dither the image in a paint or graphics program that supports dithering before importing the image into QuarkXPress.

With dithering, there are no controls available for halftone frequency or screen-element angle, since these are determined by the dithering equations.

You can use dithering to simulate a wood-cut or pointillism effect. Otherwise, use dithering only if you don't have a 300-dpi or better printer.

Using Color and Shade Controls

Even if you don't alter gray levels or screening, you can still alter how gray-scale and black-and-white bitmap graphics print by using QuarkXPress color and shade controls, available through the Style menu.

Color and shade controls do not work with color images or with vector images (such as EPS, PICT, and CGM) because they are meant to add color and shades to black-and-white and gray-scale images. The assumption is that such color changes should be done in a color graphics program.

Through the Style menu's Color option, you can replace the black parts of an image — including grays, which after all are simply percentages of black — with a color. Figure 20-16 shows the secondary menu that appears when you highlight the Color option on the Style menu. Any colors defined in the document appear in the list of colors. (Chapter 21 describes colors in depth.)

Likewise, you can make the image lighter by applying a shade through Style ⇨ Shade. Figure 20-17 shows how the gray-scale image used in figures throughout this chapter appears with a 20-percent shade applied. Each gray level appears at 20 percent of its original level, so the image remains faithful to the original value ratios, even though it prints so much lighter. This effect is handy when you want to have text overprint a photograph or other image.

You are not limited to the shade percentages displayed in the Shade drop-down menu. By choosing Other, you can set any percentage from 0 to 100, in 0.1-percent increments.

You can combine the Color and Shade options. You can print an image at 30-percent magenta, for example. You also can apply other effects, such as gray-level filters and screen settings, to the same image.

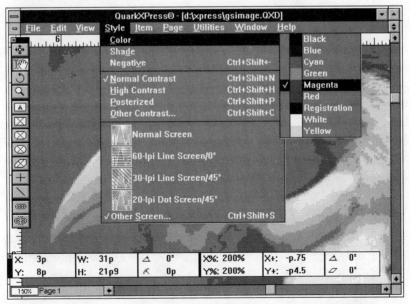

▶ **Figure 20-16:** Through Style ⇨ Color, you can apply colors to black-and-white or gray-scale images. In this figure, the image is being colored as magenta.

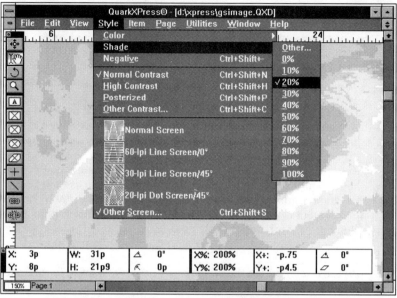

▶ **Figure 20-17:** An image with a 20-percent shade applied via <u>S</u>tyle ⇨ Sha<u>d</u>e.

Summary

▶ You can modify gray levels for 8-bit gray-scale TIFF files only.

▶ Avoid compressed TIFF formats and avoid color bitmaps in formats other than TIFF.

▶ You can apply only the Negative filter to color bitmaps.

▶ Images that have gray-level filters applied can be reset to their original settings or to other settings at any time.

▶ You can modify line-screen settings for any gray-scale or black-and-white bitmap files. Line-screen settings are available only if you use a PostScript printer, however.

▶ Your monitor cannot display line-screen frequencies finer than 60 lpi, so be sure to output samples before using finer screens on final documents.

▶ The appropriate lpi settings for a document depend on the printer, the paper, and other press-related factors. Make sure the representative at your printing plant knows how you create your negatives, as this affects the advice you get.

▶ Shade controls affect an image uniformly. Typically, shading is used to lighten an image so text can be overprinted on it. Color controls, whether used alone or with shade controls, often are used for the same effect.

Working with Color

∎∎∎

In This Chapter

▶ Setting QuarkXPress color controls

▶ Understanding process color vs. spot color

▶ Defining colors

▶ Applying colors to pictures and layout elements

▶ Creating linear color blends

▶ Establishing global trapping settings and overriding trapping locally

∎∎∎

Although color still is largely the province of high-end publishers — people producing magazines and catalogs — color is more accessible to all publishers today, thanks to the emergence of color printers, color copiers, and leading-edge desktop publishing programs. Whether you want to produce limited-run documents on a color printer, create newsletters using spot colors, or publish magazines and catalogs using process colors and special inks, QuarkXPress offers the tools you need to do the job well.

You can either use color in your graphics or apply colors to text and layout elements (such as bars along the edge of a page). Or you can use color in both ways. To a great extent, where you define and apply color determines what you can do with it.

Process color vs. spot color

Several forms of color are used in printing, but the two basic ones are *process color* and *spot color.*

Process color refers to the use of four basic colors — cyan, magenta, yellow, and black (known as a group as *CMYK*) — that are mixed to reproduce most color tones the human eye can see. A separate negative is produced for each of the four process colors. This method, often called *four-color publishing,* is used for most color publishing.

Spot color refers to any color — whether one of the process colors or some other hue — used for specific elements in a document. For example, if you print a document in black ink but print the company logo in red, the red is a spot color. A spot color is often called a *second color,* although you can use several spot colors in a document. Each spot color is output to its own negative (and not color separated into CMYK.

Using spot color gives you access to special inks that are truer to the desired color than any mix of process colors can be. These inks come in several standards, with Pantone being the most popular. (The Pantone system is also called *PMS color,* because the full name is *Pantone Matching System.*) Focoltone and Trumatch are less popular but still common standards. QuarkXPress supports all three standards.

Spot-color inks can produce some colors that are impossible to achieve with process colors, such as metallics, neons, and milky pastels. You can even use varnishes as spot colors to give layout elements a different gleam than the rest of the page. Although experienced designers sometimes mix spot colors to produce special shades not otherwise available, it's unlikely that you will need to do so.

Some designers use both process and spot colors in a document — known as *using a fifth color.* Typically, the normal color images are color-separated and printed via the four process colors, while a special element (such as a logo in metallic ink) is printed in a spot color. The process colors are output on the usual four negatives; the spot color is output on a separate, fifth negative and printed using a fifth plate, fifth ink roller, and fifth ink well. You can use more than five colors; you are limited only by your budget and the capabilities of your printing plant.

QuarkXPress can convert spot colors to process colors. This handy capability allows designers to specify the colors they want through a system they're familiar with, such as Pantone, without the added expense of special spot-color inks and extra negatives. Conversions are never an exact match, although there are now guidebooks that can show you in advance the color that will be created. QuarkXPress can convert some spot colors in a document to process colors but leave others alone, or leave all spot colors as spot colors. If you use Pantone colors, we suggest you get a copy of the *Pantone Process Color Imaging Guide: CMYK Edition* swatchbook, available from several sources, including art and printing supply stores, mail order catalogs, and Pantone itself. This swatchbook shows each Pantone color and the CMYK equivalent so you can see how accurate the conversion will be and thus whether you want to use the actual Pantone ink on it own negative or convert to CMYK.

Working with Color Pictures

When you work with imported graphics, whether they are illustrations or scanned photographs, color is part of the graphic file. So the responsibility for color controls lies primarily with the creator of the picture. It is best to use color files in EPS format (for illustrations) or TIFF format (for scans and bitmaps). These standards are de facto for color publishing, so QuarkXPress is particularly adept at working with them. (See Chapter 7, "Preparing Files for Import," for details on preparing graphics files for import.)

 QuarkXPress may lock up if you try to import color PCX or BMP bitmap files. Most, if not all, professional image-editing software can create or translate to color TIFF format, so the need to use other formats for color images should be rare.

If you create files in EPS format, do any required color trapping in the source application. Also, be sure to define any Pantone or other spot colors used in your graphic in your QuarkXPress document as well (this process is explained later in this chapter). Otherwise, the spot colors will not be color-separated when you output color separations.

Not all programs encode color information the same way. If you create EPS files in some illustration programs, colors may not print as expected. One of three things can happen:

- Each color prints on its own plate (as if it were a spot color), even if you defined it as a process color.

- A spot color is color-separated even when you define it as a spot color in both the source program and in QuarkXPress.

- A color prints as black.

Color TIFF files do not cause such peculiarities; however, only those files saved in CMYK TIFF format can be color-separated.

After you import a color graphic, you can do little to it other than resize or crop it. For color bitmaps, you can create a negative of the image through the Style ⇨ Negative option described in Chapter 20, "Working with Bitmap Images."

 Color files pasted via the clipboard should print properly after they are pasted into a QuarkXPress picture box. But problems do sometimes occur, such as dropped colors or altered colors, depending on the applications involved.

Working with Color Layout Elements

More color controls exist for layout elements you create in QuarkXPress than for imported graphics. You can do the following:

- Apply color to specific text
- Apply colors to imported gray-scale and black-and-white bitmaps (see the preceding chapter)
- Add color backgrounds to text and picture boxes
- Add color borders to boxes
- Apply color to ruling lines associated with text and to lines drawn with the line tools

In addition, by using empty picture boxes (boxes with no pictures imported into them) as shapes, you can create simple graphics, to which you can apply colors.

Defining Colors

Before you can apply any colors — to bitmap images or to layout elements — you must first define the colors. You can also define their trap values (covered later in this chapter). To define colors, select Edit ➪ Colors to open the dialog box shown in Figure 21-1. From this dialog box, you can do the following:

- Select New to add colors.
- Choose Edit to edit any color you add.
- Select Duplicate to duplicate an existing color for editing purposes.

QuarkXPress comes with several predefined colors: black, blue, cyan, green, magenta, red, registration, white, and yellow. (Registration is a color that prints on all negatives and is primarily used for crop and registration marks.) You cannot edit cyan, black, magenta, yellow, or white. You can duplicate any of the

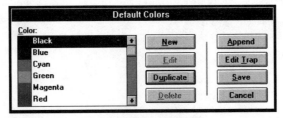

▶ **Figure 21-1:** The Default Colors dialog box.

predefined colors *except* registration and then edit the duplicates. (You can, for example, use green as a spot color and as a process color.)

As with most basic attributes, QuarkXPress lets you open the Default Colors dialog box when no document is open. If you do this, the dialog box is titled Default Colors; any changes to the color settings are automatically reflected in all subsequently created documents. If a document is open when you open the dialog box, the dialog box title is `Colors for` *`filename`*, and any color settings apply only to the open document.

You can import colors defined in other QuarkXPress documents or templates by selecting the Append button, which opens the Append Colors dialog box shown in Figure 21-2. All colors defined in the specified document or template are imported; you cannot selectively import colors. The color trap values are imported with the colors.

Any color in the current document with a name that matches that of a color in the second document or template is not overridden by the append operation. The color in the current document is preserved. QuarkXPress does not display a message saying a name collision occurred and was avoided.

For your changes to take effect, you must choose Save in the Default Colors dialog box after you finish defining colors. Choose Cancel to undo any changes you make.

The Edit Trap options are covered later in this chapter.

Because regular black can appear weak when it's overprinted by other colors, many designers create what printers call *superblack* by combining 100-percent black and 100-percent magenta. You can define superblack as a separate color or redefine the registration color as 100 percent of all four process colors, and use that as a superblack.

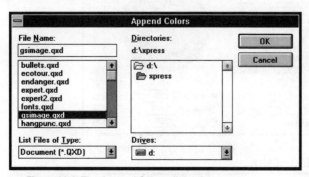

▶ **Figure 21-2:** The Append Colors dialog box.

Color models

QuarkXPress supports several *color models,* which are ways of representing colors. The supported models include: Pantone; Trumatch; Focoltone; process (CMYK); RGB (red, green, blue), which is used in monitors; and HSB (hue, saturation, brightness), which is typically used in creating paints. You can convert a color defined in any model to CMYK, RGB, or HSB models simply by selecting one of those models after defining the color.

 Colors defined in one model and converted to another may not reproduce exactly the same, because the physics underlying each color model differ slightly. Each model was designed for use in a different medium, such as paper or a video monitor.

How to define colors

You define colors in the Edit Color dialog box, which appears when you choose New, Edit, or Duplicate in the Default Colors dialog box. Figure 21-3 shows a color being defined through the CMYK model, which is the standard model used in the publishing industry. After selecting the model from the Model list box, we entered values in the Cyan, Magenta, Yellow, and Black fields. If you prefer, you can define the color values by using the slider bars or by moving the black spot on the color wheel to the desired color. Or you can use any combination of these three techniques.

In Figure 21-3, the bar to the right of the color wheel is grayed out. You use this bar to control brightness when you define colors through the HSB color model. When you use RGB and HSB color models, the arrangement of the slider bars is

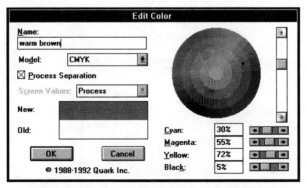

▶ **Figure 21-3:** You can define colors using any of several color models, including CMYK.

different from what you see in the figure. All three of the mix-based color models (RGB, HSB, and CMYK) use a color wheel to show the range of allowable mixtures.

You can name a color anything you want, provided you stay within the character limit of the <u>N</u>ame field. But to make it easier to remember what a defined color looks like, either use descriptive names (such as *warm brown*, as we did here) or use names based on the color settings. For example, if you create a color in the CMYK model, give it a name based on its mix, such as 30C55M72Y5K for our warm brown color — composed of 30-percent cyan, 55-percent magenta, 72-percent yellow, and 5-percent black. (Believe it or not, this naming convention is how professionals specify colors on paste-up boards.) The same system applies to the RGB and HSB models. That way, you can look at the Colors palette and immediately tell what color you'll get.

 If you edit an existing color, the old color is displayed in the box to the right of the word *Old* in the Edit Color dialog box (shown in Figure 21-3). As you define the new color, you see the new color to the right of the word *New*. If you define a color for the first time, no color appears in the field named *Old*.

Figure 21-4 shows a Pantone color being added to the QuarkXPress color list. As you can see, the fields in the Edit Color dialog box change depending upon what color model you use. When you use a spot-color model such as Pantone, Quark-XPress replaces the color wheel with a series of color swatches and their identifying labels. If you know the label, you can enter it in the field at the bottom right; alternatively, you can scroll through the list of labels.

 Keep in mind that the colors displayed are only on-screen representations and that the actual color may be different. This is particularly true if your monitor is running at 8-bit (256 hues) or lower resolution. (Most VGA boards run at 4-bit, or 16-color, resolution.) Check the actual color in a color swatch book for the model you are using. (Art and printing supply stores usually carry these swatch books.)

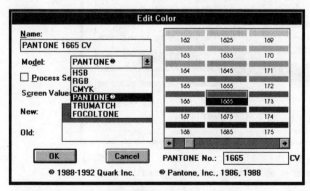

▶ **Figure 21-4:** Selecting a Pantone color.

Color-separation controls

When defining a color in any model other than CMYK, check the Process Separation box in the Edit Color dialog box, as shown in Figure 21-5; Quark-XPress then color-separates the color when you output negatives. If you do not check this box, the color outputs as a spot color on its own negative — even if you enable color separation in the Print dialog box. If you build a color using the CMYK model, the Process Separation Box will be unavailable since the color is, in effect, already color-separated.

Pantone produces a swatch book, the *Pantone Process Color Imaging Guide: CMYK Edition,* that displays actual Pantone inks next to their process-color equivalents (or *builds,* in publishing parlance) so you can see how well they translate. The builds used in the swatch book are the same ones used by QuarkXPress and other major publishing programs. You can get the swatch book from several sources, including art and printing supply stores, mail order catalogs, and Pantone itself.

In process-color printing, each color prints at a slightly different angle so that the overlap of the four colors produces evenly mixed colors. Although spot colors rarely mix with process colors, QuarkXPress needs to orient the angle of the line screen that prints the spot color, just in case there is mixing with process colors or other spot colors.

The Screen Values option in the Edit Color dialog box lets you define the screening angle for spot colors. You can pick any of the process color plates — cyan, magenta, yellow, or black — to define the screening angle. We suggest that you use the yellow plate's angle for light spot colors; darker colors can use any of the others.

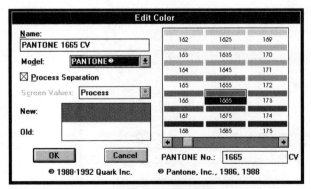

▶ **Figure 21-5:** Check Process Separation to tell QuarkXPress to reproduce a color using CMYK process-color values.

When the Process Separation box is checked, the Screen Value option is automatically grayed out; because no separate negative is produced, you do not need to assign a screening angle for it.

Applying Colors

After you define colors, you can apply them. Most dialog boxes for text and items contain a color list option, as do many options in the Style menu. All colors defined in a document appear (in alphabetical order) in any of these color lists.

When working with picture boxes, text boxes, and lines, you can apply colors by using the Colors palette (accessible through the View menu's Show Colors option) rather than invoking the dialog boxes. Figure 21-6 shows the Colors palette. This palette gives you a handy way to quickly apply colors to lines and to picture and text box backgrounds, frames, and, in some cases, contents.

The Colors palette displays a list of available colors. The palette also contains icons that let you direct how QuarkXPress applies colors to the selected box. Select the icon first and then select the color you want to apply. (The currently

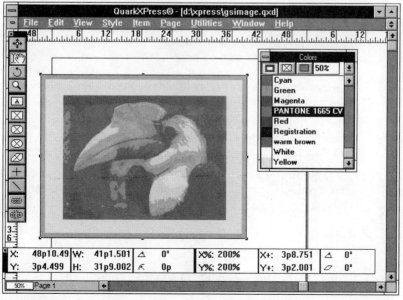

▶ **Figure 21-6:** The Colors palette.

▶ **Figure 21-7:** The icon in the Colors palette resembles a picture box if a picture box is selected.

▶ **Figure 21-8:** The icon is a line if a line is selected.

▶ **Figure 21-9:** The Colors palette with the background icon selected.

highlighted color is applied.) From left to right, the Colors palette icons are as follows:

- **Frame:** If you select this icon, QuarkXPress applies the selected color to the box frame. (If no frame is defined in the Item ⇨ Modify option for the box, no color appears. As soon as a frame is defined, it takes on the color you applied.)

- **Contents:** The contents icon changes depending upon what element is currently selected. The icon looks like a picture box if the selected item is a picture; like a text box if the selected item is text; and like a line if the selected element is a line. Choosing the icon applies the selected color to the contents of the box or line. Figures 21-7 and 21-8 show how the palette looks when you apply colors to different types of elements. Figure 21-8 also shows the line the color is being applied to.

  You can apply colors to any contents except color pictures. If you apply color to the contents of a text box, any text you subsequently enter into the text box takes on the applied color. Existing text is unaffected.

- **Background:** Selecting this icon applies the selected color to the box background. Figure 21-9 shows how the palette looks when this icon is selected.

If an option is not available for the selected item (for example, a background for a line), its icon is grayed out.

You can apply the color at different shades by editing the number in the field located at the upper right of the Colors palette. Enter any value from 0 to 100 percent, in 0.1-percent increments. You can access common percentages (multiples of 10) through the drop-down list box to the right of the field.

Creating Linear Blends

Using the Colors palette, you also can apply a *linear blend,* which is a smooth transition from one color to another. Figures 21-10 and 21-11 show examples of linear blends applied to the story's headlines.

You can apply a linear blend to a selected picture or text box. To do this, select the background icon from the Colors palette and then invoke the drop-down list box below the row of icons (the current list selection will likely be Solid, which is the default). Two radio buttons and a field appear.

The #1 radio button is selected by default, and the current background color is highlighted. (The color is White if you did not apply a color to the box). You create the linear blend from the selected color; change the color if necessary. Then click the #2 radio button and select the color you want to blend into. In the field to the right of the #2 button, enter the angle of the blend; you can enter any value from –360 to +360 degrees, in increments of 0.001 degrees. A setting of 0 degrees blends the two colors from top to bottom; a setting of 90 degrees blends the colors from left to right.

The linear blend will not display while the picture or text box is selected (this speeds redraw when making changes in or to the box). To see the effects of your blend, select another picture or text box.

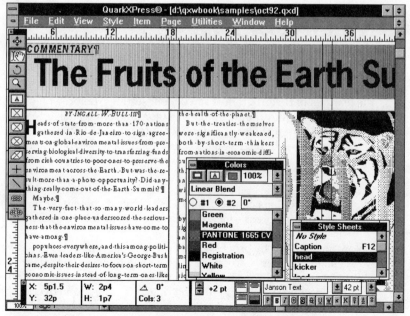

▶ **Figure 21-10:** A 0-degree linear blend between yellow and magenta.

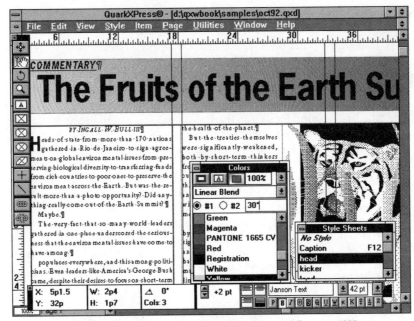

▶ **Figure 21-11:** A 30-degree linear blend between yellow and Pantone 1665.

Working with Color Traps

Color trapping — which controls how colors overlap and abut when printed — is one of the most powerful features available in QuarkXPress. It's also one that novice users can abuse terribly. If you don't know much about trapping, leave the features of the program at the default settings. Before you use QuarkXPress trapping tools, study some books on color publishing, talk to your printer, and experiment with test files you don't want to publish. If you are experienced with color trapping — or after you become experienced — you'll find QuarkXPress trapping tools a joy to use.

Trapping adjusts the boundaries of colored objects to prevent gaps between abutting colors. Gaps can occur because of misalignment of the negatives, plates, or printing press — all of which are impossible to avoid.

Colors are trapped by processes known as *choking* and *spreading*. Both make an object slightly larger — usually a fraction of a point — so that it overprints the abutting object slightly. The process is called choking when one object surrounds a second object, and the first object is enlarged to overlap the other. The process is known as spreading when you enlarge the surrounded object, so that it "leaks" into the surrounding object.

▶ **Figure 21-12:** Spreading (at left) makes the underlying color bleed out; choking (at right) makes the outside color bleed in, in effect making the area of the choked element smaller.

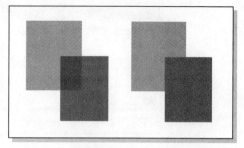

▶ **Figure 21-13:** Setting colors to overprint results in mixed colors, at left; setting them to knock out results in discrete colors, at right.

The difference between choking and spreading is the relative position of the two objects. Think of choking as making the hole for the inside object smaller (which in effect makes the object on outside larger), and think of spreading as making the object in the hole larger.

Figure 21-12 shows the two types of trapping techniques. Spreading (at left) makes the interior color bleed out; choking (at right) makes the outside color bleed in, in effect making the area of the choked element smaller.

In practice, trapping also involves controlling whether colors *knock out* or *overprint*. The default is to knock out — cut out — any overlap when one element is placed on top of another. If, for example, you place two rectangles on top of each other, they print like the two rectangles on the right side of Figure 21-13. If you set the darker rectangle in the figure to overprint, the rectangles print as shown on the left side of the figure. Setting colors to overprint results in mixed colors, as on the left, while setting colors to knock out results in discrete colors, as on the right.

Setting traps

You define trapping settings for separate documents and colors in the Trap Specifications dialog box, shown in Figure 21-14 (to open the dialog box, select Edit ⇨ Colors ⇨ Edit Traps). However, you define some default trapping settings in the Application Preferences dialog box, accessed via Edit ⇨ Preferences ⇨ Application.

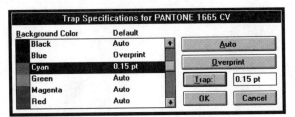

▶ **Figure 21-14:** The Trap Specifications dialog box.

The trapping settings — the defaults for all documents and standard colors — you define in the Application Preferences dialog box are covered in detail in "Color trapping," in Chapter 4, "Customizing QuarkXPress."

The title of the Trap Specifications dialog box shows the color for which you are defining trapping values. (In Figure 21-14, trapping values are being defined for Pantone 1665 CV.) In the Background Color list box, you see all defined colors — except registration, black, and white. You do not need to trap these three colors as background colors, because black and registration completely obscure any color spread into them; also, white does not "mix" with other colors and thus causes no unsightly gaps or color artifacts due to misregistration.

The list of background colors includes a color not defined via Edit ▷ Colors: indeterminate. This item is not exactly a color, but a special case used by QuarkXPress to handle multicolored backgrounds (such as a color picture or multiple color objects abutting) for which trapping information is unavailable or is conflicting.

You can choose three basic options in the Trap Specifications dialog box by selecting the corresponding button:

- **Auto:** This is the default setting for all colors; it applies whatever trapping values are set in the Application Preferences dialog box.

- **Overprint:** Overprint sets the color named in the dialog box title bar to overprint the color selected in the color list. (Except for black, colors always knock out unless you choose overprint.)

- **Trap:** Trap lets you specify an actual trapping value, which you enter in the field to the right of the button. You can enter any value from –36 to +36 points, in 0.001-point increments.

Entering a negative trapping number chokes the object that has the background color. Entering a positive number spreads the background color. The difference between the two is subtle and usually comes into play for fine elements such as text and lines. If the object using the background color is thin or has a light hue, a good rule of thumb is to spread; otherwise, choke.

Overriding traps

Because trapping depends as much on the elements being trapped as their colors, trapping tools based solely on relationships among colors would be insufficient. That's why QuarkXPress offers the ability to override trapping settings for selected objects.

To override trapping locally, you must first invoke the Trap Information palette, which is accessible via View ⇨ Show Trap Information. The contents of this palette depend on the type of object selected, but no matter what the contents, the palette works the same way. Figure 21-15 shows the Trap Information palette for a picture box.

In the figure, all three picture-box elements for which trapping is appropriate are set at Default (shown in the second column), which means they take on whatever settings were made globally in the Trap Specifications dialog box. Because there are so many possible combinations of colors, no one can be expected to remember how every color combination traps. Recognizing this, QuarkXPress displays what the default setting is in the column at right. Thus, in Figure 21-15 the defaults are as follows:

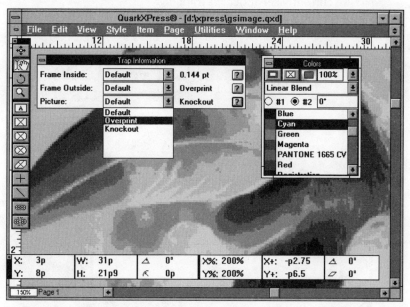

▶ **Figure 21-15:** The Trap Information palette for a picture box.

■ The default for trapping the frame color with the color of the image inside the frame is 0.144 points (which happens to be the setting for automatic trapping in this document).

■ The default for trapping the frame color with the color of the object outside (abutting) the frame is overprint; this default makes sense because the only thing abutting the frame is the paper, which is white and is thus over-printed.

■ The default for trapping the picture with the picture box background is Knockout, which is what you would expect a picture to do. However, as an example of how you can override default settings, Figure 21-15 shows the process of using the drop-down list box to change this last trapping setting to Overprint. Changing this setting causes the image to overprint the background (which the Colors palette shows is cyan), which means that the image will have a cyan background rather than the usual white back-ground that knocking out creates. Because the image is colored Pantone 1665, the result will be a muddy mixture of Pantone 1665 (a warm brown) and cyan — not a particularly attractive combination.

As a further service to explain trapping settings, QuarkXPress describes the current trapping rationale if you select the question-mark icons in the Trap Information dialog box. Figure 21-16 shows an example explanation for the picture currently set at default trapping.

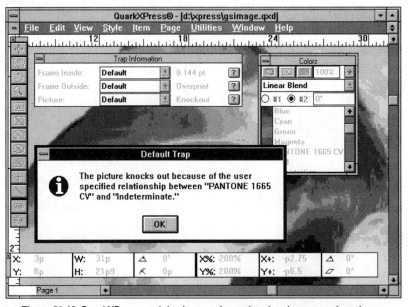

▶ **Figure 21-16:** QuarkXPress explains its trapping rationale when you select the question mark icon.

Summary

▶ TIFF and EPS formats are the best choices for imported color images. Color files in other formats can cause QuarkXPress to lock up.

▶ You can define colors using any of several color models. Colors defined in one model and translated to another sometimes print differently than the original colors because of differences between the color models that defy translation. The same is true for colors defined in any model but CMYK that are color-separated via process colors.

▶ Colors defined in models other than CMYK (process) are color-separated only if you check the Process Separation box in the Edit Color dialog box.

▶ You can import colors defined in other documents into the current document, although you cannot import colors selectively.

▶ Creating a superblack color, perhaps based on the registration color, can result in stronger blacks, especially when printing over color images and other colored elements.

▶ Using the Colors palette is a handy way to apply colors and shades to boxes and lines.

▶ The Colors palette includes a linear-blend feature for picture box and text box backgrounds.

▶ Generally speaking, when you establish trapping values, use spreading (indicated via positive numbers) for light-hued or thin elements, and choking (negative numbers) for darker or thicker elements.

▶ Use the Trap Information palette to override global trapping settings for selected elements.

PART VI

Document Management

One of the toughest parts of publishing — whether done on a desktop or via traditional means — is keeping track of the many elements that comprise the document, including the source text, graphics, and style standards. QuarkXPress offers several tools to help you manage elements within and across documents. Understanding these tools is critical to using QuarkXPress effectively, especially in an environment in which many people contribute to the final publication.

QuarkXPress's document-management tools fall into four broad categories: libraries, links, style standards, and multiplatform support.

CHAPTER

22

Using Libraries

In This Chapter

▶ Creating and using QuarkXPress libraries

▶ Displaying selected library elements

▶ Moving elements between libraries

▶ Using library elements in documents

A feature unique to QuarkXPress is the capability to create *libraries* of text and graphics. This feature is a great aid if you reuse elements throughout a set of publications. For example, you can have a library containing your corporate logos, columnists' photos, or such standard text as mastheads and postal statements. QuarkXPress does more than let you create libraries: It lets you create multiple libraries — any or all of which may be open at a time. QuarkXPress also lets you group library elements to make them easy to find.

The libraries themselves are separate files that can reside anywhere on your hard disk (or network). QuarkXPress libraries have the filename extension QXL. Because the libraries are not part of any document, any document can use them.

Creating Libraries

Before you can use a library, you must create it. Selecting Utilities ⇨ Library opens the Library dialog box shown in Figure 22-1. Through this dialog box, you can open existing libraries and create new ones. Navigate the folders and disks as you do in any Windows application until you access the folder that you want to use for the library (or that contains the library you want to load).

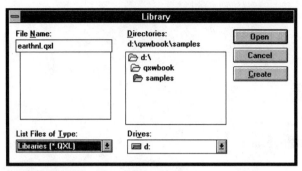

▶ **Figure 22-1:** The Library dialog box.

▶ **Figure 22-2:**
A new, empty
library.

To create a library, enter a name in the File Name field. You don't need to include the QXL extension — QuarkXPress does that for you automatically. After you enter a filename, select Create. An empty library appears in your document, as Figure 22-2 shows.

The library filename appears at the top of the library and includes the full path name (the drive and directory). Because the library window is narrow, the name may be cut off, as it is in Figure 22-2. You can resize the window by selecting any of its sides or corners, holding the mouse button down, and dragging the window side or corner.

QuarkXPress for Windows cannot read libraries created in QuarkXPress for Macintosh.

Adding Elements to Libraries

After you create your library, you can add elements from any open document or library to it. If you want to bring in elements from several documents, you can — the library window stays on-screen as you open and close documents, as well as when you open and close other libraries.

You can only put elements that are in text or picture boxes or that are created with one of the line tools into libraries. You cannot include graphics files that are not in a picture box or text files that are not in a text box. All attributes applied to the boxes — including frames, backgrounds, and colors — are retained. Graphics include all cropping, sizing, and other such information; text includes all formatting.

Although style tags are not copied from the original document into a library, text retains all formatting from the styles tags except H&J sets. In the library, QuarkXPress applies the No Style tag to the copied text. When pasted into a new document, this text will retain any character formatting, such as typeface and size. But if you want this formatting to be part of the document's style sheet, you will have to recreate the style. See Chapter 6 for details on creating style sheets. You also cannot put text boxes that contain text linked to other text boxes into a library — when you try to do so, QuarkXPress alerts you and aborts the placement.

There are two basic ways to add elements to libraries:

- **Option 1:** Use the standard cut, copy, and paste functions, either through the keyboard shortcuts (Ctrl+X, Ctrl+C, and Ctrl+V, respectively) or through the Edit menus in the QuarkXPress document and library windows.

- **Option 2:** Drag elements from documents or libraries to the destination library.

To add elements using the standard cut, copy, and paste functions, take the following steps.

▶ Steps: Adding elements to libraries with cut, copy, and paste

Step 1. Select the picture box, text box, or line you want to place in a library. Make sure that the Item tool, not the Content tool, is highlighted, because you can only cut and copy boxes with the Item tool.

Step 2. Use Copy or Cut (either through the keyboard shortcuts or the Edit menu) to put the box in the Clipboard. Use Copy unless you want to remove the box from your source document.

Step 3. Move the mouse pointer to the library window. Click anywhere in the window; two triangle pointers appear to show where the library element will be placed.

Step 4. Paste the element. (Figure 22-3 shows the Paste function being selected via the library window's Edit menu.) The element appears as a box in the library window.

You can also use the drag-and-drop approach to add elements to a library. Take the following steps to use this method.

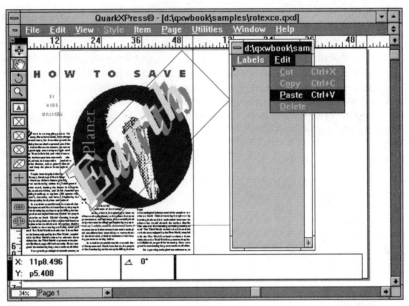

▶ **Figure 22-3:** Using the Paste function to add a library element.

▶ Steps: Adding elements to libraries with drag-and-drop

Step 1. Select the picture box, text box, or line you want to place in a library. Make sure that the Item tool, not the Content tool, is highlighted, because boxes can only be dragged with the Item tool.

Step 2. Move the element into the library window by holding down the mouse after selecting the element. Notice how the cursor changes to a pair of glasses (the library cursor) and a thin box appears when your cursor is in the library window. Figure 22-4 illustrates this part of the process.

Step 3. Release the mouse button. The element appears as a box in the library window.

If you check the Auto Library Save option in the Application Preferences dialog box (open by selecting Edit ⇨ Preferences ⇨ Application), the library is saved each time you add or delete an element. Otherwise, the library is saved when you save the current document, close the library, or quit QuarkXPress. (Preferences are covered in Chapter 1, "What Is QuarkXPress?")

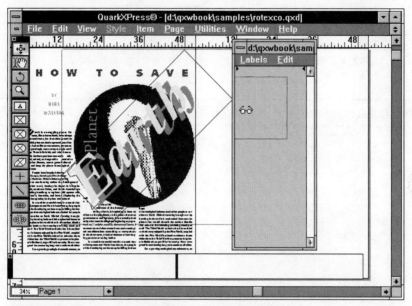

▶ **Figure 22-4:** Dragging an element into the library window.

Repeat this process for all elements (from all documents) you want to put in the library. The result is a library like the one shown in Figure 22-5. We opened several documents to get elements for this library. You may find that your libraries evolve over time, too.

▶ **Figure 22-5:** A library with text and graphics elements from several documents.

Adding Master Pages to Libraries

Moving master pages from documents to libraries is tricky because QuarkXPress offers no feature explicitly designed to do this task. Take the following steps to accomplish this task.

▶ Steps: Moving master pages to libraries

Step 1. Open or create a library to hold the master pages (select Utilities ▷ Library).

Step 2. Open the document that contains the master page you want to copy. Display the master page by selecting Page ▷ Display.

Step 3. Select the Item tool and then select all items (choose Edit ▷ Select All or use the shortcut Ctrl+A).

Step 4. Drag (or copy and paste) the items into an open library and release the mouse. All elements on the master page appear in their own library box, as shown at the top of the library window in Figure 22-6. (In the figure, the master page in the library has a darker background than the others because it is currently selected; on a color monitor, the background would be yellow or another highlight color.)

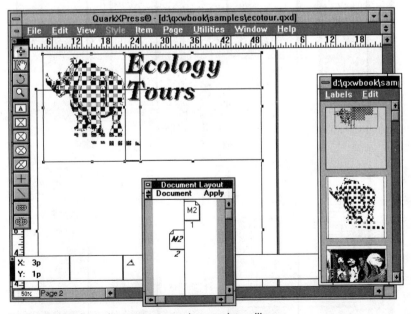

▶ Figure 22-6: Dragging master page elements into a library.

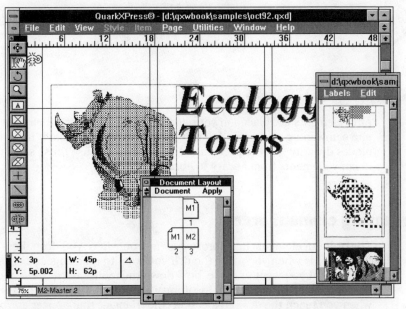

► **Figure 22-7:** Dragging the library item containing the master-page elements to the new master page.

Step 5. Open the document into which you want to copy the master page. You don't need to close the other document, but unless you intend to get other elements from it or work on it later, go ahead and close it to reduce clutter both on-screen and in the PC's memory.

Step 6. Insert a new blank master page in the second document. (Creating master pages is covered in Chapter 5, "Understanding Master Pages." Here, that master page is M2, as shown in the Document Layout palette in Figure 22-6.)

Step 7. Drag (or copy and paste) the library item containing the master-page elements to the new master page and position it where you want it. In Figure 22-7, the library's first object (the rhino illustration and the "Ecology Tours" logo) have been dragged onto the M2 master page. You may want to change the screen display to fit-to-window view so that you can better position the elements on the new master page. (To display this view, select View ▷ Fit in Window or use the keyboard shortcut Ctrl+0 [zero].)

Step 8. Use the Document Layout palette to display the master pages and rename the new master page so that you can remember what it contains.

Master pages are discussed in detail in Chapter 5, "Understanding Master Pages."

Managing Libraries

After elements are placed in your library, you can manage their order and remove unwanted elements. You can always add elements later using the techniques described in the preceding section. You can use those same techniques to copy elements from library to library.

Rearranging element order

The order of elements in a library depends on where you drop them or where the cursor is when you paste them. If you want to rearrange the order, select the element you want to move, hold down the mouse button, and move the cursor to the new position in the library window. Release the mouse button when you reach the desired location (the triangles that appear as you move the element are the insertion points).

Labeling elements

Because a library can easily grow so large that there are too many elements to scroll through, QuarkXPress lets you assign labels to elements. You then can tell QuarkXPress to display only those elements that have a particular label. In effect, you create sublibraries within a library. The process of adding a label is simple; just take the following steps.

▶ Steps: Labeling elements in a library

Step 1. Double-click the element you want to label. The Library Entry dialog box appears.

Step 2. Either type in a label, as Figure 22-8 shows, or select an existing label (a label already used in the current library) from the drop-down list box next to the Label field. Several entries can have the same label.

Step 3. Choose OK.

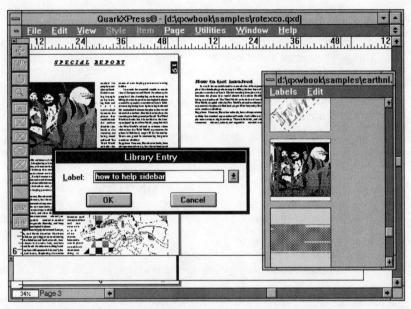

▶ **Figure 22-8:** The Library Entry dialog box.

The label does not display with the element image in the library window. To see a label, you must double-click the item to bring up the Library Entry dialog box.

After you create labels, you can use the library window's Labels menu to select which elements are displayed. Figure 22-9 shows this menu. Because All is checked, all elements are displayed. If you select Unlabeled, QuarkXPress displays all elements that are not labeled; this option is handy for those odds-and-ends library elements you want to see infrequently but need to access easily.

▶ **Figure 22-9:** The Labels menu in the library window.

Using multiple libraries

Although labels are a great way to keep the list of library elements manageable, this method is no substitute for creating different libraries to hold distinct groups of elements. Don't let the label feature be an excuse for having an un-wieldy library — when the elements in a library become too diverse, it's time to create a new library and move some elements into it. There are three ways to move elements from one library to another:

- **Option 1:** Drag the element into the new library. This option copies the element from the first library into the second while leaving the original element intact in the first library.

- **Option 2:** Use the copy command in the first library and paste a copy of the element into the second library. This option also copies the element from the first library into the second while leaving the original element intact in the first library.

- **Option 3:** Use the cut command in the first library and paste the element into the second library. The element is removed from the first library.

Figure 22-10 shows two open libraries. The one on the left contains artwork only, because this library is intended for use in any number of documents. The one on the right contains elements used often in a particular newsletter, so this library contains both text and graphics for the newsletter.

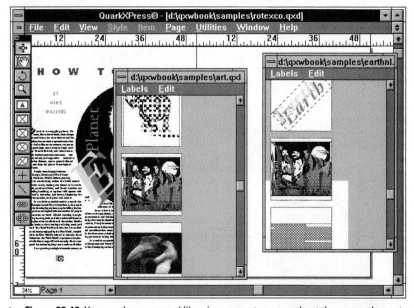

▶ **Figure 22-10:** You can have several libraries open at once and put the same element in more than one of them.

Another benefit of creating multiple libraries is that you can more readily identify the documents in which they may be useful — assuming you use logical filenames like EDPHOTOS.QXL or EARTHNL.QXL.

Deleting unwanted elements

Your libraries will evolve over time, as your document elements change. This means you sometimes need to delete library elements as well as to add them. There are two ways to delete elements:

- **Cut:** Cutting an element removes it from the library but puts a copy on the Clipboard so that you can paste it elsewhere, such as into another document or library.

- **Delete:** Deleting an element removes it from the library and does not put a copy on the Clipboard. A deleted element is erased permanently from the current library.

You can use the Edit menu, shown in Figure 22-11, to cut and delete. To cut an element, you also can use the keyboard shortcut Ctrl+X. There is no shortcut for delete. When you cut or delete an element, QuarkXPress asks you to confirm the edit, as shown in Figure 22-12.

► **Figure 22-12:** The edit confirmation message box.

► **Figure 22-11:** Use the Edit menu to cut and delete library elements.

Using Library Elements

After you create and fill your libraries, it's easy to move the library elements into your documents. Just drag them or use the cut, copy, and paste commands as you did to put elements in the library in the first place.

In Figure 22-13, the middle element (the one with the pointers above it) is being moved into a document. The dashed line shows the size of the element being copied. Library elements always paste into documents in their original size, not the smaller version displayed in the library. After you place an element into a document, you can modify it as you do any other text box, picture box, or line.

Libraries are especially helpful when you work with graphic and text elements that have special effects applied. For example, it may seem odd for us to include the *Earth* text in the library shown in the figure. After all, how often do you use the rotated word *Earth* in documents? We placed the text box in the library not so that we could reuse the word *Earth* itself, but rather its rotation, drop shadow, and color. After copying the element into a document, we can easily change the text to something else while retaining all the formatting of the original element. This technique is also handy for picture boxes that have intricate frames, special color blends, or odd shapes, and for special lines like arrowheads.

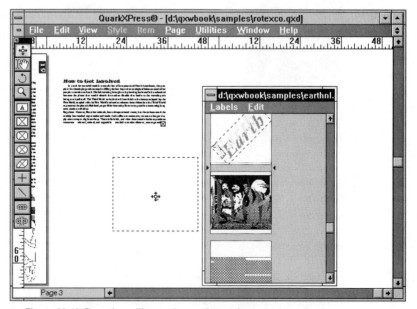

▶ **Figure 22-13:** Dragging a library element into a document.

Summary

▶ Libraries let you collect common text, pictures, and lines and make them accessible to any document, with all formatting retained. You can put complex text formatting in a library by applying such formatting to dummy text and putting that text in the library.

▶ Graphics placed into libraries maintain all links — including OLE links — to their source files.

▶ You can enlarge library windows to make their names more readable. You also can reduce library windows so that they do not cover up too much of a document.

▶ Dragging elements to a library is the easiest way to add them to a library.

▶ Make sure to select the Item tool before trying to drag or copy a picture box, text box, or line to a library.

▶ If you check the Auto Library Save option in the Application Preferences dialog box, QuarkXPress automatically saves libraries any time you change them.

▶ You can reposition the elements in a library by selecting them and moving them to a new location.

▶ Element labels let you view selected groups of library elements.

▶ Use multiple libraries to keep the number of elements in any one library manageable.

▶ You can move or copy elements between libraries.

Linking To Source Files

∎∎∎∎∎∎∎∎∎∎∎∎∎∎∎∎∎∎∎∎∎∎∎∎∎∎∎∎∎∎∎∎∎∎∎∎∎∎∎

In This Chapter

▶ Updating links to source graphics

▶ Understanding OLE and how OLE objects and links differ from standard objects and links

▶ Updating links to OLE objects

▶ Exporting text

∎∎∎∎∎∎∎∎∎∎∎∎∎∎∎∎∎∎∎∎∎∎∎∎∎∎∎∎∎∎∎∎∎∎∎∎∎∎∎

Document elements such as text and graphics may change, and you need to ensure that your document contains the latest version of all elements. In addition, you sometimes need to make sure that any changes you make to text in a document are made to the original text files, because you may want to use the same text in other documents. Both these problems can be solved with a process known as *linking*. QuarkXPress supports several types of links, which are detailed in the sidebar "Understanding links."

QuarkXPress offers features that address several linking issues, although in some areas it offers no support at all. QuarkXPress is particularly adept at two kinds of links: links (static) and OLE (dynamic) links for graphics. QuarkXPress is weak, however, at making text links.

Understanding links

QuarkXPress supports several types of links to source files, particularly graphics. The terms can be confusing, especially because people tend to use the word "link" generically, no matter what kind of link they are referencing. Links in QuarkXPress fall into two classes: static links to files and dynamic links to objects.

Static links are the standard links common to most publishing programs: When you import a graphics file, QuarkXPress records the location of the file and its date and time stamp. The next time you open a document, QuarkXPress looks to see if the graphic is in its expected location and if its date and time stamp has changed (if so, the graphic has been updated). QuarkXPress does this for two reasons: First, by linking to the original graphic, QuarkXPress needs to make only a low-resolution image for use on-screen, which keeps the document size manageable and screen-redraw time quick. (When printing, QuarkXPress substitutes the actual high-resolution graphic.) Second, by checking the links, QuarkXPress gives the layout artist the opportunity to use the latest version of a graphic. You can choose among the options for QuarkXPress to: always load the latest version, make you decide, or ignore any updates. If the graphic is not where QuarkXPress expects it to be, the program asks you to find the graphic.

Dynamic links are possible with a new capability offered by Windows 3.1 (and via Publish and Subscribe on the Macintosh via System 7). They differ from static links in two significant ways: First, they are links to *objects*, not entire files — for example, you might have a link to a range in a spreadsheet or to part of a graphic. Second, the links can be updated any time, not just when you open a document. Dynamic links are established through a technology called OLE (described in detail later in this chapter), which lets programs communicate with each other and share objects among them.

There are two basic types of dynamic links: object linking and object embedding. A *linked object* has a *live* (automatic) connection between QuarkXPress and the program that created the object. If the linked object is changed in its original program, the new version is automatically sent to QuarkXPress, which automatically updates the object in your layout document. An *embedded object* has a manual link to its source object and program. If the embedded object is changed in the source program, you must tell the program to update QuarkXPress. You can also tell QuarkXPress to ask all source programs if any embedded objects have changed. In either case, the update occurs only when you request it.

Working with Graphics Links

You can bring graphics into QuarkXPress documents in two ways: You can import them through the File ⇨ Get Picture command or use the Windows clipboard to copy a graphic from another Windows application directly into QuarkXPress. Both methods have their advantages:

- The primary advantage to using the import method is that you can create a link to the original graphic in case the graphic is changed or moved.

- The primary advantage to using the clipboard method is that you can copy into a document graphics that QuarkXPress ordinarily cannot import. The Windows Clipboard translates them to a format QuarkXPress can read.

When you open a QuarkXPress document, QuarkXPress checks the links to any imported graphic. These links are created automatically when you import the file; no special effort on your part is needed. QuarkXPress looks for two things: to see if the file is where it is supposed to be, and to see if the file has changed since the last time it was accessed (QuarkXPress looks at the file's date and time stamp to determine this second factor).

If the file is missing or has been modified, QuarkXPress displays the alert box shown in Figure 23-1. You can select Cancel, which tells QuarkXPress not to worry about the problem, or you can choose OK to invoke the Missing/Modified Pictures dialog box, shown in Figure 23-2. (A file might be missing because the file was deleted; moved to a different disk, such as for backup; or renamed after being edited.)

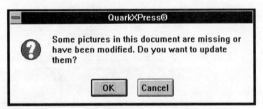

▶ **Figure 23-1:** QuarkXPress warns you if files are missing or have been modified.

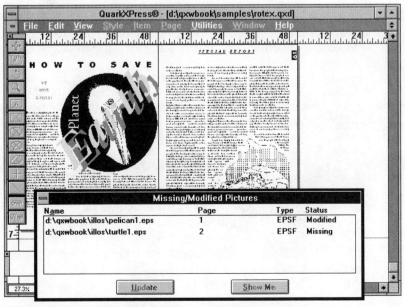

▶ **Figure 23-2:** The Missing/Modified Pictures dialog box.

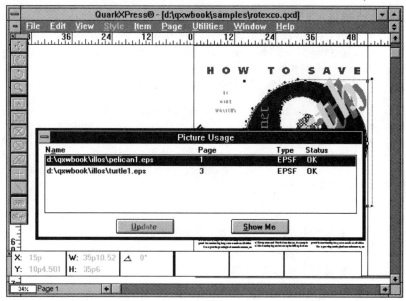

▶ **Figure 23-3:** The Picture Usage dialog box.

The Missing/Modified Pictures dialog box gives you several pieces of informa-tion about the graphics that are missing or have been modified. These include the full filename (including the last known location), the page each graphic appears on, the type of graphic format, and the graphic's status (OK, Missing, or Modified). OK appears only after you update a graphic.

If you don't update files when you open your document (by selecting Cancel in response to the alert box or by not making selections in the Missing/Modified Pictures dialog box), you still see the graphics in your document, as Figure 23-2 shows. What you see is a low-resolution copy of your graphic that QuarkXPress creates when importing a graphic. This version is not appropriate for printing and should not be used in place of the real thing: it exists only to show you what graphic you placed, in case you don't remember the graphic by name.

If you decide not to update a graphic link when you first load your document, you can do so later through the Utilities ⇨ Picture Usage dialog box, shown in Figure 23-3. This box works the same way as the Missing/Modified Pictures dialog box. You can use the Picture Usage dialog box to substitute new graphics for missing graphics, because QuarkXPress doesn't know (or care) whether the new links are to the same graphics.

If you need to see the graphic to remember which graphic a filename refers to, select the filename and then choose Show Me. QuarkXPress displays the screen version of the graphic on the page on which it occurs. You should be in a normal (100%) or reduced view so you can see enough of the image when Quark-XPress displays it.

Updating missing graphics

To update the link to a missing graphic, select the filename and then choose Update. Then move through the drives and directories available through the Find *filename* dialog box, shown in Figure 23-4. QuarkXPress uses the standard Windows dialog box to search for missing graphics. In the figure, the file is located in a different directory than the one it was imported from. If you choose OK, you update the link to the graphic and return to the Missing/Modified Pictures dialog box. You see confirmation of your selection in the dialog box and can update any other files. Once you've found the file, it will no longer say "missing," but it may say "modified" if the newly located file is more recent than the original. Choose Update again to update the link to the file.

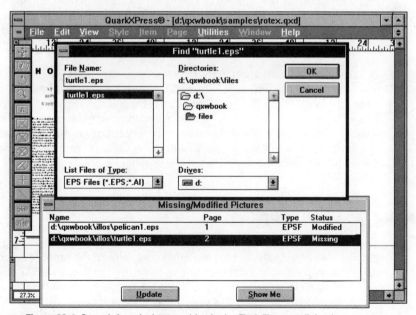

▶ **Figure 23-4:** Search for missing graphics in the Find *filename* dialog box.

Picture Usage			
Name	**Page**	**Type**	**Status**
d:\qxwbook\illos\pelican1.eps	1	EPSF	Modified
d:\qxwbook\banta.doc	2	????	Wrong Type

[Update]   [Show Me]

▶ **Figure 23-5:** QuarkXPress tells you when a file is not in a supported graphics format.

Note that only files whose extensions match a particular file type (in the figure, EPS) appear in the File Name list. You can specify other extensions, available from the list in the drop-down menu under the List Files of Type option, in case the file has been renamed to a different extension.

Macintosh users are accustomed to seeing an icon that identifies the file type. DOS — and thus Windows — uses a three-letter extension to identify file types. However, these extensions are mnemonic labels only. DOS doesn't care if you really use them or not, since it assumes the program loading the file will figure out the file type and whether the program can handle it. For example, even though EPS files usually have the extension EPS (or AI if created in Adobe Illustrator), you can use any extension you want.

QuarkXPress is smart enough to determine whether a file you load is in a graphics file format it can support. Figure 23-5 shows how QuarkXPress alerts you to a file mismatch in the Picture Usage dialog box (accessed via Utilities ➪ Picture Usage). If the newly loaded file is not in a supported file format, QuarkXPress will not load it, and you will have to try to update the graphic link again to a file in a supported format. In the document itself, QuarkXPress retains the low-resolution screen representation of the original graphic.

Updating modified graphics

The process for updating a modified graphic is simpler than updating a missing graphic, because QuarkXPress already knows where the graphic is located. To update a graphic, select the filename and choose Update. QuarkXPress prompts you with an alert box and asks you if it is OK to update the file. (You also can cancel the update through this dialog box.) If you choose OK, QuarkXPress creates a new low-resolution screen representation and updates its link to the modified graphic. You also see the graphic's status change to OK.

Finishing the update process

When all missing or modified graphics are updated, their names disappear from
the Missing/Modified Pictures dialog box. Whether you were working with missing or modified graphics (or both), you may be puzzled about how to leave the
Missing/Modified Pictures (or Picture Usage) dialog box, because it does not
offer an OK button. To close the dialog box, use the Control box in the upper-
left corner of the dialog box. Either double-click the box or single-click it and
select <u>C</u>lose.

It's possible to complete all of these steps without any of the updates taking
place: If you do not save your document, none of the updates are saved.

Working with OLE Links

Windows 3.0 brought with it a powerful feature called *OLE*, which is usually
pronounced like the Spanish word *olé* and stands for *object linking and embedding*. This feature lets you create *live links* directly between applications —
which means that when you make changes to text or graphics in the program in
which you originally created them, the text or graphics are instantly and automatically updated in other programs that use them. Through object embedding, you can double-click a graphic in QuarkXPress that was originally created
in CorelDRAW, for example, and CorelDRAW is automatically launched (you
then make any changes there). See the following sidebar, "Understanding OLE,"
for a more detailed explanation of OLE.

Macintosh users may recognize this feature as System 7's Publish and Subscribe capability. OLE and Publish and Subscribe accomplish the same thing.
The main difference is that the user of a source application on a Mac must explicitly publish a file to make it available for subscribing, whereas the user of a
Windows source application needs only to copy or cut a graphic or text to put
it on the Clipboard for linking.

Creating different OLE links

To create an OLE object link, you select the object in the source application and
then use the application's copy function to put it in the Windows Clipboard,
just as if you were copying any other information among Windows applications.
An OLE server automatically tells the Clipboard that it is an OLE server, and the
Clipboard passes that information on to any OLE client you try to paste the
object into.

Only the most recently copied object resides in the Clipboard, because the
Clipboard can hold only one object.

Understanding OLE

As powerful as OLE can be, it also can be a little confusing. First, you must learn the terms *linking* and *embedding*. And then you must learn the terms OLE *clients* and OLE *servers*.

With OLE, programs can communicate with each other and share objects — a range in a spreadsheet, a selection of text, part of a graphic. Unlike the static links created when you import a graphic (as described earlier in this chapter), an OLE link need not be a link to an entire file. And an OLE link can be changed at any time. How and when the OLE link is changed depends on the type of OLE link: linked objects or embedded objects.

A linked object is a *live* (automatic) link. In such a link, when both the application that created the material and any applications that link to the material are running, any change in the original material is automatically made to the linked versions. So if you link part of a Microsoft Excel spreadsheet to a QuarkXPress document, for example, and you change the data in the spreadsheet, the data in the QuarkXPress document is updated automatically. (If all the applications aren't open at once, the updates will take place when you later open the linked document or launch the source application, as described next.

An *embedded object* is similar to an object that you copy by cutting and pasting it through the Windows Clipboard. The difference is that the embedded object also includes information on the location of the original material and the program you used to create it. In most cases, if you double-click an embedded object, the source program launches so you can modify the material (any other application files also using the material are updated, as well). If you embed Excel spreadsheet data in QuarkXPress, double-clicking the picture box that contains the data launches Excel (spreadsheet data is treated as a graphic, not as text, when brought into QuarkXPress via OLE). Any changes you make to the data are not reflected in your QuarkXPress document until you tell QuarkXPress to update all OLE objects.

Not all Windows programs support OLE. And some support it only as a *client* or only as a *server*. QuarkXPress is a client: It can accept linked files but cannot be the source of a link (the program in which the object was created). An OLE server is a program (such as Excel) that can serve as the source of a link. Some programs can be both.

In QuarkXPress, you have several paste options for an OLE object. You choose these options in the Edit menu, as Figure 23-6 shows. Your options are:

- **Paste:** This is the normal, unlinked paste function.

- **Paste Special:** This option gives you a choice of normal, embedded, and linked paste functions.

- **Paste Link:** This is the same as the linked paste function. (It is also placed here to make it easily accessible.)

The Paste Special dialog box, shown in Figure 23-7, offers the full range of OLE paste functions. The dialog box displays the source and type of data being pasted. In the example shown in the figure, the material being pasted is a

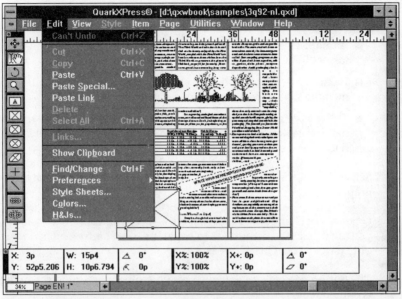

Figure 23-6: The three paste commands, two of which are related to linked objects, reside in the Edit menu.

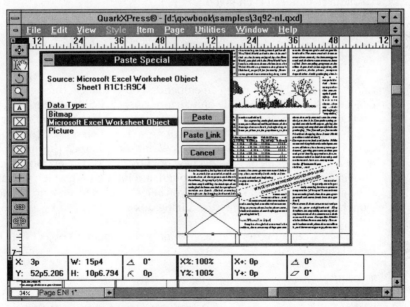

Figure 23-7: The Paste Special dialog box.

specific range of data in an Excel spreadsheet. The Data Type field lets you specify the format in which the data is pasted. Your choices are:

- **Bitmap:** This setting converts the source object into the Microsoft BMP format before pasting it.

- **Picture:** Select this option to convert the source object into the Windows metafile WMF format before pasting it.

- **The source's native format:** Choose this setting to retain the native (original) format of the source object. In the figure, the original format of the data is an Excel worksheet.

Select the source's native format unless you want the material converted to a graphic format.

QuarkXPress handles all OLE objects — even data and text — as graphics, so you must select a picture box to paste the object into. You cannot edit OLE data or text objects in QuarkXPress.

The button you click to actually paste the object determines whether the object is embedded or linked:

- The Paste button embeds the object, so the object must be manually updated.

- The Paste Link button links the object, so it is updated automatically if the source material is changed.

If you select the Paste Link option from the Edit menu, you create an OLE object link using the source's native format. This is the simplest way to create an OLE link.

Another method for creating an embedded object link is through the Insert Object dialog box, accessible only by pressing Ctrl+Shift+I after selecting a picture box with the Content tool. Figure 23-8 shows the resulting dialog box, which lists file types from all applications installed on our PC that are OLE servers. Double-clicking a file type causes Windows to launch the appropriate application and open or create a new document. (The Insert Object dialog box also lists generic formats such as Sound and Picture, for which you may not have an appropriate OLE server; if you select such a format, no application will launch and you will return to this dialog box.)

The Insert Object option creates an embedded (manual) object link, not a linked (live, or automatic) object.

The difference between Insert Object and the Paste options described earlier is that Insert Object creates a link directly between OLE applications; the Paste options move objects through the Windows Clipboard, so the source application need not be running.

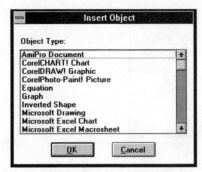

▶ **Figure 23-8:** The Insert Object dialog box lets you create embedded objects from any available OLE server.

Once Windows launches the source application, you can create the desired object. If you want to use a previously created object, open the file containing it and use the application's copy and paste commands to move the object from the original file's window to the new object's window. (Use the Window menu and its tile or cascade options to display multiple windows so you can switch among them, or use the Window menu's list of open windows to move from one to another.) After you create (or move) the object, use the source application's File menu to update QuarkXPress with the new object. Figure 23-9 shows the menu for Corel-CHART, which offers a wide range of OLE link options. Other programs may offer only the Update option.

You need not save the new object in a file; closing or exiting the source application saves the object in a special file that Windows uses to keep track of such OLE objects. (For example, in the CorelCHART example here, the new object was automatically named XPress0000.)

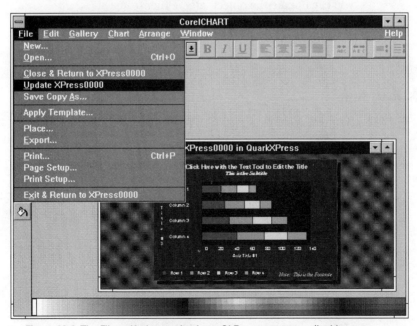

▶ **Figure 23-9:** The File ➾ Update option in an OLE server program (in this case, CorelCHART) tells all active programs using an object to substitute the updated version of the object for the current version of the object.

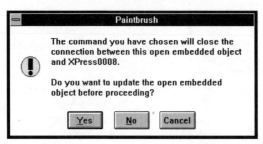

▶ **Figure 23-10:** The alert dialog box that appears If
you update an object in an OLE server and quit
without updating.

If you do not use the Update (or equivalent) command in the source application's File menu, the alert box shown in Figure 23-10 (here, from Microsoft
Paintbrush) gives you the chance to do one of the following:

■ Update QuarkXPress with the new object.

■ Not update QuarkXPress with the object; the link is still maintained so that
you can update the object later, either from QuarkXPress or from the
source application.

■ Cancel and return to the source application.

Updating links

QuarkXPress offers several features for managing OLE links. For any OLE object
in your document, you can use the Edit ➪ Links option to check or change link
settings. Figure 23-11 shows the Links dialog box. The Links field shows the
status of all OLE objects in your document. (You need not select an OLE object
for this menu option to be available, as long as there is at least one OLE object
in the document. If the menu option is grayed out, there are no unupdated OLE
objects in the current document.) The Links dialog box offers two sets of controls, one for the update settings and one for the link settings.

The update settings are:

■ **Automatic:** This specifies a live link. It is the default for objects pasted
through Edit ➪ Paste Link or through the Paste Link button in Edit ➪ Paste
Special.

■ **Manual:** This establishes an embedded link.

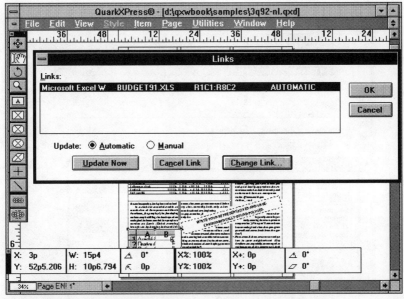

► **Figure 23-11:** The Links dialog box.

The link settings are:

- **Update Now:** This usually is used for an embedded (manual) link. If you use it on an automatic (live) link, it checks with the source application to see if anything has changed, as with linked objects whose source applications are not running or that change when QuarkXPress is not running.

- **Cancel Link:** This severs the link and makes the pasted object a regular pasted object, turning it into a bitmap or illustration within the Quark-XPress document.

- **Change Link:** This lets you change the file to which the material is linked — but not the application. When you use only a selected range of spreadsheet material or other data, the range settings in the original link are used and cannot be changed, so make sure the new file has the data you want in that same range. Figure 23-12 shows the Change Link dialog box that appears when you select this option.

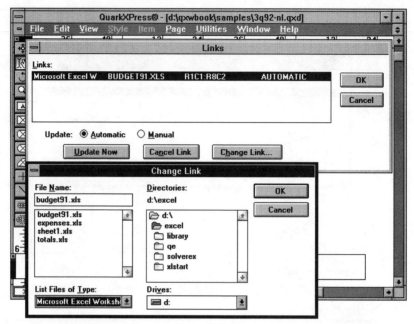

▶ **Figure 23-12:** Change the source file for OLE objects through the Change Link dialog box.

When you open a document containing OLE objects, QuarkXPress displays the alert box shown in Figure 23-13. If you choose Yes in response to the alert box, QuarkXPress tries to update the links.

If you try to update a link — whether through the alert box displayed when you open a document or through the Update Now button in the Links dialog box — and the OLE server (source) application for a link is not running, you see a message that says the link cannot be updated. In the Links dialog box, the status changes from Manual or Automatic to Unavailable; the QuarkXPress document uses its internal copy of the object until the OLE server application is available again. At that time, any live (automatic) links are updated automatically; you must use Update Now for embedded (manual) links.

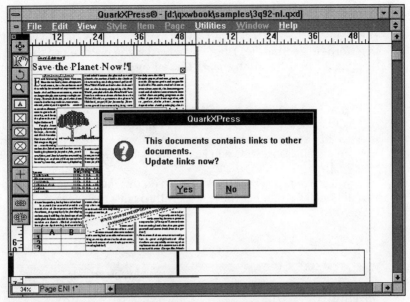

▶ **Figure 23-13:** QuarkXPress gives you the option of having it try to update links.

Working with Text

QuarkXPress offers fewer features for text links than it does for graphics links. Its text-link features are essentially limited to export capabilities.

Loading the latest text

One of the few omissions in QuarkXPress is the ability to link text so you can keep versions of your source text current with your layout. This ability is particularly handy if you want to ensure that your layout uses the latest version of text that changes periodically, such as a price list. Unfortunately, even with the OLE capabilities, you cannot get around this omission, because QuarkXPress treats OLE objects as graphics, not as text.

The only workable option is to reimport changed source text. Before you do this, first select all the old text with Edit ⇨ Select All and then delete or cut it.

Exporting the latest text

Fortunately, QuarkXPress offers a way to save changed text in your document to a word-processing file. This is beneficial if you need to use the text in other documents or just want to ensure that all versions of text are the same throughout the office.

To export text, you must first select the text with the Content tool. You can highlight specific text to export, or you can just make sure that your text cursor is active in a story you want to export. After you are ready to export, invoke the Save Text dialog box, shown in Figure 23-14, by selecting File ➪ Save Text.

Now you are ready to save your text. To do this, take the following steps. (Note that although we number these steps 1 through 4, you need not follow the same order.)

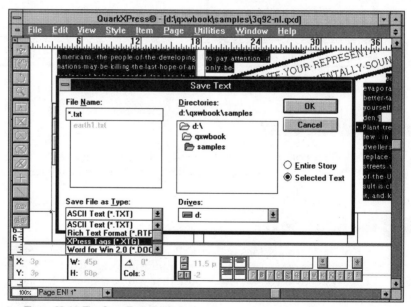

▶ **Figure 23-14:** The Save Text dialog box.

▶ **Steps: Saving text for export to a word processor**

Step 1. Decide what file format to save your text in. Choose a format from the drop-down list box to the right of the Save File as <u>T</u>ype field (at the bottom left of the dialog box). QuarkXPress saves documents in all formats it imports in.

Pick your word processor's native format unless you want to export the text for use in other QuarkXPress documents. In that case, use the XPress Tags format, which includes all the codes needed to bring over style tags and formatting.

Step 2. In the <u>D</u>irectories and Dri<u>v</u>es fields, specify where you want to place the file.

Step 3. Give the text a filename. If you don't type in an extension, the extension listed for the file type selected is used.

Step 4. Choose either <u>E</u>ntire Story or Selected Text. If you choose <u>E</u>ntire Story, QuarkXPress exports all text in the current text box and all text boxes linked to it (via the automatic text box or the Linking (chain) tool). This is the same as using <u>E</u>dit ➪ Select <u>A</u>ll before invoking the Save Text dialog box. If you choose the Selected Text button, QuarkXPress exports only the selected (highlighted) text.

Not all programs (or all versions of a program) support all formatting available in QuarkXPress, although most Windows programs support the vast majority of formatting features.

Another way to "export" text is to copy it to the Windows Clipboard and paste it into your word processor or other program. But text copied via the Clipboard loses all formatting, including such character formatting as font and size, and such paragraph formatting as indentations and leading. Special symbols should not be lost if you accessed them via Character Map or the ANSI codes. However, this is not guaranteed if you use a different typeface in your word processor than in the QuarkXPress document, because not all fonts have all characters available.

■■■

Summary

▶ QuarkXPress checks the status of graphics files when it opens a dialog box, letting you update links to missing or modified graphics.

▶ Graphics brought into QuarkXPress via the Windows Clipboard are copied directly into the document and thus have no links to their source.

▶ You can update missing or modified links later (rather than right after loading a document) via the Picture Usage dialog box.

▶ QuarkXPress checks to see if updated graphics are in a supported file format; those that are not are marked in the Picture Usage dialog box.

▶ QuarkXPress supports live links via OLE technology. It can have live links that are automatically updated as well as embedded links that are updated when you ask QuarkXPress to update them.

▶ Selecting Edit ⇨ Paste Link is the fastest way to create an OLE live link.

▶ You can specify whether an OLE object is converted to a graphics format when it is pasted by choosing Edit ⇨ Paste Special.

▶ QuarkXPress treats all OLE objects — even text — as graphics, so you must select a picture box for import. You cannot edit OLE text objects in QuarkXPress.

▶ Canceled (severed) links leave a copy of the OLE object in your document as a graphic.

▶ The Save Text dialog box lets you save parts of a story or an entire story in several word processing formats.

▶ Exporting text in the XPress Tags format lets you use that text in other QuarkXPress documents with all style and formatting information retained.

▶ Avoid using the Clipboard to copy text from QuarkXPress to your word processor, because all character formatting is lost.

■■■

Using QuarkXPress in a Workgroup Environment

In This Chapter

▶ Sharing common elements with other QuarkXPress users

▶ Transferring document and general preferences (including kerning, colors, and spelling exceptions) to other documents

▶ Creating common-use libraries and graphics

▶ Sharing styles, H&J sets, and master pages among documents

▶ Transferring files between Macintosh and Windows versions of QuarkXPress

▶ Using file-transfer tools

Working Together Effectively

Publishing is rarely a single-person enterprise. Chances are that the creators of your text and graphics are not the same people who do your layout. In many environments, it's likely that a good number of people are involved in layout and production. (See Chapter 26, "Printing Techniques," for file-management tips related to sending documents to service bureaus.)

By its very nature, publishing is a group activity, and so publishing programs must support workgroups. Yet a PC is, as its name so clearly states, a *personal* computer. That makes it easy to work on a PC without worrying about how your setup and work style might affect others. QuarkXPress lets you create your own balance between the individual and the workgroup.

The key to working effectively in a workgroup environment is to establish standards and make sure it's easy for everyone to stick to them. A basic way to do this is to place all common elements in one place, so that users always know where to get standard elements. This practice also makes it a simple matter to maintain (add, modify, and delete) those elements — which is essential, because no environment is static.

- If you don't use a network, keep a master set of disks and copy elements from the master into a directory on each person's PC. Use the same directory name on all PCs. Update the directories each time a standard element changes on the master disk.

- If you do use a network, keep a master set of disks anyway. Networks do go down, and you want your files accessible when that happens. Create a directory for your standard elements on a network drive accessible to all users. Update this directory each time a standard element changes on the master disk.

Some standard elements can be accessed easily from a common directory, because QuarkXPress can import certain elements that are stored outside QuarkXPress documents. These include graphics files, libraries, kerning tables, spelling dictionaries, and even default preferences.

Other elements reside within documents and templates and cannot be saved in separate files. These elements include edited tracking tables, style sheets, hyphenation-exception dictionaries, H&J sets, color definitions, master pages, and picture-contrast specifications. But style sheets, H&J sets, and color definitions can be appended (imported) from one document to another, and master pages can be copied among open documents.

Standardizing Preferences and Other QuarkXPress Files

When working in a document, all changes you make via the preferences dialog boxes, the hyphenation dictionary, the kerning and tracking tables, color definitions, and picture-contrast specification are saved with the document as part of its preferences. If you want to use them in another document, you may be out of luck and have to re-create them in that other document. The following sections explain what preferences you *can* standardize.

The XPRESS.PRF file

For most general preferences (see Chapter 6, "Creating Style Sheets") and global settings, if you change the preference when no document is open, QuarkXPress stores the modified settings in a file called XPRESS.PRF, which resides in the \XPRESS directory on your PC. The exception is picture-contrast specifications, which you can define only for specific graphics, and not for global use.

If you keep the XPRESS.PRF file current with your preferences, you can apply the preferences to all previously created documents. To do this, open the documents. If QuarkXPress detects a difference between your QuarkXPress master preferences (the preferences in the XPRESS.PRF file) and the document's preferences, it automatically displays the dialog box shown in Figure 24-1. To apply the preferences in the XPRESS.PRF file, select the Use XPress Preferences button. (Newly created documents always use the most current XPRESS.PRF settings.)

Preferences are covered in detail in Chapter 1, "What Is QuarkXPress?" and Chapter 4, "Customizing QuarkXPress."

Although XPRESS.PRF is stored in the directory in which you installed QuarkXPress (usually \XPRESS), you can tell QuarkXPress to use an XPRESS.PRF file stored elsewhere. On a network, this means that all users can access the same XPRESS.PRF file. If you take this approach, make sure everyone understands *not* to change the global preferences without permission, since all users are affected by any change.

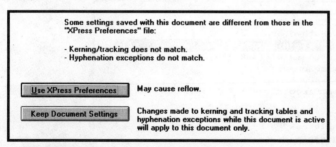

Some settings saved with this document are different from those in the "XPress Preferences" file:

- Kerning/tracking does not match.
- Hyphenation exceptions do not match.

Use XPress Preferences — May cause reflow.

Keep Document Settings — Changes made to kerning and tracking tables and hyphenation exceptions while this document is active will apply to this document only.

▶ **Figure 24-1:** Apply master preferences to existing documents through this dialog box.

To tell QuarkXPress to use an XPRESS.PRF file stored somewhere other than the default directory, you need to edit the QUARK.INI file in the \WINDOWS directory on each system. To edit this file, take the following steps.

▶ Steps: Editing QUARK.INI for XPRESS.PRF use on a network

Step 1. Load QUARK.INI in a word processor or text editor (such as Windows' Notepad) and add a line that indicates where the common XPRESS.PRF file resides. In Figure 24-2, this added line is highlighted. You can use any drive or directory; we used N: for the drive in the figure because that is our network's drive name. We used \XPRESS\MASTER\ as the directory because that name makes it easy to remember what kinds of files reside there.

Step 2. If you use a word processor, save the modified QUARK.INI file as an ASCII (text-only) file. (Saving the file in a text editor such as Notepad automatically saves it as ASCII.)

Step 3. For the revised QUARK.INI file to take effect, you must exit Windows and restart it.

If there is no XPRESS.PRF file in the directory you specified, QuarkXPress creates one automatically the next time you load the program.

```
[QuarkXPress]
XPressPath=d:\xpress\
XPressPrefs=n:\xpress\master\xpress.prf
AppWinLoc=(0,0)-(628,446) 0
MaximizeApp=0
MaximizeDoc=1
CurrentDirectory=d:\qxwbook\samples

[Installer]
InstallerReadPath=a:\
DoneRegistration=1
```

▶ **Figure 24-2:** The highlighted line in this figure specifies where the common XPRESS.PRF file resides.

Kerning tables

Like changes to tracking tables, changes to kerning tables are part of a document's preferences unless you make the changes when no document is open. QuarkXPress provides a method to export and import kerning tables, so you can transfer kerning information among documents. (This feature is not available for tracking tables.)

Kerning and tracking tables are covered in detail in Chapter 12, "Understanding Character Spacing."

After you change kerning values for a particular face, you can export the new values as a text file. You can then import the text file into other documents. At the top of Figure 24-3 is the Kerning Values dialog box (accessed via Utilities ⇨ Kerning Table Edit). At the bottom of the dialog box are the Export button, which creates the kerning file, and the Import button, which loads previously created kerning files. The figure also shows the Save As dialog box that appears when you select Export. Kerning files are given the extension KRN, and you can save them in any drive or directory.

Because each face in a typeface has its own kerning table, be sure that your names include some sort of code for the face. In the example illustrated in Figure 24-3 (in the Save As dialog box), we use a hyphen to separate the typeface

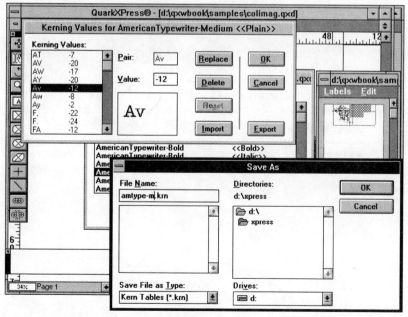

▶ **Figure 24-3:** The Import and Export buttons in the Kerning Values dialog box let you exchange kerning values among documents.

name (AMTYPE, short for American Typewriter) from the face (M, for medium). You might want to use the same name as the font's printer file but with the extension KRN.

When you import kerning tables, QuarkXPress displays a similar dialog box, called Open. When you select a kerning table to import, its values display in the Kerning Values list in the Kerning Values dialog box.

Note that these values are not yet part of the current document's preferences (or, if no document is open, they are not part of the QuarkXPress master preferences). You must select each pair whose values you want to apply and choose Replace to make them part of the current preferences. After you are done, be sure to choose OK to save the changed kerning table.

By periodically exporting kerning tables and then importing them into Quark-XPress when no documents are open, you can update the global kerning preferences set in XPRESS.PRF, so all future documents use the new kerning values. You can update previous documents by choosing Use XPress Preferences when opening such documents.

Color definitions

It's not unusual to want to keep color definitions consistent across documents. This practice lets you ensure that everyone uses your corporate-identity colors, if you have them, instead of someone's approximations.

Color definition is covered in detail in Chapter 21, "Working with Color."

You can import colors created in other documents through the Append button in the Colors dialog box (accessed via Edit ➪ Colors), as shown in Figure 24-4. All colors not in the current document are imported from the other document. Any trapping settings are also imported for each color.

Any colors whose names match in both documents are not imported into the current document. QuarkXPress does not alert you that such conflicts have been avoided.

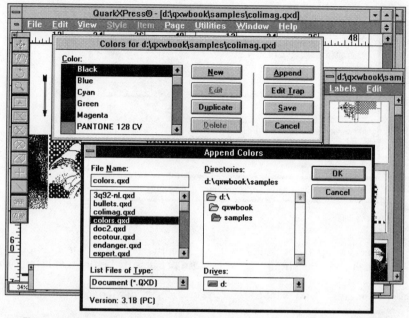

▶ **Figure 24-4:** The Colors dialog box and its corresponding Append Colors dialog box.

Spelling dictionaries

To add words to the built-in auxiliary spelling dictionary, QuarkXPress requires that you create an auxiliary dictionary (via Utilities ▷ Auxiliary Dictionary) or open an existing one. Figure 24-5 shows the Auxiliary Dictionary dialog box. Any number of documents can use the same dictionary.

Auxiliary dictionaries are covered in detail in Chapter 17, "Editing Text."

If you create a new auxiliary dictionary (via the Create button), the words in the current dictionary (if the document has one) are *not* copied into the new dictionary.

Unfortunately, you cannot create your own auxiliary dictionaries by using a word processor to edit or merge together several auxiliary dictionaries, so it's easy to end up with auxiliary dictionaries that differ widely among documents and PCs. However, this should not have a major effect on your documents,

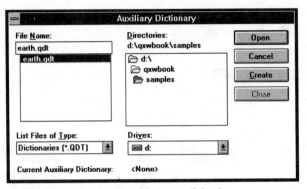

▶ **Figure 24-5:** The Auxiliary Dictionary dialog box.

because spell-checking is not part of actual layout and production — most spell-checking should occur in word processors before text is imported.

Sometimes you want to remove an auxiliary dictionary from a document. To do this, choose Close in the Auxiliary Dictionary dialog box.

Standardizing Source Files and Libraries

Perhaps the most obvious elements to standardize are *source elements* — the text and graphics you use in your documents. This is especially true if you use common elements, such as logos, in many documents.

The simplest way to guarantee that everyone uses the latest version of these common elements is to keep the elements in a standard directory (either on each PC or on a network drive). This practice works well for the first version of a text or graphic element, but it does not ensure that the element is updated in QuarkXPress documents if the element is changed after being imported.

Graphics and text files

For text files, there is no easy solution to the problem just described, because QuarkXPress has no text-link feature. But you can put common text contained in a QuarkXPress picture box into a library (described later). This procedure should address most needs — for example, mastheads, postal information, and standard sidebars containing such material as customer-service information.

For graphics files, using either OLE or regular links — and keeping common elements in a common location — can ensure consistency across documents.

File links are covered in detail in Chapter 23, "Linking to Source Files."

Libraries

QuarkXPress libraries are a great aid to keeping documents consistent. Because libraries are stored in their own files, you can put common libraries in common directories. For many people, libraries offer more benefits besides just linking to graphics files, because all attributes applied to the elements and their picture boxes are also stored in the library.

Libraries are covered in detail in Chapter 22, "Using Libraries."

Graphics you put in libraries also retain any links — whether regular import links or OLE links — so you don't have to worry about losing this information when you store graphics in libraries.

Establishing Standard Styles, H&J Sets, and Master Pages

In the course of creating documents, you may develop templates that you want to use again and again. QuarkXPress can save a document as a template; templates take the filename extension QXT rather than the document extension QDT. The only difference between a template and a document is that when you save a template, you must choose Save As rather than Save in the File menu. This ensures that when you use the template, you do not overwrite the template but instead create new documents based on it.

While the optimum approach is to design a template before creating actual documents, the truth is that no one can foresee all possibilities. So even if you create a template (and you should) that incorporates a style sheet, H&J sets, and master pages you want to use in all new documents, you can expect to modify your template at some point. As you use the template to work on real documents, you generally encounter situations that call for modifications and additions to the template.

Whether or not you use templates, you still may need to transfer basic layout elements, such as styles and master pages, from one document to another. QuarkXPress offers import capabilities for styles (and the related H&J sets), and you can copy master pages among documents.

Styles

The Style Sheets dialog box (accessed via Edit ↩ Style Sheets) contains the Append button, which lets you import styles from other QuarkXPress documents and templates. Figure 24-6 shows the dialog box and the Append Style Sheets dialog box that appears when you select the Append button. Note that the List Files of Type drop-down list box lets you narrow or expand the types of files that display in the File Name field above it.

Style sheets are covered in detail in Chapter 6, "Creating Style Sheets."

When you import styles from one document to another, all styles in the source document with names that do not match style names contained in the current document are imported. Styles with names that are the same as those in the current document are not imported, to prevent existing styles from being overridden. If you *want* existing styles to be overridden, you must edit the style tag in the current document so that its settings match the settings in the other document.

You can import from several documents by clicking Append after importing styles from a document; this reinvokes the Append Style Sheets dialog box. After importing, make sure you select Save in the Style Sheets dialog box to save the imported styles in the current document (or in the general preferences).

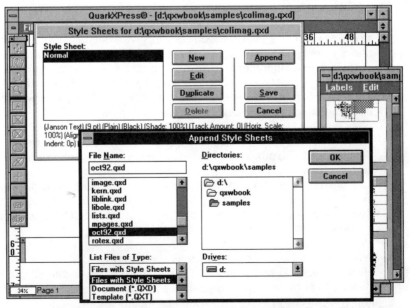

▶ **Figure 24-6:** The Style Sheets dialog box and the Append Style Sheets dialog box.

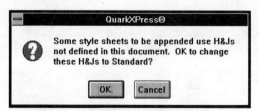

► **Figure 24-7:** QuarkXPress alerts you that style sheets you are importing use H&J sets not defined in the current document.

If an imported style uses an H&J set not defined in the current document, QuarkXPress displays the alert box shown in Figure 24-7. You can change those H&J preferences to the Standard H&J set or cancel the import. Because you can import H&J sets from documents, we suggest you cancel the import, import the H&J set (as described next), and then import the styles.

If you import styles when no document is open, you copy all new styles into your global defaults (those stored in the XPRESS.PRF file we discussed earlier in this chapter). This is a handy way to bring new styles into your default settings without affecting existing styles.

If you want to replace an existing style (whether in your default settings or in a document) with a style that has the same name in another document, you have only two choices. You can modify the style yourself, or rename or duplicate the style in the other document before importing it. If you choose the latter method, you can delete the original style and rename the newly imported version back to the original name.

You can import H&J styles from several documents by choosing Append after importing styles from a document; this reinvokes the Append Style Sheets dialog box. After importing, choose Save in the Style Sheets dialog box to save the imported styles in the current document (or in the general preferences).

H&J sets

Importing H&J sets is similar to importing styles. Open the H&Js dialog box (select Edit ➪ H&Js) and then select Append to open the Append H&Js dialog box, shown in Figure 24-8. Note that the List Files of Type drop-down list box lets you narrow or expand the types of files that display in the File Name field above it. Any H&J set with a name used by an H&J set in the current document is not imported.

H&J sets are covered in detail in Chapter 13, "Understanding Paragraph Spacing."

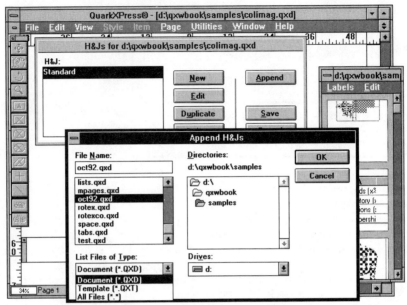

▶ **Figure 24-8:** The H&Js dialog box and its Append H&Js dialog box.

If you import H&J sets when no document is open, you copy all new H&J sets into your global defaults (those stored in the XPRESS.PRF file we covered earlier). This is a handy way to bring new H&J sets into your default settings without affecting existing H&J sets.

If you want to replace the existing H&J sets (whether in your default settings or in a document) with sets that have the same names from another document, you have only two choices: modify the H&J set yourself, or rename or duplicate the H&J set in the other document before importing it. If you choose the latter method, you can delete the original H&J set and rename the newly imported version back to the original name.

Master pages

You follow a different process for moving master pages among documents. Unlike styles and H&J sets, you do not import or append master pages from one document to another. Instead, you drag elements among open documents, just as though you were dragging boxes among pages or among documents.

To move master pages among documents, take the following steps.

▶ Steps: Moving master pages among documents

Step 1. Open the document containing the master pages you want to copy and then open all documents you want to copy them to. So you can see all documents at once, use the <u>W</u>indow ▷ <u>T</u>ile command to arrange the windows containing QuarkXPress documents so they appear side by side, rather than overlap. (<u>W</u>indow ▷ <u>C</u>ascade arranges the windows so they overlap, with the window title for each window visible. You can always drag and resize QuarkXPress document windows just like any Windows window.)

Step 2. Select each window one at a time and switch each to thumbnails view (choose <u>V</u>iew ▷ T<u>h</u>umbnails).

Step 3. Drag a document page that uses the master page you want to copy into each open document. The master page is copied automatically with the document page. Figure 24-9 shows the result; the Document Layout palette shows that the copied document page uses master page M2, which is the master page copied with the document page. In the source document, that master page was named M1; the name in the target document is Mx, where x is the next available master-page number. Because our target document already had a master page named M1, QuarkXPress named the copied master page as M2.

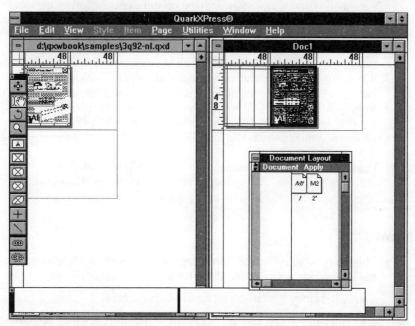

▶ **Figure 24-9:** Copying a document page from one document (at left) to another (at right) also copies its master page (shown as M2 in the Document Layout palette).

Because the master-page numbers may be renumbered as you move master pages among documents (no two master pages in a document can use the same number), we recommend that you *name* your master pages so that you can more easily tell which master page does what.

Copying a document page among documents automatically copies the associated master page, so you may end up having unwanted master pages in some documents. You can remove unwanted master pages manually. Alternatively, you can avoid copying a master page from one document to another by copying the group of boxes and lines that make up a document page rather than copying the document page itself.

Chapter 5, "Understanding Master Pages," covers master pages in detail.

Working in Mixed Mac and Windows Environments

This entire section covers differences between the Mac and Windows.

As a cross-platform application, QuarkXPress appeals strongly to all sorts of users who deal with "the other side." These include corporate users whose various divisions have standardized on different platforms, service bureaus whose clients use different machines, and independent publishers or layout artists who deal with a range of clients.

Quark did a very good job making its Macintosh and Windows versions compatible — the features are virtually identical, and Version 3.1 on both platforms can read Version 3.1 files produced on the other. (You need a free XTension from Quark in order for the Mac version to read Windows files; this XTension is actually an import filter that works with the File ⇨ Open command just as word processing filters work with File ⇨ Get Text.)

However, differences between Windows (and DOS) and the Macintosh do exist, and they add a few bumps along the road to cross-platform exchange.

Filenames

The most noticeable difference between Windows and Macintosh operation is the file-naming convention. Macintosh files follow these rules:

■ Names may contain as many as 31 characters.

■ You can use any character except for colons (:), which are used internally by Macintosh system software to separate the folder name (which is not visible on-screen) from the filename.

- Uppercase letters are considered to be different from the same letters in lowercase. The system perceives a file named *ADDRESSES* as different from a file named *addresses* or *Addresses*.

Windows files follow these rules:

- Names are limited to eight characters.

- Names may have a extension of up to three characters. Programs often add the extension automatically to identify the file type. A period separates the filename from the extension, as in FILENAME.EXT.

- You can use any characters in a filename except for most punctuation: pipes (|), colons (:), semicolons (;), periods (.), commas (,), asterisks (*), equal signs (=), plus signs (+), brackets ([and]), less-than symbols (<), greater-than symbols (>), question marks (?), slashes (/), and backslashes (\). DOS uses all of these marks to separate parts of paths (file locations, such as drives and directories) or to structure commands. You can, however, use a period as the separator between a filename and an extension.

- Case does not matter. *FILE*, *file*, and *File* all are considered the same name. If you have a file named *ADDRESS,* and you create or copy a file named *address, ADDRESS* is overwritten.

When you import Mac QuarkXPress files and any associated graphics into Windows, you must change the Mac names into names that are legal in Windows. You must do this not just for the QuarkXPress document but for any associated files, including kerning tables, graphics, and auxiliary dictionaries.

If you rename the files, either on the Mac before transferring them or on the PC during transfer, the original names are still used within the QuarkXPress document itself. When QuarkXPress tries to open these files, it searches for them by their original Mac names.

The simplest way to ensure that you don't have problems with incompatible names is to use DOS file-naming conventions even on your Mac files. This may gall Mac users, but it saves everyone a lot of headaches. (The Mac has no problem handling Windows filenames, since Windows file-naming rules don't violate any Mac file-naming rules.) When naming your files, don't forget to use the correct file extensions, which are listed in Table 24-1.

The extensions in Table 24-1 are the standard extensions that programs such as QuarkXPress expect, and they are the extensions that display in the list of files when you open, import, or save a file. However, you can enter any extension you want when opening, importing, or saving a file. For example, if you are using File ⇨ Get Picture to import an EPS file, QuarkXPress will display all files with the extensions EPS and AI, because it knows those are the standard extensions for such files. However, you can type in a name like *LOGO1.PS* for an EPS file, and QuarkXPress will import it, even though it doesn't have a standard extension and thus doesn't appear in the file list.

Table 24-1: Windows and DOS Filename Extensions

Extension	File type
QuarkXPress	
KRN	Kerning tables
QDT	Auxiliary dictionaries
QXD	Documents
QXL	Libraries
QXT	Templates
Text	
DOC	Microsoft Word for Windows
RTF	Rich Text Format
TXT	ASCII (text only)
WP	WordPerfect
WRI	Microsoft Write
XTG	XPress Tags
Graphics	
AI	Adobe Illustrator files
BMP or RLE	Microsoft bitmap files
CGM	Computer Graphics Metafiles
CT	Scitex continuous tone scans
DRW	Micrografx Windows Draw files
EPS	Encapsulated PostScript files
GIF	Graphics Interchange Format files
MAC	MacPaint graphics files
PCT	PICT files
PCX	PC Paintbrush files
PLT	HPGL plots
TIF	TIFF files
WMF	Windows metafiles

By choosing the All Files option in the QuarkXPress dialog boxes for opening and importing, you can instruct the program to display all files — not just those with standard extensions — in the file list. If you try to load a file that is not in a format QuarkXPress can determine and accept, you will get an error message.

To avoid any confusion, we suggest you name your files with the default extensions (most programs will automatically add these extensions for you if you don't enter an extension yourself).

Although you can use other extensions for graphics files, the extensions in this table are typical.

Font differences

Although major typeface vendors such as Adobe Systems and Bitstream offer typefaces for both Windows and Macintosh, these typefaces are not always the same on both platforms. This is especially true of typefaces created a few years ago, when multiplatform compatibility was not a goal for most users or vendors. Differences can occur in three areas:

■ The internal font name — the one used by the printer and type scalers such as Adobe Type Manager — may not be quite the same for the Mac and Windows version of a typeface. An alert box appears to show you which fonts used in your document are not on your PC (or Mac).

Use the Font Usage dialog box or the Find/Replace dialog box (covered in Chapter 17, "Editing Text") to replace all instances of the unrecognized font name with the correct one for the current platform.

■ Even if typefaces use the same internal names, the font files' tracking, kerning, and other character-width information may be different on the two platforms, possibly resulting in text reflow. Check the ends of all your stories to make sure text did not get shorter or longer.

■ Symbols do not translate always properly. Even when created by the same vendors, the character maps for each font file differ across platforms, because Windows and the Macintosh use different character maps. This is complicated by the fact that some vendors didn't stick to the standard character maps for any platform or didn't implement all symbols in all their typefaces.

Proofread your documents and note which symbols are incorrect, and then use the Find/Change dialog box to replace them with the correct symbol. (Highlight the incorrect symbol and use the copy and paste commands to put it in the Text field, instead of trying to figure out the correct keypad code.)

To minimize these problems, use a program such as Altsys Fontographer or Ares Software Corp. FontMonger to translate your TrueType and PostScript files from Mac to Windows format or vice versa. (Both programs are available in both Mac and Windows versions.) This ensures that internal font names, width information, and symbols are the same on both platforms.

When you bring QuarkXPress for Macintosh files into QuarkXPress for Windows, QuarkXPress automatically remaps characters from their Mac positions to their Windows positions. This remapping assumes that both the Mac and Windows versions of the typefaces use the standard Mac and Windows character maps. For some typefaces, this assumption is false (especially symbol typefaces such as Zapf Dingbats and Sonata). You can tell QuarkXPress not to remap characters for specific typefaces by adding a line to the QUARK.INI file, which resides in the WINDOWS directory. Take the following steps to edit your QUARK.INI file.

▶ Steps: Editing QUARK.INI to prevent character remapping

Step 1. Load QUARK.INI in a word processor or text editor and add a line telling it what typefaces not to remap. In Figure 24-10, this added line is highlighted. Note that there are no spaces anywhere on the line. The typeface name should be spelled and capitalized exactly as the typeface name appears in the typeface lists in QuarkXPress dialog boxes and the Measurements palette. For example, although the typeface's proper name is ITC Zapf Dingbats, the name that QuarkXPress (and other Windows programs, as well as printers and image setters) know it by is ZapfDingbats. These names should have no spaces within them and should be separated by commas only (no spaces between names, either).

Step 2. Make sure you save the modified QUARK.INI as an ASCII (text-only) file. If you use a text editor such as Notepad, saving the file automatically saves it in ASCII format.

Step 3. For this changed QUARK.INI to take effect, you must exit Windows and restart it.

Unfortunately, there is no definitive way to know which typefaces QuarkXPress will map correctly between Windows and the Mac or which need no remapping. Nor is there an easy way to know which typefaces have kerning and tracking differences between the two platforms. You should experiment with your documents on both platforms so that you can address these issues before you are

```
[QuarkXPress]
XPressPath=d:\xpress\
AppWinLoc=(0,0)-(614,422) 0
MaximizeApp=1
MaximizeDoc=0
CurrentDirectory=d:\qxwbook\samples
DoNotTranslate=Carta,Sonata,ZapfDingbats

[Installer]
InstallerReadPath=a:\
DoneRegistration=1
```

▶ **Figure 24-10:** Adding this line to the QUARK.INI file prevents the incorrect remapping of typefaces that have identical character mappings on Windows PCs and Macintoshes.

on deadline. Create a QuarkXPress document that uses all the special characters you are likely to use (or just use every character available); then print it on both platforms to see what happens. Likewise, print several typical documents on both platforms to see how spacing differs for the typefaces you use.

Although this exercise will not prevent problems, it will let you know which problems exist so that you can schedule time to fix them. You may, for example, need to change mismapped symbols to the correct ones, or change tracking values in a style tag on a document moved to the Mac so that the printed result matches that in the Windows original.

Transfer methods

Moving files between Macs and Windows PCs now is easier than ever before, thanks to a selection of products on both platforms that let each machine read the other's disks. Here is a brief summary of the major products:

- **DaynaFile** (Dayna Communications): This external Mac drive comes in two versions that enable a Mac to read DOS 5 ¼-inch and 3 ½-inch floppies, so you can copy files back and forth.

- **Apple File Exchange** (provided in Apple Computer's System software for each Mac): This utility lets you use 3 ½-inch DOS disks in an Apple SuperDrive (the high-density, 1.4MB drives). It does not work with 800K drives and is generally a more difficult method than others in this list.

■ **Macintosh PC Exchange** (Apple Computer): With this product, you can use DOS disks in a SuperDrive. The program also enables the Mac to recognize files immediately and to know what applications are compatible with each type of DOS file. You don't need to use a program to copy the files (as you do when you use Apple File Exchange) — you can just use the standard drag and drop techniques.

■ **DOS Mounter** (Dayna Communications): This is similar to Macintosh PC Exchange, except that it also works with other types of media, such as SyQuest and tape drives.

■ **AccessPC** (Insignia Solutions): This is similar to DOS Mounter.

■ **MacLinkPlus/PC** (DataViz): This includes file translation, not just file transfer.

■ **Mac-in-DOS** (Pacific Microelectronics): This is similar to Apple File Exchange — except that it runs on DOS and Windows PCs, using their 1.4MB, 3 ½-inch disks to read to and write from Mac 1.4MB disks. (It is the only non-Mac product listed here, since Macs traditionally have shouldered the burden of cross-platform compatibility.)

Another option is to transfer files via a cross-platform network, if you are using one.

The Macintosh assigns a hidden file, called a *resource,* to each file; this hidden file tells the Mac what icon to display for the file and what program to launch if you double-click the file. Windows and DOS files have no such hidden files, so PC files appear as either TeachText or DOS binary files when you move them to the Mac. (AccessPC, DOS Mounter, and Macintosh PC Exchange can be set to create these hidden files automatically based on the DOS file's extension.) To load DOS files with no accompanying hidden file into QuarkXPress (or other Mac applications), you must first load your application and then use the File ⇨ Open command.

Be warned that not all Mac applications display TeachText or DOS binary files in their File ⇨ Open lists — such applications mistakenly assume that these files couldn't possibly be compatible because they are missing the hidden file information. You must use a program such as Apple's ResEdit program to create the hidden file — and at this point, you need the help of a Mac guru, because a mistake could corrupt your file irreparably. Fortunately, Mac QuarkXPress doesn't suffer from this problem.

■ ■

Summary

▶ Put common elements in common locations, whether or not you use a network. If other users know where the elements are and can access them easily, they are likely to use your common elements, encouraging consistency.

▶ If you use a network, you can have all Windows QuarkXPress users share a common set of default preferences. To do this, modify the QUARK.INI file in each user's \WINDOWS directory.

▶ Export modified kerning tables and then import them into QuarkXPress when no document is open. This makes them part of your default preferences, so they apply to all subsequently created documents.

▶ Use the Append buttons in the Colors, Style Sheets, and H&J Sets dialog boxes to import other documents' settings into the current document. If no document is open, you import settings into general preferences.

▶ When you create a new auxiliary spelling dictionary, any words in the current dictionary are *not* copied into it, so you cannot build new auxiliary dictionaries based on existing ones. Neither can you create auxiliary dictionaries in a word processor.

▶ Use DOS conventions for naming files, even for Mac files. This assures smooth file transfer between Windows and Mac versions of QuarkXPress.

▶ Use a font-translation program to translate Mac fonts to Windows format (or vice versa). This ensures that fonts are compatible and identical on both platforms. Otherwise, symbols may not map correctly, spacing may differ, and document font names may not match system font names.

■ ■

PART VII

Printing

QuarkXPress is designed for professional publishers, so it offers a host of printing controls for everything from laser printers to image setters. At first, these controls might seem daunting. But you'll soon realize that you don't have to use most of them for routine tasks, such as printing to a laser printer. And after you determine the proper settings for advanced devices, such as image setters, you won't need to change them very often.

To take full advantage of QuarkXPress's printing capabilities, you need to do two things: You need to set up your printer(s) correctly, and you need to know how to use QuarkXPress's printing controls to get the desired results.

CHAPTER

25

Setting up Printers

• •

In This Chapter

▶ Setting up Windows options for PostScript and PCL 5 printers

▶ Choosing a printer other than the Windows default printer

▶ Overriding Windows printer default settings

▶ Selecting printing options for PostScript image setter style sheets

• •

Windows Setup

QuarkXPress printing controls work hand in hand with Windows controls. What follows is an overview of those controls. If you have a more complex setup or would like to understand Windows better, we recommend that you refer to the Microsoft Windows reference manual, as well as *Windows For Dummies,* by Andy Rathbone (IDG Books, 1992). When you install Windows or add a printer, configure your printers through the Windows Control Panel. Select the Printer icon to open the Printers dialog box and then choose <u>C</u>onnect to open the Connect dialog box, in which you specify the port connection for each printer. Figure 25-1 shows the Printers dialog box and the Connect dialog box.

Keep in mind that you should also configure Windows for your service bureau's printer, unless you intend to rely on the service bureau to set up controls for line screen and resolution.

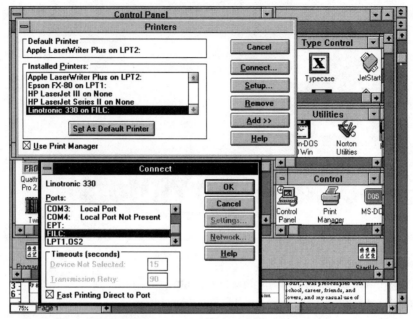

▶ **Figure 25-1:** The Printers dialog box and its Connect dialog box.

 The following steps apply if you use Windows 3.1. Windows 3.0 has similar functions, but they sometimes reside in different dialog boxes or have different names. Because QuarkXPress is designed for use with Windows 3.1, not Windows 3.0, we do not include instructions for Windows 3.0 here. For full explanations of all the Windows printer configuration options, consult your Windows documentation.

The following steps install and configure printers for all Windows applications, including QuarkXPress. Remember that the settings you establish here are the defaults for Windows. When you print a specific job from QuarkXPress or any Windows program, you can override any of these settings from within the program.

▶ Steps: Setting up printers for Windows applications

Step 1. The first step is to install your printer (which you most likely did when you installed Windows). Use the Add >> button in the Printers dialog box to add more printers.

Step 2. After installing printers, tell Windows which port (connector) they are attached to on your PC. Use the Connect button to do this, as shown in Figure 25-1. Always check the Fast Printing Direct to Port box unless it is grayed out — this significantly speeds up printing. Uncheck this box only if you have problems printing.

Step 3. If you plan to output to files (perhaps for use by a service bureau), install the appropriate printer and select FILE: or FILC: as a port connection. This tells Windows to direct the output to a disk file rather than to a PC port. (FILE: and FILC: are identical; which one appears in the list of port connections depends on your system configuration.)

Step 4. If you typically print complex files, such as files containing many downloaded fonts, bitmap graphics, detailed EPS files, or blended or gradient fills, you might want to change the Timeouts settings in the Connect dialog box. Select 999 in the Transmission Retry field to disable job timeout. This tells Windows not to stop transmitting the file, even if it gets no response from the printer. Otherwise, Windows stops trying to print the job. (Sometimes the printer is working fine, but it doesn't respond to Windows while it works on a particularly complex part of the document.) If your documents are not that complex, use a value of 45 seconds for LaserJet printers and 90 seconds for PostScript printers. The Device Not Selected field tells Windows how often to check if the printer is connected and ready to print. The default setting of 15 seconds is fine for most users. If you want to disable this feature (perhaps you have to manually switch to an active printer in a multiprinter environment), change the setting to 0 seconds.

Step 5. If you configure a printer connected to a serial (COMx:) port, the Settings dialog box offers further setup options. To open the Advanced Settings dialog box, shown in Figure 25-2, first click the Connect dialog box's Settings button (it is grayed out for other types of ports). This opens the Settings for COMx: dialog box. Choose Advanced to open the Advanced Settings for COMx: dialog box. Set the values to match those required by your printer (these requirements should be specified in the printer's manual). The Advanced Settings dialog box, also shown in Figure 25-2, should rarely be used, because it requires a thorough understanding of your PC's physical configuration. The two values, Base I/O Port Address and Interrupt Request Line (IRQ), tell your PC the "address" of your printer, both in the PC's system memory and on the motherboard. The defaults should work unless you have other devices in your PC that don't follow conventional assignments.

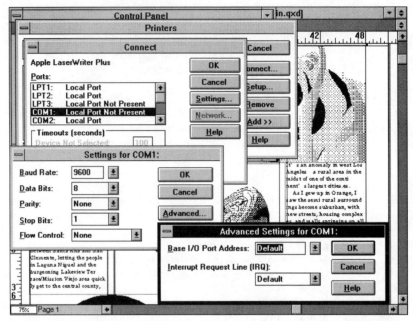

▶ **Figure 25-2:** The Settings and Advanced Settings dialog boxes used for serial printers.

Step 6. After configuring the connections, select one printer as the default printer. Choose whichever printer you output to most of the time. Select the printer name and then click the Set As Default Printer button in the Printers dialog box. You are now ready to configure Windows for each printer's specific abilities.

The setup instructions from this point on are specific to your printer. The following two sections detail the steps for setting up PostScript printers — standard for publishing work — and for later models of the Hewlett-Packard LaserJet printers (using the PCL 5 language) — standard for office printing.

Many LaserJets and compatibles, such as the LaserJet II series, use the PCL 4 language. This is fine for text-intensive publishing, but if you use many graphics, we suggest you upgrade to a PCL 5 or PostScript printer. Settings for PCL 4 printers are similar to those shown here for PCL 5 printers.

▶ Steps: Completing Windows setup for PostScript printers

Step 1. Follow the steps in the preceding section, "Setting Up Printers for Windows Applications."

Step 2. In the Printers dialog box, select the name of the printer you want to set up and then choose Setup. This opens the dialog box for that specific printer, as shown in Figure 25-3. Here, you can establish default settings for paper orientation, paper trays, paper sizes, and number of copies.

Step 3. Select the Options button to open the Options dialog box, in which you can establish further printer settings. You can specify whether you want to print to the printer or as an EPS file; whether to send the PostScript header (it should be sent in most cases); and whether to use the printer's color features (this box is grayed if the printer is not a color printer). You also can set page margins and scaling (scaling usually is left at 100 percent). If you select Encapsulated PostScript File, you can also enter the name of that file, which is used every time you print. If you leave the filename blank, you are prompted to specify a filename each time you print. Leaving it blank is the best option, because you then can create several EPS files with names that mean something for each specific job.

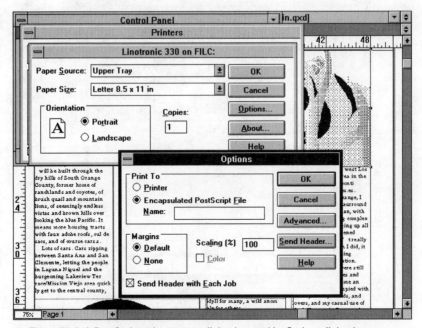

▶ **Figure 25-3:** A PostScript printer setup dialog box and its Options dialog box.

Printing to file and *printing as an EPS file* are not necessarily the same thing. Printing as an EPS file produces a file that any PostScript printer can print. Printing to a file without selecting the EPS option produces a file that only the specific PostScript printer you select can print. Use the EPS file option whenever you create a file for use by a service bureau.

Step 4. To specify how the printer handles fonts and imaging, select the Advanced button in the Option dialog box. This opens the Advanced Options dialog box, shown in Figure 25-4.

Step 5. In the first part of the dialog box, you can tell Windows how to handle TrueType fonts. This is covered in detail in Chapter 3, "The Windows Environment." For laser printers, you can leave the settings at the defaults (which substitute the PostScript fonts Helvetica, Times, and Courier for the TrueType fonts Arial, Times New Roman, and Courier New, respectively). For image setters, check the Use Printer Fonts For All TrueType Fonts box. This ensures that the exact fonts you use in your document are printed, even if they are TrueType fonts that must be downloaded.

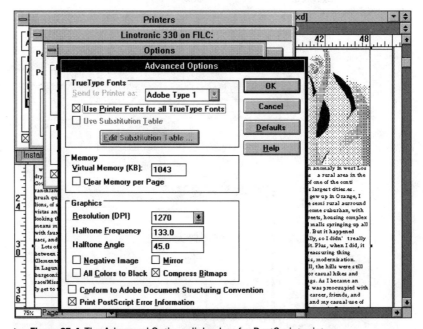

▶ **Figure 25-4:** The Advanced Options dialog box for PostScript printers.

Step 6. The Virtual Memory field tells the printer how much memory to reserve for downloaded fonts and for processing complex images. Leave this setting unchanged unless your service bureau or equipment manager tells you otherwise. The value entered in the Virtual Memory field depends on the amount of memory installed in your printer.

If you or no one else knows how much memory is installed in your printer, print the TESTPS.TXT file that Windows loaded in your \WINDOWS\SYSTEM directory when you installed your Windows software. Printing this files causes the printer to report how much memory it has. Print this file from DOS by typing the command **COPY C:\WINDOWS\SYSTEM\TESTPS.TXT LPT1:** (this command assumes that C: is the hard drive on which you installed Windows and that your printer is connected to LPT1; if this is not the case, substitute the name of the correct drive and printer port).

Step 7. Set options in the Graphics section of the Advanced Options dialog box to reflect your printer's capabilities as well as the kind of documents you typically produce. For example, you'll want 150-line screens and 2540 or higher dpi if you are outputting to an image setter and printing on a web-offset press, as for a four-color magazine. You'll want 110-line screens and 1270 dpi if outputting to an image setter and printing on a small-run press, as you might to create a black-and-white newsletter.

You don't always want to choose the finest settings for your target printer; doing so can create output that is finer than the printing press can reproduce, resulting in smudging. Similarly, if you output to negatives (film) on an image setter, you can use a higher resolution than if you output to RC paper. The photographic process your service bureau or press bureau uses to create negatives from the RC output can't distinguish halftone dots that are too fine. In either case, the result is murky or spotty, or halftones and grays are dropped. For example, the dots in a 2540-dpi image are finer than the plastic or paper printing plates typically used in low-volume printing can reproduce. If you try to create a negative from RC paper output at 2540 dpi, the camera will not see the fine dots, and your image quality will suffer. See the sidebar "Understanding lpi" in Chapter 20, "Working with Bitmap Images," for more details.

Step 8. When printing to film, check Negative Image and Mirror, so output is right-reading, emulsion-side-down. Otherwise, the output is left-reading, emulsion-side-up. Before enabling Negative Image or Mirror (usually done when outputting to negatives), check with your service bureau to see if its printer's internal settings take care of these concerns. They usually do.

Step 9. Check Compress Bitmaps unless doing so causes your bitmaps to print coarsely (this sometimes happens when bitmaps are compressed). Checking this option reduces print times and file sizes.

Step 10. Leave All Colors to Black unchecked, since you'll likely want colors converted to gray shades instead when printing to black-and-white printers.

Step 11. Check Conform to Adobe Document Structuring Convention if you are printing to file and want your service bureau to establish all the settings listed in the Graphics section of the dialog box. These Graphics options are then grayed out. If you want to retain control over the printing settings, do not check this box. As a practical matter, leave the box unchecked.

Step 12. Check Print PostScript Error Information. If something goes wrong during printing, a page prints out identifying the problem so you and your service bureau can more easily track down the cause of it.

Choosing Defaults resets all the settings in the Advanced Options dialog box to Windows default settings.

▶ Steps: Completing Windows setup for PCL 5/LaserJet III printers

Step 1. Follow steps 1 – 6 under "Setting Up Printers for Windows Applications" (in the first part of this chapter).

Step 2. In the Printers dialog box, select the printer you want to set up and then select the Setup button to open the dialog box for that printer, as shown in Figure 25-5. In this dialog box, you can choose paper trays, paper sizes, and graphics resolution (150 dpi is fine for proofing, but use 300 dpi for presentation-quality output). You also can specify which font cartridges are installed and set page protection. The Page Protection option lets you tell the printer to reserve memory (the amount is based on the page size you select from the drop-down menu). This option is available only if you have at least 2 megabytes of memory in your printer. Leave Page Protection unchecked unless you have problems printing your pages (you'll typically see the error code 21 on your printer's message panel).

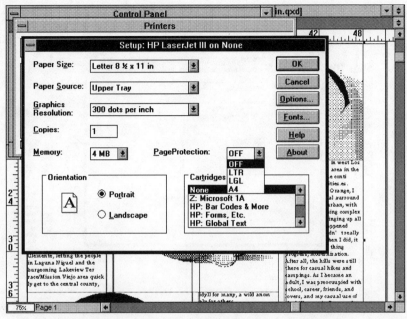

▶ **Figure 25-5:** The Setup dialog box for a PCL 5 printer.

Step 3. If you use soft fonts (downloaded fonts in Hewlett-Packard's Intellifont format) instead of TrueType, Adobe Type Manager, or another type scaler, use the Fonts button in the Setup Dialog box to specify which fonts to download and where to download them. If, for example, you have different PCL printers with different font cartridges, you can specify which fonts need to be downloaded to which printer so that, no matter where you print, the needed fonts are available. You can also download fonts "permanently" — meaning until the printer is turned off — rather than for each job.

Step 4. Finally, select the Options button to open the Options dialog box (shown in Figure 25-6), which offers you more setup choices. To determine the output quality of pictures, select a setting from the Gray Scale drop-down list:

■ Use the Photographic Images setting if your document contains many scans or other gray-scale bitmap images. This tells the PCL printer to use a dithering pattern optimized for such images. (A dithering pattern is an irregular pattern of black dots used to simulate grays.)

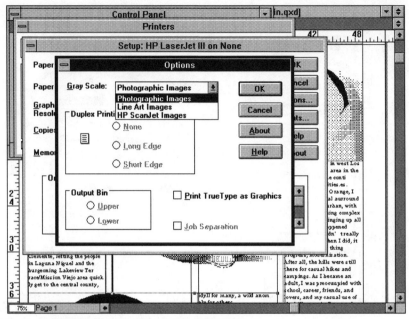

▶ **Figure 25-6:** The Options dialog box for PCL 5 printers.

- Use the Line Art Images setting if your document contains drawings done in vector formats such as CGM and Windows metafile. This tells the PCL printer to use a dithering pattern optimized to retain the sharp lines and edges typical in such illustrations.

- Use the HP ScanJet Images setting only if you use the HP ScanJet scanner.

- If your document contains both bitmap and vector images, you must decide which type of image you'd rather sacrifice clarity on. Using the Photographic Images setting is usually the better option in this case. Vector art tends to hold up better when dithered at Photographic Images settings than bitmap art does when dithered at Line Art Images settings.

Step 5. Check the Print TrueType as Graphics box only if you use TrueType fonts sparingly. This option speeds printing, because it saves Windows from having to download the TrueType fonts. But if you use more than a dozen or so TrueType characters, this advantage disappears, and for text-intensive pages, using this option slows printing time. Generally, it's best to leave this option unchecked.

Step 6. Choose from the options in the duplex printing and output bin sections of the dialog box and then specify whether you want Job Separation enabled or not. This option — not available for all PCL 5 printers — tells the printer to shift each new document in the paper tray, as some photocopiers do, to help you identify which stacks of papers belong together.

QuarkXPress Setup

When you print a document in QuarkXPress, you have access to all Windows printer setup options as well as to QuarkXPress options. Select File ⇨ Printer Setup to access the QuarkXPress Printer Setup dialog box, shown in Figure 25-7. If you then select the Options button, you enter the Windows Options dialog box for your printer, as described in the preceding sections.

The other options in the QuarkXPress Printer Setup dialog box are also available in the Windows printer-setup dialog boxes. QuarkXPress makes them available in the Windows printer-setup dialog boxes so you can conveniently override any of these common publishing settings for the current job.

Changes you make in the QuarkXPress Printer Setup dialog box are saved as part of your current document's preferences. Except for halftone frequency, you cannot make any changes to printer setup part of your default QuarkXPress preferences. (To change the default halftone frequency, close all documents, open a new document, change the setting in the Printer Setup dialog box, choose OK, and close the new document.)

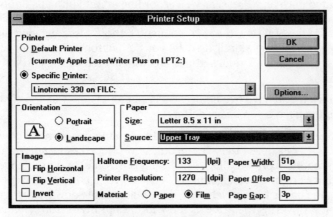

▶ **Figure 25-7:** The QuarkXPress Printer Setup dialog box.

Through the QuarkXPress Printer Setup dialog box, you can temporarily change printers without having to reset any of your Windows printer settings. This is particularly helpful if you have several printers (for example, on a network), or if you print to file occasionally for output at a service bureau but do most of your printing on a laser printer. By selecting Specific Printer and then choosing an installed printer from its drop-down list, you can change printers quickly.

 This ability to change printers is similar to the Macintosh Chooser utility, except that in Windows programs, you can change printers from within the current program rather than having to switch to the Chooser utility.

QuarkXPress's Printer Setup dialog box has several publishing-oriented options. The first four options in the following list are grayed out if you select a non-PostScript printer, because only PostScript image setters support these functions:

- **Printer Resolution:** This lets you set the dpi for image setters, which often support multiple output resolutions.

- **Paper Width:** This lets you tell QuarkXPress the width of the roll of RC paper or negative film used in the image setter's paper cartridge, to allow for correctly centered pages

- **Paper Offset:** Paper Offset lets you set a margin for the image setter's paper or film roll.

- **Page Gap:** This option lets you separate pages by a specified amount. (Otherwise, pages output right next to each other, which you don't want if you have bleeds or registration marks.) Pick a value that is enough to separate pages without wasting paper or film, such as 3 picas (½ inch). This gap does not occur between pages within spreads if the Spreads option is checked in the Print dialog box (described in the next chapter).

- **Halftone Frequency:** Here, you specify the line screen for all elements created in QuarkXPress, as well as for line art and bitmaps imported into QuarkXPress. Note that you can set individual halftone settings for TIFF files via the Style ⇨ Other Screen menu option. Also, high-end illustration programs such as CorelDRAW let you set halftone settings for EPS files they create. These individual settings are not affected by the entry in this dialog box.

- **Material:** You have two choices — Paper and Film — to specify the printing medium used by an image setter.

- **Image:** You are offered a trio of settings that let you control how an image prints. Check Invert to have the output produced as negatives (do this if you routinely print to film). Check Flip Horizontal to output pages printed to film as right-reading, emulsion-side-down. Unchecking Flip Horizontal sets the pages to print left-reading, emulsion-side-down, a less common choice. (Invert is the same as the Windows printer-setup Negative Image setting, found in the Advanced Options dialog box. And Flip Horizontal is the same as the Mirror setting. Both are described earlier.) The Flip Vertical box is used rarely. You might want to check this box when you want the orientation of a page to match its orientation on a printer's signature form (the group in which negatives are stripped together to create the large printing plates).

Summary

▶ Make sure Fast Printing Direct to Port is enabled in your Windows printer setup.

▶ Install any printer used by your service bureau, even if you don't have that device, so you can select from its options when printing to file.

▶ You can override Windows defaults for a specific document using the Options button in the QuarkXPress Printer Setup dialog box.

▶ Change the Timeouts settings in the Windows printer setup (either for the default or just for specific documents) when you print complex documents. This prevents the printer from giving up on the job prematurely.

▶ Have all TrueType fonts downloaded if you are printing to an image setter, rather than substituting PostScript fonts for those that have PostScript counterparts. This prevents minor misadjustments in character spacing caused by slight character differences in the two formats.

▶ Printing to file and printing as an EPS file are not the same, even if a PostScript printer is selected. Use the EPS option when creating files that will be output on a different PostScript printer than your own.

▶ Choose resolution and halftone settings based on your printer and press considerations, not just on the capabilities of the PostScript output device.

▶ Use Negative Image and Mirror in the Windows printer setup or Invert and Flip Horizontal in the QuarkXPress printer setup when outputting to negatives that you want to be right-reading, emulsion-side-down (a typical orientation for negatives).

▶ Use the Compress Bitmaps option for PostScript printers in the Windows printer setup to keep file size smaller.

▶ Use the Print PostScript Error Information option in the Windows printer setup to get a report of errors that occur while printing.

▶ In the QuarkXPress Printer Setup dialog box, set a Page Gap of about 3 picas (½ inch) when outputting to an image setter. This prevents bleeds and registration marks from running into the next page while wasting a minimum of paper or film.

Printing Techniques

In This Chapter

▶ Using PCL printers as proofing printers for PostScript jobs

▶ Selecting printing options such as collation and number of copies

▶ Specifying options used in image setters, such as registration marks and color separation

▶ Printing color separations

▶ Working with service bureaus

Printer Considerations

It used to be that there was a clear choice between PostScript and PCL (the language used in Hewlett-Packard LaserJet printers): PostScript was the printer language required for professional printers, while PCL was fine only for "business" documents — primarily textual reports and presentations.

Although PostScript remains the only viable choice for those who output work to image setters for publication in magazines, newsletters, and other consumer-oriented media, PCL is now worthwhile for producing a broad range of publications in which 300-dpi resolution is sufficient. Such publications still tend to be internal publications, but PCL is increasingly acceptable for use in technical documentation, short-run newsletters, press releases, and the like.

What made PCL viable for mid-range publishing? For one thing, improvements in its image handling, a result of the more advanced HPGL graphics language that comes with the new PCL 5 page-description language. For another, improvements in typeface rendering, brought about by type scalers such as TrueType and Adobe Type Manager and by the increasing availability of PCL soft fonts.

Despite these improvements, we believe PostScript printers are a must for professional publishers. Only PostScript printers can handle EPS graphics, the format favored by most artists because it lets them create and use more design

Printing terms

Ganging is taking several images and color-separating them (via traditional means, not within QuarkXPress) at one time. This saves money but means the camera operator cannot optimize the color balance for each image. You can also gang photos when creating halftones.

Creating negatives for printing — including the generation of halftones, color separations, and overlays, and any stripping in of individual elements' negatives into the final page's negatives — is called pr*epress,* or *prep* for short. It encompasses all activities between layout and printing, including scanning and creating negatives, whether directly from an image setter or indirectly from the shooting of a negative from a layout's paste-up board.

The final negatives are photographed onto a *plate,* which can be made of metal, paper, or other material. There is one plate for each color. The plates are mounted on a *press,* and the ink well for each plate is filled with the appropriately colored ink. The paper is then run through the press. Printing from plates is called *offset printing,* since the image is transferred (offset) from one medium (the negatives) to an intermediary (the plate) before being printed onto another medium (the paper). (In photocopying, by contrast, the image is applied directly to the paper from the imaging drum.) Offset printing is also known as *lithography.*

In *web printing* (so-called because the huge sheets of paper look like webs when running through the giant printing presses), the negatives are stripped together on to a large plate.

This method is used primarily for large documents like magazines and catalogs, since it allows for many pages to be handled at once.

Saddle-stitching means to fold sheets and staple them along the fold, as in many magazines, brochures, and newsletters; the name comes from the fact that the sheets are placed in a saddle for stitching (stapling) and folding. Only a saddle-stitched document can have an element in the centerfold that prints across the two pages without misregistration, since the centerfold is a continuous sheet. *Perfect binding* means to cut all the sheets and stack them together and then glue them together with a wrap-around cover. The part of the cover that holds the pages together is called a *spine,* and the magazine or book title is usually printed on the outside of the spine.

Magazines and books are usually printed in *forms,* which is a set of pages that is printed at one time on a very large sheet of paper. These pages are not consecutive. Instead, they are ordered by the folding order: Take a sheet of paper, fold it length-wise and then twice width-wise (it will look somewhat like a magazine). Trim the tops and bottoms so the pages are held only along one side, like a magazine (this is what printers do for perfect-bound publications). Now number the pages. If you fold it out, you will see that the numbers on the folded-out sheet — the form — is not in consecutive order. Printers must figure out this order before st*ripping* the negatives together that make up a publication.

effects than any other language. Service bureaus use PostScript only, so if you output to film, you must use PostScript. And more typefaces are available in PostScript Type 1 format than in any other, which makes it the standard font format for service bureaus.

Because PCL printers are a corporate standard for PC users, however, Quark-XPress recognizes their wide availability. It enables you to use these printers both for mid-range documents and for proofing documents that will eventually be output on a PostScript image setter. If you use a PCL printer as a proofing printer, be aware of these limitations:

■ EPS graphics do not print.

■ TIFF images do not print in high resolution. Instead, QuarkXPress substitutes a lower-resolution image.

■ Color-separation, even for proofing, is unavailable. Nor can you print colors as grays — they appear in solid black or in dithered patterns.

■ Thumbnail printing is unavailable.

Printing Options

To print a document, select File ➪ Print (or the shortcut Ctrl+P) to open the Print dialog box, which is shown in Figure 26-1. Change any options and choose OK, and QuarkXPress sends your document to the printer. (To set up your printer, use the Setup button. To set up or add new printers to Windows, select the Windows Control Panel's Printer icon, which opens the Printers dialog box. Both are described in the preceding chapter.)

Windows 3.1 supports drag-and-drop printing. If you are in the Windows File Manager and the Print Manager icon is minimized and visible, you can select a QuarkXPress document (hold down the mouse button after selecting the file), drag it to the Print Manager icon, and then release the mouse button. Windows launches QuarkXPress and prints the file according to the default settings in the Print dialog box.

Basic options

It's likely that for most printing jobs, you only need to worry about the first two settings in the Print dialog box: Copies, which lets you specify how many copies of your document print, and Pages, which lets you specify whether all pages print or just a selected range of pages.

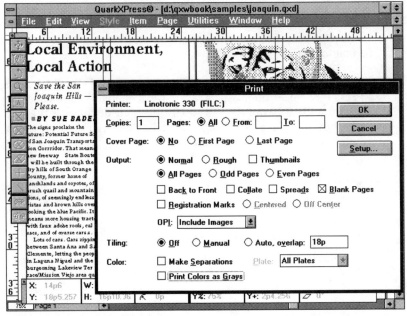

▶ **Figure 26-1:** The Print dialog box.

If you use the From and To options to select a range of pages to print, and you used the QuarkXPress section-numbering feature to create multiple sections in your document, you must enter the page numbers exactly as they are labeled in the document. (The label for the current page appears in the lower-left corner of your document screen.) Include any prefix used and enter the labels in the same format (letters, roman numerals, or regular numerals) used in the section whose pages you want to print. Alternatively, you can indicate the absolute page numbers by preceding the number with a plus sign (+).

For example, suppose you have an eight-page document with two sections of four pages each. You label pages one through four as AN-1 through AN-4 and label pages five through eight as BN-1 through BN-4. If you enter BN-1 and BN-4 in the From and To fields of the Print dialog box, QuarkXPress prints the first four pages in the section that uses the BN- prefix. If you enter +5 and +8, QuarkXPress prints document pages five through eight — which again includes BN-1 through BN-4.

Other options that frequently come in handy are:

■ **Cover Page:** This lets you specify whether a cover page prints. The options are First Page and Last Page, which determine where the cover page falls in the output tray. The cover page includes the document name and the date and time printed.

■ **Normal and Rough:** Select Normal to print graphics and Rough to suppress them. Suppressing graphics for proof copies speeds printing and is especially appropriate when you are printing the page to read the text or to look at other nongraphics aspects.

■ **Thumbnails:** If you check Thumbnails, QuarkXPress prints reduced versions of the document pages, printing eight pages per sheet. This is handy when you want to take a layout sample or storyboard to a meeting without having to bring a large stack of sheets. (This option is available only with PostScript printers.)

■ **All Pages, Odd Pages, and Even Pages:** These settings let you control which pages are output. This is useful if you want to do duplex (two-sided) copying and thus need the even and odd pages separated. Note that these settings do not override the settings for the Pages option (at the top of the dialog box). If you select a range of pages in the Pages option and then choose All Pages, Odd Pages, or Even Pages, QuarkXPress applies that option to the range. So, for example, you can print all odd pages from page 3 through page 78.

■ **Back To Front:** If you check this option, QuarkXPress reverses the printing order of the document pages. When you output a document to a printer whose pages print face up, the document is in order when done printing.

■ **Collate:** Check this option to keep pages in sequence when you print multiple copies of a document. When Collate is set at the default — which is unchecked — QuarkXPress prints all requested copies of one page, then all copies of the next page, and so on, because this speeds printing time significantly.

■ **Spreads:** Checking the Spreads box tells QuarkXPress to print facing pages as contiguous output (assuming your paper size allows it or you output to an image setter that uses a roll of RC paper or film). This overrides odd/even page options, which is grayed out if Spreads is selected.

 You may not want to use the Spreads option when outputting to an image setter if you have bleeds, because there will be no bleed between the spreads. If you use traditional perfect-binding (square spines) or saddle-stitching (stapled spines) printing methods, where facing pages are not printed contiguously, do not use this option.

■ **Blank Pages:** If you uncheck this option, QuarkXPress suppresses the output of blank pages. The default setting is checked, but you'll probably want to change this if you use the All option for Pages.

Advanced options

QuarkXPress offers several advanced printing options designed for publishing users. Options not available for non-Postscript printers (such as color options) are grayed out in the Print dialog box.

- **Registration Marks:** If you check this box, QuarkXPress prints registration marks. (Printers use registration marks to determine where to cut pages when they trim the paper used on the press to the page size actually used in the printed document.) When you output color separations, QuarkXPress also includes a color bar in the output, so the printing press operator can check that the right colors are used with the right negatives. If you check Registration Marks, you have the added option of selecting Centered or Off Center registration marks. Centered is the default. Use Off Center when your page size is square or nearly square; this makes it easy for the press operator to tell which sides of the page are the left and right sides and which are the top and bottom sides, thus reducing the chances that your page will be accidentally rotated.

- **OPI:** This setting tells a high-end prepress system how to handle TIFF and EPS graphics. The drop-down menu gives you three choices: Include Images, which tells the prepress system to use the TIFF files embedded in the file; Omit TIFF, which tells the system to substitute a higher-resolution image (which you provide to the service bureau separately) but to apply any image control done within QuarkXPress (this is the most typical setting for prepress systems); and Omit TIFF and EPS, which tells the prepress system to use its images instead of your TIFF and EPS images (this is used only on a few prepress systems). If you and your service bureau don't use a prepress system (such as a Scitex), leave this setting at the default, which is Include Images. Otherwise, check with the prepress operator.

- **Tiling:** QuarkXPress gives you three *tiling* options: Off, Manual, and Auto. Tiling takes an oversized document and breaks it into several pieces, called *tiles,* that you then reassemble. You can use this in creating posters, for example. If you choose Off, no tiling occurs. If you choose Auto, Quark-XPress determines where each tile breaks. If you choose Manual, you decide where the tiles break by repositioning the ruler origin in your document. For all pages selected, QuarkXPress prints the tiled area whose upper-left corner matches the ruler's origin. Repeat this step for each tiled area. Choose the Manual tile option if certain areas of your document make more logical break points than others. No matter whether you choose Auto or Manual tiling, you can select the amount of tile overlap by entering a value in the overlap field. You can enter a value between 0 and 6 inches.

Figure 26-2 shows how to reposition the ruler origin (the cross-hair box that appears below the document Control menu). Select the origin and hold the mouse button down. Then move through your document to the new position (you'll probably want to note the ruler values as you move), releasing the mouse button at the new location. The thin dashed lines under the 0 on the top ruler and to the right of the 0 on the side ruler indicate the location of the current origin as you move through the document.

▶ **Figure 26-2:** To use manual tiling, reposition the ruler origin for each tile.

Working with the Print Manager

If you hold the Shift key while clicking the OK button in the Print dialog box, QuarkXPress displays a printing status report for your document. But that status box only tells you what goes on between QuarkXPress and Windows. The actual printing is handled between Windows and your printer. Windows provides a program called Print Manager that lets you monitor and delete jobs being sent to the printer. The accompanying figure shows the Print Manager dialog box. To invoke Print Manager, switch to the Windows Main group (unless you moved Print Manager out of this group) and double-click Print Manager.

If you are printing complex jobs or multiple documents in queue, you might want to minimize the Print Manager and then occasionally double-click it or switch to it via the Task List to check your documents' status. If you have more than one printer, Print Manager displays the status of each one, as the figure shows.

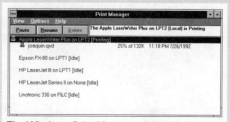

The Windows Print Manager dialog box.

- **Make Separations:** If you check this option, QuarkXPress prints a separate sheet (usually a film negative) for each color. QuarkXPress makes separate sheets for the colors you specify in the Plate list box. (Color options are covered in detail in the next section.)

- **Print Colors as Grays:** If you check this box, QuarkXPress translates colors to gray values. This is handy for printing proof copies on noncolor printers. It is also helpful if you have a color image that you cannot otherwise convert to gray scale for use in a black-and-white document. If this option is unchecked, colors might appear as solid whites or blacks if printed to a noncolor printer.

Color Separations

With its built-in color separator, QuarkXPress offers the controls you need to handle both four-color and spot-color printing, as well as printing that mixes the two.

See Chapter 21, "Working with Color," for details on how to define colors and an explanation of the difference between four-color and spot-color color printing.

When you select Make Separations in the Print dialog box, you can choose which colors have plates printed, as Figure 26-3 shows. You can print plates for the four process colors (cyan, magenta, yellow, and black) and for any colors defined in the Edit ⇨ Colors menu as spot colors. Colors translated to process colors in the Edit Color dialog box do not display (see the next section). If the Colors palette is visible, you can quickly scroll through the list of colors defined for your document, although it does not distinguish between spot colors and colors created through process colors.

The default setting of All Plates works for most jobs. Although a large list of colors appears, plates are output only for those colors actually used on each page. Thus, if you use yellow, black, and magenta on page two but use cyan, yellow, magenta, and black on page three, QuarkXPress outputs three plates for page two and four plates for page three. The only exception is that QuarkXPress always prints a plate for black, even if you do not use black in your document. Because press operators expect a black plate for each and every page (if for no other reason than they need the piece of negative on their presses), QuarkXPress makes sure they get it.

If you do not select All Plates, you can select only one color at a time for printing. You typically select plates one at a time if you want to proof (whether on a color or black-and-white printer) specific color plates, or if you need to reprint a plate whose negative was lost or damaged.

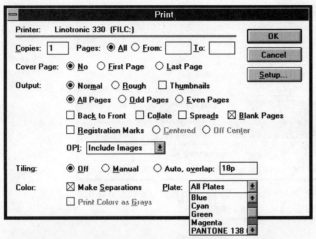

▶ **Figure 26-3:** Select plates to print from the Plate drop-down list.

Spot colors and separations

It's very easy to accidentally use spot colors such as red and Pantone 111 (say, for picture and text box frames) in a document that contains four-color TIFF and EPS files. The result is that QuarkXPress outputs as many as six plates: one each for the four process colors, plus one for red and one for Pantone 111. You might expect the red to be separated into 100 percent each of yellow and magenta (which is how red is printed in four-color work). And maybe you expect QuarkXPress to separate the Pantone 111 into its four-color equivalent (11.5-percent yellow and 27.5-percent black). So why doesn't QuarkXPress do this?

By default, each color defined in QuarkXPress — including the red, green, and blue that are automatically available in the Edit ⇨ Colors menu — is set as a spot color. And each spot color gets its own plate, unless you specifically tell QuarkXPress to translate the color into process colors. You do so by checking the Process Separation box in the Edit Color dialog box, described in Chapter 21. Figure 26-4 shows that dialog box for Pantone 111 set as a process color. Check the Process Separation box to make sure that extra plates aren't printed unexpectedly.

If your work is primarily four-color work, either remove the spot colors such as blue, red, and green from your Colors dialog box or edit them to make them process colors. If you make these changes with no document open, they become the defaults for all new documents.

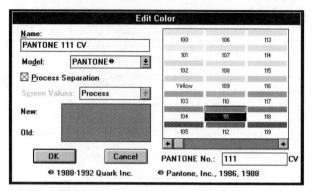

▶ **Figure 26-4:** Check Process Separation in the Edit Color dialog box to translate spot colors into process colors.

If you do some spot-color work and some four-color work, duplicate the spot colors and translate the duplicates into process colors. Make sure you use some clear color-naming convention, such as Blue P for the process-color version of blue (which is created by using 100 percent each of magenta and cyan).

The same is true when you use Pantone colors (and Trumatch and Focoltone colors). If you do not check the Process Separation box in the Edit Color dialog box (choose Edit ⇨ Colors ⇨ New), these colors are output as spot colors. Again, you can define a Pantone color twice, making one of the copies a process color and giving it a name to indicate that. Then all you have to do is make sure you pick the right color for the kind of output you want.

You still can mix process and spot colors if you want. For example, if you want a gold border on your pages, you have to use a Pantone ink, since metallic colors cannot be produced via process colors. So use the appropriate Pantone color, and don't check the Process Separation box when you define the color. When you make color separations, you get five negatives: one each for the four process colors and one for gold. That's fine, because you specifically wanted the five negatives.

Supported elements

QuarkXPress color-separates any colors you define in QuarkXPress. Thus, if you use colors for text, frames, backgrounds, or other such elements, QuarkXPress produces plates for them. The plates are output either as part of the process-color plates or separately as spot colors, depending on how you defined the colors. But QuarkXPress might not color-separate imported images the way you expect.

First, QuarkXPress can color-separate only certain types of color image files: those in the CMYK version of TIFF; those in an EPS file created by an illustration program that can specify color information properly; and those in the DCS (Document Color Separation) format, which is a form of EPS.

Second, for EPS files that use spot colors, the spot color must be defined in QuarkXPress (in the Edit Color dialog box) using the same name as used in the EPS file. For example, if you define a color called Bright Orange in CorelDRAW, define the same color — using the same values — with the same name in QuarkXPress. Likewise, if you use Pantone 111 in an Adobe Illustrator document, make sure you define Pantone 111 in QuarkXPress.

Service Bureau Issues

Service bureaus are great: They keep and maintain all the equipment, know the ins and outs of both your software and your printing press requirements, and turn around jobs quickly. At least, most of the time. Working with a service bureau involves commitment and communication between both parties. They need your business; you need their expertise and equipment.

To ensure that you get what you want (fast, accurate service) and that the service bureau gets what it wants (no-hassle clients and printing jobs), make sure you both understand your standards and needs. As the customer, keep in mind that the service bureau has many customers, all of whom do things differently. Service bureaus likewise must not impose unreasonable requirements just for the sake of consistency, because customers can have good reasons for doing things differently.

Paying attention to a few basic issues can help you establish a productive relationship with your service bureau.

Sending documents vs. output files

First, do you give the service bureau your actual QuarkXPress documents or do you send an EPS file? The answer depends on several things:

- A document file, even if the graphics files are copied with it, takes less space than an EPS file created from your document. That means fewer disks or cartridges to sort through and less time copying files from your media to theirs.

- A document file can be accidentally changed, resulting in incorrect output. For example, a color might be changed accidentally when the service bureau checks your color definitions to make sure that spot colors are translated to process colors. Or document preferences might be lost, resulting in text reflow.

- A service bureau may not have your fonts, and if it doesn't, it can't print your document from the document file unless you give it your fonts. With an EPS file, you presumably have Windows download all fonts you know the service bureau doesn't have (right?).

- The service bureau cannot edit an EPS file. So the service bureau can't come to your rescue if you make a mistake such as forgetting to print registration marks when outputting the EPS file or specifying landscape printing mode for a portrait document.

Basically, the question is whom do you trust more: yourself or the service bureau? Only you can answer that question. But in either case, there is one thing you can do to help prevent miscommunication: Provide a proof copy of your document.

Give the service bureau a proof with all images placed, shades indicated, and colors marked (include information about whether they are process or spot colors). Also, indicate what trapping settings you specified, if any. Also include a list of all fonts used. The service bureau uses these tools to see if its output matches your expectations — regardless of whether you provided a document file or EPS file.

Determining output settings

A common area of miscommunication between designers and service bureaus is determining who sets controls over line screens, registration marks, and other output controls. (Document-specific controls are covered in the "Printing Options" section earlier in this chapter; related global settings are covered in the previous chapter.) Whoever has the expertise to make the right choices should handle these options. And it should be clear to both parties who is responsible for what aspect of output controls — you don't want to use conflicting settings or accidentally override the desired settings.

For output controls on gray-scale images (covered in detail in Chapter 20), the layout artist should determine these settings and specify them on the proof copy provided to the service bureau.

If the publication has established production standards for special effects or special printing needs or if the job is unusual, we recommend the layout artist determine the settings for such general controls as the registration marks (set in the Print dialog box) and the printer resolution (set in the Printer Setup dialog box).

But for issues related to the service bureau's internal needs and standards, such as how much gap between pages, we recommend that the service bureau determine this. If you are sending the service bureau EPS files, instead of QuarkXPress documents, you will have to enter such settings in the Printer Setup dialog box before creating the file, so be sure to coordinate these issues with the service bureau in advance.

Issues related to the printing press (such as which side of the negative the emulsion should be on), should be coordinated with the printer and service bureau. Again, let the service bureau enter this data unless you send EPS files.

In all cases, determine who is responsible for what aspect of output controls and ensure everyone does not specify a setting outside his or her area of responsibility without first coordinating with the other parties.

 Smart service bureaus do know how to edit an EPS file to change some settings, such as dpi and line-screen, that are encoded in those files, but don't count on them doing that work for you except in emergencies.

Providing the right graphics files

Whether sending QuarkXPress documents to a PostScript service bureau or to a prepress service bureau, make sure to include all the necessary graphics files. If you forget any, QuarkXPress substitutes the low-resolution screen representations. Yes, QuarkXPress displays an alert box about missing files (if you specified checking for links in the document preferences), but a harried operator might inadvertently ignore the alert.

Don't forget about graphics linked via OLE, either. These must be replaced with graphics imported the standard way or cut-and-pasted as regular objects, not live links. Otherwise, you again get the low-resolution screen representation in your output.

When you work with prepress service bureaus, be very clear about any OPI settings. And make sure the bureau knows which high-resolution scans to substitute for your TIFF (or EPS) files. Again, providing printouts with the images in place helps the service bureau ensure that the right graphic is substituted in the right place, with the right settings.

Providing font files

Similarly, consider providing copies of your font files (the TTF files for TrueType and PFM and PFB files for PostScript) on disk to the service bureau — just in case the bureau doesn't have them. If you send EPS files to the service bureau for output, just provide the PFB files in case the operator has to download them to the image setter. (The Font Usage dialog box lists fonts used in your QuarkXPress document.)

Don't forget to provide font files for typefaces used in EPS graphics imported into your document. (These don't display in the Font Usage dialog box.)

Ensuring correct bleeds

When you create an image that bleeds, it must actually print beyond the crop marks. There must be enough of the bleeding image that if the paper moves slightly in the press, the image still bleeds. (Most printers expect ⅛ inch, or about a pica, of *trim* area for a bleed.) In most cases, the document page is smaller than both the page size (specified in QuarkXPress through the File ⇨ Document Setup option) and the paper size (specified through Windows Printer Setup option), so the margin between pages is sufficient to allow this. If your document page is the same size as your paper size, the paper size limits how much of your bleed actually prints: any part of the bleed that extends beyond the paper size specified in the Windows Printer Setup is cut off. (This is a problem in how PostScript controls printing, not in QuarkXPress.)

Figure 26-5 shows examples that illustrate the effects of page and paper size on bleeds. The gray boxes indicate the final printed sizes after pages are trimmed at the printing plant.

- The document page on the left is smaller than the page size (9.5 × 12 inches), so its bleeds extend beyond the crop marks, giving the printer sufficient leeway in case of paper misalignment. The printer's paper size must be 11 × 14 inches (legal size) to accommodate this page size.

▶ **Figure 26-5:** The effects of page size on bleeds.

■ The document page on the right is the same size as the paper and page size (8.5 × 11 inches), so the paper boundary chops off anything bleeding past it. Even though the document looks OK in QuarkXPress, the trim area is insufficient for a reliable bleed in the output document.

Make sure your service bureau knows you are using bleeds and whether you specified a special paper or page size, because that may be a factor in the way the operator outputs your job (see the next section).

Sending oversized pages

If you use a paper size larger than US letter size (8.5 × 11 inches), tell the service bureau in advance, because it might affect how the operator sends your job to the image setter. Many service bureaus use a utility program that automatically rotates pages to save film, because pages rotated 90 degrees still fit along the width of RC paper and film rolls. But if you specify a larger paper size to make room for bleeds or because your document will be printed at tabloid size, this rotation might cause the tops and/or bottoms or your document pages to be cut off.

We've worked with service bureaus who forgot they loaded this page-rotation utility, so the operator didn't think to unload it for our oversized pages. It took a while to figure out what was going on, because we were certain we weren't doing the rotation (the service bureau assumed we had) and the service bureau had forgotten that it was using the rotation utility.

Working with Macintosh service bureaus

Although QuarkXPress 3.1 for the Macintosh can read Windows files if the XTension to do so is installed, try to avoid giving Windows files to a Mac-based service bureau. After all, fonts can be different between platforms, resulting in mismapped characters (even though QuarkXPress seeks out the most common mismaps and corrects them automatically when transferring files between the two platforms). You might also end up with incorrect fonts (some font names are different across platforms) or with character spacing that differs enough to cause reflow.

If your service bureau doesn't have a Windows PC with QuarkXPress, provide an EPS file instead of your document file. If you have large files because of complex graphics, use a SyQuest cartridge. With a program such as Insignia Solutions' AccessPC or Dayna Communications' DOS Mounter, your Mac-based service bureau can read a SyQuest cartridge formatted on a Windows or DOS PC — something your service bureau may not realize is possible. (SyQuest cartridges, which can hold up to 88 megabytes of data, are practically the standard method of file exchange for Mac users at service bureaus.)

■ ■

Summary

▶ You can use PCL printers as proofing printers for jobs that ultimately will be output to PostScript image setters. Be aware, however, that EPS files and high-resolution TIFF files do not print and color-separation features are not available.

▶ If you want to print a selected range of pages from a document that has multiple sections, use the exact page-numbering scheme (including the prefix) for the desired section when you specify pages to print. An alternative is to use absolute page numbers, indicated with a plus sign (+) before the page number.

▶ Check the Rough box in the Print dialog box to have QuarkXPress suppress the printout of graphics. This is handy when you need to proof text but don't want to wait for graphics to print.

▶ Avoid using the Spreads option if you output to negatives and use bleeds across the spread.

▶ Check the Process Separation box in the Edit Color dialog box for any spot colors you want separated into process colors. Otherwise, they print on their own plates.

▶ Make sure to define any colors you use in EPS files in QuarkXPress as well. Otherwise, the colors print as black or white.

▶ If you want to color-separate TIFF files, save them in the CMYK version of the TIFF format. Likewise, make sure that EPS files using color come from illustration programs that can properly encode color information so QuarkXPress can color-separate the colors.

▶ Give your service bureau a proof printout of your document, with colors, shades, and graphics marked. Also list fonts used and any trapping values set.

▶ When you send your QuarkXPress document to a service bureau, be sure to send all graphics files. Replace OLE live links with imported files or cut and paste the graphic directly into QuarkXPress.

▶ Provide font files for all fonts the service bureau does not have. To be on the safe side, you might simply provide all fonts used — including those in the document's EPS files.

▶ Make sure your paper size is big enough to provide a trim area for bleeds.

▶ Alert your service bureau to the use of bleeds or oversize pages.

■ ■

PART VIII

Appendixes

B ecause publishing involves so many aspects — different needs for different types of publications, organizational approaches, and skill sets — the key to effectively using desktop technology is tailoring the tools to your process. You first need to get the right tools for the job and then know how to combine the tools' capabilities to accomplish your design goals.

The following three appendixes detail three types of tailoring for QuarkXPress users. Appendix A, "Application Tips," shows how to use the various QuarkXPress features covered throughout the book to produce real-world documents — how to make the whole greater than the sum of the parts. Appendix B, " Installing and Reconfiguring QuarkXPress," explains how to customize your QuarkXPress installation so you can add or delete import filters and some features. Appendix C, "Extending QuarkXPress's Capabilities," describes QuarkXPress's powerful XTensions feature, which allows you to add functions to QuarkXPress, and describes some of the XTensions available for Windows users.

APPENDIX A

Application Tips

Introduction

Seeing is believing. There's no better teacher than experience. Clichés, perhaps, but truths nonetheless. This book is designed to teach you QuarkXPress from a process point of view, describing how to apply QuarkXPress tools and explaining the underlying theory and techniques you need to know to use those tools effectively.

The best way to get a sense of how you can complete different publishing projects by combining the many tools, theories, and techniques covered in this book is to look at some real-life examples. The following sections contain a representative sample of documents in five major categories: advertisements, brochures, documentation, newsletters, and magazines. All the samples you see are real documents created in QuarkXPress. And even though they were done by different people at different companies in different parts of the country, they share some underlying design principles: simplicity, focus, flow, and restrained embellishment. (And you might even notice similarities in typeface selections!)

Creating Advertisements

An ad must grab the reader's attention. To do that, it must be visually distinct from other ads and from surrounding editorial material. But it must not be annoying, or it creates a negative impression that's worse than making no impression. Furthermore, the message of the advertisement must be immediately clear to readers — or they won't spend much time reading the ad (12 seconds is a reported average) even if they do notice it.

▶ **Figure A-1:** A clean, simple ad design.

Clean and Simple

The ad in Figure A-1 takes a straightforward design approach: simple graphics, clean typefaces, and reversed-out lettering. The graphics are line drawings created in Adobe Illustrator, imported into QuarkXPress, and then enhanced with QuarkXPress drawing features.

For example, the designers rotate the videocassette — already positioned at an angle in the original graphic file — another 10 degrees to make it more dynamic. In Figure A-2, you see the rotation amount highlighted in the Measurements palette. To produce the text on the videocassette label, the designers create the text in QuarkXPress, place it in a text box, rotate it, and then group it with the videocassette's picture box (Item ➪ Group).

The videocassette player incorporates several QuarkXPress effects. First, the gray videocassette slot is added as an empty picture box with a half-point frame and a gray background. These settings are established in the Frame Specifications dialog box (Item ➪ Frame), as shown in Figure A-3.

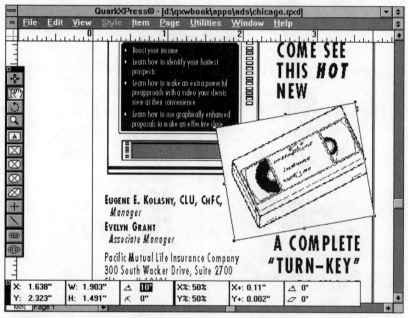

▶ **Figure A-2:** The videocassette and the label text are rotated and grouped together.

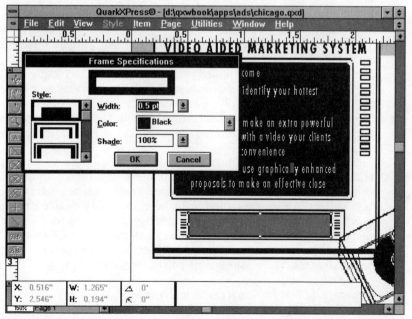

▶ **Figure A-3:** A framed picture box creates the videocassette slot on the video player.

▶ **Figure A-4:** The videocassette player picture box knocks out of the headline's gray background above it.

The text on the video monitor is created by adding a QuarkXPress text box with a solid black background (set via the Colors palette or Item ⇨ Modify). The text box contains white text (applied via Style ⇨ Color). The picture box that holds the videocassette player is given a solid white background so it knocks out of the gray band above it, as illustrated in Figure A-4. That band is a text box with a gray shade applied as the background (set via the Colors palette); it is sent back (Item ⇨ Send Backward) so it displays behind the videocassette player.

The text in the ad is set almost wholly in variants of the sans serif typeface Futura: Condensed Medium for text, Condensed Extrabold for the title, and some oblique (the proper name for a sans serif typeface's italic variant) and bold variants for emphasis and text labels. The serif typeface Palatino is used only for the banner identifying the advertiser (Pacific Mutual) — this juxtaposition of typefaces clearly delineates the ad message from its sponsor. To lend class to the advertiser's name, the designers use the QuarkXPress small caps feature (set via the Measurements palette or Style ⇨ Type Style).

Designers: Robert Francisco and John Frick, Jr.
Company: Pacific Mutual Life Insurance Company

Type as Art

As you can see from the ad in Figure A-5, which announces award winners, you can use type as art. Although the ad includes a picture of the award and corporate logos, the emphasis is on the text. This is especially appropriate because the ad appears in a trade journal *(Columbia Journalism Review)* whose design is low-key and nongraphical. Rather than creating a look that is jarring compared to the journal's stolid design, the designer — who happens to be one of the authors of this book — relies on sophisticated typographic effects to provide visual counterpoint to the editorial.

The text in the ad follows the typographic standards used by the association sponsoring the awards: Cheltenham for body copy and Century Oldstyle Bold and Goudy Oldstyle (roman and italic) for embellishments such as headlines and labels. The use of style sheets ensures that the formatting for each type of text is applied identically in all instances. In all the styles, text is centered, with hyphenation turned off.

Announcing the Winners of the

Seventh Annual Computer Press Awards

for works appearing in 1991

PRINT MEDIA

Macworld
MAGAZINE
(over 50,000 circ.)

Computers in Accounting
MAGAZINE
(under 50,000 circ.)

PC Week
NEWSPAPER
(over 50,000 circ.)

Computer Retail Week
NEWSPAPER
(under 50,000 circ.)

Windows Watcher
NEWSLETTER

ELECTRONIC MEDIA

Business World, ABC News
TELEVISION
PROGRAM

Computing Success!,
Business Radio Network
RADIO PROGRAM

Computer Club,
Prodigy Services
ON-LINE
PUBLICATION

ARTICLES

Peter Krass,
Information Week
NEWS STORY
(computer pub.)

G. Pascal Zachary and
Stephen Kreider Yoder,
Wall Street Journal
NEWS STORY
(general-interest pub.)

Preston Gralla,
PC/Computing
FEATURE
(computer pub.)

Elizabeth Corcoran,
Scientific American
FEATURE
(general-interest pub.)

Douglas Adams, *MacUser*
OPINION/
EDITORIAL

Deborah Branscum,
Macworld
COLUMNIST

Russell Ito, *MacUser*
PRODUCT REVIEW:
HARDWARE

Craig Stinson,
PC Magazine
PRODUCT REVIEW:
SOFTWARE

BOOKS

David O. Arnold,
*Computers and Society:
Impact!*
(Mitchell/McGraw-Hill)
NONFICTION

Microsoft Corp.,
Microsoft Excel: Step by Step
(Microsoft Press)
INTRO HOW-TO:
SOFTWARE

Neil Salkind,
*Getting Started with the
Apple Macintosh*
(Microsoft Press)
INTRO HOW-TO:
SYSTEMS

Jesse Berst, Stephen
Roth, Olav Martin Kvern,
and Scott Dunn,
Real World PageMaker 4
(Bantam Computer Books)
ADVANCED HOW-TO:
SOFTWARE

Raj Jain,
*The Art of Computer
Systems Analysis*
(John Wiley & Sons)
ADVANCED HOW-TO:
SYSTEMS

▲ For a complete list of winners and runners-up, or for information on entering the awards, write Horizon Communications, 8865 Morro Rd., Ste. A2, Atascadero, CA 93422.
▲ For information on the Computer Press Assn., write 7000 Bianca Ave., Van Nuys, CA 91406.

Awards Sponsored By

Computer Press Association
Promoting Excellence in Computer Journalism

◉CITIZEN

▶ **Figure A-5:** A type-intensive ad design.

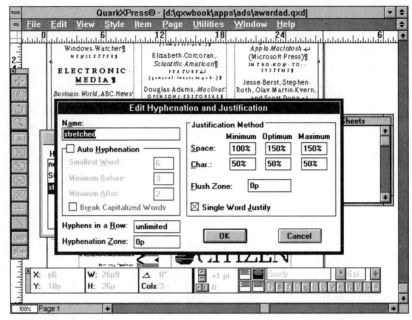

► **Figure A-6:** Creating a new H&J set for the Division and Category heads.

Creating an H&J set (Edit ➪ H&Js ➪ New) that has character spacing set to 50 percent for minimum, optimum, and maximum achieves the text spacing used for the Division and Category heads. Figure A-6 shows these settings. Establishing the same value for all three character-spacing settings ensures that all text using the H&J set is spaced uniformly. The style tags for the Division and Category heads reference the new H&J set (Edit ➪ Style Sheets ➪ Edit ➪ Formats) instead of the Standard H&J set. You can accomplish the same thing by using the tracking setting for each style (in the Paragraph Formats dialog box). But using a common H&J set means that you only need to change the spacing in one place; changes to the H&J set affect all styles referring to that H&J set.

Triangles created with the Zapf Dingbats typeface serve as bullet characters in the ad, replacing the traditional en bullets (filled circles). The triangle motif works well because it evokes the pyramid shape of the awards logo. To determine which keyboard character accesses the desired Zapf Dingbats symbol (*s*, in this case), you can use the Windows 3.1 Character Map utility, as shown in Figure A-7.

One-point rules, created with the Orthogonal Line tool, provide boundaries between the three main elements — the ad logo and title, the list of awards winners, and the contact information and sponsor logos. Figure A-8 shows a close-up view of one of these rules and the Measurements palette, which reflects the rule specifications.

Designer: Galen Gruman
Company: Computer Press Association

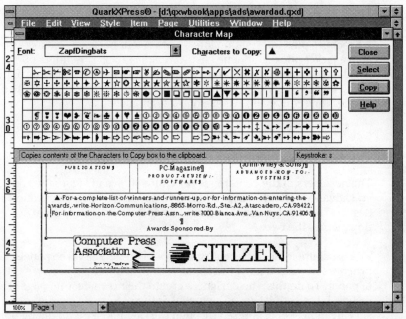

▶ **Figure A-7:** Using the Windows 3.1 Character Map.

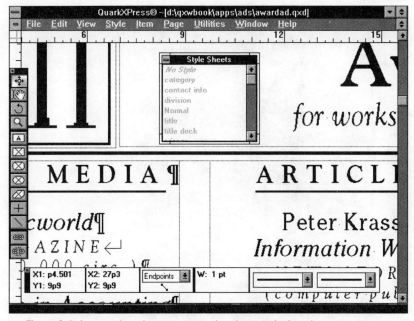

▶ **Figure A-8:** A one-point rule separates major elements in the ad.

Designing Brochures

A brochure puts information into a convenient package — usually small enough to fit in a jacket pocket, attaché case, or display rack. Brochures often contain a proposal or data meant to reassure or attract investors (such as an annual report), which means they not only must communicate information, but also must be engaging while conveying a sense of professionalism.

Fold-out Poster

The designers of the conference brochure shown in Figures A-9 and A-10 use several advanced QuarkXPress features to accomplish the publication's ambitious design. The client originally wanted a brochure and a separate poster. This solution merges the two.

The brochure folds out into six panels — two tiers of three panels each. When the brochure is opened fully, the conference schedule appears across the entire sheet of paper. To do this, the designers create their own custom page size, 33×20.75 inches, by selecting File ⇨ Document Setup or File ⇨ New. Figure A-11 shows these specifications being entered through the Document Setup dialog box.

▶ **Figure A-9:** The front cover of a six-panel brochure.

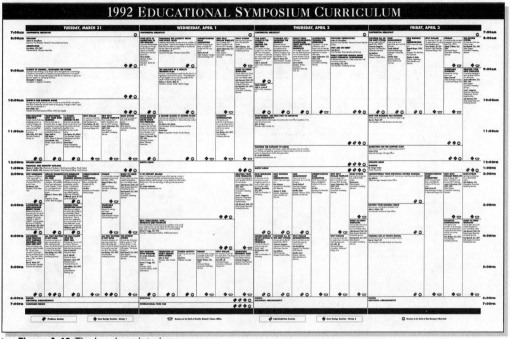

▶ **Figure A-10:** The brochure interior.

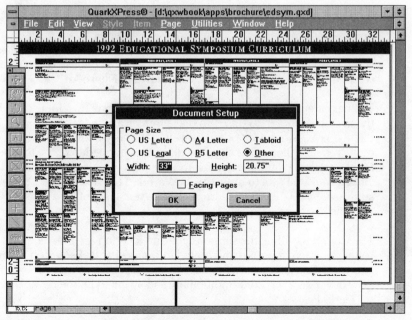

▶ **Figure A-11:** Creating a custom page size in the Document Setup dialog box.

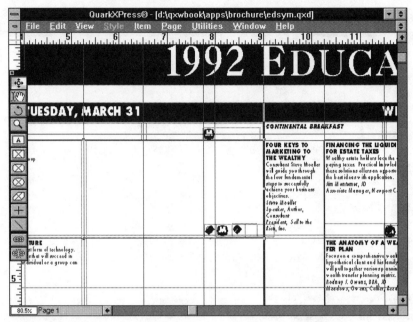

▶ **Figure A-12:** Using column guides and ruler guide lines to align elements.

The first step in creating the brochure is to set up a grid for the four main text boxes — one for each day of the conference agenda — and then create the six columns (by adding text and picture boxes in each column for the session descriptions and icons) in each main box. The designers use column guides and ruler guide lines to align elements, as shown in Figure A-12.

The next step is to delineate each session's text box by adding rules between them. One approach to this is to place frames around the text boxes. Because the text boxes abut each other, however, it's very difficult to control the width of the resulting lines. The slightest difference in overlap of the text boxes' frames causes a difference in line thickness. So the designers instead use the Orthogonal Line tool to draw the lines around the text boxes. You see the results in Figure A-13. The text boxes have a text inset of 3 points so the text does not abut the lines.

The icons describing the session type and location are created in Adobe Illustrator and then imported and scaled in QuarkXPress. Each icon is placed by hand and then grouped to the appropriate text box, as illustrated in Figure A-14. (The cover art is created traditionally and stripped in; the cover text is created in QuarkXPress.)

▶ **Figure A-13:** Lines around the text boxes are added using the Orthogonal Line tool.

▶ **Figure A-14:** Grouping the icons to the appropriate text box.

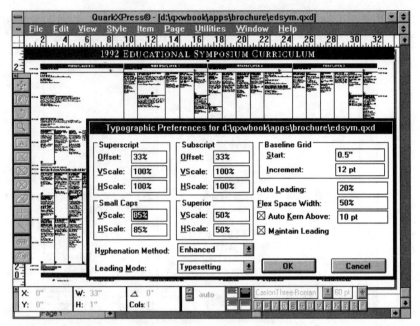

▶ **Figure A-15:** Text specifications are entered in the Typographic Preferences dialog box.

In keeping with the client company's typographic look, the text is set primarily in variants of Futura. The title is set in Caslon 3, using very slight small caps (85 percent). Figure A-15 shows the text specifications set in the Typographic Preferences dialog box.

To output the large sheet required to produce this brochure, the designers use the tiling option in the Print dialog box (File ⇨ Print), as you see in Figure A-16. Even so, the size is larger than the image setter can accommodate. So the designers send the document to the service bureau in reduced size (not shown here; this is specified via File ⇨ Printer Setup ⇨ Options) and enlarge it later through traditional photographic means.

Because this enlargement is necessary, the designers send the document to the image setter at super-high resolution (via File ⇨ Printer Setup). This way, the resolution approaches normal when the piece is enlarged. Figure A-17 shows the resolution settings in the Printer Setup dialog box.

No colors are applied to the text box backgrounds so there are no grainy effects from the enlargement and no mismatches between colors when the tiles are pieced together. Instead, the colors are added traditionally, using spot-color plates created by hand.

Designers: Robert Francisco and John Frick, Jr.
Company: Pacific Mutual Life Insurance Company

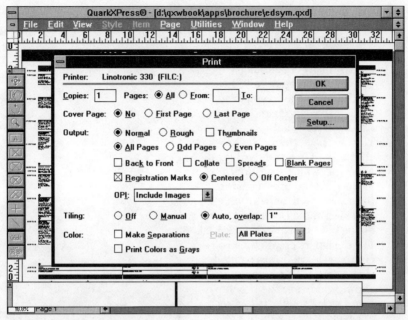

▶ **Figure A-16:** The tiling option is selected to accommodate the oversize page needed for the brochure.

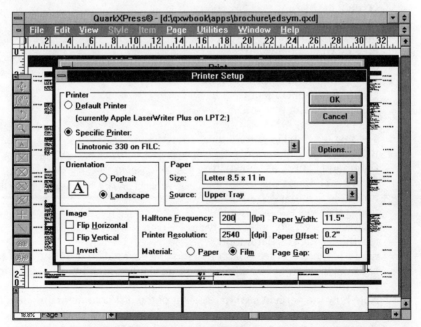

▶ **Figure A-17:** Super-high resolution is specified in the Printer Setup dialog box.

Annual Report

The design of the brochure shown in Figure A-18 is typical of a style used by many organizations: As you can see in Figure A-19, the brochure has one column of text accompanied by charts.

The odd page size of the brochure (to fit in a standard legal envelope, which measures 4⅜ × 9½ inches) requires a custom page size (4 × 9 inches), which is specified in the Document Setup dialog box, shown in Figure A-20. The designers create the brochure in QuarkXPress using facing pages. This technique allows you to see the brochure pages side by side, just as readers eventually see them.

The charts are created in Adobe Illustrator, but their titles are created in QuarkXPress as separate text boxes. The photography on the cover and elsewhere is created traditionally and stripped in. Picture boxes with gray backgrounds are used in the QuarkXPress document to indicate photograph placement.

The text is set in ITC Garamond, with numerals set in Adobe Garamond Expert, as shown in Figure A-21. Using this typeface for its old-fashioned, traditional numerals gives the brochure a more conservative, authoritative feel than using ITC Garamond's

PACIFIC MUTUAL

Report to Policyowners 1991

▶ **Figure A-18:** This annual report features a straightforward, businesslike cover design.

modern numerals (see Chapter 14 for a more detailed description of the two styles of numerals). Headlines appear in Univers Medium and Medium Oblique.

Note how the percent sign to the right of the last column of numbers (next to 8.86) is placed in its own small text box, outside the large text box. This ensures that numerals align consistently against the column's outside margin. (You

Table of Contents

Company Description

Founded in 1868 by Leland Stanford, Charles Crocker and Mark Hopkins, Pacific Mutual Life Insurance Company is the largest domestic life and health insurer in California. With nearly $50 billion in total assets and funds under management, Pacific Mutual, together with its subsidiaries, is also one of the nation's largest financial institutions. It has more than $37 billion of individual and group life insurance in force and over 4,000 employees and associates nationwide. Furthermore, it is rated A+ (Superior) by A.M. Best, AA+ by Standard and Poor's, AA+ by Duff & Phelps and A1 by Moody's.

Financial Highlights

(In Millions)	1991	1990	Change
Company Assets	$ 10,650	$ 9,783	8.86%
Additional Funds Under Management	38,939	30,715	26.78
Total Capital[1]	476	425	12.00
Total Revenues	2,572	2,570	0.07
Individual Life Insurance in Force	25,812	21,116	22.24
Net Investment Income	830	724	14.64

[1] Total Capital includes surplus and mandatory securities valuation reserve.

2

Assets and Funds Under Management
Dollars in Billions

22.88 27.24 35.52 40.50 49.59
87 88 89 90 91

■ Funds Under Management
■ Company Assets

Total Capital[1]
Dollars in Millions

343 366 392 425 476
87 88 89 90 91

Total Revenues
Dollars in Millions

2.18 2.09[2] 2.34 2.57 2.57
87 88 89 90 91

Individual Life Insurance in Force
Dollars in Billions

12.73 14.11 16.38 21.12 25.81
87 88 89 90 91

Net Investment Income
Dollars in Millions

528 640 665 724 830
87 88 89 90 91

[1] Total Capital includes surplus and mandatory securities valuation reserve.

[2] Beginning in 1988 all Pacific Mutual group life and health business was transferred to PM Group Life Insurance Company.

3

▶ **Figure A-19:** The report interior also combines straightforward text and charts.

cannot define a tab stop to be outside its text box to, in this example, align the percent symbol in the first row.) The text box containing the percent symbol is grouped to the other text box.

Designers: Robert Francisco and John Frick, Jr.
Company: Pacific Mutual Life Insurance Company

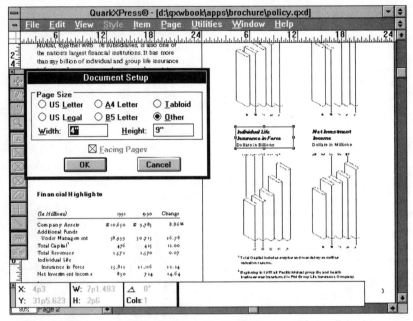

▶ **Figure A-20:** A custom page size is specified in the Document Setup dialog box.

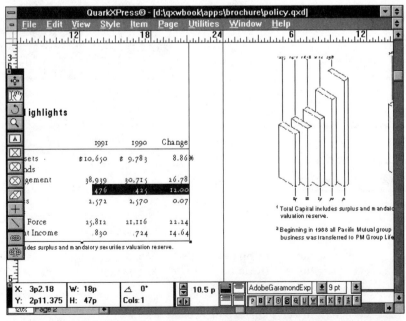

▶ **Figure A-21:** Numerals are set in the traditional Adobe Garamond Expert typeface to create a more conservative look.

Producing Documentation

When you create documentation, you face an unenviable task. Documentation must not appear as if it is "designed" — if the image gets in the way of the message, the design has failed. This means that the design must stay in the periphery, aiding comprehension while not calling attention to itself.

Quark practices what it preaches: The company designed and laid out the QuarkXPress for Windows manuals in QuarkXPress for Windows. In Figures A-22 and A-23, respectively, you see the cover of the QuarkXPress for Windows Reference Manual and an interior page of the book.

Figure A-24 shows a page of the manual as it is being created in QuarkXPress. The design is simple, using a minimum number of master pages and style tags. Text is in two-column format, and type is limited to Futura Medium and Extrabold for headlines and graphic callouts (labels) and ITC Stone Serif for body text. Stone Serif Semibold is used to highlight commands in text. All text within a chapter is created as one story so that last-minute changes don't cause headlines to separate from their text, which can happen if headlines are in separate text boxes.

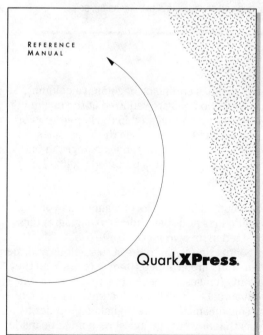

▶ **Figure A-22:** The cover of the product documentation for QuarkXPress for Windows.

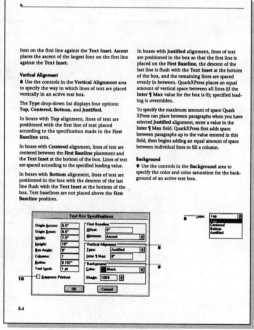

▶ **Figure A-23:** An interior page of the documentation manual.

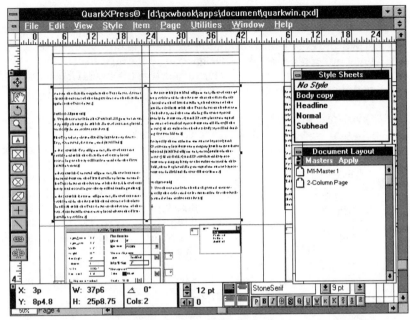

▶ **Figure A-24:** The number of master pages and styles is kept to a minimum, as is fitting for a no-frills design.

To prevent widows and orphans (single lines ending or beginning a column), the style for the body text specifies that two lines are required at the beginning or end of each paragraph. These settings are established in the Paragraph Formats dialog box (Edit ⇨ Style Sheets ⇨ Edit ⇨ Formats) via the Keep Lines Together option, shown in Figure A-25. QuarkXPress arranges paragraph breaks to follow this setting. Similarly, the Standard H&J set is modified (Edit ⇨ H&Js ⇨ Edit) to allow no more than three hyphens in a row.

Graphics are placed below the text columns in a free-form manner, as you see in Figure A-26. The designer uses guidelines and ruler guides to align graphics and callouts, each of which is contained in its own picture or text box. The callout text boxes, the ruling lines connecting them to the screen shots, and the picture boxes containing the screen shots are grouped (Item ⇨ Group), so they can be moved as one unit if the layout changes. Screen shots are captured via a screen-capture utility program from actual QuarkXPress documents and then pasted directly into QuarkXPress. This means there are no linked graphics to move from PC to PC — it also means that any change in a screen must be made manually in the document.

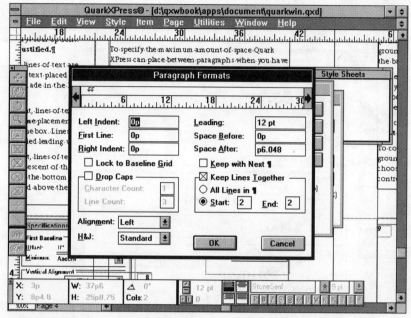

▶ **Figure A-25:** Style settings in the Paragraph Formats dialog box prevent widows and orphans.

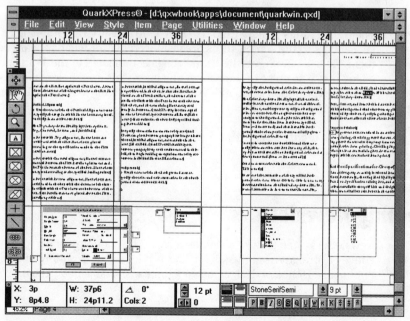

▶ **Figure A-26:** Callouts and graphics are placed in individual text boxes or picture boxes.

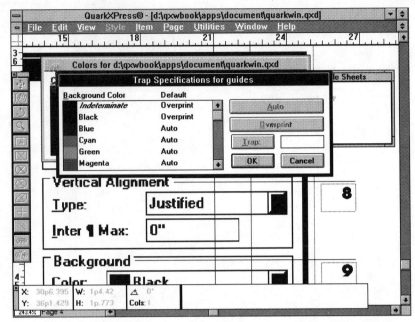

▶ **Figure A-27:** Connecting lines are set to overprint black and indeterminate colors.

The trap settings (Edit ⇨ Colors ⇨ Edit Trap) ensure that ruling lines connecting callouts to the screen shots are visible no matter what appears beneath them. Figure A-27 shows the trap settings established in the Trap Specifications dialog box. The color of the connecting lines (this spot color is named *guides*) is set to overprint black and indeterminate colors. (*Indeterminate* includes imported and pasted images.)

Designers: Creative Services Dept.
Company: Quark, Inc.

Creating Newsletters

Newsletters often feature a simple design. The economy of design is meant to convey a straight-from-the-source, earnest look. But economy of design does not mean absence of design; instead, it means *understated* design.

Company Newsletter

A company newsletter — whether distributed to employees, clients, or customers — requires both simplicity and visual interest. An overly designed newsletter seems out of place for a company document, while a sloppily designed newsletter harms the company's image, branding it cheap or inept. Subtlety and attention to detail are the keys to a successful design.

In the sample newsletter shown in Figures A-28 and A-29, a three-column grid gives the layout flexibility while retaining its simplicity. Text flows in the two inside columns, while the thin third column is a free-form area that holds some captions and the newsletter masthead. Photographs are allowed to cut into the third column as well.

▶ **Figure A-28:** The cover page of a sample company newsletter.

▶ **Figure A-29:** The other pages from the sample newsletter.

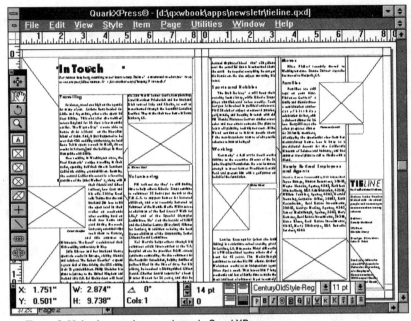

▶ **Figure A-30:** Laying out the newsletter in QuarkXPress.

In Figure A-30, you see pages of the newsletter being laid out in QuarkXPress. Each column is contained in a separate text box (which makes it easier to move elements around while experimenting with the layout). If a new story begins in the middle of a column, it begins in its own text box. Picture boxes with hairline frames (Item ➪ Frames) indicate the placement of photographs, which are stripped in manually.

To create the white-on-black *F* drop cap in the headline, the designers place the capital *F* in its own text box; set the background to black (via the Colors palette or Item ➪ Modify); and set the text to white (Style ➪ Color). The baseline is shifted up 10 points (Style ➪ Baseline Shift) to center the cap vertically in its text box, as shown in Figure A-31. (Because the *F* is selected, QuarkXPress highlights it by reversing its color, so it appears black-on-white in the screen shot. But you can see the black background on either side of the *F*; this is the text box's true background color.) The drop cap typeface is Futura Extrabold, but the letter is scaled to 46 percent (Style ➪ Horizontal Scale). This creates a highly condensed version of the typeface.

To keep the rest of the headline from touching the text box containing the drop cap, the designers give the text box a right-side runaround of 6 points (Item ➪ Runaround). The runaround is set in the Runaround Specifications dialog box, shown in Figure A-32. A left runaround is not needed since there is no text to the left of the drop cap. The bottom runaround of 1 point ensures the drop cap won't bleed out of the background.

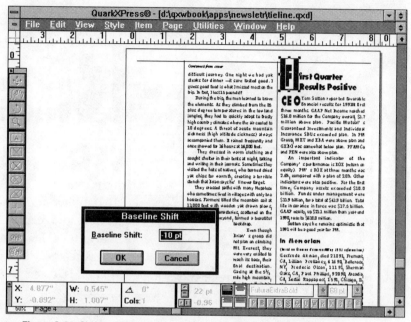

▶ **Figure A-31:** Shifting the baseline 10 points centers the drop cap vertically in its text box.

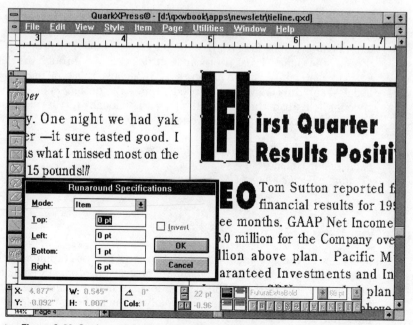

▶ **Figure A-32:** Setting a right-side runaround for the drop cap.

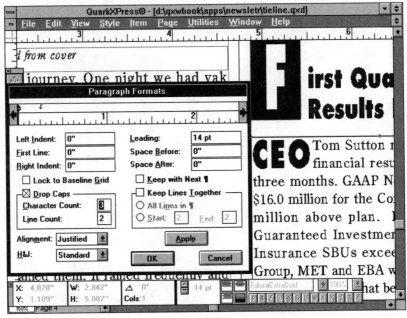

▶ **Figure A-33:** Setting a drop cap through the Paragraph Formats dialog box.

The body text contains one other drop cap — which actually is a three-letter drop cap. Such a drop cap is unusual, but it works well here because the three letters comprise the first word of the paragraph: *CEO*. The drop cap is created through the QuarkXPress drop cap feature, accessed through the Paragraph Formats dialog box, shown in Figure A-33. Because this type of drop cap is unusual — and thus unlikely to be used often — the designers do not define a style for it. Instead, they format the paragraph locally (Style ⇨ Formats). (The newsletter's cover page has a two-letter drop cap created the same way.)

Designers: Robert Francisco and John Frick, Jr.
Publication: TieLine
Company: Pacific Mutual Life Insurance Company

Association Newsletter

Many newsletter designers who lack the resources for graphics rely on typographic and layout treatments to create professional-looking, engaging newsletters. The design of the association newsletter *Network News*, shown in Figures A-34 and A-35, relies almost solely on such effects: typefaces, ruling lines, and shaded elements.

The front page contains a bug advertising a story on page three — a handy device that draws readers into the newsletter. This complements, but does not replace, the table of contents at the bottom of the page. Figure A-36 shows the Text Box Specifications (Item ⇨ Modify) for the bug. The bug is centered in a gray box, with 1-point rules above and below. As shown in the figure, the Vertical Alignment feature is used to center the text vertically in the box. The Measurements palette is used to center the text horizontally. The rules are drawn with the Orthogonal Line tool and then grouped with the text box containing the bug text. The background is created by using Item ⇨ Modify (you can also use the Colors palette).

To add ruling lines to boxes, you must use the Orthogonal Line tool. But there is a simpler way to assign rules to paragraphs: by using styles. In the sample newsletter, the dateline paragraph is accented with a 0.75-point rule above and a 1.5-point rule

▶ **Figure A-34:** The cover page from an association newsletter.

below. To accomplish this, a style called Dateline is created, and rule settings for the style are established through the Paragraph Rules dialog box (Edit ⇨ Style Sheets ⇨ Edit ⇨ Rules), which you see in Figure A-37. The dateline paragraph is then tagged with the Dateline style. The Dateline style also is set to automatically indent the text from both the left and right by 6 points. To make the rules span the full width

▶ **Figure A-35:** An interior spread from the association newsletter.

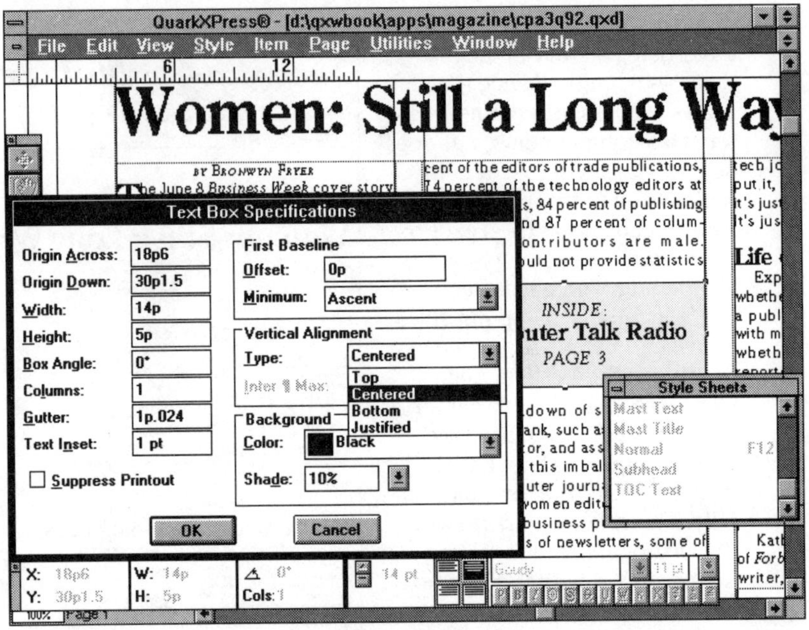

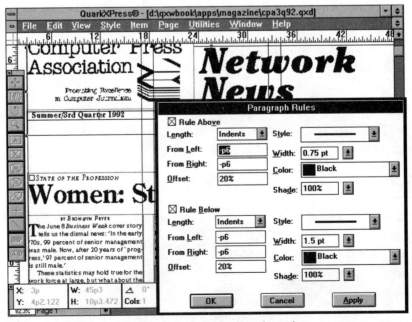

▶ **Figure A-36:** The Text Box Specifications settings for the cover page bug.

▶ **Figure A-37:** Rules are assigned to paragraphs through a style.

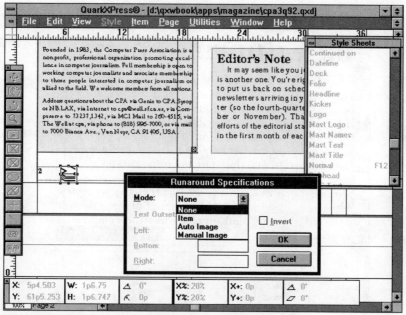

► **Figure A-38:** The association logo is incorporated into the folios.

of the text box, the rule length settings for the style are changed to –0p6 (6 points) for both the right and left.

As you see in Figure A-38, the association logo appears as part of the newsletter folios. This subtly reinforces the association's sponsorship of the newsletter (which is sent to both members and nonmembers). The logo is placed in its own picture box, 3 picas from the page number. To prevent any folio text from wrapping around the logo, picture box runaround is turned off (Item ⇨ Runaround). To save effort, the folios (including the logo) are placed on the master pages, so they automatically repeat on all pages. (If you press Ctrl+3 in the text box in which you want the page number, QuarkXPress substitutes the current page number — which means folios are numbered automatically.)

Newsletter text often jumps to (continues on) another page, and you must alert readers to this fact. QuarkXPress makes this easier by offering keyboard shortcuts you can use to automatically insert the page number in your Continued on . . . and Continued from lines. Press Ctrl+2 to insert the number of the page the story continues from; press Ctrl+4 to insert the number of the page the story jumps to.

For this approach to work, you must link the story's text box to other text boxes making up the story, and the *Continued* line must appear either with

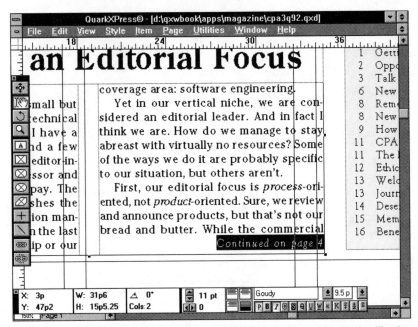

▶ **Figure A-39:** Using the line break character at the end of a line retains line justification.

the story's text or in a text box contained in the story's text box — not in an independent text box. (If the continued line were in an independent text box, that box would have to be linked to the text boxes containing the story.) The first approach — putting the *Continued* line in the story's text box — can cause problems: If the text reflows, the *Continued* line might move.

In Figure A-39, notice that even though we put the cross reference in the story's text, the line before the *Continued* line remains fully justified, even though text is interrupted by the *Continued* line. Using the line break character (Shift+Enter) rather than a regular paragraph break (Enter) at the end of the line keeps the line justified.

Designer: Galen Gruman
Publication: Network News
Company: Computer Press Association

Designing Magazine Elements

Magazine designers get to experiment a lot — design is a fundamental part of their readers' expectations. Some magazine designers create the opening page(s) for each article completely from scratch; others use a set of standard designs and tweak them to fit the needs of the images (which themselves are created with the standard designs in mind).

But proponents of both approaches develop a consistent design for the table of contents. Like the cover design, the table of contents design helps define the magazine's tone. A table of contents can be gaudy — with screened-back, full-color illustrations under the type — or it can be plain. The best designs combine images and text to the detriment of neither, while easily answering the reader's question: "What's in this issue?"

Alternating Contents Pages

Traditionally, the table of contents appears across two facing pages. One way to make it stand out is to have it appear on two alternating pages, which is the approach used by *IEEE Software* magazine, shown in Figure A-40.

Sometimes, the table of contents appears on two right pages or two left pages; other times, it begins on a right page and continues on a left page, as shown in Figures A-41 and A-42. This design gives the reader two chances to find the contents. It also gives the advertising department prime space to sell, because almost everyone reads the contents pages.

When the table of contents is split in this manner, feature articles typically are listed on the first contents page, and departments and the masthead appear on the second.

Another way to make the table of contents more prominent is to use a type-intensive design, as done in the *IEEE Software* contents pages. This creates a

▶ **Figure A-40:** *IEEE Software* magazine cover.

▶ **Figure A-41:** The first contents page in *IEEE Software* magazine appears on a right page.

▶ **Figure A-42:** The second contents page falls on a left page.

visual contrast to the graphically laden ads. Notice that the *IEEE Software* design uses only two typefaces — Goudy and Futura Condensed — but incorporates many variations of those two typefaces. These variations clearly delineate elements and add interest without being distracting.

The designer uses colors picked up from the cover illustration to highlight page numbers on the contents pages. The cover illustration is partially repeated in the table of contents; the image is stripped in manually. Using the same colors creates unity between the image and type while adding visual interest. Because the colors change every issue, the designer defines a process color for each major color element, then simply changes the color definition (Edit ⇨ Colors ⇨ Edit) each issue. Applying colors this way prevents color clutter and ensures that the right color specs are applied to the right elements. Figure A-43 shows the color named "numerals" being applied to the contents' page references. You can also see the colors defined for other standard elements, including "logo" and "Masthead Background."

To achieve the white-on-black text for the title banners, the designer creates a 13-point black rule below for the style Headings (Edit ⇨ Style Sheets ⇨ Edit ⇨ Rules), as illustrated in Figure A-44. The text baseline is shifted 2.5 points (Edit

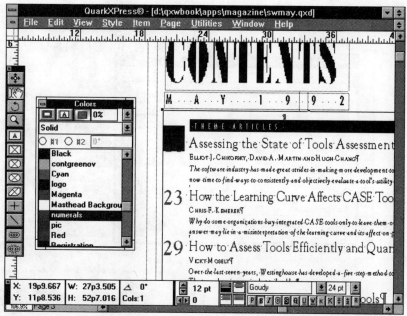

▶ **Figure A-43:** Using labels like "logo" and "numerals" for colors lets you change colors each issue for standard elements while ensuring that the correct new colors are applied to the right elements.

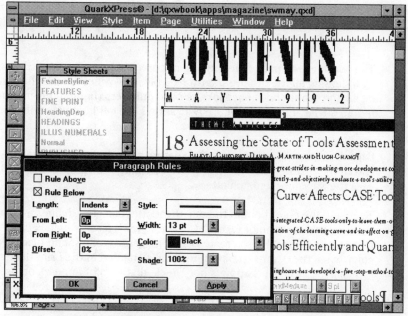

▶ **Figure A-44:** A black rule serves as the background for white banner text.

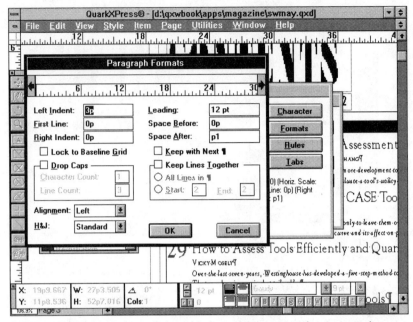

▶ **Figure A-45:** Paragraphs are indented 3 picas so the page numbers can overhang.

⇨ Style Sheets ⇨ Edit ⇨ Character), which brings the white text down into the black rule (note how the selected text falls below the on-screen highlighting area).

The overhanging page numbers are not created by using an outdent or tab, but by indenting all the other paragraphs 3 picas — which equals the width of two digits and the trailing space for the page numbers (finding this measurement requires trial and error). Figure A-45 shows the left indent specifications for the Features Byline style tag.

Page numbers are tagged with the Feature style, but are made larger than the rest of the text tagged with that style. To enlarge the page numbers, the designer uses the Measurements palette.

To create the color behind the masthead, the designer defines a color and specifies it as a process color (Edit ⇨ Colors ⇨ New), as shown in Figure A-46. This means that QuarkXPress creates cyan, magenta, yellow, and black plates for the color when the color-separation feature is enabled in the Print dialog box (File ⇨ Print). If Process Separation is not checked, the color appears on its own plate,

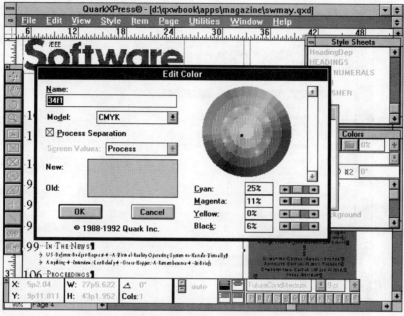

▶ **Figure A-46:** The masthead color is defined as a process color.

as a spot color, which is useful when you want to use process colors along with such spot colors as metallics and neons that cannot be created accurately through process colors. The logo, which is created in CorelDRAW and imported into QuarkXPress, is also in color; it too is created as a process color, so it color-separates when printed.

To apply the color, the designer simply selects the text box, clicks the background icon in the Colors palette (you can also use Item ⇨ Modify), and selects the color, as illustrated in Figure A-47.

Designer: Dirk Hagner
Publication: IEEE Software
Company: IEEE Computer Society

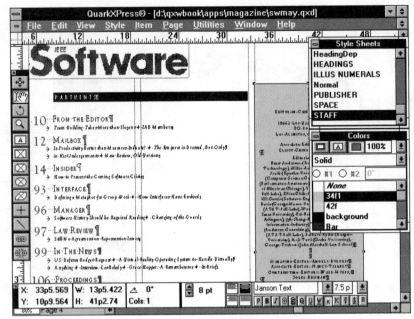

▶ **Figure A-47:** Color is applied to the masthead through the Colors palette.

Facing Contents Pages

Although placing the table of contents on alternating pages gives the reader two opportunities to find the contents, using the traditional, facing-pages design delivers everything in one package. It also gives the designer more room to experiment and to tailor the contents to different graphics each issue. In Figures A-48 and A-49, you see the cover and table of contents pages for *IEEE Computer Graphics and Applications.* The designer repeats a slice of the cover (created electronically and output digitally with the rest of the contents) on the left page, and uses an image from one of the feature articles on the right page. The two pictures below that image are stripped in traditionally, because they were not provided electronically to the magazine. With QuarkXPress, you can handle both traditional and electronic images.

As this design proves, graphic elements can do more than look pretty — they can refer readers to particular articles or departments. By placing a page number next to a graphic or overprinting it on the corner of the graphic, you can call attention to a particular element in the magazine. To accomplish this effect in QuarkXPress, all you need to do is create a text box, enter the text, and format the text and box attributes (typeface, size, color, backgrounds, and so on) in the usual ways, as shown in Figure A-50.

In this design, text boxes also are used for page numbers in the contents text. Because of this approach, no indents need to be set for the contents text, although page numbers must be moved manually if the text length changes.

One way to add a distinct appearance to a table of contents is to use the magazine logo as a graphic element. In this example, the designer specifies a CMYK process-color build to the logo in Aldus FreeHand and then uses the Colors palette in QuarkXPress to apply the same color to the text titles and page numbers. Figure A-51 shows these colors being applied. Another effect is to create a

▶ **Figure A-48:** *IEEE Computer Graphics* cover page.

logo as an EPS or other vector file and make the logo itself transparent while making the rest of the shape (usually the rectangle it sits in) a solid color (white). After placing the logo graphic in a picture box, you can give the box a linear-blend fill, so the logo color changes smoothly from one color to another.

One small feature that designers often overlook when creating contents pages — especially when text lines are fairly wide, as in this example — is hyphenation. When you use wide lines, hyphenation is not necessary, and it can look awkward to break a word after a few characters when there clearly is no visual reason to keep those few characters on the line. This is especially true if the text is not

▶ **Figure A-49:** This publication uses the traditional, facing-pages design for its table of contents.

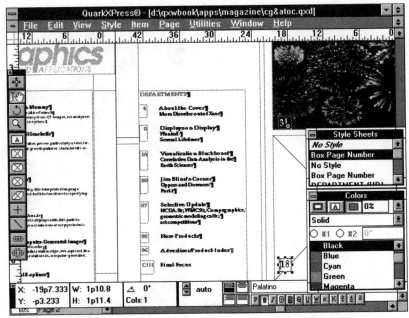

▶ **Figure A-50:** Page numbers are placed in their own text boxes and formatted to overprint the graphics.

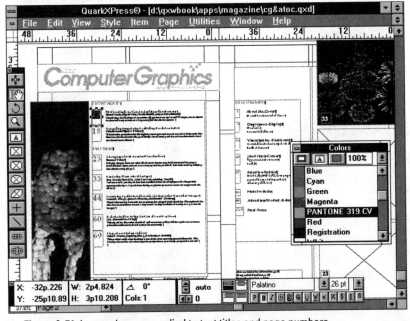

▶ **Figure A-51:** Logo colors are applied to text titles and page numbers.

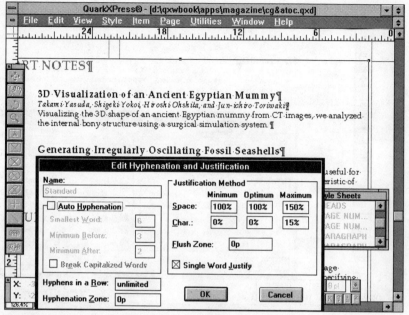

▶ **Figure A-52:** Turn off hyphenation when using wide lines of text.

justified. If you use wide lines, turn off hyphenation for the Standard H&J set (Edit ➪ H&Js ➪ Edit) by unchecking the Auto Hyphenation box, as shown in Figure A-52.

As with the other example publications shown, this magazine restricts its type-faces, relying on variety within the typeface to provide visual differentiation among text elements rather than using a ransom-note approach to typography. In the contents page, the only typeface used is Palatino. In Figure A-53, you see the complete list of typefaces used in this document, as shown in the Font Us-age dialog box (Utilities ➪ Font Usage). (Although Helvetica also appears in the list of typefaces, it is used on other pages of the magazine, not on the contents pages.) Using a serif typeface throughout the contents pages makes the logo, which is set in a sans serif typeface, more distinct.

Designer: Vic Grenrock
Publication: IEEE Computer Graphics and Applications
Company: IEEE Computer Society

▶ **Figure A-53:** This magazine uses only one typeface — Palatino — in its contents page. This keeps the visual focus on the magazine's graphics, not its text.

APPENDIX

B

Installing and Reconfiguring QuarkXPress

• •

Installing QuarkXPress for Windows is easy, especially if you've installed other Windows applications. QuarkXPress has an install program that automates the process for you. But it also lets you customize your installation: you decide what program components to install, such as import filters, OLE support, drag-and-drop printing support, and help files. If you don't install a component and later decide you want that feature, you can install just that component.

Starting the Installation

Start the install program from Windows Program Manager, insert Disk 1 of your QuarkXPress disks and then select File ➪ Run. In the Run dialog box, type **A:INSTALL** in the Command Line field and then choose OK. (If your install disk is in drive B:, enter B: instead of A:.) It doesn't matter whether you type the command in lowercase, uppercase, or mixed-case letters — Windows doesn't pay attention to case when dealing with file and program names.

After a few seconds, the dialog box shown in Figure B-1 will display, giving you the chance to continue or abort the installation. The QuarkXPress for Windows Installer dialog box then appears, asking you what drive and directory you want QuarkXPress installed on. The default is C:\XPRESS. You may change this to another drive (such as D:) or directory (such as QXP) or both by editing the existing name or entering a new name. Figure B-2 shows this dialog box set to the default.

▶ **Figure B-1:** The first dialog box you see when you start the installation process.

▶ **Figure B-2:** QuarkXPress asks which drive and directory you want to install the program on.

You now decide whether to install all the QuarkXPress files — including graphics import filters, bundled XTensions (word processing import filters and the kerning and tracking editors), OLE support, drag-and-drop printing support, on-line help, update documentation (readme) files, and sample documents — by choosing OK or selecting from the available files by choosing Customize.

Customizing the Installation

If you choose Customize, the Select Items to Install dialog box appears, as shown in Figure B-3. A check mark appears next to all group folders (directories) to be installed. (Here, we have unchecked the Sample Files folder.) As you select an item (by single-clicking it), the Install highlighted item box will be checked if a check mark appears next to the item in the list; it will be unchecked if no check mark appears. By clicking that box, you control whether an item will be installed or not. If you uncheck a folder, all folders and files within it are automatically unchecked. Also, the item's destination location will appear in the Path field. If that location is not grayed out, you may change the location by editing the pathname.

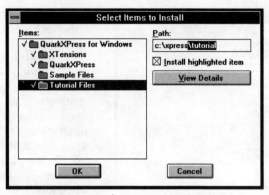

▶ **Figure B-3:** The Select Items to Install dialog box.

These group folders contain other groups (subdirectories), which you can also select or deselect for installation. Choosing View Details reveals the items within a folder. (If you select an item that is not a folder, this button will be grayed out and say No Details.) In Figure B-4, you can see the items for the Tutorial Files folder. These groups are indented beneath the folder they reside in. (Note that the View Details button has changed to Hide Details, and choosing that button with the Tutorial Files folder selected hides all the folders within it.) If you select a folder within the Tutorial Files folder, you could view the folders and files within it for selection or deselection.

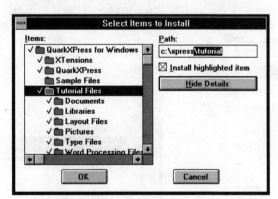

▶ **Figure B-4:** Choosing View Details (which then becomes Hide Details) reveals subdirectories within the four main program directories.

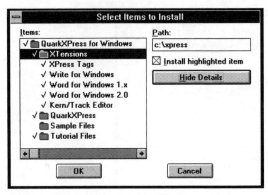

▶ **Figure B-5:** Highlight individual files in any directory for installation.

Figure B-5 shows the subdirectories in the QuarkXPress for Windows folder and the files within its XTensions folder. You could select import filters that you do not plan to use and deselect them by unchecking the Install highlighted item box. Later, if you decide to add an XTension, you would uncheck all the previously installed XTensions (as well as all other Items), leaving only the ones you want to add checked. QuarkXPress then installs only that XTension. You can use the same process to deselect or select graphics filters and other program elements.

Once you have selected and deselected program elements, choosing OK returns you to the QuarkXPress for Windows Installer dialog box. Choose OK to continue the installation.

Completing the Installation

The installation dialog box shows the installation status and lists each file as it is being installed, as shown in Figure B-6. (You can abort the installation by pressing the F3 key.) When QuarkXPress needs to install files from another disk, you'll see a prompt like that shown in Figure B-7.

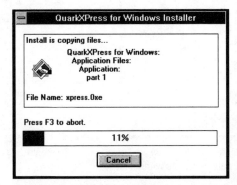

▶ **Figure B-6:** QuarkXPress informs you of the files it is installing.

▶ **Figure B-7:** QuarkXPress prompts you to change disks during installation.

► **Figure B-8:** QuarkXPress asks if you want a program group and icon created in Program Manager.

If this is the first time you've installed the program, you will be asked to register the program by filling out a series of questions on-screen. You must answer each question (you will get a beep and a message telling you information is missing if you do not). QuarkXPress asks you to insert the registration disk that comes with the program and then writes the information to that disk. At this point a registration code is added to your first install disk. If you reinstall the program later, such as after upgrading disk drives or adding filters, you will not be asked for this registration information or code as long as you reinstall from the same install disk.

Once the installation is complete, the installer program asks whether you want a Program Manager group and icon created for you. Figure B-8 shows this dialog box. If you choose Yes, QuarkXPress will create the program group shown in Figure B-9. (You can resize and reposition this group window just like any other.) If you would rather have the QuarkXPress icon in an existing group, go ahead and choose yes, and then drag the QuarkXPress icon to the group you want to keep it in. You can then delete the QuarkXPress program group by making it active and then pressing Delete.

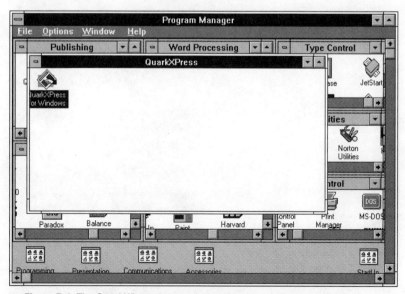

► **Figure B-9:** The QuarkXPress icon and program group in Program Manager.

You can change the name, shortcut key, or icon at any time by entering the Program Item Properties dialog box via File ➪ Properties. You can install a program in more than one program group by pressing Ctrl and then dragging and dropping the icon to the desired group.

Adding and Deleting Filters

If you want to add import filters for word processors or graphics, you must reinstall QuarkXPress. You cannot simply copy the files from the install disks via the DOS COPY command or Windows File Manager, since those files are compressed and only the QuarkXPress installer can decompress them. (If you add third-party XTensions or filters, follow the instructions on their install disks.)

To remove filters, use the DOS DEL command (or ERASE) or File Manager to delete the appropriate filter. Graphics filters have the extension FLT, while word processing filters have the extension XXT (they are actually XTensions). Note that if you delete filters supplied with QuarkXPress, they will still appear in the Get Picture and Get Text dialog boxes. Because these filters take up little room, we suggest you install them all and not remove any later.

Extending QuarkXPress's Capabilities

● ●

Years ago, the developers of QuarkXPress for Macintosh decided not to try to make the program all things to all people by adding a sinkload of features that would inhibit performance and make the program too feature-laden to use effectively. Instead, the developers created an architecture for what Quark calls *XTensions* — add-on programs that Quark and other developers can create to target the needs of specific users.

For example, those seeking to work on complicated tables need not resort to the techniques we described in Chapter 16; instead, they can buy an XTension that automates most of the formatting. And users who want to have sophisticated controls over the output of four-color images — the kind of prepress work normally done by an expert color separator on a $50,000 system — can buy an XTension that gives them these controls. Others can get an XTension that tracks individual elements in a file, which is extremely helpful in workgroup publishing environments where you need to maintain a check-off list for approval by each department.

The XTensions approach lets you customize QuarkXPress to meet your needs without burdening your system or users with unneeded functions. This approach has proven so successful that the latest version of PageMaker on the Macintosh offers a similar feature, called Additions, and future versions of Ventura Publisher are planned to offer the same abilities to plug in specialty features through Extensions.

Because of their popularity with Macintosh users, many companies that have developed XTensions for the Mac version of QuarkXPress expect to sell versions for Windows users. What follows are brief descriptions of several such XTensions planned for release in late 1992 and early 1993. You can expect to see even more developed, and a good way to keep current with what's available is through XChange, an independent users and developers group that both develops XTensions and serves as a clearinghouse between users and XTensions developers. The following XTensions are available from XChange as well as from their developers (if contact information is listed).

XChange membership is $99 per year in the U.S. and $149 per year in other nations. XChange can be reached at the following locations:

- 4243 Starflower Dr., Fort Collins, CO 80526; 800-788-7557, 303-229-0656, fax 303-229-9773

- 73 Upper Richmond Rd., 5th Floor, Putney, London SW13 2SZ, England; 44-0-81-877-9771, fax 44-0-81-877-9770

- Postbus 171, 7400 AD Deventer, The Netherlands; 31-5700-36622, fax 31-5700-30474

Color blends: Cool Blends lets you extend the gradient fill feature in the Colors palette to apply nonlinear blends, such as starburst, circular, and rectangular blends, to box backgrounds. Quark Inc., 1800 Grant St., Denver, CO 80203; 800-788-7835, 303-894-8888, fax 303-894-3399.

Color image control: SpectreSeps QX automatically translates standard color (RGB) TIFF files into the CMYK format needed by QuarkXPress for color separations. It lets you set prepress controls (such as undercolor removal, gray component replacement, custom screen angles, and dot ink gain correction) both globally and locally for specific images. Pre-Press Technologies, 2443 Impala Dr., Carlsbad, CA 92008; 619-931-2695, fax 619-931-2698.

Hyphenation control: Dashes lets you set hyphenation levels, so you can establish preferential hyphenation within words. It also lets you remove discretionary hyphens within selected text (QuarkXPress has no way to find and replace discretionary hyphens). Dashes is available in many languages, including English, Spanish, Italian, Portuguese, French, German, Dutch, Bokmål, Nynorsk, Swedish, Danish, Icelandic, Turkic, Russian, and Finnish. CompuSense Ltd., Avondale House, The Square, Ballincollig, Cork, Ireland; 353-21-871-394, fax 353-21-874-513.

Miscellaneous: Bob and Son of Bob both extend the QuarkXPress interface. Features include the abilities to drag a color from the Colors palette onto box elements and to use multiplication and division in any numeric-entry field (such as entering ¾ instead of .75). Quark Inc., 1800 Grant St., Denver, CO 80203; 800-788-7835, 303-894-8888, fax 303-894-3399.

Printing: PinPointXT prints detailed PostScript error messages, which is particularly helpful for service bureaus in diagnosing errors in QuarkXPress jobs.

Spell checking: SpellBound lets you use as many as five spelling checkers for multilingual documents. Dictionaries are available for major western and eastern European languages. The English dictionary offers features not found in QuarkXPress's built-in dictionary, including interactive "guess" mode and control over capitalization of found and corrected words. CompuSense Ltd., Avondale House, The Square, Ballincollig, Cork, Ireland; 353-21-871-394, fax 353-21-874-513.

Table editing: ProTabsXT lets you set up complex tables and reformat them on-the-fly. Software XTensions, 4609 B-5 NW Sixth St., Gainesville, FL 32609, 904-371-9722, fax 904-377-7566.

Index

IDG BOOKS

IDG Books Worldwide is part of International Data Group, one of the leading publishers of information on computers, software, and technology for over 25 years. Many of our books bear the endorsements of our widely read magazines — *PC World, Infoworld, Macworld,* and *Publish* — publications considered by millions of readers as authoritative guides to the world of desktop computing.

Whether you're new to computers or looking for in-depth advice on sophisticated subjects, IDG has the right computer book for you. Carefully written by recognized experts, IDG Books are consistently praised for their high quality content, innovative design, and superior value.

Windows For Dummies

by Andy Rathbone

A light-hearted "…For Dummies" approach that clears up Windows confusion — covers basics from installation nightmares to troubleshooting problems.
$16.95/$21.95 Canada
ISBN: 1-878058-61-4

1-2-3 For Dummies

by Greg Harvey

An entertaining yet thorough guide for new or reluctant Lotus 1-2-3 users. Features all the 1-2-3 fundamentals you need and simple tricks that make you look good. Free Pull-Out "Cheat Sheet" of key commands and functions.
$16.95/$21.95 Canada
ISBN: 1-878058-60-6

WordPerfect For Dummies

by Dan Gookin

Dan Gookin, author of IDG's blockbuster bestseller, *DOS For Dummies,* shows you the absolute basics (for non-science majors) of WordPerfect 4.2 through 5.1. Free Pull-Out Cheat Sheet & Function Key Reference.
$16.95/$21.95 Canada
ISBN: 1-878058-52-5

PCs For Dummies

by Dan Gookin and Andy Rathbone

The non-nerd's guide to PC configuration, upgrading and repair. System hardware and popular peripherals explained — for the computer phobic!
$16.95/$21.95 Canada
ISBN: 1-878058-51-7

Excel For Dummies

by Greg Harvey

The best beginner's guide to Excel 4 for Windows — today's fastest growing spreadsheet program.
$16.95/$21.95 Canada
ISBN: 1-878058-63-0

UNIX For Dummies

by Mark Schulman

The fun and friendly guide that takes the mystery out of UNIX. Covers all the UNIX essentials: from file and directory management to pipes, filters, security, passwords, and more!
$19.95/$26.95 Canada
ISBN: 1-878058-58-4

IDG Books Worldwide Registration Card

QuarkXPress for Windows Designer Handbook

Fill this out — and hear about updates to this book and other IDG Books Worldwide products!

Name _____

Company/Title _____

Address _____

City/State/Zip _____

What is the single most important reason you bought this book? _____

_____

Where did you buy this book?
- ❑ Bookstore (Name: _____)
- ❑ Electronics/Software store (Name: _____)
- ❑ Advertisement (If magazine, which? _____)
- ❑ Mail order (Name of catalog/mail order house: _____)
- ❑ Other: _____

How did you hear about this book?
- ❑ Book review in: _____
- ❑ Advertisement in: _____
- ❑ Catalog
- ❑ Found in store
- ❑ Other: _____

How would you rate the overall content of this book?
- ❑ Very good   ❑ Satisfactory
- ❑ Good   ❑ Poor
- Why? _____

What chapters did you find most valuable? _____

What chapters did you find least valuable? _____

What kind of chapter or topic would you add to future editions of this book? _____

_____

Please give us any additional comments. _____

_____

How many computer books do you purchase a year?
❑ 1   ❑ 6-10
❑ 2-5   ❑ More than 10

What are your primary software applications?
_____
_____
_____

Thank you for your help!

❑ I liked this book! By checking this box, I give you permission to use my name and quote me in future IDG Books Worldwide promotional materials. Daytime phone number_____ .

❑ FREE! Send me a copy of your computer book and book/disk catalog.

Fold Here

Place
stamp
here

IDG Books Worldwide, Inc.
155 Bovet Road
Suite 610
San Mateo, CA 94402

Attn: Reader Response / QuarkXPress

Order Form

Order Center: (800) 762-2974 (7 a.m.–5 p.m., PST, weekdays)
or **(415) 312-0650**
Order Center FAX: (415) 358-1260

Quantity	Title & ISBN	Price	Total

Shipping & Handling Charges

Subtotal	U.S.	Canada & International	International Air Mail
Up to $20.00	Add $3.00	Add $4.00	Add $10.00
$20.01–40.00	$4.00	$5.00	$20.00
$40.01–60.00	$5.00	$6.00	$25.00
$60.01–80.00	$6.00	$8.00	$35.00
Over $80.00	$7.00	$10.00	$50.00

In U.S. and Canada, shipping is UPS ground or equivalent. For Rush shipping call (800) 762-2974.

Subtotal _____

CA residents add applicable sales tax _____

IN residents add 5% sales tax _____

Canadian residents add 7% GST tax _____

Shipping _____

TOTAL _____

Ship to:

Name _____

Company _____

Address _____

City/State/Zip _____

Daytime phone _____

Payment: ☐ Check to IDG Books   ☐ Visa   ☐ MasterCard   ☐ American Express

Card # _____   Expires _____

Please send this order form to: IDG Books, 155 Bovet Road, Suite 610, San Mateo, CA 94402.
Allow up to 3 weeks for delivery. Thank you!

BOB101392

Fold Here

Place
stamp
here

IDG Books Worldwide, Inc.
155 Bovet Road
Suite 610
San Mateo, CA 94402

Attn: Order Center / QuarkXPress